Baseball Autograph Handbook

A comprehensive guide to authentication and valuation of Hall of Fame autographs

By Mark Allen Baker

Editor & photography - Christine Orioli Baker

Graphics - Thomas Gilhooly

Autograph valuation panel
Rich Altman
Ted Elmo
Daniel Ginsburg
Bob Schmierer
Pat Quinn

Published in United States of America
by Krause Publications Inc., Iola, Wisconsin.

Library of Congress: 89-83584
ISBN: 0-87341-124-2

First Edition

Table of Contents

Dedication

To Ford William Baker, my father, who played professional baseball from June 15, 1951, to July 28, 1953, with both the New York Yankees and the New York Giants organizations. In addition to showing Branch Rickey his first fork ball, he also pitched against, played with, and was coached by many of the players in this book.

To Marilyn Allen Baker, my mother, who made so much possible.

Preface

This book has been a project I have wanted to undertake for many years and I am honored to have Krause Publications as its publisher. The book combines over 20 years of autograph collecting experience, together with seven months of extensive research. Many hours were spent searching the files at the National Baseball Library in Cooperstown, N.Y., and walking the floors of the Baseball Hall of Fame. Over 4,000 photographs were taken and, along with access to many personal collections just as expansive, together provided an outstanding base of research materials.

This book was written for every baseball autograph collector who loves the hobby as much as I do. Through these pages I have tried to share with you every important piece of information I could find to make your collecting easier and more enjoyable. My inspiration has been my experiences, years of collecting with little information, errors that have cost me personally and financially — mistakes you the reader will not have to make.

For the new collector, I hope this book entices you to continue collecting and helping all of us preserve the memories of the game we love. For the expert, I hope this book can be a valuable research tool, and hopefully move you to share your knowledge with the hobby.

Collecting baseball autographs, specifically as it applies to the elite in the Hall of Fame, has never been as popular as it is today. Thousands attend card shows and pay a considerable fee to attain a single signature of their boyhood hero. Others will spend hours at the ballpark creating signature masterpieces to adorn their mantel, as showpieces for their love of the game. Whatever the approach, style or motivation, there has been precious little information available about the treasures we seek or acquire, until now.

Nothing is more personal than an individual's signature. This fact should remain paramount in your mind as you progress through the pages of this book. No baseball player is obligated to comply with your autograph requests, therefore all of us should learn to approach this task with the utmost in courtesy. Not all players will comply, and by respecting their attitudes, we can preserve the hobby for those who will.

In addition to respecting the attitudes of the baseball players, we must begin to respect those expressed by our peers, fellow collectors, promoters and dealers. Although the hobby is enjoyable and sometimes profitable, it is also complex, making expertise scarce and mistakes commonplace. As a group we must dedicate ourselves to the education and preservation of our hobby.

Some of the information presented within this book will require updating in future editions, some of it may even be controversial. Please keep in mind that the intent of this book is to educate the collector, with hopes of preserving the integrity of the hobby. Any collectors wishing to correspond on information represented in this book may feel free to do so.

It is my sincerest wish that you find this book not only useful and functional, but a valuable asset for all your baseball autograph collecting needs.

Mark Allen Baker
P.O. Box 2492
Liverpool, NY 13089

Foreword

When the time came to choose someone to write the foreward of this book, as a collector there were many choices, but only one of them was obvious — Joseph Wheeler Sewell. To the experienced collector no player has been more humble and congenial with autograph requests, or as willing to share with the public his love for the game he played so well.

To those who are not familiar with Joe's accomplishments, let me enlighten you. Joe Sewell has the fewest strikeouts per at bats — .016 — of any major league player. During his 14 seasons with the Indians and the Yankees, he struck out only 113 times. (By comparison, Reggie Jackson struck out 171 times just during the 1968 season.) Joe played in 1,103 consecutive games and ended his career with a lifetime batting average of .312. One of the greatest shortstops to play the game, he racked up 3,262 putouts and 5,221 assists during his career.

Joe's foreward typifies baseball's mystique and nostalgia. His induction into the Hall of Fame in 1977 brought to a crescendo, not to mention the public spotlight, his career. Through his numerous responses to collectors across the country, he has shared a warmth that so few other players have been able to give. I am indeed so proud and thankful to the Sewell family, who endured so much personal tragedy over the months preceeding my request, for working with me on this project.

To Joe,
Thanks for remembering us.
The Collectors

Joe Sewell (Courtesy National Baseball Library, Cooperstown, N.Y.)

Baseball is a game I have loved and played all my life. I was born on Oct. 9, 1898, in the small town of Titus, Alabama. My father was a country horse-and-buggy doctor. I had three brothers which made up a good part of a baseball team. Baseball was the only sport we knew in my day. We knew very little about football and nothing about basketball or golf. Baseball was a year-round sport for us. How we learned the rules of the game, I don't remember, but it took very little special equipment, so it became our game. We could use anything for a bat or ball. I remember the time I took one of my newly knitted wool socks to make a ball. Needless to say, my mother didn't appreciate it.

Baseball became my love throughout high school and into college at the University of Alabama. I entered college at the age of 16 years. My younger brother, Luke, was only 14 years old when he entered. While in college, I played for the University and during the summer I played for a semi-pro league, which was legal for a college player at that time. I was signed by the New Orleans Pelicans in 1920 — my senior year in college — for no bonus, but I was given $300 to buy some clothes. I played for New Orleans for about six weeks and then was sent to the Cleveland Indians after the beaning death of Ray Chapman. Following Ray's death, Cleveland used Harry Lunte at short, but he pulled a hamstring. They then used Joe Evans, who usually played outfield. They needed a shortstop as they were in a pennant race with the Chicago White Sox and the New York Yankees.

When I arrived in Cleveland, they were completing a series with the Yankees. I sat that first game on the bench. That game Babe Ruth hit his 28th and 29th home runs of the year. I saw some great infield and outfield play. Doc Johnson had five hits for five at-bats and stole home. Elmer Smith made some great fielding plays. Needless to say, I felt out of place.

The second day in Cleveland we played Philadelphia. This was only the second major league game I had ever seen. I was standing at my locker next to George Burns when manager/player Tris Speaker told me I was to play that game. George gave me three bats from his locker. They were Ty Cobb model bats. One of them I used throughout my entire baseball career. It was 35" long and weighed 40 ounces. My first time at bat I hit a line drive off Scott Perry to left-center which was caught by Tilly Walker. My second at bat, I hit a triple over third base. From that time, I have never been nervous at the plate.

Cleveland won the pennant that year, beating the Yankees by two and a half games, with the help of Walter Mails who was called up shortly before me. We won the World Series against Brooklyn, winning five of nine games.

During that year I played on three championship teams. The University of Alabama won the Southeastern Conference, the New Orleans Pelicans won the Southern League and Cleveland won the Series. Another highlight that year was meeting Ty Cobb. Cobb had always been my idol, but I had never seen or met him until our first game with Detroit. When Cobb walked onto the field, I was in awe. He was neatly dressed in a clean uniform, the greatest specimen of man I had ever seen. When I first shook his hand, I was even more thrilled. We became good friends throughout our careers. Cobb was the greatest ballplayer I have ever seen. He could hit, throw, field, slide, and think better than any player, and he would do anything necessary to beat you. Off the field there could not be a nicer and more courteous person.

In 1931 I was released by Cleveland and went to the Yankees where I played with Ruth, Gehrig, Dickey, Combs, and a great group of players. In my opinion, the 1932 Yankees were the greatest ball team ever assembled. Eight players off that one team are in the Hall of Fame. During my years with the Yankees, I roomed with Lou Gehrig at spring training and on the road. There could not have been a nicer or more dedicated baseball player. Our wildest night was going to a movie after the game. We were rooming together when the symptoms of his disease first appeared. We were playing at Detroit in 1933. Lou hit a ball to right field (a yard higher and it would have been a home run), turned and fell at the plate, not moving. He was taken from the field, but played the next day.

Babe Ruth was the greatest power hitter I have ever seen. He could do it consistently. If he had been pitched to like power batters of today are pitched to, he would have hit well over 100 home runs in 1927. I well remember the third game of the 1932 World Series which has caused a controversy about Ruth pointing to centerfield and then hitting a home run. During that series, there was friction between the Yankees and Chicago Cubs concerning the Cubs not giving Mark Koenig a full share of the Series money even though he was instrumental in the Cubs winning the pennant. Koenig had played with the Yankees and was friends with the Yankee team, and when the Cub players voted to give him only a one-half share this upset his Yankee friends. Charlie Root was pitching for the Cubs.

Ruth was cursing Burleigh Grimes, Bob Smith and Jeff Bush on the bench. Ruth took two strikes then stepped out of the batter's box. Holding his hat in his left hand, he pointed to center field and hit the next ball over the centerfield wall, through a tree full of small boys watching the game. Sam Byrd, who was sitting next to me, made the comment, "Look at those kids fall out of that tree!" I was there and saw it; it happened that way.

Baseball is a fun game with many funny stories, but one of the funniest was seeing Smead Jolley make three errors on one ball in Cleveland in the early 1930s. We were playing the White Sox and the grass was damp from a misty rain. Glenn Myatt hit a line drive to Jolley in rightfield. The ball hit the grass and skipped like a rock on water and went through Jolley's legs before he could get down to field it. The ball continued until it hit the right-field wall. It bounced back through Jolley's legs again for error number two. He turned and ran after the ball finally catching up with it. Myatt was rounding second base. Jolley braced himself and threw the ball about 15 rows up in the stands. You could hear him all over the field say "My God, I didn't know I could throw a ball that far." Needless to say, Myatt made a home run.

During my career I faced many great pitchers, but I don't ever remember going to the plate and not feeling confident I could hit any pitcher. The only pitcher I felt uncomfortable with was Dutch Leonard, a hard throwing left-handed spitball pitcher who played for the Red Sox and then Detroit. He didn't hesitate throwing at you, which was common in those days. Our Cleveland pitchers would throw at Ruth's feet. This was our way of holding his home runs down. The greatest left-handed pitcher, in my opinion, was Lefty Grove, and the greatest right-handed pitcher was Walter Johnson.

We traveled on non-air-conditioned trains most of my career, but we did have private cars; two in Cleveland and three when I played for New York. The Yankees had one car just for the news media. After each game we had a short time to rest, then talk to the news media, and when we left the stadium there was always a crowd of autograph seekers. They might follow us all the way to our hotel room, and most players were cooperative with the fans and media because without them we would have no job.

Baseball is a game I loved to play. I awakened each morning ready and anxious to play. I did not have to get myself mentally ready. I was always ready. I feel that some of the deficiencies affecting baseball today are the excessive salaries and long, no-trade contracts which may decrease a player's incentive to play at full capacity each day. In my day, there was always someone to fill your shoes if you let down. A great baseball player must be able to throw, field, hit, run, slide, and think. You may be deficient in one or two of these and become only a good player. Most of the baseball fans of today have never seen a great ballplayer. There aren't many.

Baseball has given me a great life. I have made many friends which I have cherished throughout the years. My return to Cooperstown each year gives me a chance to recall a lot of those memories and renew life-long friendships. To be inducted into the Baseball Hall of Fame in 1977 was the greatest thrill of my life. When I was playing ball I never even considered it. I was associated with and played with a lot of great ballplayers, but they never thought about the Hall of Fame. They played ball for the love of the game. A boy who loves baseball first wants to be able to play professional ball, then play in the major leagues, and then the ultimate goal is to be inducted into the Baseball Hall of Fame. With God's help, I was able to accomplish all these in my lifetime.

Since retiring from baseball, I have continued to receive baseball fan mail and baseball memorabilia almost daily. I have been honored to sign this memorabilia because, in my opinion, it keeps the enthusiasm of baseball, old and modern, in the minds of the true baseball fan as the nation's number one pastime. I have become acquainted with many interesting people. They are not only interested in the memorabilia, but also in the history of baseball. Without their interest, baseball and the great players of my era may be forgotten.

Joseph Wheeler Sewell

Baseball, Cooperstown and the Hall of Fame

Nobody would ever have dreamed that a simple game played with a ball made out of various types of parchment and catgut, and a bat hand-crafted from selected lumber, used by two opposing teams played on a field with four bases, 90 feet apart, forming a diamond, would grow into our National Pastime — baseball. Its foundation is attributed to a multi-faceted man by the name of Alexander Joy Cartwright, a New York City drafts-man, bank cashier and surveyor. Cartwright was of British descent and familiar with the English game of rounders and other games relating to the use of balls and bases. From 1842 to 1845 a group of New York City men spent their time playing assorted versions of evolutions of a new game called "baseball," first at a Manhattan park area at 47th Street and Fourth Avenue — soon to be the depot of the Harlem River Railroad, followed by a lot on Lexington Avenue and 23th Street where the first baseball club, the Knickerbockers of New York, was organized on Sept. 13, 1845.

By the year 1846, Cartwright had polished the rules of the game, eliminating many of the carryover regulations of rounders including the edict that provided for a runner to be retired when being hit by a thrown ball. The new rules added much to the organization of the game including foul lines and additions to the magic attraction to the number nine — nine players and nine innings. Cartwright's Knickerbockers practiced for weeks before offering an open invitation to any challenger. How appropriate indeed that the first baseball game between two teams was played near his home at Elysian Field in Hoboken, N.J., June 19, 1846, the Knickerbockers challenged by the New York Nine. The final score was Knickerbockers 1, the New York Nine 23 (21 or more "aces" [runs] won the game). Unfortunately the Knickerbockers' star player had decided to umpire the first historic game rather than play, his name was Alexander Cartwright.

Cartwright, aroused by the discovery of gold in 1849, headed west for San Fransico, with frequent stopovers to profess his knowledge of the game of baseball. Five weeks after he had arrived in California Cartwright booked passage back to New York City via China. During his return home, he developed a sickness that made it necessary for him to be put ashore and convalesce in the Hawaiian Islands. Cartwright remained there until his death, July 12, 1892.

Meanwhile the Knickerbockers went on playing, with blue trousers, white shirts and straw hats — the first club to wear uniforms — defeating nearly all their opponents. It was in 1856, that British born Henry Chadwick was to witness his first Knickerbocker game against the Gothams, though his love was cricket, his paramount interest was soon to be baseball. He joined the *New York Clipper*, a show business and sports journal, in 1857. Frustrated by the method of scorekeeping, he created the box-score appearing in the June 16, 1857, issue of the *Clipper*. It was from Chadwick's accounts that Americans would learn baseball idiosyncrasies — "balk," "fungo" and "assist." He was elected to the first organization

The National Baseball Museum and Hall of Fame opened in Cooperstown, N.Y., in 1939, the "centennial" of the national pastime's legendary invention by Abner Doubleday. This is a scene from the dedication ceremony. (Courtesy National Baseball Library, Cooperstown, N.Y.)

in baseball, The National Association of Baseball Players, a formal player's group organized at a New York convention on March 1, 1858. The association adopted most of Cartwright's rules with only slight modifications. New York became a hotbed for baseball with many teams competing in local challenges. By 1857, baseball clubs, thanks to Cartwright's seed, began to spring up across the United States. The Excelsiors of Brooklyn became the first team to tour in 1860, stopping in Albany, Troy, Rochester and Buffalo.

The troops from both sides of the Civil War (1861-1865) spread baseball fever throughout their journeys, often referencing the sport in soldiers' letters and diaries. It was from the Civil War that the major in command at Fort Sumter, the man who ordered the first cannonball be fired at the Secessionists, emerged — General Abner Doubleday. It was claimed that Doubleday, while a cadet at West Point Military Academy, drew up the first crude baseball rules and on a plot of land just off Main Street in Cooperstown, N.Y., played the first game of baseball with former classmates at Cooperstown Classical and Military Academy in 1839.

Enter the beautiful village of Cooperstown, nestled in the serenity of Otsego County, just a quick southeast trip from Utica and slightly over an hour's drive southwest from Albany. Following the Civil War, baseball grew with great enthusiasm. Alfred J. Reach of Brooklyn, N.Y., became baseball's first professional player in 1867 for the Philadelphia Athletics. The Cincinnati Red Stockings became baseball's first professional team in 1869, ten men drawing $9,500.

The first professional league began in 1871, the National Association of Professional Ball Players. Its first president was Morgan G. Bulkeley. The forerunner of the National League had as its first pennant winner the Philadelpia Athletics.

In 1876, while pitching for Chicago, Albert Goodwill Spalding founded A.G. Spalding & Bros., which soon became the exclusive supplier of baseballs and bats for professional use. Additionally, they began to publish the *Official League Book* (rule book) and *Spalding's Official Baseball Guide* (records book).

The American Association made its appearance in 1882 lasting a decade until it merged with the National League into a 12-club league in 1892. The league was reduced to eight clubs in 1900, allowing Ban Johnson's Western League to expand and change its name to the American League. Capturing talent the likes of Lajoie, Young, Flick and Keeler, the anarchy forced the National League to recognize Johnson's offspring as legitimate in 1903.

Claims of baseball's ancestry persisted, among them one from Abraham G. Mills, the third president of the National League, who proclaimed at a dinner in 1889 that patriotism and research had established that baseball was native to America and not descended from the English game of rounders. As years passed little resistance to the Cooperstown theory was shown until 1905, when Henry Chadwick, now editor of the *Spalding Baseball Guide* wrote about his schoolboy experience playing rounders in England some 70 years previous. Chadwick's description of rounders was very convincing and few doubted the similarities of the two games.

A.G. Spalding, annoyed by Chadwick's proclamation from his own presses, sought to put the issue to rest by appointing a distinguished committee to investigate the origin of the game. The prominent committee was chaired by A.G. Mills. Also on the committee: Morgan G. Bulkeley, former governor, National League President (1876) and sitting senator from Connecticut; Arthur P. Gorman, senator from Maryland, former player and ex-president of the National Baseball Club of Washington, D.C.; Nicholas E. Young, former player and fifth president of the National League (1884-1902); Alfred J. Reach and George Wright former baseball standouts and, like Spalding, now equipment manufacturers, and, James Sullivan, president of the Amateur Athletic Union.

The committee's limited research over the next three years consisted of a pile of correspondence and unsubstantiated claims, with the chief evidence coming from Spalding himself who submitted a letter written in 1907 by a Colorado mining engineer named Abner Graves. Graves, then in his mid-eighties, recalling some 68 years earlier, explained how his classmate Doubleday explained the game of "base ball or town ball" behind a Cooperstown tailor shop during a game of marbles. On Dec. 30, 1907, the unanimous conclusion was: "Baseball is of American origin and has no traceable connection whatever with rounders or any foreign game." The final committee report also read, "the first scheme for playing baseball, according to the best evidence obtainable to date, was devised by Abner Doubleday at Cooperstown, New York in 1839."

The Mills Commission Report was contained in the 1908 *Spalding Guide*. Henry Chadwick, editor of the *Guide* immediately offered a rebuttal. Graves's recollection of playing "base ball" in "Phinney's pasture" off Main Street in Cooperstown remained the most conclusive evidence.

Overlooked by the committee and possibly forgotten by Graves was the fact that in the summer of 1839 Doubleday was a cadet at the United States Military Academy. According to school policy he was confined to post because he was between his first and second years of attendance. Doubleday would have been considered AWOL had he been in Cooperstown. Ironically, Doubleday and Mills were well acquainted, in fact it was Mills who organized the honor guard at Doubleday's funeral in 1893.

The controversy subsided until 1930, when the citizens of Cooperstown were negotiating the purchase of "Elihu Phinney's pasture," a cow pasture with a brook running through the middle, where Graves had claimed Doubleday played the first game. A baseball field was constructed on the site with minimal accommodations for visitors in small wooden stands. It remained in rough original condition until 1939 when the Village Board of Trustees transformed the site into a ballpark of professional league qualifications.

One day in 1935, in the nearby village of Fly Creek, just a stone's throw from Cooperstown, a farmer came across an old trunk in his attic where it had been stored untouched for years. Opening the trunk released the memories and relics belonging to a Cooperstown schoolboy by the name of Abner Graves. The farmer, a descendent of Graves, pored over the relics from the past — old books covered with dust, faded pictures and a unique antique baseball unlike any he had seen. His homemade relic was stuffed with cloth, torn and misshapen. There was no doubt that the ball belonged to the young schoolboy who testified later in life that the game of baseball was invented in Cooperstown — Abner Graves. The find was soon labeled the "Abner Doubleday baseball" and cast a legendary spell on the local belief that the game's origin was Cooperstown.

The antique baseball was purchased for $5 by Stephen C. Clark, a native of Cooperstown, and heir of the Singer sewing machine family. Following his purchase Clark conceived the idea of exhibiting the relic with other baseball related memorabilia in the Cooperstown Village Club. The project undertaken by Alexander Cleland on Clark's behalf attracted so much interest that the idea for a national shrine for the sport began. Meanwhile, Clark was conceiving even bigger plans for his hometown, a giant celebration to mark the centennial of baseball which, according to the Doubleday legend, would occur in 1939. Clark presented a proposal for an all-time all-star team selection to Ford C. Frick, president of the National League. Frick not only fully endorsed the idea, but suggested a shrine to the sport. Cleland wrote and visited baseball enthusiasts throughout the country, seeking relics for display. Through Frick, Cleland was able to gain the support of William Harridge, president of the American League, and of baseball's first commissioner — Kenesaw Mountain Landis. From all parts of the country relics were sent to join the Doubleday Ball, the beginnings of a huge baseball memorabilia collection and America's first museum devoted to a sport. Frick's idea for a Hall of Fame met with enthusiastic response and plans were immediately made to erect a National Baseball Hall of Fame and Museum to be formally dedicated in 1939, the year of Baseball's Centennial.

In January, 1936, the first election for enshrinement was held. Of the many players in nomination only five received the necessary 75 percent vote necessary for induction. Out of 236 ballots, Ty Cobb appeared on 222, Honus Wagner and Babe Ruth on 215, Christy Mathewson on 205, and Walter Johnson on 189 ballots. During the next three years, 21 more selections were named bringing the total number to 26 for induction on June 12, 1939.

Baseball's four ranking executives of that era dedicated the National Baseball Hall of Fame and Museum as part of the official ceremony that day. Three ribbons were cut, one red by Ford Frick, one blue by William G. Bramham — president of the National Association of Professional Baseball (minor) Leagues, and one white by William Harridge. Commissioner Landis then spoke the words that will forever echo from the walls of the Museum: "I now declare the National Baseball Hall of Fame and Museum in Cooperstown, New York, the birthplace of baseball, officially open. May it forever stand as a symbol of clean play and good sportsmanship."

Eleven of the 25 baseball immortals inducted through 1939 attended the dedication: Ty Cobb, Walter Johnson, George Sisler, Nap Lajoie, Tris Speaker, Grover Alexander, Honus Wagner, Cy Young, Connie Mack, Babe Ruth and Eddie Collins. Each walked through the door of the shrine when his name was announced and uttered a few comments in the microphone on the podium in front of the hall. Ovations greeted each as the crowd overspilled into Main Street, each person seeking a glimpse of these baseball legends.

The Postal Department, by a special act of Congress in 1939, issued for the first time a commemorative stamp in honor of a sport — baseball. Designated as the first place of

An all-time all-star lineup gathered for the Hall of Fame dedication ceremonies in 1939. Standing (left to right): Honus Wagner, Grover Cleveland Alexander, Tris Speaker, Larry Lajoie, George Sisler and Walter Johnson. Seated (left to right): Eddie Collins, Babe Ruth, Connie Mack and Cy Young. (Courtesy National Baseball Library, Cooperstown, N.Y.)

sale was the Cooperstown post office, with United States Postmaster General James A. Farley presiding.

Following the original dedication in 1939, a new wing was added on July 25, 1950, and on Aug. 4, 1958, the Hall of Fame Gallery was dedicated. The firm of Moore & Hutchins of New York was chosen as architects for the impressive 85x43' brick and steel construction. Black marble columns supporting a lofty ceiling, lead visitors over raised aisles with alcoves that display each inductee's carved biography plaque. A marble centopath at one end of the Gallery salutes those players who served in the Untied States Armed Forces, while at the opposite end is a wall dedicated to the Baseball Hall of Fame Cup presented to the winner of the Annual Hall of Fame Game.

Though the Hall of Fame will forever commemorate baseball, Cooperstown, will forever be haunted by the legacy of Abner Doubleday. A mystery shrouded by fantasy and lore, each new decade spawns more disbelievers. Claims of baseball's origin has spanned the creative gamut, from claims that an ancestral version of baseball was played in the Nile Valley in the time of the pharohs to accounts from Revolutionary War soldiers. In some respects baseball's true origin is irrelevant, in fact the mystery surrounding it makes the sport all that more intriguing. Cooperstown is the embodiment of the qualities America stands for, somehow untouched or less touched by the commercialism and the modern values that seem so far removed from our past. I have been many places in my life, but in my mind and in my heart there is no place I would rather be than Cooperstown, New York.

Hall of Fame roster

Henry Aaron
Grover Alexander
Walt Alston
Cap Anson
Luis Aparicio
Luke Appling
Earl Averill
Frank Baker
Dave Bancroft
Ernie Banks
Al Barlick
Edward Barrow
Jake Beckley
Cool Papa Bell
Johnny Bench
Chief Bender
Yogi Berra
Jim Bottomley
Lou Boudreau
Roger Bresnahan
Lou Brock
Dan Brouthers
Mordecai Brown
Morgan Bulkeley
Jesse Burkett
Roy Campenella
Max Carey
Alexander Cartwright
Henry Chadwick
Frank Chance
Happy Chandler
Oscar Charleston
Jack Chesbro
Fred Clarke
John Clarkson
Roberto Clemente
Ty Cobb
Mickey Cochrane
Eddie Collins
Jimmy Collins
Earle Combs
Charles Comiskey
Jocko Conlan
Thomas Connolly
Roger Connor
Stan Coveleski
Sam Crawford
Joe Cronin
Candy Cummings
Ki Ki Cuyler
Ray Dandridge

Dizzy Dean
Ed Delahanty
Bill Dickey
Martin Dihigo
Joe DiMaggio
Bobby Doerr
Don Drysdale
Hugh Duffy
Billy Evans
Johnny Evers
Buck Ewing
Red Faber
Bob Feller
Rick Ferrell
Elmer Flick
Whitey Ford
Rube Foster
Jimmie Foxx
Ford Frick
Frankie Frisch
Pud Galvin
Lou Gehrig
Charlie Gehringer
Josh Gibson
Bob Gibson
Warren Giles
Lefty Gomez
Goose Goslin
Hank Greenberg
Clark Griffith
Burleigh Grimes
Lefty Grove
Chick Hafey
Jesse Haines
Billy Hamilton
Will Harridge
Bucky Harris
Gabby Hartnett
Harry Heilmann
Billy Herman
Harry Hooper
Rogers Hornsby
Waite Hoyt
Cal Hubbard
Carl Hubbell
Miller Huggins
Catfish Hunter
Monte Irvin
Travis Jackson
Hugh Jennings
Ban Johnson

Walter Johnson
Judy Johnson
Addie Joss
Al Kaline
Tim Keefe
Wee Willie Keeler
George Kell
Joe Kelley
George Kelly
Mike Kelly
Harmon Killebrew
Ralph Kiner
Chuck Klein
Bill Klem
Sandy Koufax
Nap Lajoie
Kenesaw Landis
Bob Lemon
Buck Leonard
Freddie Lindstrom
John Lloyd
Ernie Lombardi
Al Lopez
Ted Lyons
Connie Mack
Larry MacPhail
Mickey Mantle
Heinie Manush
Rabbit Maranville
Juan Marichal
Rube Marquard
Eddie Mathews
Christy Mathewson
Willie Mays
Joe McCarthy
Tom McCarthy
Willie McCovey
Joe McGinnity
John McGraw
Bill McKechnie
Ducky Medwick
Johnny Mize
Stan Musial
Kid Nichols
James O'Rourke
Mel Ott
Satchel Paige
Herb Pennock
Ed Plank
Charles Radbourn
Pee Wee Reese

Sam Rice
Branch Rickey
Eppa Rixey
Robin Roberts
Brooks Robinson
Frank Robinson
Jackie Robinson
Wilbert Robinson
Edd Roush
Red Ruffing
Amos Rusie
Babe Ruth
Ray Schalk
Red Schoendienst
Joe Sewell
Al Simmons
George Sisler
Enos Slaughter
Duke Snider
Warren Spahn
Al Spalding
Tris Speaker
Willie Stargell
Casey Stengel
Bill Terry
Sam Thompson
Joe Tinker
Pie Traynor
Dazzy Vance
Arky Vaughan
Rube Waddell
Honus Wagner
Bobby Wallace
Ed Walsh
Lloyd Waner
Paul Waner
John Ward
George Weiss
Mickey Welch
Zack Wheat
Hoyt Wilhelm
Billy Williams
Ted Williams
Hack Wilson
George Wright
Harry Wright
Early Wynn
Tom Yawkey
Carl Yastrzemski
Cy Young
Ross Youngs

Rules for election to The Baseball Hall of Fame by members of The Baseball Writers' Association of America

1. Authorization — By authorization of the Board of Directors of the National Baseball Hall of Fame and Museum, Inc., the Baseball Writers' Association of America is authorized to hold an election every year for the purpose of electing members to the Baseball Hall of Fame from the ranks of retired baseball players.

2. Electors — Only active and honorary members of the Baseball Writers' Association of America, who have been active baseball writers for at least ten (10) years, shall be eligible to vote. They must have been active as baseball writers and members of the Association for a period beginning at least ten (10) years prior to the date of election in which they are voting.

3. Eligible Candidates — Candidates to be eligible must meet the following requirements:

(A)   A baseball player must have been active as a player in the Major Leagues at some time during a period beginning twenty (20) years before and ending five (5) years prior to election.

(B)   Player must have played in each of ten (10) Major League championship seasons, some part of which must have been within the period described in 3 (A).

(C)   Player shall have ceased to be an active player in the Major Leagues at least five (5) calendar years preceding the election but may be otherwise connected with baseball.

(D)   In case of the death of an active player or a player who has been retired for less than five (5) full years, a candidate who is otherwise eligible shall be eligible in the next regular election held at least six (6) months after the date of death or after the end of the five (5) year period, whichever occurs first.

4. Method of Election

(A)   BBWAA Screening Committee — A Screening Committee consisting of baseball writers who are elected by the BBWAA at their Annual Meeting. This Screening Committee shall consist of six members, with two members to be elected at each Annual meeting for a three-year term. The duty of the Screening Committee shall be to prepare a ballot listing a minimum of thirty (30) names in alphabetical order. The nominees listed on the ballot shall be eligible candidates who (1) receive a vote on a minimum of five per cent (5%) of the ballots cast in the preceding election or (2) are eligible for the first time and are nominated by any one of the six members of the BBWAA Screening Committee.

(B)   An elector will vote for ten (10) eligible candidates appearing on the ballot, or fewer if he feels that he

13

cannot in fairness vote for ten (10) candidates, that he believes to be most entitled for election to the Baseball Hall of Fame.

(C)   Any candidate receiving votes on seventy-five per cent (75%) of the ballots cast shall be elected to membership in the Baseball Hall of Fame.

5. Voting — Voting shall be based upon the player's record, playing ability, integrity, sportsmanship, character, contribution to the team(s) on which the player played and not on what he may have done otherwise in baseball.

6. Automatic Elections — No automatic elections based on performances such as a batting average of .400 or more for one (1) year, pitching a perfect game or similar outstanding achievement shall be permitted.

7. Time of Election — The duly authorized representatives of the Association shall prepare, date and mail ballots to each elector no later than the 15th day of January in each year in which an election is held. The elector shall sign and return the completed ballot within twenty (20) days. The vote shall then be tabulated by the duly authorized representatives of the Association.

8. Certification of Election Results — The results of the election shall be certified by the Secretary of the Baseball Writers' Association of America and transmitted to the Commissioner of Baseball and to an officer of the National Baseball Hall of Fame and Museum, who shall review and release the results for publication.

9. Amendments — The Board of Directors of the National Baseball Hall of Fame and Museum, Inc. reserves the right to revoke, alter or amend these rules at any time.

July 1986

Rules for election to the National Baseball Hall of Fame by members of Baseball Hall of Fame Committee on Baseball Veterans

1. Name — The Committee shall be known as the Baseball Hall of Fame Committee on Baseball Veterans.

2. Number — The Committee shall consist of twenty (20) members: namely a Chairman and nineteen (19) members. Membership of this Committee shall be selected from former baseball players who are members of the Baseball Hall of Fame, individuals now or formerly connected in an official capacity with baseball, members of the Baseball Writer's Association of America and baseball broadcasters. An officer of the National Baseball Hall of Fame and Museum, Inc. shall act as non-voting Secretary.

3. Method of Appointment — The Committee shall be appointed by the Board of Directors of the National Baseball Hall of Fame and Museum, Inc. who shall have the sole power to fill all vacancies caused by the expiration of the term of an appointment, death, physical or mental incapacity, resignation or failure to perform the duties assigned to the Committee or to participate in its activities.

4. Term — The term of each appointment is for six (6) years and expires on the date of the election of a successor or on December 31st of the year on which the appointment expires whichever is earlier.

5. Duties — The Committee shall consider all eligible candidates and hold elections every year. It shall have such further duties as may be assigned to it from time to time by the Board of Directors of the National Baseball Hall of Fame and Museum, Inc.

6. Eligible Candidates — Candidates to be eligible must be selected from:

(A)   Major league players who have competed in at least ten (10) championship seasons and who have been retired as players for at least twenty-three (23) years. Those whose careers began after 1945 must have received one-hundred (100) or more votes in one (1) or more elections of the Baseball Writers' Association of America.

(B)   Baseball Executives and/or Managers and/or Umpires who have been retired from organized baseball as Baseball Executives and/or Managers and/or Umpires for at least five (5) years prior to the election. The five (5) year waiting period shall be reduced to six (6) months for anyone who has reached the age of sixty-five (65).

(C)   Players (1) who played in at least ten (10) years in the Negro Baseball Leagues prior to 1946; or (b) whose service in the Negro Baseball leagues prior to 1946 and in the Major Leagues thereafter aggregates of at least ten (10) years; and (c) who are not otherwise eligible for election to the Hall of Fame.

(D)   No member of the Baseball Hall of Fame Committee on Baseball Veterans can be elected to the Hall of Fame while he is a member of the Committee.

7. Number to be Elected — The Committee is authorized to elect each year no more than two (2) members to the National Baseball Hall of Fame from those eligible under Paragraph 6.(A), (B) and (C) but no more than one (1) from those eligible under Paragraph 6.(B).

8. Time and Place of Election — Elections shall be held at such time and place as the Chairman of the Baseball Hall of Fame Committee on Baseball Veterans may designate. Upon the application of three (3) members of the Baseball Hall of Fame Committee on Baseball Veterans special elections may be held at such time and place as designated in the application.

9. Voting — A quorum of twelve (12) members is required for an election. An affirmative vote of at least 75% of the members of the Committee present at the election shall be necessary for election of a candidate to membership in the National Baseball Hall of Fame. No proxies are permitted.

10. Minutes — The Committee shall keep minutes of its meetings, one copy of which is to be placed on file at the National Baseball Hall of Fame and Museum.

11. Rules — The Committee shall make such further rules as it may wish for the conduct of its affairs.

12. Automatic Elections — No automatic elections based on performances such as a batting average of .400 or more for one (1) year, pitching a perfect game or similar outstanding achievement shall be permitted.

13. Amendments — The Board of Directors of the National Baseball Hall of Fame and Museum, Inc. reserves the right to revoke, alter or amend these rules at any time.

July, 1987

The philosophy of collecting

"To understand the collector, you must first understand the game," perhaps this Harwellism will help. Ernie Harwell is a recipient of the Ford C. Frick Award (1981), a Hall of Fame caliber award to honor a broadcaster for meritorious service to baseball and his profession. In a personal tribute to Harwell, which I also believe best exemplifies why an individual would devote part of his life to collecting, I have styled a verse similar to Ernie's "The Game for All America."

Baseball, the game

Baseball, the game, is the memories we all have, of playing catch with our fathers on a warm summer day. Our first trip to a major league park. The smell of fresh popcorn. Shouts from concessionaires, "Programs. Get your programs here." Little boys and girls dressed in caps, with baseball mitts half their size, dreaming of catching a foul ball. Fresh roasted peanuts and hot dogs that by some miracle taste better at the ballpark than in your own home.

Old men in caps, sharing detailed accounts of innings long past, as if the game had only been yesterday. Youngsters shouting for autographs along a chainlinked fence, at players a mere decade older than themselves. Scouts sitting behind home plate, armed with a radar gun in one hand and a cigar in the other, checking the speed of a 19-year-old pitcher from Tampa.

Baseball, the game of strategy and statistics, of reflexes and reactions, where heroics are fleeting moments, transformed into indistinguishable feats in the box score of tomorrow morning's paper.

A game governed by a man dressed in a blue shirt with a polka dot tie, who proclaims the only rite of Spring most of us understand, "Play Ball."

Baseball, the game, is names of rookies we can't pronounce or spell, like Yastrzemski, trying to rebuild a legend left by a man named Williams. It's a veteran named Ryan throwing a 90 mile an hour fastball by a batter who remembers collecting the pitcher's first baseball card.

From Robby, Pee Wee, Campy and the Duke, to Tommy, Joe and Luke. It's Sandy, Candy, Connie and Judy. It's Catfish, Rabbit, Ducky and the Iron Horse. From Dizzy and Daffy, Dazzy and Dickey to Whitey, Yogi, Casey and Mickey, any way you cut it, it's baseball.

A piece of white ash from the timbers of upstate New York, trying to send two pieces of cowhide with 108 stitches, 284 feet over an eight-foot wall. It's nine innings, nine players and 90 feet.

Baseball, the game, is for those who play and a dream for those who don't. It's our yearning, just for one minute, to step inside a fantasy, into the World Series footsteps of Larsen, Mazeroski, or Kirk Gibson. It's the voices of our youth: Mel Allen, Red Barber, Ernie Harwell, Harry Caray, Bob Prince and Vin Scully. It's the thrills up your spine when Bob Sheppard's voice rang from the P.A. system in Yankee Stadium. "Now batting, #7, Mickey Mantle."

The game is also Branch Rickey, Bill Veeck, Max Patkin, Al Schacht, and Brooklyn's Hilda Chester "The Bell of Ebbets Field." It's "The National Game" or "Take Your Girl to the Ball Game" or even, "Take Me Out to the Ball Game." It's languages like Stengelese or Yogisms.

It's written in the rules that the objective of each team is to win by scoring more runs than the opponent, a goal that can be translated in concept to almost every objective in life.

Baseball, the game is fond memories of a time that was, and dreams of what will be.

Baseball memorabilia collectors are a unique and specialized group of individuals, varying widely in social, financial and occupational backgrounds. The collectors are as diverse as the game they love, with the only common denominator being the sport of baseball. Each group of collectors has its own specialty niche; concentrating on individual players, teams, leagues or events. Regardless of specialization, all are driven by the same goal, to seek out the finest attainable pieces for their collections.

Perhaps the easiest way to segment the hobby would be to divide it into two categories: Collections based on subject, those items collected as sets or based on material type, and general collecting. Subject collections contain letters, documents, uniforms, caps, hats, bats, newspaper clippings, advertisements and more relating to one particular subject or person. Special collections can concentrate on specific teams or leagues. Frequently subject collections concentrate on one particular individual, such as Babe Ruth, Mickey Mantle, Pete Rose or Joe DiMaggio. Subject collections concentrating on one individual are usually fascinating, filled with every type of item imaginable surrounding a life and career. They often contain autographed cards, equipment, advertisements and even letters from friends. Though limited in appeal, perhaps, they stand as lasting monuments to a single person's achievements.

Subject collections are particularily popular among institutions and museums. The material is significant to the institution or museum because the source material, in original form, is sought for research purposes. Subject collections are also a haven for the private collector, frequently relating to individuals or teams that the person shares fond memories of. Several of the finest subject collections have been formed by baseball executives or owners. Most collectors have limited access to professional baseball and therefore must acquire their items through other channels.

Generally, private collectors and institutions try to purchase items that relate to specific key events or milestones of the individual's career, though some routine autograph samples may exist for comparison purposes. Demand is usually high for material containing historical content or relics commemorating such an event, therefore many general collectors should expect to pay premium dollar.

Subject autograph collectors often find themselves branching out into other areas of baseball memorabilia. This process is a natural evolution, taking their interests beyond its original intent and into areas requiring additional education if any level of expertise is expected to be obtained. You will find that some special collectors and many institutions are more interested in the subject being collected than the autographs obtained.

Private collectors often form collections centering around a common achievement such as "The 500 Home Run Club" or "The 3,000 Strikeout Club." Also popular are team-signed baseballs and team-issued collectibles — books, patches, and unusual items or souvenirs.

Collecting items based on material type or sets is also very popular, for example: autographed cachets, postcards, bats, balls, pennants, cards or books. Collectors taking this approach are less interested in particular individuals and more concerned with the collection as a whole. Accessibility to this type of autographed material varies significantly with the material. Generally, set collectors will go to great lengths, sparing little expense to complete their collections. Often set collectors will pursue their objectives based on the accessibility of the material to be autographed, rather than the autograph itself.

Material type or set collecting takes tremendous patience and is clearly the most demanding form of the three. Frustration is commonplace. However, once the object of completing a difficult collection is accomplished, the results are most rewarding.

Subject collectors and institutions migrate little towards material or sets collecting, this is primarily due to the lack of research value associated with this form. There are always exceptions, of course. A complete set of autographed World Series programs would no doubt be of value to the researcher.

The most common form is the personal or general collector whose interests are primarily circumstantial. The casual collector often has a collection filled with many unrelated items. The items were often obtained in person or purchased at a very reasonable price. Many dealers are general collectors, since their material will have a wider appeal and thus attract a better volume of business. The general collector is often a novice whose interest is only limited by his imagination. When purchasing from a general collector it is wise to take a little extra time evaluating the autograph. Since the item was likely purchased impulsively, the concern for its authenticity or quality was probably less than by that of a subject or type collector.

Although there are relatively few who purchase autographed material solely as an investment, this number is growing annually. The investor as a collector is a subject unto itself.

As a collector you will no doubt fall into one or more of the categories previously defined. It is important and in your best interest to know the collecting goals and characteristics of each form, since you will one day acquire material from one of these sources. Keep in mind your own evolution as a collector, and chart your personal goals. Be realistic, cautious, frugal and above all, have fun.

The history of writing materials

It still amazes me that so many autograph collectors and dealers actually approach acquisition very haphazardly. At the shows I have attended in the past dealers have been approached by people selling autographed materials that, to the uneducated, appear to be rare finds. A careful inspection of some of the material often yields evidence to the contrary.

At a recent show I walked from table to table viewing various assortments of autographs. I found not only significant variations from known authentic autograph styles, but that the very writing materials alone proved the signature was not genuine. For example, felt tip pen signatures from Connie Mack and Mel Ott were being offered, even though each was deceased years before such writing material became available. Another dealer offered a ball point pen sample of Cap Anson who was deceased a good 20 years before such material became popular. It is typical for a purchaser of autographed material to put emphasis on the style and characteristics of the signature, but one must learn to take into account the material on which or with which it is written.

The knowledge of writing instruments and materials can only enhance a baseball autograph collector's chances of obtaining a genuine signature. Writing instruments have had many stages of development, changes that every autograph collector should be aware of.

Pens & Inks

Even the Bible refers in the Old Testament to the presence of ink, and although this evolution was a slow process, the reference point for the baseball autograph collector begins with the use of iron gall inks that were in general use well into the 20th Century. Iron gall inks consist of iron salts mixed with gall nuts, posing a significant danger to manuscripts until the early 1900s due to their evaporation characteristics that often leave heavy acid deposits that erode the material to which the ink is applied.

The evolution of pens saw the goose-quill pen displace the reed pen, common until the 7th Century, and remain the world's most common writing instrument until well into the middle of the 1800s. Because all these pens required quill or metal points (circa 1893), and held only enough ink for a few words of writing, they required the writer to constantly access an open ink bottle. Since this method was such a nuisance, inventors tried for years to invent a pen that would hold a fair quantity of ink. It wasn't unitl 1884 that the first fountain pen was marketed in the United States by L.E. Waterman. An immediate success, fountain pens poured into the market for many years to follow.

Baseball autograph collectors should be aware that every member of the Baseball Hall of Fame could have signed an autograph with a fountain pen. However, due to the pen's introduction near the end of their lifetime, some Hall of Famers probably did not have the opportunity to sign very many signatures in fountain pen. They include Alexander Cartwright, Henry Chadwick, John Clarkson, Edward Delahanty, William Ewing, James Galvin, Michael Kelly, Charles Radbourn and William Wright.

The ballpoint pen is not a 20th Century invention, although its commercial success is due primarily to the United States Army adopting its use in 1944. John Loud, an inventor, received the first United States patent for such a device in 1888, but it was Laszlo Jozsef's design patented in 1937 that was finally commercially accepted. The ballpoint pen has virtually driven the fountain pen out of the market.

The fiber-tip pens were placed on the market in 1951 strictly for commercial use as a consumer goods marker. After some Japanese enhancements the pen was reintroduced and popularized around 1964. Since a significant number of Hall of Fame inductees were deceased prior to 1964, the collector should refer to Materials Analysis Chart III prior to purchasing a fiber-tip sample.

Following 1964 a variety of colored inks were introduced for fiber-tip pens. Many of the inks introduced were not permanent, and a few days' exposure to sunlight can badly fade the signature. Many studies are now being conducted by various private collectors and institutions to identify the deterioration characteristics of these inks.

The mid-1970s found the advent of the Sanford's Sharpie, a highly water resistant, permanent, large fiber-tip marker that writes on virtually every surface. Since its introduction this marker has become the ad hoc standard writing device of the hobby. Unfortunately, when applied to a variety of surfaces, such as baseballs or certain papers, the ink begins to bleed into the material and will significantly discolor while deteriorating the signature. Tests conducted on certain surfaces show a bleeding of twice the thickness of the signature in just five years. Additionally, many collectors are moving away from signatures in Sharpie because of the inability to clearly distinguish the characteristics (individual letters) of the autograph due to the thickness of the pen combined with material surface distinctions.

The 1980s have brought about the introduction of many interesting devices, such as the Pen-Touch marker manufactured by Sakura Color Products Corporation of Japan. These gold or silver markers come in three sizes and are permanent and quick drying. The opaque ink writes on a variety of surfaces, including bats and baseballs. The signatures are particularly notable due to the addition of Xylene, which is a common ingredient of permanent markers, to the ink. Xylene is very harmful or fatal if swallowed; parents should exercise extreme caution if their child intends to use these instruments. The ink's aging characteristics are unknown at this time, but similar to other permanent ink predecessors, they are expected to show significant decomposure on various materials over time. Signatures using this type of marker often have uncharacteristic qualities due to inconsistent ink flow.

For serious collectors who are concerned with the preservation of autographs, it is possible to obtain "material safety data sheets" (MSDS) from every manufacturer that clearly explains an ink's ingredients.

Of equal importance, as stated previously, is for parents to encourage children collecting autographs to use only water-based markers which contain a CP or AP seal of approval. Exposures to permanent markers can produce a variety of symptoms including dizziness, fatigue, headaches and other effects associated with solvents.

Pencils

The pencil has been a popular writing device since the discovery of "lead" strips in 1564. In 1789 the word "graphite" was coined for the discovered substance. Due to the limited supply of graphite at the time, a move was made to combine the material with other substances such as clay. Though a variety of pencils had been developed, the modern day device centers around a 1795 patent by N.J. Conte of France. Pencil leads were square in the early days, and it was not until 1827 that the leads became round or octagonal due to developments by the Dixon Pencil Company.

Pencils have always been a common writing device around the ballpark, primarily due to their being given away with the purchase of scorecards for recording the game's events.

Many fine autographed pieces surface in the market, but unfortunately the inability to authenticate many factors of pencil signatures detracts from purchasing materials in this form. A novice should be discouraged from purchasing items in this form without the advice of an expert.

Paper

Until about 1800, almost all paper was made from rags, except for occasional experimentation with other fiber sources. The invention in 1840 of a machine that could grind wood chips into fiber, accompanied by a process to chemically disintegrate wood in 1851, paved the way for a permanent replacement for rags. The years following 1851 led to widespread growth of inexpensive printing of newspapers and books.

As man attempted to revolutionize the production of paper, the quality has deteriorated over the years. In comparison to hand-made samples, machine-made paper is poor. Many collectors predict that with the advent of very sophisticated inks, applied to very poor quality papers, the life cycle for future autographs will be substantially reduced.

The modern day collector finds most baseball autographs adorning photographs, equipment, or paper. Few typewritten letters seem to enter the market, however many of the tougher signatures to find may adorn such samples. Many baseball executives in the Hall of Fame routinely signed typewritten letters; they include: Ed Barrow, Warren Giles, Branch Rickey, Albert Chandler, and many others. Though the first patent for a home printing machine was issued in 1714, the first practical implementation did not obtain a patent until 1868. The machine, manufactured by E. Remington & Sons, reached the market in 1874. Experts estimate there were over two million typewriters in use in the United States by 1910. It is fair to conclude that every member of the Baseball Hall of Fame could have signed a typewritten letter. It should also be pointed out that those members deceased before 1900, with the exception of the active baseball executives, likely signed only a few. Collectors wishing to authenticate such samples may want to compare the piece with similar dated correspondence. Comparison points should center around fonts or typestyles, kerning or space between the letters, and character alignment.

Collectors are encouraged, as a part of their normal acquisition procedure to study the characteristics of the tool used to autograph the item. As you have probably already concluded, the writing device used to sign the autograph can be just as revealing as the signature in determining the authenticity of an item. Additionally, study of the evolution of the printing and photography industries could also prove very beneficial to an autograph collector's future acquisition needs. Aging and deterioration characteristics of materials are also useful in authenticating autographs, not to mention their value in preservation. Three materials analysis charts have been provided for your convenient reference to writing instruments used by members of the Baseball Hall of Fame. The year of death of each Hall of Famer is noted in parentheses.

Materials analysis — Chart I

Players who couldn't have signed in fountain pen (1884).
* — denotes unlikely (limited time)   ** — very unlikely

Alexander Cartwright (1892)*
Mike Kelly (1894)*
Harry Wright (1895)*

Materials analysis — Chart II

Players who couldn't have signed in ballpoint pen (1944)
* — denotes unlikely (limited time)   ** — very unlikely

Cap Anson (1922)	Buck Ewing (1906)	Tom McCarthy (1922)
Jacob Beckley (1918)	Rube Foster (1930)	Joe McGinnity (1929)
Roger Bresnahan (1944)**	Pud Galvin (1902)	John McGraw (1934)
Dan Brouthers (1932)	Lou Gehrig (1941)	James O'Rourke (1919)
Morgan Bulkeley (1922)	Bill Hamilton (1940)	Ed Plank (1926)
Alexander Cartwright (1892)	Miller Huggins (1929)	Hoss Radbourn (1897)
Henry Chadwick (1908)	Hugh Jennings (1928)	Wilbert Robinson (1934)
Frank Chance (1924)	Ban Johnson (1931)	Amos Rusie (1942)
Jack Chesbro (1931)	Addie Joss (1911)	Al Spalding (1915)
John Clarkson (1909)	Tim Keefe (1933)	Sam Thompson (1922)
James Collins (1943) **	Willie Keeler (1923)	Rube Waddell (1914)
Charles Comiskey (1931)	Joe Kelley (1943)**	John Ward (1925)
Roger Connor (1931)	King Kelly (1894)	Mickey Welch (1941)
Candy Cummings (1924)	Judge Landis (1944) **	George Wright (1937)
Ed Delahanty (1903)	Christy Mathewson (1925)	Harry Wright (1895)
		Ross Youngs (1927)

Materials analysis — Chart III

Players who couldn't have signed in felt tip pen (1964).
* — denotes unlikely (limited time)   ** — very unlikely

Cap Anson (1922)	John Evers (1947)	Kid Nichols (1953)
Frank Baker (1963) **	Buck Ewing (1906)	James O'Rourke (1919)
Ed Barrow (1953)	Rube Foster (1930)	Mel Ott (1958)
Jacob Beckley (1918)	Pud Galvin (1902)	Herb Pennock (1948)
Chief Bender (1954)	Lou Gehrig (1941)	Ed Plank (1926)
James Bottomley (1954)	Josh Gibson (1941)	Hoss Radbourn (1897)
Roger Bresnahan (1944)	Clark Griffith (1955)	Eppa Rixey (1963) **
Dan Brouthers (1932)	Bill Hamilton (1940)	Wilbert Robinson (1934)
Mordecai Brown (1948)	Harry Heilmann (1951)	Amos Rusie (1942)
Morgan Bulkeley (1922)	Rogers Hornsby (1963) **	Babe Ruth (1948)
Jesse Burkett (1953)	Miller Huggins (1929)	Al Simmons (1956)
Alexander Cartwright (1892)	Hugh Jennings (1928)	Al Spalding (1915)
Henry Chadwick (1908)	Ban Johnson (1931)	Tris Speaker (1958)
Frank Chance (1924)	Walter Johnson (1946)	Sam Thompson (1922)
Oscar Charleston (1954)	Addie Joss (1911)	Joe Tinker (1948)
Jack Chesbro (1931)	Tim Keefe (1933)	Dazzy Vance (1961)
Fred Clarke (1960)	Willie Keeler (1923)	Arky Vaughan (1952)
John Clarkson (1909)	Joe Kelley (1943)	Rube Waddell (1914)
Ty Cobb (1961)	King Kelly (1894)	Honus Wagner (1955)
Mickey Cochrane (1962)	Chuck Klein (1958)	Bobby Wallace (1960)
Eddie Collins (1951)	Bill Klem (1951)	Ed Walsh (1959)
James Collins (1943)	Nap Lajoie (1959)	Paul Waner (1965) *
Charles Comiskey (1931)	Judge Landis (1944)	John Ward (1925)
Tom Connolly (1961)	John Lloyd (1964) **	Mickey Welch (1941)
Roger Connor (1931)	Connie Mack (1956)	Hack Wilson (1948)
Candy Cummings (1924)	Rabbit Maranville (1954)	George Wright (1937)
Kiki Cuyler (1950)	Christy Mathewson (1925)	Harry Wright (1895)
Ed Delahanty (1903)	Tom McCarthy (1922)	Cy Young (1955)
Hugh Duffy (1952)	Joe McGinnity (1929)	Ross Youngs (1927)
Bill Evans (1956)	John McGraw (1934)	

The autograph collector's language

Like other specialty groups which share a common interest, the baseball autograph and memorabilia collector has evolved his own form of communication based on neccessity. The form of communication adopted was the language of the autograph collector, slightly modified, to save time and money while delineating new terminology for descriptive purposes. Today abbreviations for conversations or advertising are widely accepted by the hobby community, requiring a novice to learn this skill prior to extensive participation.

The word autograph, used as a verb, often refers to writing one's signature on or in something. To a baseball enthusiast, what that signature is on or in is almost as important as the autograph itself. The item autographed can span over a century worth of memorabilia, from Yankee Stadium chairs, game used player bats, uniforms, advertisements, bottles and baseball spikes to caps, arm casts, pine tar cans and tickets. The greater significance the subject matter, the more appealing to the collector.

The true collector seeks items that shed historical perspective on the subject's life and his accomplishments. Additionally, many collectors fully realize the research appeal of a collection focused specifically upon an element of baseball's history, or time period significant to the sport's development.

True collectors and research professionals describe their materials with the colloquialisms indicative of the game's evolution. The novice collector must therefore study not only the language of the autograph collector, but the terminology and history of the game of baseball. For example, if a collector is reading an ad in a hobby publication and notices the following item of interest: "For sale: Autographed Mickey Mantle - H&B, K100 (Fungo) LS, 125 burn-branded, signed on barrel, small chip on knob, best offer"; it will be in his best interest to have some level of understanding prior to contacting the individual advertising the item.

A handwritten letter, a typed letter or a signed document are some of the most popular material sought by the baseball autograph collector. A handwritten letter is a correspondence entirely in the hand of, and signed by, the author. Often referred to as a "holograph letter," its more common name is "autographed letter signed" or "A.L.S." A.L.S. are often upon personal stationery and much easier to authenticate than an autograph on an index card. Autograph samples from baseball's executives are commonly found on typewritten letters (T.L.S. - "typed letter signed") or on player contracts or documents (D.S. - "document signed").

Additional items such as handwritten notes (A.N.S. - "autograph note signed") or typewritten notes (T.N.S. - "type note signed") are also common forms of communication. Notes are easily distinguished from letters due to a lack of a formal salutation (Dear Billy,) and a lack of a complimentary close (Sincerely, George).

Postcards, particularily those issued by the National Baseball Hall of Fame, are extremely popular. Postcards are abbreviated P.C. or A.P.C.S. for "autographed postcard signed" and

H.O.F.P.P. for "Hall of Fame Plaque Postcard." There have been hundreds of styles of postcards issued over the past decade, with only the popular styles included in a separate section in this book.

Other popular items include "personal bank checks" (P.B.C.), index cards (3x5s), baseball cards (commonly abbreviated by manufacturer and year, 1957T - 1957 Topps), "cut signatures" (C.S.) and photographs (commonly abbreviated by size and finish - 8x10" glossy).

Each year that passes yields tremendous growth in collecting baseball autographs, particularly those elite members in the Hall of Fame. With so many new collectors entering the hobby every year, it was just a matter of time before some of the larger national collectors realized this niche's market potential and began to advertise in many of the trade publications. Their presence will require a greater understanding of manuscript and printing terminology, since they will use abbreviations from these areas in describing their material.

Size abbreviations derived from book printing
Folio: 19x25" large single sheets, folded once to create four pages.
Broadside: Above sheet not folded, but printed on one side.
8vo: Octavo - 8x6" book or manuscript.
4ro: Quarto - 12x8" book or manuscript.
12mo: A sheet 6x4"
Note: Vertical dimensions customarily given first.

Exact reproductions are frequently referred to as "facsimilies." Dealers and manufacturers will on occasion offer facsimilies for sale. These exact reproductions vary significantly in quality and in some cases may require an expert to determine authenticity. The field of printing and publishing has matured so significantly over the past 25 years that facsimilies can now be created easily, with an astounding level of detail.

Athletes from every sport commonly utilize facsimilies in the form of a photograph (copyphoto) of an original autographed photograph, or a photograph that has had a signature printed (screened) upon it. The photographs are so well done that the novice collector is easily convinced of its authenticity. Printed facsimilies are easily identified due to the lack of ink variance in the strokes of the signature. The screening process in printing lays down

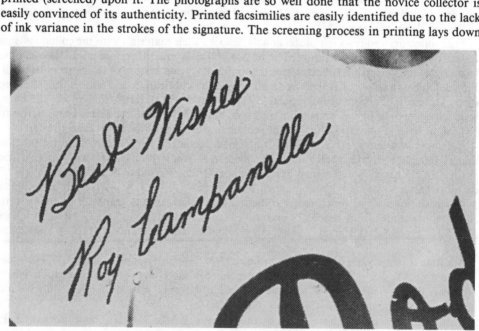

Facsimile signature of Roy Campanella printed on the front of a postcard.

ink very uniformly, a characteristic very easy to spot with a magnifying glass. Photographed facsimilies however, will require careful surface examinatin for the presence of writing material pressure lines and ink.

With the advent of computer based technology, facsimile reproduction can now be achieved on devices such as laser printers, electrostatic copiers, thermal printers, pen plotters, ink jet printers and a host of others. As technology improves and becomes more affordable, better and cheaper facsimilies will find their way into the collector's marketplace, forcing all of us to observe greater caution when buying autographed material.

The rubber stamp is perhaps the most popular facsimilie method used today. Stamped signatures are often easy to identify due to their uniform inking and often haphazard form of application. Examples most common to baseball collectors include Hall of Famers Roy Campenella and Joe Cronin.

Frequent terms used by an autograph collector

Autograph quotation signed: A.Q.S. - a familiar signed quotation attributable to the author.

Bid: the amount of money one is willing to pay for a particular lot of items.

Cachet: a special design, in honor of an event or person, printed on an envelope.

First Day Cover: F.D.C. - an envelope, usually bearing a cachet and bearing a stamp canceled on the first day it was available for sale.

Holograph: writing sample in the hand of the author that may or may not be signed

Legal size: 8½x14" standard paper size (U.S. government 8x12½")

Letter size: 8½x11" standard paper size (U.S. government 8x10½")

Lot: group of materials sold at one time.

Provenance: the record of ownership of an item or collection.

Collectors who are preparing to sell their items through autograph catalogs or auctions must be acquainted with the language of their audience in order to properly describe the material being offered. For each item it is customary to give the author's name, description of material signed, date of writing, addressee of letter, origin, condition, and a description of content. If uncertainty surrounds any item described, provide an explanation. For example, if an item was not dated, try to make an effort ("Probably 1910-1915" or "Circa 1889"). Abbreviations such as n.d. - "no date" or n.p. - "no place of writing was given" are also acceptable if they will not be confusing to the audience. A description of physical condition of the item being offered is absolutely essential. Nothing is more disturbing to a collector than to receive an item in unsatisfactory condition, not to mention that it is the quickest way to lose a customer. It is important to explain physical factors of each item being offered that affect its future value, such as deterioration, stains, missing corners, personalization (Can it be matted out if owner desires to frame the piece?), creases and tears (Can they be repaired?).

The language of the baseball autograph collector is indeed unique, requiring some advanced preparation and commitment. In the chapters ahead there will be many more terms to be discussed as they relate to the definitions and descriptions of the materials being autographed.

Acquiring baseball autographs

In order to establish a significant collection of baseball autographs, the collector should place considerable emphasis on his acquisition procedures. Each collection should be a balance of the collector's personal and financial goals, which will determine the method of acquiring an item. A collector should pursue the procurement path most applicable to meeting his goals. If one's goal is to obtain the autographs of all the members of the Hall of Fame who played in the 1980s, then surely the avenues of acquisition would be much different than a goal of collecting an autographed piece of original game-used equipment from every member of the baseball shrine.

A novice to the field of baseball autograph collecting will have only a handful of really experienced collectors to consult. The lack of expertise in the field has been reciprocal to the amount of accurate information available on the hobby. Though there are very experienced autograph collectors in other fields of interest, few can shed light on the evolutionary signatures of the Hall of Fame inductees. Generally, a veteran private collector may share his acquisition strategy or contacts, but personal or general form collectors (usually dealers), will be very reluctant to quote sources. Books, both on autograph collecting and baseball in general, are very important resources. The numerous newsletters and trade publications can also be helpful.

Collectors' organizations can also be forums for meeting other hobbyists and sharing information. A novice should exercise caution in choosing an organization, because not all groups are of equal value. The good organizations will spend time sharing their knowledge and expertise on the hobby. Often the more advanced groups will even acquire the services of various experts in the field to lecture and educate their members. The groups that have stressed education and professionalism have done a great service for the hobby. Groups not worth joining are those which spend most of their time disparaging other collectors, selling their merchandise, or passing along inaccurate information. Remember, mere membership in an organization doesn't make an expert. Some of the finest collectors in the hobby prefer to pursue their collecting goals outside of organizations. Many organizations publish directories of their members, or willingly pass along information about fellow members' collecting interests, resulting in some collectors preferring anonymity for security reasons.

Recently I conducted a phone study in which I contacted many of the autograph dealers who commonly place full-page advertisements in the hobby's periodicals. When asked which dealers were reputable and which weren't, I was shocked by the results. Not only did the dealers freely exchange their information, but they disparaged many individuals based on isolated incidents and unsubstantiated claims. Additionally, they disparaged most of their local competitors, some of which belonged to the same autograph clubs as themselves. They also recommended to me a few dealers whose reputation has been questionable. Most admitted they had no formal training in autograph authentication.

In 1985, I was interested in purchasing some unique autographed baseball memorabilia and contacted a prominent promoter who dealt in materials of this kind for his advice on dealers to purchase from. To make a very long story short, he highly recommended to me a dealer who ended up selling me a rash of forged material, finally costing me $2,000. There was no way to recoup my loss, forcing me to destroy the forged material. As a collector you must learn to acquire material using methods that are most comfortable to you and involve the least amount of risk. Collectors should learn to use their own judgement and not that of others, which may be biased positively or negatively to one source or another.

Other than having a collection just given to you, there are six methods of acquiring baseball autographs:

1. Personal correspondence with the individual.
2. Direct requests to the individual.
3. Purchasing at an auction.
4. Purchasing from a dealer or promoter.
5. Purchasing items from related sources - antique dealers.
6. Trading.

Few collectors are fortunate enough to correspond directly with the individual or inherit an autograph collection, therefore acquisition is primarily through the five other methods. Prior to 1980, requesting a Hall of Famer's autograph by mail was an inexpensive way to begin a baseball autograph collection. Few requests were refused, particularly if common courtesy was used and a self-addressed stamped envelope was included. For a collector whose concern was content, the results varied with each player. Following 1980, the success rate of acquiring a signature through the mail fell off dramatically. The decrease was attributable to the increase in popularity of collecting baseball Hall of Fame signatures, resulting in an overwhelming number of requests through the mail and the dramatic increase in personal appearances at autograph shows. Obtaining signatures via direct mail requests to the individuals has an unpredictable success rate. Requests can easily be lost, misplaced for long lengths of time, ignored, or even returned with signatures in facsimile form or from a secretary.

The most convenient way of acquiring an autograph is to buy it from a reputable dealer. An established dealer will often offer a wide variety of autographed material. All material offered for sale should be at a fixed price for each item and carry a guarantee of authenticity.

Direct requests to the individual — when that request results in the desired autograph — is the most satisyfying method of autograph acquisition. It is also the only way to absolutely guarantee the authenticity of an autograph. Here, Lou Gehrig signs a baseball for a youngster. (Courtesy National Baseball Library, Cooperstown, N.Y.)

With each item purchased, the dealer should provide a reasonable return policy. As a courtesy to the dealer, the buyer should also promptly return any item found unsatisfactory. A 14-day return policy is common among many baseball autograph and memorabilia dealers. The buyer should always have a full understanding of the dealer's return policy prior to purchasing an item. If a prominent or valuable item is involved, the buyer may want to request a letter of authenticity that also includes a clear description of the return policy. It is also not uncommon for a buyer of a major autographed piece to require a provenance, or history, of the item's origin. It is always beneficial for the novice collector to develop a good relationship with an established dealer. Dealers can be particularly helpful in locating difficult to find items for your collection. The collector may want to provide the dealer with a "want list" of items needed for his collection. If such a list is provided to a dealer, the collector should indicate price range, condition and time frame of the desired acquisition.

Collectors should also request to be added to the dealer's mailing list for future catalogs or sale notifications. To insure that the collector's name remains on such a list, it is a common courtesy to buy at least one item from the dealer on a periodic basis or purchase the catalogs. Receiving catalogs is a good method of comparison shopping and learning each dealer's specialties. Usually the items in a dealer's catalog are only a small part of the available stock, a call or visit should provide a better knowledge of the inventory. The importance of buying only from established and reputable dealers cannot be stressed enough; it will reduce the likelihood of potantial problems resulting from the purchase of forged or stolen merchandise.

The collector should be aware that dealer prices for similar items may vary. Dealers usually price their items based on their local appeal, existing stock, their own knowledge of the item's worth, their own interest in the item, scarcity, and the price they paid for the item. Knowing the characteristics of the dealer will help determine where to find the best deals in his catalog. For example, a catalog from a bat specialist may contain miscellaneous autographed equipment. Since the dealer's primary interest is bats, the inclusion of the equipment was probably an afterthought and therefore bargains may be found in this section. On the contrary, if the dealer's expertise is bats, he may have paid little attention to the necessary authentication characteristics of the other equipment offered, and the collector therefore may be running a risk in purchasing the equipment from him. If a dealer does offer an appealing item, it is suggested that a potential buyer act promptly. "Good deals" are usually gone within hours of the receipt of the catalog or advertisement.

Upon ordering an item from a dealer, the collector should provide immediate payment or notification if other than prompt payment is expected. Upon receipt of the item, the collector should verify the dealer's description and inspect for any unexpected flaws, possibly incurred through shipping. If the item meets the collector's expectations the deal is complete, if not the item may be returned.

Acquiring autographed material at a baseball card show that features special guests signing items is also a common method of collecting. By the time you add up the price of an admission ticket, the price of an autograph ticket, parking, any items you purchase to have autographed, not to mention the value of your time waiting in line, you may have a less than cost effective approach to collecting. What is valuable, however, is your personal experience in meeting the individual and insuring that the signature you obtain meets your expectations. Autograph shows are the recommended means of having scarce and valuable items signed.

Auctions have long been commonplace in the hobby publications. Until recently, mail auctions predominated. However, the entry of some of the largest New York auction houses into the baseball memorabilia field, and the growing popularity of telephone auctions have expanded the arenas for competitive bidding. Typically auctions are platforms for the sale of highly sought-after items, autographs and baseball memorabilia normally unavailable through local dealers or shows. Participation in an auction can be very exciting and offer many collecting advantages. Bargains can be had for the shrewd buyer, and overpriced items can become the possession of many an uneducated bidder. Collectors and dealers study collectible purchases at auctions as a guideline for gauging market demand. Not all auctions are market indicators. Those sparsely attended or poorly publicized will yield significantly lower prices, while well-publicized auctions may find two or three collectors bidding feverishly high for the same piece. Mail auction participation depends on the quality of the material being offered, catalog or advertisement presentation, terms and conditions of the auction, as well as the reputation of the seller. Since many auctions do not guarantee the authenticity of the item, the buyer bids at his own risk.

A buyer, new to the method of acquiring autographs via auctions, should consider hiring an agent to act on his behalf. The agent, who is often a well established dealer, will also provide the buyer with his opinions on authenticity, scarcity and value. The common fee for dealer services is about 10 percent. Remember, that once a buyer employs the services of an agent, he cannot refuse the items purchased on his behalf. A buyer employing the services of an agent should clearly explain in advance the goals and objectives of their relationship. This will insure that an agent does not bid in excess of the buyer's purchasing budget, or purchase an item of a condition unacceptable to the buyer. Each auction has bidding restrictions, therefore a strategy should be set by both the buyer and agent in advance to assure some level of success. Advanced estimates for lots may be provided by the auctioneer, however, these are just that, "estimates." Often items can be purchased significantly higher or lower than these figures.

Commonly, when auction houses receive two identical mail bids, the first bid received is deemed the winning bid. At auctions the bidder closer to the lectern, in case of an identical bid from the floor, is declared the winner. The buyer should understand the rules for identical bidding in advance of the auction.

Over the past few years, auctions have, in my opinion, improved in the quality and scarcity of the material being offered to the public. Mail auctions are common and usually attract large participation from the hobby. The only weakness has been the sellers' inability to stick to a prompt closing time in the case of auctions which offer the option of telephone bidding. Too many auctions end up being a fiasco during the final minutes of bidding. Some bidders have even been called the day after the close of an auction for a final bid, a method which is totally inappropriate. Auctioneers who fail to close auctions promptly lose the respect of all the bidders participating. The only time an unsuccesssful bidder should be contacted after the close of an auction, is if the successful bidder has reneged (failed to honor his winning bid) and the unsuccessful bidder is now highest bid. If the unsuccessful bidder is contacted in this manner after an auction has closed, he has no obligation to honor his bids. To honor unsuccessful bids in this manner is clearly a courtesy extended to the seller. A buyer should beware of auctions from the same auctioneer that consistently contain the same material. This is usually an indication that the material is unsatisfactory or the auctioneer is not following acceptable auction guidelines.

It is also possible for collectors to obtain autographs from parallel hobby enthusiasts. This could range from antique stores, book collectors, coin collectors and even jewelers. Knowledge of baseball autographs and memorabilia is often poor in these areas, since this is not the vendor's primary source of interest. The buyer should approach acquisition here with extreme caution. You can find bargains, but the likelihood is minimal and the risk of an unauthentic piece being purchased is considerably higher than the previously mentioned sources.

Acquiring signatures by combing over items at flea markets or material from a casual collector at a card show is tempting, though time-consuming and unlikely to uncover quality items. Additional problems can also arise when authenticity, scarcity, or value become an issue. Local card shows and flea markets are filled with self-proclaimed autograph and memorabilia experts, often substantiated by only limited contacts with players and a general collection of 50 or fewer signatures. A collector should exercise caution when purchasing items from these sources, since their knowledge is often limited and in some cases inaccurate.

A good source for acquiring autographs is fellow collectors. Additionally, you can share your experiences and collecting needs to form a better base of hobby knowledge. An inexperienced collector can really benefit by such a relationship. Choose collectors whose opinions and practices you respect. If an expensive item is being purchased don't hesitate to ask the fellow collector for a written statement of authenticity that includes a return policy. A reputable collector will gladly oblige such a request.

Trading is also a recommended form of acquiring autographed material. Many collectors have established a wonderful network of collectors to trade with all across the country. This by far is the most rewarding form of acquisition, since you often receive items to fill your needs, while supplying items to fill another collector's wants. The hobby is filled with some interesting people, this is one way of getting to know them.

Acquisitions are the source by which great collections are built. It is important for each collector to choose the means that best suit his particular goals. The novice is encouraged to acquire only the finest materials available from the sources he feels most comfortable with and at a reasonable budget level. The collector's satisfaction is of utmost importance. A collector should never acquire an item that he is the least bit uncomfortable with. Be conscious of all the elements surrounding acquisition and enjoy the thrill of building an outstanding collection.

Hints for acquiring autographs through the mail

☆ Always include a self-addressed stamped envelope (SASE) for convenient response. Please be sure that the enclosed envelope is of proper size to house the returned material, and that proper postage is affixed.

☆ Be brief, personal and sincere with your request. Exhibit in a few sentences your genuine interest in, and knowledge of, a player's career. Courtesy is paramount.

☆ Avoid form letters. In addition to being inpersonal and unflattering, the letters typically have a low response rate.

☆ To avoid confusion and disappointing responses, requests should be succinct and specific. If personalization is desired, please clearly indicate it in your request.

☆ Be conscious of a player's time by including no more than one or two items to be autographed.

☆ Be reasonable with your expectations. Some players receive hundreds of requests a day and have little time to read a request, let alone respond to it.

☆ Don't risk sending expensive items through the mail. Although I am astounded by the accuracy and promptness exhibited by the U.S. Postal Service, most collectors are not in position to replace lost merchandise.

☆ Be creative with your request. Prior to sending out your letter collectors should ask themselves these questions: What is unique about my request that will make a player want to respond? Will my request stand out among the hundreds of others he receives? What would be my reaction to such a request?

Baseball autograph acquisition evaluation

This chart/scoring system was developed to aid the collector in determining his acquisition risk for a particular piece of autographed baseball memorabilia.

Question	Score	Possible Points
1.) How would you rate the scarcity of the item autographed? 5 4 3 2 1 (Abundant) (Scarce)	_____	5
2.) Can the autographed item be dated? (Yes = 5, No = 1)	_____	5
3.) Rate the value of the autographed item: 5 4 3 2 1 (High) (Low)	_____	5
4.) Does the autographed item show any signs of alteration or variation from known characteristics? (Yes = 1, No = 10)	_____	10
5.) Does the writing instrument used conform in origin to the signee's lifetime? (Yes = 5, No = 1)	_____	5
6.) Was the material obtained through a reputable source? (Yes = 10, Unsure = 5, No = 1)	_____	10
7.) Is the source you obtained the item from willing to provide any guarantees, return policy, letter of authenticity, etc? (Yes = 10, No = 1)	_____	10
8.) Signature characteristics: (Score each) (Yes = 10, Unsure = 2, No = 0) — Does the capitalization conform to known examples?	_____	10
— Does the signature size conform to known examples?	_____	10
— Does the character formation conform to known examples?	_____	10
— Does the signature slant conform to known examples?	_____	10
— Does the style (flamboyance) conform to known examples?	_____	10
Total —	_____	100

Note: A "no" answer to any question after #5 should make you reconsider your purchasing plans.

Scoring:
   7-60 high risk   60-80 moderate risk   80-100 little risk

Collector's checklist for mail ordering

Is there a minimum order?

What are the postage and handling costs?

What types of payments are accepted — VISA, MasterCard, etc.?

Is there a minimum credit card order?

What amount of sales tax is required?

Can items be reserved?
Does the dealer ship to post office boxes?
What are the proper insurance costs?
Are there volume discounts available?
Do I have to include a SASE (self addressed stamped envelope) with the order?
Can items be shipped outside the continental United States?
Can I be added to the dealer's mailing list?
Does the dealer accept COD (cash on delivery) orders?
If CODs are accepted, what type of payment does the dealer prefer?
If I pre-order an item and change my mind at a later date, can I be refunded?
Can items be sent on approval?
Are foreign funds accepted?
Are all sales final?
What is the dealer's return policy?
When should I expect delivery?
How is the item being delivered?
Is there a money-back guarantee?

Common mail bid auction rules

☆ Postage and insurance are typically added to the invoice.

☆ Most auctions do not allow "buy" or unlimited bids. A "buy" is when the auctioneer is told by a bidder to buy the lot for a reasonable cost mutually determined, commonly 10% above previous bid.

☆ Commonly lots are not to be broken into individual items, therefore bidders are requested to bid by lot.

☆ The highest bid should represent the maximum selling price of the lot, no additional charges beyond postage and handling should be added to the total.

☆ Invoicing by seller should commence within 10 days after closing date of the sale. Payment upon receipt of invoice is expected promptly. Included with the invoice, and provided by the seller, should be a SASE (self-addressed stamped envelope) as a courtesy to the highest bidder.

☆ Mail bid sales commonly close two weeks from date of auction publication, unless otherwise stated by seller.

☆ As a guarantee that the highest bidder will honor his bid, seller may require a deposit. This deposit is typically not returned if high bidder fails to honor his bids, it shall however be applied as partial payment against the bid made by the highest bidder. Any deposit requested by seller must be clearly stated in the catalog or advertisement. Any deposits being held by seller from unsuccessful bidders must be returned promptly following the close of the auction.

☆ Any item not properly described — condition or grading, year, manufacturer — by the seller may be returned by the highest bidder. All items should be guaranteed authentic by the seller.

☆ A seller should allow a grace period of up to two weeks upon receipt of buyer for returns from highest bidder.

☆ A seller has the right to reject a bid for any reason whatsoever.

☆ A bidder is obligated to honor any and all bids submitted.

☆ Any unusual exception to common mail bid rules for an auction must be clearly stated by the seller in the auction catalog or advertisement.

☆ A pre-registration procedure may be requested in order to simplify bidding procedure on the final day of the auction.

☆ A seller should be accessable during specific times during the auction's duration in order to answer questions from bidders.

☆ A seller may request minimum bid increases over previous bid.

Autograph variations

The most fascinating yet perplexing aspect of collecting autographs is the seemingly endless anomalies of the signature.

Anomalies or deviations are simply the departure from the usual method of signing one's name. These variations can be related to a person's mood, health, age, circumstance, popularity, writing tool and the item the signature is placed upon. Any person's signature may vary due to those factors; as human beings our signatures are inconsistent, determined by circumstance.

I have written many articles over the past three years which attempt to educate the novice collector in signature variations. Since then, the hobby has grown dramatically. Anyone who has witnessed the autograph lines at shows or spent endless hours in line for an autograph session at the Otesaga Hotel in Cooperstown can certainly verify this statement. Though the hobby has grown in number, our autograph education quotient, if such a thing existed, would show less impressive improvement. This is perhaps justifiable considering the increased volume of superstar shows, larger number of dealers and greater number of new hobbyists entering this facet of collecting.

Failure to identify an authentic autograph due to individual changes or evolution is a common problem faced by both the novice and experienced collector. A good example is the signature of Don Mattingly. In 1984 his signature was usually very small. When asked to autograph baseballs he would, instinctively not sign on the "sweet spot." The "D" in Don was rounded and less pronounced. The double "tt" in Mattingly was often very open and recognizable as two loops. The "g" in Mattingly had a much longer decender, or lower portion stroke, and the "y" was similar to a simple vertical stroke. The "i" was dotted often with a round circle.

In 1987, Mattingly's signature was a stark contrast. The "D" in Don had doubled in size and was eliptical in nature versus round. The "tt" in Mattingly was thinner in stroke and often not recognizable as two loops. The "ly" ending changed completely to an opposite direction sweep. To an inexperienced collector, or someone who obtained a version in 1984, the 1987 Mattingly signature might be incorrectly denounced as "not authentic." In contrast, early Mattingly autographed material might be passed over by collectors familiar with his current signature due to the significant variance.

Unless an autograph deviation is associated with a particular major event or period of time, pinpointing its origin is usually very difficult. There are, of course, dramatic autograph variations associated with a major illness or accident, as is the case with Walter Alston and Roy Campanella.

Collectors and dealers are not spending adequate time identifying these variations. The result is some outstanding authentic autograph values unrecognized by inexperienced collectors, and self-proclaimed autograph experts giving worthless authentication advice to novice collectors. A good collector or dealer is aware of the ongoing evolution of the subject's signature, and studies autographs with care and patience. Additionally, more and more collectors are realizing how difficult it is to authenticate signatures and how painstaking the task undertaken by experts to determine the origin of an autograph really is. Sources such as the Baseball Hall of Fame, periodicals and private collections continue to play a vital role in obtaining authentic examples for comparison. Inexpensive photocopies from these sources can be accumulated into a comprehensive reference file for study and comparison.

Complicating issues even further have been many of the modern day players being taught "autograph avoidance" by veteran players. Techniques these stars teach range from the "sign while you walk method" to shortening the signature for speed/convenience. I have even witnessed situations where players have signed other names or even scribbled illegibly upon a baseball. Unfortunately, because of these tactics autograph authenticators of the future will have great difficulty determining if a signature is genuine.

To complement a reference file, an autograph collector should be aware of autograph anomalies that can be traced to a subject's life. Knowledge of major events and their ramifications upon an individual's handwriting or signature can aid a collector in authentication. I remember passing up the opportunity to purchase some nice 1960s memorabilia autographed by Pete Rose because I was unfamiliar with the non-looped "P" and "R" capitalization exhibited in his early signatures. I later learned that as Rose's popularity soared, so did the flamboyance of his signature.

Autograph anomalies come in many forms including, but not limited to the following:

Capitalization

Example: Mickey Mantle (1954), Capital "M" in Mickey slanted to the right, with beginning stroke starting at the highest point of the signature above the top of the "k". Capital "M" in Mantle same characteristic as first capital "M", with greater separation between the two loops.

Mickey Mantle (1985), Capital "M" in Mickey slants slightly to the right, with beginning stroke starting about the height of the "c" and descending dramatically down and to the right to form the familiar dramatic loop at the beginning of Mickey and repeated slightly smaller with the capital "M" in Mantle.

Variations of Bill Dickey's signature through the years.

34

Signature size
Example: Don Mattingly (1983), signed inconspicuously small, compared to his much larger and bolder style of today.

Character formation
Example: Since 1976, George Brett has made the following modifications to his signature:
1.) Changed the "G" in George completely in form from what once resembled a "G" to a form more like a "J".
2.) Kept the "e" in George, but dropped the "o" and the "r".
3.) Extended the descender of the "g" in George and tightened the loop in the "e".
4.) "B" in Brett not eliptical, smoother in form.
5.) "r" in Brett is not connected to "rett".
6.) "e" has been tightened up and often appears closed up or solid in Brett.
7.) "tt" in Brett shows more loop formation and has been slightly extended.
8.) "tt" in Brett is now crossed by the final stroke versus an independent crossing of both.

Signature slant
Example: Carl Hubbell's autograph (pre mid-1970s) had a 20-30 degree slant right, versus post-1980s' stiff, squared off, 0-10 degree slant left.

Legibility
Example: Mike Schmidt's autograph varies depending on the circumstance surrounding the request, from a crisp example where most characters are legible to a rendition often recognized only by the "M" in Mike.

Flamboyance
Example: Reggie Jackson's flamboyant autograph of today is a departure from his stiff "Reginald M. Jackson" signature of the 1970s.

If any of the above were not difficult enough to keep track of, add to it the combination of two or more of the elements to create what is commonly known as a style variation. Style variations are commonplace, particularly among certain players. Since a person never signs the exact same signature twice, variations naturally occur. These variations can be subtle or in great contrast depending on the environment. Style variations most often occur during the beginning and ending stroke of a signature or in the capitalization.

During the past few decades I have witnessed the following style variations in the authentic autograph of Joe DiMaggio:
1. Capitalization:
   — "J" in Joe seven different styles
   — "D" in DiMaggio eleven different styles
(Note: Styles in capitalization vary in size, beginning and ending of character stroke, slant, character formation and flamboyance.)
   2. "oe" in Joe has remained relatively consistent over the years, varying slightly in size and slant.
3. I have seen the "e"at the end of Joe connect to the "D" in DiMaggio. (very rare)
4. The "i" in DiMaggio varies considerably in slant, size and where the "i" is dotted — above the "M", below the top stroke of the "M" and even in the middle of the "M".
5. "Maggio" in DiMaggio has varied little, with the exception being the size of the "gg" descending loops and slant.
6. The construction of the second loop of the "M" in DiMaggio is always smaller in size and angled inward, often touching the end of the first loop.
7. I have seen the beginning character stroke of the "M" in DiMaggio, start on the bottom (very rare), instead of the top across from the finishing character stroke of the "D" (common).
8. The slash stroke below the "io" and at the end of the signature has been consistently there, however a mystery as to the reason.

Studying signature variations is a never-ending task, complicated by circumstances and cost. A majority of the signatures you will find will exhibit one or more of the style variations listed here. It is important to remember that during a subject's life deviations will occur. Sometimes inconsistencies are significant like the examples given, on other occasions they will be less dramatic. The most common conclusion after examining a signature that exhibits style variations, is for a buyer to deem it unauthentic. A collector or dealer should be warned that disparagement, or the attempt to discredit someone, is a crime. If you feel an item is not authentic, simply do not buy it. Remember that if the burden is placed on you to prove beyond the shadow of a doubt that an item is not authentic, could you? Style variations are a collector's nightmare. More often than not they are dismissed as forgeries, allowing a better-educated buyer an opportunity to purchase the collectible.

Variations of Joe DiMaggio's autograph.

Forgery detection

Of greatest concern to the modern day collector of baseball autographs is the possible acquisition of a forged signature. A collector is reminded that this is a concern faced by every niche of the hobby. From cards to uniforms, authenticity is paramount. In the last five years there has been a proliferation of salesmen's uniform samples, card reprints and phony autograph signatures, all of which dramatically increase the collector's chances of picking up a fake item.

The rapid growth of the hobby combined with the overall lack of accurate information has fueled the influx of unauthentic items. The purchasing power of new collectors entering the hobby, inexperienced with the necessary authentication techniques, is a tempting scenario to many unscrupulous individuals. It is imperative that every collector, regardless of which facet of the hobby he participates in, spends as much time acquiring a thorough knowledge of authentication techniques as he does adding new items to his collection. If becoming an authority yourself is not an option, you must develop a relationship with someone you can trust who has a thorough knowledge in your specific area of collecting. There are only a handful of experts in this field, predominantly private collectors who have spent years acquiring the skills and materials necessary to support their own area of collecting. Since your likelihood of obtaining an expert's service is minimal, the burden of education rests primarily on your shoulders.

Many experts have had formal training and are professionals in their field. Often these experts have spent over 20 years authenticating everything from literary manuscripts to presidential correspondence. Though experts certainly have the authentication skills, few of them have the background knowledge in baseball required to fully assess many items, another obstacle the collector must acknowledge. An expert is generally not a dealer at a show selling 20 Willie Mays or Pete Rose signatures, nor is it likely to be a show promoter whose claim to fame may be owning 30 old signatures of Don Mattingly or Bob Feller.

The process of authenticating autographed material is meticulous and requires dedication. In the area of baseball collectibles, it requires an in-depth knowledge of the game and its individual personalities, as well as demanding a thorough knowledge of the characteristics and environmental factors that can help differentiate between a forgery and an authentic signature. These characteristics and factors include: the signature habits of the signer, the writing materials available to the player during that period, paper, ink, the signer's age and even health.

In addition it is useful to have some knowledge of the correct methods of comparing handwriting samples and the impact of all the factors previously mentioned. Many of the factors and characteristics considered in an examination of a signature may not, by themselves, provide conclusive proof of authenticity. Many collectors have mistaken a genuine autograph for a forgery due to a variation in one of these factors. In many cases the uncharacteristic quality of the signature can be attributed to an extreme or unusual circumstance during the signing. For example, the excitement of a moment, such as reaching a career milestone or winning the World Series, can dramatically affect an individual's autograph.

Collectors should be aware of the existence of many unusual items. At first glance an item may appear questionable, however, through careful inspection it proves authentic. As an example, I once witnessed a women going through an autograph line to obtain the signature of Reggie Jackson on a baseball already signed by Babe Ruth and other players who have reached the 500 home run plateau. This type of item, though authentic, could create skepticism among future potential buyers. If the paper or item was manufactured after the purported lifetime of the individual's signature adorning the item, or the sample exhibits the use of tools that didn't exist during a specific period, then the item is clearly a forgery. Collectors should, however, not presumptuously conclude, based on cursory examination, that a particular item is not genuine. The experienced and knowledgable collector can often find examples of signatures adorning many unique items that have been overlooked by the less informed.

Tools

Tools for authentication have never been better. Many government agencies are using sophisticated computer based image processing equipment that can lift signatures off of any item. Using sophisticated scanning technology, the images can be manipulated, enlarged, or edited in a vast number of ways for comparison. Signatures can actually be reconstructed and merged with other samples to determine authenticity. In the future these sophisticated tools, now priced around $75,000, will evolve into low cost versions that will eliminate many of the conventional methods currently used by the authenticator.

Until this equipment becomes cost effective for the collector, the microscope will remain a practical alternative. Through the lens of a microscope the authenticator can examine specific characteristics of letter formation, pen stroke and line weight. Various sources of light can also be used to detect the existence of materials such as pencil and assorted ink types.

Perhaps the most necessary, affordable and useful tool remains the magnifying glass. Of utility to the advanced collector may be an opaque projector. Both of these tools are particularly effective in comparing signature traits.

The collector will also find that the use of test plates is helpful in forgery detection. Test plates are measuring devices, typically made of glass or clear plastic, etched with various scaled grids at a variety of angles. Though most often used for typewritten letters, they can be especially useful in measuring character size, and the ratio of the individual letter to an entire signature. Additionally, signature slant characteristics can easily be identified by using test plates.

Recognizing characteristics

Regardless of the tools employed in the process, authentication begins with a good reference collection of examples (or reproductions) of original baseball autographs. Most serious collectors have an extensive file of original baseball signatures obtained in person or from credible sources such as estates and legal documents. Politely requested, most dealers and some private collectors will exchange reproductions of original material, as it is in their best interest to raise the buying public's level of knowledge. It is the goal of this book to provide the collector with a strong base to complement his reference collection. It is important for the collector to continue to update these references, as the signature process is an evolutionary one.

Revealing elements that seem to be consistent with many forgeries relate to the manner in which a signature was placed or positioned and the material signed. Normal handwriting, as most of us are aware of, is produced with very smooth strokes, consistent in strength and notably careless in detail. This does vary depending on the device used; fountain pen versus Sharpie, and the material being signed; a flat item such as a postcard versus a baseball or bat. The exceptions are often the writing of ill or aging individuals, commonly exemplified by the signatures later in life of Carl Hubbell, Frankie Frisch, Elmer Flick, Earl Averill and Walter Alston.

If you are an observant collector you will find that certain characteristics are common to many forged signatures and are fairly easy to detect. They include: unusual or uncommon breaks in a signature; an unusual change in stroke thickness as a result of stiff starts or ends instead of flying starts or endings; or unusual roughness in upward or downward strokes, indicative of a slow and careful reproduction. Roughness in the strokes is not enough to certify a signature is fake. As mentioned previously, tremors in the writing of an individual can result from age or ill health, as witnessed by comparing early examples of a player's signatures to those later in his life. In fact, the collector should be more speculative of a recently obtained smooth signature of a Charlie Gehringer or Luke Appling, than a rough example.

The most common mistake made by beginning collectors, is the failure to recognize authentic earlier material. Signatures mature and may change considerably over the lifetime of an individual. Notable examples are Carl Hubbell, Mickey Mantle, Joe DiMaggio, Pete Rose and Hank Aaron.

The material that the autograph adorns can readily unmask a fake. That is why significant attention should be paid to learning the manufacturing process and identification of items commonly autographed. The collector should study printing or manufacturing dates of baseball cards, postcards, and baseballs, as well as the deterioration characteristics of the various types of material. To a lesser degree it is also helpful to study the specific characteristics of various inks. There are sophisticated testing techniques available for determining the age of inks. However, like image processing equipment, they are beyond the budget of the average collector.

Pencil, as a writing device, is a completely different scenario. Pencils were, and are still, rarely used for letters and documents, but they were very commonly used at the ballpark, traditionally being given away with the purchase of a scorecard. A forged pencil signature is the most difficult of all to detect, because it can simply be retouched, and is extremely difficult to judge stroke direction. Experts may be able to determine stroke direction by examining the paper fibers with the use of a microscope, however this is not typically done by the average collector. Definitive conclusions based on pencil signatures are nearly impossible based on the writing alone, and therefore pencilled autographs are not recommended purchases for the novice, or even wary, collector.

The traced signature is a common forgery technique. This method quite simply involves placing a signature on a light table, then tracing over it in pencil. Ink is then applied over the pencil or to an indented surface if no pencil is used, and the pencil is erased or the surface rolled to smooth out the indentations. Signatures of this type have very unnatural characteristics, such as smooth, non-spontaneous curves, and are therefore easy to detect. Careful microscopic evaluation will reveal the indentations or erasure marks. Facsimile signatures show little to no variations from sample to sample, uncharacteristic of how an individual signs his name.

Another technique used by the forger is the false aging of paper. The techniques used are similar to those demonstrated in grade school and involve soaking in lemon juice or tea, then applying heat. A majority of quality autographed material is on good paper, therefore absent of dirt, holes or other distinct flaws. The discoloration of paper is a natural process and thus easily identified by an expert.

Recently the most popular technique has been to add a forged signature to old paper, resulting in a "feathering" of the signature. The ink exhibits uncharacteristic traits due to an abnormal amount of absorption by the paper. Commonly the signatures are added with other genuine examples, to throw the collector off guard. The forged signatures are most often added at the edge or bottom of the material, as to not conflict with an authentic sample. If the item is detected as a forgery, the genuine autographs can be clipped by the forger and recycled. Material commonly found with forged signatures include the 1939 First Day of Issue baseball centennial stamp cachet, stock certificates, old baseball club or hotel stationery, postcards, and old baseball guides. By far the most commonly forged signature on the market today, based on my examination of material available for sale, is Lou Gehrig.

What should you look for?

The collector should try to recognize characteristics unique to each individual's writing, such as specific letter formations. Pay detailed attention the following: the way the individual crosses a "t" or dots an "i" all capital letters, loops on lower case letters such as "e", "a" and "o", natural breaks, finish strokes on the letters "v", "w" and "g", and the tendency to extend or abbreviate characters at the conclusion of the signature, exemplified by Carl Yastrzemski.

Additional peculiarities include specific variations before and after particular letters, connections between letters, angular or straight formations and the spacing between letters. Bluntness in the beginning and ending strokes, slant and length should also be reviewed. The letter "s" is also a suggested reference, as it often varies in angularity, curvature, roundness, size and proportions. Samples worth noting are Duke Snider and Eddie Mathews.

The pressure and movements of the pen can also be studied, specifically the upward and downward strokes for width and application variation.

Bill Terry, Dizzy Dean, Don Drysdale and Red Ruffing are also good examples to study character slants in particular letters such as "f", "y", "h", "n" and "z." The proportions of these individual letters should be compared to the other characters in the individual's signature.

Forgery fear

If you are going to collect or deal in baseball autographs and memorabilia you will some day experience "forgery fear." It's commonplace for the experienced in the hobby, but difficult to face as a novice. As a dealer you may have an individual stroll up to your table and claim that everything or portions of the material are not authentic, despite the fact that some of the autographs may have been obtained in person. There is a certain breed of individual, who despite their obvious lack of formal education or knowledge in the field, feels a necessity as a self-proclaimed expert to cast judgement on your material. I will never forget setting up at a show, where a dealer who was not exhibiting came up to my table and told me some of my autographed 3x5" cards "didn't look good." My reply was that if I found out that this was indeed true, that he was going to have some explaining to do in court, since I purchased the material from him three years ago at a flea market.

Another buying ploy you may encounter as a dealer involves a group of individuals teaming up to denounce a particular item on your table to be a forgery, only to set "forgery fear" in your mind so that you might part with the item at a ridiculous price, now doubtful of the item's authenticity.

Often individuals will even buy items from a dealer specifically to resell. If the individual is unsuccessful at selling the merchandise, he returns the unsold items claiming that it is forged material and intimidates the original seller into taking the merchadise back.

Circumstances also arise due to competition. At every show dealers will have equivalent merchandise priced above or below the other dealers in attendance. It is natural to be competitive, or even jealous of someone's material, however it is against the law to disparage or discredit another dealer with claims that his material is not authentic. If you are going to attempt this strategy you should be well aware of the legal circumstances surrounding your claims and be willing to accept the consequences. This matter will be elaborated on in the ethics portion of this book.

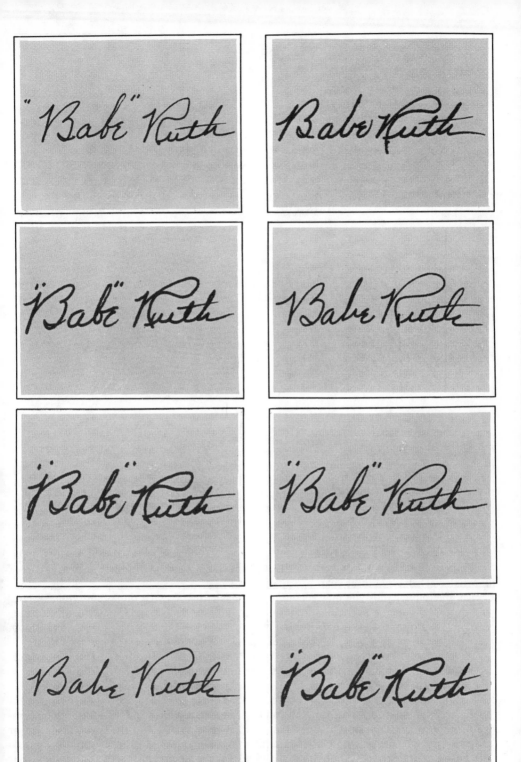

Each of these "Babe Ruth" signatures is a forgery

Each of these "Lou Gehrig" signatures is a forgery

Suggestions

The acquisition of autographed baseball memorabilia should be handled with care if the collector is at all concerned with preserving the value and integrity of his collection. Here are some suggestions that are reinforced by other chapters in this book:

★ Buy your material from an established and reputable dealer or obtain them in person. Qualify dealers yourself, by first purchasing small amounts of material easily verified for authenticity. Use your own judgement in determining whether a dealer is reputable; taking the advice of other dealers is a risk.

★ Stay away from questionable material. If you can't explain the anomalies of a piece, how are you going to be able to sell it when such a time arises?

★ If you run across any questionable material at a dealer's table, and you feel a need to express your concerns, do so in private.

★ Do not make any public claims of forgery, unvalidated or unsubstantiated, that could lead to legal ramifications. If an item does not look good don't buy it.

★ Usually, the more expensive the autographed item, the less likely it is a forgery. An autographed bat is less likely to be fake versus the same signature on a postcard.

★ Try to collect material that can be dated, such as baseballs and cards.

★ Stay away from signatures in pencil, unless you consider yourself an expert.

★ Do not be intimidated as a dealer or collector. Have faith in your own ability to make an accurate judgement based on your knowledge.

★ If you experience a bad transaction with another dealer or collector simply don't deal with him anymore.

★ Quality will vary from one dealer to the next, and so will expertise. Try to deal with individuals who specialize in the areas you are collecting.

★ Maintain an up-to-date clip file of authentic signatures for comparison.

★ If you find an expensive item that you want to purchase, it may be worth spending a few dollars to have it authenticated by an expert.

★ Cautiously inspect all autographed material over 30 years old before making a purchase. Material from members of the Hall of Fame inducted in the last 30 years, with the exception of those deceased prior to induction, is generally available and abundant in a variety of forms. You will find a lot more forged Babe Ruth signatures than those of Ted Williams.

★ Meticulously study older signature samples. A person's signature can vary extensively with age and health.

★ Always be familiar with a dealer's return policy prior to a purchase.

★ Don't immediately discount the authenticity of unusual items, there are many unique items in this market.

The threat of forgery is not unique to autograph collecting, it is a concern to anyone who deals with any type of valuable merchandise. It is a threat that can be dissipated by education and following the suggestions of those who have made mistakes in the past. With a thorough knowledge of the characteristics of forgeries and genuine signatures, the expert can determine the authenticity of virtually all the materials examined. There will always be a small percentage that exemplify both characteristics, that fact must be accepted by both the collector and the hobby. Baseball autograph collecting is a wonderful way to cherish the memory of an individual, and with the commitment of everyone in the hobby to educate themselves on forgery detection it will continue to be an enjoyable pursuit.

Collection organization and display

One of the greatest satisfactions for a collector of baseball autographs and memorabilia is to display his collection. Whether a collection is large or small, thick or thin, round or flat, proper attention to the display, storage and organization should be of utmost importance to the collector. A haphazard approach to any of these factors may lead to serious damage to the material. Dealers should also pay particular attention to the proper display of materials at shows to insure that items are handled properly in order to preserve the value of these materials.

For the autograph collector a file cabinet is often suitable for storage. Storage of the files is most often vertical, however due to size it may be necessary to store some items horizontally. File cabinets come in a variety of sizes and models. Collectors are encouraged to explore which cabinet fulfills their particular needs.

Each collector's filing system is unique to his own collection. Whatever filing system you choose should allow the greatest flexibility, while providing necessary reference information about each acquisition. There is nothing more frustrating to a collector than not being able to identify the background of an acquisition. Each file cabinet should contain a listing of each file it houses. If necessary, you may even want to store your more expensive items in individual folders to avoid any potential mishandling problems associated with an abundance of material in one file. Collectors are also encouraged to have copies and transcripts of their valuable materials to be used as reference pieces, again to avoid mishandling of the original item. The collector will also find it most useful to have a file drawer dedicated to reference materials, catalogs, related clippings and articles about collecting.

To avoid security problems, collectors are encouraged to store valuable items in a safety deposit box at the local bank. If a piece from a collection is needed, it is best to make a copy and use it for your needs. Fireproof cabinets and safes are also very useful for the collector. For collectors with a very large collections that they wish to keep at home, I recommend a home security system. Architectural drawing cabinets are also very handy for the storage of autographed artwork, posters and other large format items.

For preservation purposes acid-free file folders are recommended, or sheets of acid-free paper inserts placed on both sides of the item, in the manilla folder. These items can be purchased from large stationery companies and some commercial art supply outlets. The collector should be wary of all other types of storage material unless a clear description of the item's composition is available. Since the deterioration characteristics of many new inks are unknown, it is suggested that collection pieces should never be in contact with other pieces in the same folder. If archival quality preservation materials are not in line with a collector's budget, acetate pages can be used. Routine inspection of the material is suggested when stored in this manner to avoid any potential problems. If you choose to store items this way, you must accept the associated risks.

Cataloging may seem a chore to most collectors, however, in the long run it usually is well worth the effort. Each collector should choose the cataloging system that best suits his needs. These systems can range from a loose-leaf binder approach to separate index cards for each item. Cataloged information should include: Name, description of the item — size, form, etc. — date of the material, any unique characteristics of the piece, date of purchase, purchase price, and who it was purchased from.

A reference file containing values is also extremely useful. Before disposing of any hobby periodicals, clip the ads offering the types of material you typically purchase. If you know that you may eventually purchase an autographed Stan Musial bat, for example, it may be handy to have a convenient listing of values and possible sources.

Though it is common for museums and libraries to mark items with acquisition numbers or stamps, this is not a procedure I recommend to the average collector. Autographed items often change hands. It is in the best interest to all parties not to alter the piece in any way. If a collector is compelled to have a reference to a piece, a photograph or copy should suffice.

Sharing your collection through attractive and informative displays can be a source of great gratification for the collector and for the beholder, as an educational experience. Each collector should take as much pride in displaying his collection as he did in acquiring it. To properly display a collection one should first be aware of proper preservation methods and the various factors affecting deterioration. The collector should consult the "Autograph preservation" chapter in this book prior to beginning a display.

To thoroughly appreciate a display, every collector should pay a visit to the National Baseball Hall of Fame and Museum in Cooperstown. The officers and staff of the museum have done a wonderful job in recreating the excitement and nostalgia surrounding the game. Few people realize the amount of time and research necessary to create one of these masterpieces, and indeed "masterpiece" is a proper term for many of the exhibits.

If a trip to Cooperstown is not possible, you may want to visit a local library or museum to study display techniques.

Often displays will have leaflets or brochures available to the viewer to guide him logically and concisely through the exhibit. The leaflets or brochures should provide the viewer with all the information necessary to thoroughly appreciate the collection. There is nothing more frustrating to a viewer than to see an item, the significance of which to the display is not clearly understood.

When displaying items of one individual it is important to do so chronologically. For example, if you were displaying a collection of Joseph E. Cronin material, you would guide the viewer through early highlights of his career before and during his years in Pittsburgh, then through his days in Washington and his first season as a manager in 1933. Finally, an overview of his last days in Boston and into his career as a baseball executive, ending with his induction into the Hall of Fame. Collateral material in the form of clippings, photographs and artwork can nicely complement an autograph exhibit.

If a general exhibit is to be created, try to find a common denominator of some kind to tie the entire collection together. Viewing general collections can often be confusing, so try to provide as much information as possible to the viewer.

How a collection is displayed is also very important. Display cases vary in size, styles and accessibility. Be aware of the display conditions prior to creating an exhibit. Choose items for a display that are particularly indicative of the message you are trying to communicate, over the space you have available. Too much or too little material can confuse a viewer. Attention should be paid to image placement, size and even color. Eye-catching displays often have tasteful backdrops with interesting arrangements of a variety of forms. A display of Babe Ruth material on or with a backdrop of Yankee Stadium can be quite impressive. If an upright case is used, pay particular attention to the careful attachment of autographs to the material surface being used to display the item. If an autographed item you are displaying has more than one page, for example the front and back of a single page, then an acceptable practice is to copy the page without the traditional closing (and signature) of the autographed letter, and place it alongside the original in the display. This will provide clarification to the viewer.

Commonly overlooked in creating an exhibit is lighting. As most collectors are certainly aware, direct sunlight or constant artificial light can damage autographed material. Fluorescent lighting is commonplace in libraries and other institutions. If the fluorescent lighting is not properly filtered to screen out harmful rays, they may cause damage to items left in display cases over a long period of time. In addition, many display cases that have built in lighting generate heat, which affects the humidity and thus impacts the material inside the case. A collector should use discretion, based on the types of material being exhibited, to choose the most effective form of lighting. Indirect lighting, not directly focused on the display, outside of the display case is most common.

Security is paramount when exhibiting a collection open to the public. Choose to exhibit autographed material only in locked display cases. A collector should be aware that even locked cases are vulnerable to alternative sets of keys that can access a case and crafty thiefs who can execute alternative methods of entering a case. Collectors who wish to display in areas large enough to merit above average security precautions are advised to procure an insurance policy to cover possible damages. Generally speaking a collector who is exhibiting at a library or art gallery will often find that the institution has taken more than adequate security precautions to safeguard their facility. If proper precautions are followed, displaying an autograph collection can be an educational experience to the public and a source of personal gratification for the collector.

Baseball autographs and memorabilia normally attract large audiences due to the popularity and widespread appeal of the game. A collector choosing to display his personal collection is providing a wonderful service to the community while encouraging others to pursue collecting. Each collection is a unique tribute to baseball and should be preserved for the benefit of future generations. Combined as hobbyists, our collections far exceed what is generally available for public viewing. To preserve and provide for display of such materials is a rewarding experience for all.

Autograph preservation

So often I have seen collectors spend hundreds of dollars for a piece of autographed baseball memorabilia, that just hours later will end up stuck on some shelf in a closet or basement, unprotected from the elements of deterioration. Deterioration is often a subtle process taking place over a long period of time. As the collector's knowledge of deterioration factors increases, he will find there is much one can do to prolong this inevitable process. If the collector decides to ignore preservation, he assumes the risk for any damage to his collection.

Many serious collectors have amassed large and valuable collections, posing a variety of storage and preservation concerns. As the hobby has matured the collector has equally evolved into eclectic acquisitions of greater significance to not only his own collection, but to the history of baseball. Many historical items now in the possession of the collector will no doubt end up somday in a museum, even that of the Hall of Fame. This is precisely why preservation knowledge has become a major responsibility to most advanced collectors.

This section will address the principal causes of deterioration, conservation problems, and dealing with professional conservators. If you find portions of this section too technical for your present needs, please realize that as your collecting habits mature, you may eventually utilize this information. A majority of autographed baseball memorabilia consists of paper-based products, therefore our discussion will center on principal causes of paper deterioration.

There are many causes of paper deterioration: the collector himself; environmental elements such as light, temperature, and humidity, and the paper's own characteristics and reaction to the other elements' chemical makeup.

The collector as a cause of deterioration is by far the most managable. Since the creation of paper, mankind has put paper through its paces. Paper has experienced almost every circumstance conceivable, from exposure to direct sunlight to being taped, torn or glued. Fortunately, autograph collector awareness seems to be improving, so this form of deterioration shows signs of subsiding over the years to come.

A common practice among collectors is to illuminate an autograph that is on display. Unfortunately, the greater the amount of light striking a paper object, the greater the fading and decomposition. The combination of both visible light and ultraviolet light can cause severe discoloration, brittleness and fading. To complicate the issue even more, combining the light factors with other materials that have chemical detrioration characteristics, such as various types of ink, can create an autograph collector's nightmare.

Ultraviolet radiation has two primary sources, sunlight and fluorescent light. To control these elements various types of filtering can be used. Professional framers commonly use assorted grades of Plexiglas to shield out the unwanted radiation.

Incandescent lights, such as those commonly used in household lighting fixtures, pose no threat in the generation of ultraviolet radiation, however if directed at an autographed item from too close a distance, can generate excessive heat that may damage an item. Since light is needed to properly view an image, a suggested lighting of a 100-watt bulb no closer than three feet from the autograph is a good rule of thumb.

Excessive heat and humidity are also great contributors to deterioration. High humidity, in excess of 70 percent, often leads to mold generation. Molds combine with paper to create "foxing," a group of reddish-brown spots that are most destructive. Since these molds are colorless, they are very difficult to detect. Professional conservators generally maintain temperatures between 65-70 degrees, with a relative humidty of about 50 percent. To avoid any problems, try to keep your collection area dry with good ventilation to exchange the air. It is also recommended to frequently inspect your collection for any signs of deteriortion, especially in climates that are indicative of excess conditions. If a collector purchases a piece that shows signs of excess deterioration, he may want to employ the skills of a professional conservator to chemically treat the material.

Any time one type of material comes in contact with another, a chemical reaction takes place. Combining various types of paper, adhesives, inks, synthetic materials and natural materials can result in severe chemical migration. Paper that is high in acidic content often will discolor and spread its serious damage to any other material it is in contact with. The advent of modern technology has created thousands of forms of adhesives, most of which have destructive characteristics. Inks also have migration characteristics; they can spread, flake, and fade, leaving little trace of the original signature. To reduce chemical reactions, collectors are urged to purchase higher grade materials with characteristics less prone to deterioration. Additionally, a collector is urged to procure the services of professionals who are familiar with proper mounting and framing procedures.

Even the materials used to manufacture the paper can play a destructive role. Numerous additives are used in the manufacture of paper, however it is the acidity content that is most destructive. Brittle or discolored paper can result when the acidity in the paper is activated by moisture. Chemically this form of destruction can be arrested through a process called deacidification. Commonly used by professional conservators, deacidification works to neutralize the acidity. Acid-free papers and cardboards are used for the production of special books, archival envelopes and boxes and slip sheets. This "permanent" or "buffered" material is used to isolate elements from many of the destructive forces of deterioration.

Thanks to the efforts of many organizations concerned with the preservation of civilization's records, alkaline paper is being requested more and more for the printing of books or journals. The alkaline reserve is stored in the paper for future neutralizing of acidity.

As a collector, the fate of your collection is in your own hands. Certainly the processes are available to curtail deterioration, however, economically they may not at all be feasible. As a collector you must learn to budget a percentge of your funds toward the acquisition of preservation materials.

In addition to budgeting for preservation materials, the following suggestions are recommended:

★ Storage area temperature: 65-70 degrees

★ Storage area humidity: 40-60 percent

★ Keep the storage area free from all environmental pollutants.

★ Consult your local library or museum for any helpful preservation techniques.

★ Try to maintain as stable an environment as possible for temperature and humidity.

★ Protect your materials from ultraviolet radiation by using Plexiglas framing or other shielding materials.

★ Keep the surface of the autographed item free from contact with other materials.

★ Avoid high-intensity lighting that could generate damaging temperatures above 70 degrees.

★ Never display an item in direct sunlight.

★ Display and storage cabinets should be designed and purchased to accommodate your specific size, weight and ventilation needs.

★ Follow all directions for any type of containers used in storage.

★ Periodically check all storage areas for any signs of deterioration.

★ Monitor air flow and exchange characteristics.

★ Avoid smoking, eating and drinking near valuable autographed material.

★ When framing autographed material, be sure to request that acid-free archival materials be used. Also, be aware of any deterioration characteristics the autographed item exhibits before framing and determine the impact framing might have on the piece.

★ Avoid using adhesives. If one must be used, try to purchase some specially developed paste from a dealer. If you're ambitious you may want to call the local museum for their paste recipe, made from natural ingredients.

★ Invest in acid-free archival supplies for better collection preservation: acid-free folders for paper based material, acid-free boxes for uniforms, special racks or holders for bats and baseballs. Photographs should be stored in acid-free envelopes.

★ Avoid handling unprotected autographed items.

★ Never store any valuable material with other items, such as newspaper clippings, that are very acidic.

★ Photographic materials, due to their chemical base, should be isolated and stored in areas separate from other materials. It is advised to consult professional conservators on specific materials handling such as old negatives and plates.

A collector is advised to seek the expertise of a professional conservator to handle cetain deterioration problems. This may or may not be cost effective. If an item has historical significance, however, it is the proper alternative. All collectors are warned against trying to preserve their baseball autograph and memorabilia collections via professional methodology without proper training. The following items should be handled by a professional conservator:

★ Deacidification

This process reduces deterioration, and involves a very sensitive chemical regimen.

★ Restoration/replacement

This involves items from uniforms to bats and is a highly controversial process that could impact the future salability of the item. It is best to consult hobby experts for their advice prior to an undertaking of this kind. Additionally, experts in this type of historical preservation are very difficult to find.

★ Tears, folds and missing pieces

Paper-based product repair is a highly complex procedure, and in no way should be considered by a collector. Fabric preservation is also very specialized and only experts should be considered to handle the repair of valuable uniforms. The decision to repair an autographed item is very subjective. Collectors deciding to do so must be willing to accept the responsibility. Most collectors would gladly choose no repairs at all over a badly repaired autographed item.

★ Stain removal

Be it a uniform or an autographed letter, stain removal involves special cleaning agents that could result in considerable damage to an item. Never try this procedure yourself.

★ Adhesive removal

Adhesives are commonly used to repair paper-based products. Eventually they may discolor or spread stains to material they are in contact with. Elimination of the stain and removal of the adhesive is very difficult, and the solvents used may also damage the item.

★Mounting and demounting

Mounting is used to reinforce badly weakened paper. Autographed items can be mounted on a variety of materials by a professional conservator. The least favorable form of mounting is lamination, only used as a last resort for restoration of a badly damaged item.

Demounting can be a very involved process. Since many people who frame or mount items are not properly trained, a variety of adhesion techniques can be encountered. A collector is encouraged to not undertake either process, unless properly trained.

As a means of educating the autograph collector, many local frame shops, galleries, institutions, and conservation centers will offer various degrees of education through workshops or classes. All collectors are encouraged to take advantage of these offerings. If a collector seeks the services of a professional conservator, contacting your local museum or art galleries is a good source for such information.

Professional conservators will require a careful examination of an item before giving a price quotation. For most collectors the services of these experts will not be affordable. It is useful though, for collectors to familiarize themselves with the services available and the associated costs. For those collectors who can afford a professional conservator, prior to acquiring their services the following information should be sought:

☆ What are the risks associated with the repair or treatment?

☆ Has the conservator performed the repair or treatment before?

☆ What type of approval is required before work can begin?

☆ What are the total costs associated with the service?

☆ What level of success can be expected with the service?

☆ How long will the service take, and when and how will the item be returned to the collector?

☆ Will a detailed report or outline of services performed be provided upon completion?

☆ What is the quality level of the materials being used on your item?

It is suggested that prior to a restoration or preservation attempt, a detailed photographic record be taken by the collector. This will act as a protection mechanism for the collector to verify the quality of the service.

It is the responsibility of each collector of autographed baseball memorabilia to preserve the collection for the generations to follow. To do so will require a commitment to preservation, not strictly financial in acquiring the proper materials, but in the form of education as well. Remember, many institutions such as the Hall of Fame depend on donations from collectors. It would be a grave injustice to the game of baseball not to care for the many precious historical items in our possession.

Hobby ethics

The autograph hobby has matured to a point where a chapter on ethics certainly is appropriate. Ethics are a system of moral values or commonly accepted guidelines that are practiced by hobby participants. Although they vary slightly from hobby to hobby, they are generally based on the same set of standards. This chapter is clearly subjective and not all points may be agreed upon, but for a novice entering the hobby it should lay down a foundation for the basic rules governing the acquisition of baseball autographs. Authoring a chapter on ethics leaves one vulnerable to criticism, since no two people share identical viewpoints. Readers are forewarned of the personal nature of this chapter and encouraged to accept it as such.

The hobby of collecting baseball autographs and memorabilia overall is a genuinely positive experience. Little corruption or dishonesty, in respect to the vast entirety of the hobby, has affected the market. If commonly accepted practices are adopted early by the novice, they should become habitual, thus setting standards for those to follow and assuring the integrity of the hobby.

The acquisition of baseball autographs is an interaction of a multitude of individuals — players, manufacturers, promoters, dealers and collectors. It involves an underlying trust, or mutual obligation to each other, the hobby and the game of baseball.

Most autographed baseball memorabilia, when purchased through honest sale, passes a clear title of ownership to the collector. A collector should be warned that the content of a letter for example, has first right of publication given to the writer or his legal heir. This may vary slightly depending upon local legislation. It is the obligation of the vendor, not the purchaser, prior to transaction to clear title of the autographed item. If a purchaser following a transaction learns that the item's title is in question (such may be the case of a stolen item), the purchaser should immediately notify the seller. Depending upon the elapsed time since the transaction, I feel it is the seller's responsibility to accept return of the material. For example, an autographed official league baseball with a single signature upon it would be difficult to prove origin since in most cases there are no identifiable markings made on the item. Additionally, there are thousands of certain identically autographed items available in the market.

"Let the buyer beware." Without a guarantee the buyer takes the risk of quality upon himself. A seller has an obligation to honesty, and at all times should try to maintain a certain acceptable level of integrity. Many dealers purchase an overwhelming amount of material, and since knowledge level varies from dealer to dealer, it is possible for a dealer to unknowingly purchase unauthentic material. A collector should be aware of this fact and exercise caution with all purchases. If an item proves not to be authentic, it is in both the collector's and dealer's best interest to handle the matter with the utmost of professionalism. Unsubstantiated allegations do little to solve disputes. Both parties should work together to rectify the problem. I have purchased unauthentic items from many good and reputable dealers who were just not knowledgable of the origin of an item, and as reputable dealers, worked with me to accomplish a solution. Because a dealer once made a mistake in purchasing unauthentic material, doesn't make him a bad dealer. Dealers also must educate themselves. Hopefully through books like this they won't have to do it at the purchaser's expense. It is very difficult for any dealer to overcome a bad reputation, but it is a true injustice to add to it unsubstantiated allegations from other dealers or collectors. The more business a dealer does, the greater likelihood of a problem occurring. Too often I have witnessed other people take advantage of a dealer's mistake, by disparaging him with hopes of increasing their own business.

Credibility is also a two-way street, and collectors too have reputations to maintain. Collectors should utilize common courtesy in all transactions. For example, if a dealer assists you in finding or procuring an item for you at your request, you have an obligation to purchase the item. Too often dealers have had cash tied up in inventory never claimed by the collector. The collector also has a responsibility to return items in the same condition that they were received.

In regard to stolen merchandise, a collector should be particularly cautious in acquiring items which he believes may have belonged to a public archive or private collection. A collector who unwittingly purchases stolen property should reach a mutually acceptable solution to the problem with the responsible seller. The seller should then assume some or all of the monetary loss to the buyer.

Often public archives, and occasionally private collectors, will mark or tag their autographed material for easy recognition. For institutions or collectors who have no intention of ever selling the piece, this methodology, if properly done, is an acceptable practice. This identification process is not recommended to the novice collector, as improper marking may damage the item.

Authenticity of autographed material should be guaranteed by the dealer to the best of his ability. Collectors should try to assess the degree of authenticity risk associated with each item by trying to interpret the seller's knowledge. Purchasing an autographed bat from a dealer who collects both autographs and bats is of less risk than purchasing the same item from an antique or stamp dealer. Since no one is infallible, there should be some concern on the part of the collector if the dealer fails to offer proof of authenticity. Once the item has been acquired, the burden of proof of authenticity will fall to the new owner.

The threat of forgery always exists. Dealers who are unsure of the legitimacy of a signature should communicate their concern to prospective buyers. Reproductions or facsimiles should be clearly labeled as such in order to not confuse the buyer. If a buyer, be it a dealer or collector, feels that an item being offered is not legitimate, it is best to pass the item by, and if you feel compelled to communicate the information to the dealer, it is best to do so very sincerely and in private. One form of deception is for one dealer to pass along claims of forgery or concern about another dealer's material, only to make himself sound like an expert or to simply steer the client's business to his own merchandise. As a collector it is best to draw your own conclusions. Dealers are also advised to follow the same advice when buying from a collector. If material doesn't appear authentic, simply don't buy it. Remember, experts spend hours meticulously authenticating autographs, to do so presumptiously at a show, after only minutes spent viewing an item, is ludicrous.

As the hobby has grown in magnitude, so have the tricks and sales techniques used by the crafty purchaser. A common technique is for a group of collectors to try to intimidate dealers by proclaiming merchandise questionable in authenticity, only to achieve a lower price. Another technique is for a dealer to purchase autographed items from another dealer, and failing to re-sell them, returning whatever items didn't sell with claims of forgery, intimidating the dealer to redeem merchandise. Dealers should be cognizant of these purchasing techniques and knowledgable of their merchandise.

The hobby has become extremely competitive. Every dealer is seeking better sources for quality material at lower costs. There just hasn't been enough supply to fulfill the collectors' demands. I have witnessed show promoters intimidating other dealers to reveal sources, by proclaiming their material unauthentic. As a dealer you have no obligation to do so; if you choose to reveal sources for your material you may jeopardize that portion of your business. Confidentiality in transactions is a must; for a collector it is a security concern, and as a dealer you livelihood may depend upon it. A dealer has no right to reveal a collector's interest without his permission. Likewise a collector should respect in confidence a dealer's transaction.

As a hobby we have seen accelerated growth, bringing with it temptation and demand. Without adhering to a code of ethics we are damaging our integrity as a trade. Novice collectors are encouraged to maintain a strong ethical code and to use knowledge as the ultimate advantage. Many collectors have spent thousands of hours researching the hobby, and still are not absolute experts. This fact should speak for itself.

Baseball autograph values

What factors determine the value of baseball autographs? Is value simply a matter of supply and demand? How does the popularity of the player affect value?

The simplest answer is that an autograph is worth only as much as one is willing to pay for it. In actuality, however, there are many factors that determine the value of baseball autographs. These factors include: supply and demand, scarcity, the significance of the item and the popularity of the player. To a dealer, knowing what factors impact the value of an item is absolutely essential. To a novice or casual collector, little or no significance is placed on such factors.

There are a wealth of ways to collect baseball autographs. Simply stated, an autograph involves placing a signature on a piece of material. So simple a task, yet so complex in nature in that every signature is unique. The burden of value assessment is most often dependent on the knowledge of the appraiser. Some areas of the hobby are privileged to have price guides available, yet the complexity of the factors listed above often yield substantially different viewpoints on value. Since it has become practically impossible for every collector or dealer to be completely knowledgeable in each area, often collectors will specialize in particular niches of greatest interest. As with virtually all collectibles, having an item appraised by a knowledgeable dealer who specializes in the particular area will no doubt yield a higher appraisal than the assessment of one who is unfamiliar with that area.

Of paramount importance to any collector or dealer is the quality of the autographed item. Value is impacted by quality, thus a purchaser should be fully aware of the effect of condition on an item purchased for future resale. Additionally, care should be taken in evaluating not only the authenticity of the autograph, but the genuineness of the item on which the signature appears. Many an authentic autograph has adorned a replica uniform, store-bought bat or reprinted program.

The popularity of collecting the autographs of members of the baseball Hall of Fame has some dealers projecting limited availability or a shortage of certain players. Though players such as Martin Dihigo, Tim Keefe, Pud Galvin, Oscar Charleston, Tom McCarthy and Candy Cummings can be elusive, the fact that more collectors are searching for these items should help in flushing them out of family or friends' collections that have been hidden in attics for years. Naturally, this search also leads to a higher price for items offered for sale. If you ask any collector who is close to completing an entire set of inductees, would they rather see a rare item offered to the public at a high price or continue searching for years for the signature, most would opt for paying the additional cost. The greater the publicity, the higher the likelihood that items will turn up in the market. For example the movie *Eight Men Out*, portraying the legacy of the 1919 "Black Sox" has resulted in an unearthing of many of the team members' scarce signatures, like Ed Cicotte.

Another reminder to collectors is the fact that the earliest date of birth of an individual in the Hall of Fame is 1820 (Alexander Cartwright). With this in mind it is fair to assume that many autographed items are still in the possession of family members. Often these items will be offered to the public through private dealers, auction houses or the families themselves. Many relics will no doubt be donated to the Hall of Fame in Cooperstown. The fact that the Hall of Fame does not purchase items certainly gives the collector a competitive edge. Collectors are indeed fortunate that few major insitutions such as libraries have entered the field to date. Institutions often have significant funds to acquire scarce items and seldom resell collections, therefore taking many sought-after items out of public circulation.

There has been a noticeable entrance by antique, stamp and coin dealers into the baseball autograph market. The participation by these individuals should add to the availability of items. The purchaser, however, is advised to use caution in the aquisition of materials from all sources not specializing in particular areas. The seller's ability to guarantee authenticity should be qualified well in advanced of any purchase. Generally speaking for single signatures on generic items such as 3x5" index cards, autograph values are generally consistent. Autographed plaque postcards, baseballs and photographs vary little, unless the player is deceased. Little has been known, up to now, about the signature habits of many of the deceased players. This fact contributes highly to the variances in price. For example, John "Monte" Ward, a brilliant man and scholar, authored and signed many correspondences, yet in the market a collector may pay much more for a Ward signature than for a scarcer Joe Kelley autograph. A reminder to all collectors: Age sometimes has little to do with the value of an autograph.

The content of an autographed letter or significance of an item such as a bat, affects the value of an item. Good content and historical significance command high prices. Scarcity also contributes to value, for example, a simple signature of Martin DiHigo or John Lloyd carries a high price regardless of the surrounding content. Letters of lesser known individuals may also command a high price because of contents.

Autographed letters of great content are often found among Hall of Fame executives, for example a letter dated July 1, 1921, from Ban Johnson to August Herrmann, President of the Cincinnati Baseball Club, it reads:

Dear Sir:

I was served with a notice from the State's Attorney's office asking that you hold yourself in readiness to act as a witness in the trial of the indicted White Sox players and gamblers in the World's Series of 1919. I am not prepared to say when you will be summoned, but I want you to be ready to appear at the request of the State's Attorney, Judge Crowe.

Kindly communicate with me immediately on receipt of this letter, with the thought you are prepared to go through and clean up this tremendous scandal in baseball as a man, and one who is ready to serve the best interests of the game.

I am-

Yours truly,
Ban Johnson

This correspondence would most certainly be a very valuable, as well as exciting, addition to a serious historical collection. As a baseball autograph and memorabilia collector it is important to establish a budget that meets your personal financial goals, while providing you an opportunity to enrich your collection. Obviously the more affluent collector can afford to be selective in his acquisitions. Regardless of budget, however, it is important to acquire wisely. The serious collector should ask himself, what significance does this item bring to my collection? Is the item comparable in quality to the other items in my collection? Will the item maintain its value over time? These are questions that only a serious collector who has established goals for his collecting can answer. The casual collector usually acquires autographs haphazardly, with little regard to the questions that a serious collector may ponder. To the casual collector value, though respected as a factor in acquiring the autograph, is secondary to the thrill of having possession of the signature.

Contents, circumstance, style and medium

A bat used by Pete Rose in 1985, during his "Countdown to Cobb," would certainly be worth more than a comparable bat used during a less significant baseball season in Rose's career. Some specialized collectors seek items dated specifically during certain periods of baseball's history. A spring training coach's uniform of a Hall of Famer is of lesser value than those used during his playing days.

Collectors of autographed baseballs are often discriminating as well, choosing only to purchase single signatures in ink on official league baseballs. To this type of collector certain factors have greater appeal and command a better price. A signature not on an official baseball, regardless of whether the collector needs it or not, is of no interest to this type of specialized hobbyist. I have seen many a collector pass by a scarce signature because it didn't fit their buying criteria. To compromise on one piece is to compromise on the entire collection in the minds of this discriminating type. It is an attitude that aggrevates many dealers, but gains the respect of many collectors.

Collectors also try to choose autographed letters of individuals which discuss the subject most associated with the individual. A letter from Kenesaw M. Landis, as Commissioner, to Connie Mack discussing gambling at the ballpark would be of greater interest and value than a letter from Landis to his dentist discussing overdue payments. Landis was a hard-nosed, rough-edged Commissioner who often took a steadfast position on difficult matters as exemplified in the following letter to Connie Mack on June 19, 1939:

"That gambling thing comes to me from all quarters, including complaints from fans to whom the gambling activity is offensive, particularily including in this the slimy character of the rats that are carrying the things on. Our clubs at least can keep after these vermin and by throwing them out of the parks on their heads and thus pestering and bedeviling them with no let up, we can at least have the personal satisfaction."

Obviously, this letter is of great value and interest to the serious collector.

Autographed game-used equipment is highly sought by collectors. The value of these items often limits purchases to only the most affluent in the hobby. A collector who possesses a strong knowledge of the game, however, can often spot young players who have not yet realized their potential and capitalize on the purchase of their memorabilia at an affordable price. Collectors who purchased items of Nolan Ryan in his earlier days can certainly attest to this claim.

The value of a collectible can also be affected by the manner in which an item was signed. Collectors often object to shortened signatures such as "Reggie J." (Reggie Jackson) or "C.G." (Charlie Gehringer). These signature variations detract from the value of an autographed item.

The tools a player uses to sign an autograph can also affect the value of an item. Autographed official league baseballs in ink pen can command a greater value than those signed in other assorted ink types. Signatures in pencil, also have a reduced value from those signed in ink.

Scarcity, supply and demand

Scarcity or no scarcity, if there is no demand for a particular piece of autographed baseball memorabilia, the price will remain low. On the contrary, if the supply is hearty and demand strong, prices will be high. As all experienced businessmen realize, supply and demand are inseparable. Autographed memorabilia from Babe Ruth has always been in great demand. Even though he signed frequently, the supply continues to be insufficient to meet the needs of the collector. Those dealers who have offered Babe Ruth single signature baseballs over the past five years have commonly seen record purchase prices set. Similarly, prices for signatures on Hall of Fame plaque cards have been disproportionately higher than comparable signatures on 3x5" cards due to the demands of the specialized collector.

The demand for Hall of Fame signatures has been so strong that some players have resorted to stamped facsimile, secretarial, and machine-signed autographs. Massive correspondence leaves little time for prominent individuals to attend to their everday needs. Most players who are still signing by mail will limit signature requests, while other may go so far as to charge a fee. The result is not unpredictable: a limited supply of authentic signatures forcing prices upward. The largest contributor to inflated prices has been the advent of the baseball card superstar shows. Hall of Famers are now being paid exorbitant fees to sign for the paying public; a public who just years before could attain their signature through the mail or at the ballpark for free. During the next few years, it will be interesting to see if the pent-up demand is still strong enough for the shows to continue to be successful.

Collecting has its share of fads as well. There may be a run on a particular player due to an unpredictable circumstance. The massive public awareness of the Billy Ripken Fleer baseball card error in 1989, is one unfortunate example. One wonders what this autographed card might fetch in the years to follow. The autographed items and memorabilia of any person who is elected to the Hall of Fame are always immediately in demand. The many collectors of complete sets will certainly require an example. Recently deceased players are also in demand, often commanding two to three times what an average autograph from this individual would have commanded prior to his death. In the case of an unpredictable circumstance claiming the player's life, demand can skyrocket, as exemplified by the reaction of collectors following the death of Roberto Clemente.

In recent years the market has been periodically flooded with the signatures of certain players, due to a massive personal acquisition or an increased attendance by that player at baseball card shows. The result is often lower prices than what an individual might have paid if they had attended the show to obtain the autograph. Additionally, expect a temporary decrease in value until all the autographed material is fully absorbed by the public.

Condition and association

Condition can also affect value, particularly if the autographed item will require repair of any kind. Naturally it is expected that game used memorabilia reflect wear, but severe damage such as uniform tears, or missing bat pieces will affect value. Aging characteristics are expected to be exhibited by autographed baseball and memorabilia. The most common characteristics in paper collectibles are light stains, discoloration due to fading, general wear and occasional folds. Other forms of collectibles share many of the same characteristics. Bats will show stains, discoloration, and dents, while uniforms will exhibit loose threads, stains, and discoloration. Perhaps the greatest tragedy a collector will face is that ink fades, and there is no acceptable method of correcting it. A collector is warned to never attempt to retrace a signature, for fear it will be mistaken as a forgery. I have seen so many beautiful autographed baseballs deteriorate to a point that makes them almost worthless. Recently, I was allowed to examine the shelves of autographed baseballs in the basement of the Hall of Fame. Not surprisingly, deterioration has also claimed some of these examples.

Auctions, assessments and investments

Auctions, whether from auction houses or dealers, vary significantly in quality items, assessed value and guarantees. Unfortuantely, the hobby has not matured enough to include value appraisals as part of each lot offered. This is primarily due to the inexperience of the auctioneer. Most auctioneers fear that if values are too high no one will bid, and if too low many a bidder will be disappointed. The truth is that if a fair market value can be placed on the item, it should be quoted so that everyone will benefit.

Most of the auctions being conducted in the hobby today are a combination of both mail and phone bidding. The quality of these auctions varies with the knowledge and professionalism of the auctioneer. Any smart autograph collector should demand, prior to entering a bid, a copy of the item being sold for evaluation. This simple procedure could eliminate much of the dissatisfaction associated with auctions. Every auctioneer should have copies available of all the items being offered, especially if the item could command a significant price. The copies should be clear and crisp, a montage shot with an 8½x11" item reduced 20 times is not acceptable. Any auctioneer not willing to offer a collector this service should become suspect in the minds of the collector. Often this is a way for dealers to camouflage bad or unsalable merchandise. I once requested from an auctioneer, running two full-page ads in a trade periodical, copies of a few of the items pictured in his ad, because the pictures were so small that I could not recognize whether the signatures were genuine nor could I properly assess the value of the item. I enclosed a check to generously cover his expenses. To my dismay I received my letter back with a handwritten note written in the corner, that the gentleman was out of town, accompanied with another copy of the ad delivered via Federal Express. Though I appreciate the hasty delivery, this response was suspect and obviously unacceptable. Unprofessionalism of this nature is unacceptable, and as collectors you are better off making your purchases elsewhere. Since these types of auctions are impacted by so many circumstances, they cannot be an accurate assessment of fair market value.

Appraisals are also very difficult, yet required for insurance purposes. Appraisals vary significantly, particularly if the collection consists of many unique items. Normally insuring a collection will require numerous appraisals of replacement value. Since appreciation and inflation affect a collection's value, the appraisal should be reconducted every five years.

Baseball autographs and memorabilia as an investment can be a dangerous commodity. Though prices have shown significant increases, investments in many would-be superstars or future Hall of Famers could yield a loss for the collector. A word to the wise collector: He who buys primarily for investment purposes and is not familiar with price fluctuations, baseball and the impact a player's performance has on the memorabilia market, could someday be faced with a loss. Collectors who acquire wisely can invariably, usually over a long period of time, see their collections increase dramatically in price.

Remember it is not the dealers who set prices, it's the buying public, the collectors themselves. Your willingness to pay a certain price for an item has an impact. While there is little doubt in my mind that a Joe DiMaggio autographed basebll will always increase in value, even the Yankee Clipper has a price threshold at which the collector refuses to purchase the item. As a collector you should monitor the prices charged for items and gradually develop an awareness of values.

Collecting Hall of Fame postcards

The last portion of a visit to the National Baseball Hall of Fame and Museum is usually the Gallery. Long black marble columns supporting a high ceiling lead viewers into raised alcoves that house each member's plaque. It's hard to believe that players such as Lou Gehrig, who played 16 years, can have their accomplishments condensed into 40 words on these plaques that will forever immortalize them. Some tributes are short, under 30 words, like Hugh Duffy's which reads, "Hugh Duffy — Brilliant as a defensive outfielder for the Boston Nationals, he compiled a batting average in 1894 which was not to be challenged in his lifetime — .438." Other tributes, like that of Herb Pennock can run over 60 words. Plaques can alter the way a player is remembered for years to follow. Carl Hubbell became renowned for his 1934 All-Star game performance when he struck out Ruth, Gehrig, Foxx, Simmons and Cronin in succession because it appeared on his Gallery tribute. A Hall of Fame plaque is truly unique, as only one will be made and it will forever adorn the walls in Cooperstown.

The first plaque postcards officially offered at the Hall of Fame were printed in black and white by the Albertype Company, of Brooklyn, N.Y. The front of the Albertype postcards, other than lacking the depth provided by color photography, is almost identical in style to those offered today by the museum. The back of the postcard carried a simple acknowledgement line, located in the middle of the postcard and the word "POST CARD" offset to the right. The Albertype postcards were offered from about 1936 through 1952. At the time of issue only 30 out of a possible 62 players could have autographed this postcard, the others were deceased prior to the issue. Albertypes are difficult to find, making a complete unsigned collection a challenging feat. They do surface on occasion and are highly sought-after.

Rarest among the Albertypes, due to the limited time available for this player to autograph the postcard, is that of John J. Evers, inducted in 1946 and deceased on March 28, 1947. Contrary to previously published information, George Wright who died Aug. 21, 1937, was elected to the Hall of Fame at the Chicago baseball convention weeks after his death, therefore a signed Albertype postcard would be impossible. Additionally, Judge Landis and Herb Pennock were also deceased just weeks prior to their election, confirmation that any autographed Albertype postcards of these two individuals would certainly be forgeries. Paul Waner, who was inducted in 1952, would be the last conceivable player whose induction preceeded the final printing of the Albertypes, who could have autographed the postcard.

From its creation to 1953, attendance at the Hall of Fame reached 714,595, a figure now that takes only a few years to amass. Though Albertypes were for sale for years following their final printing, it is easy to understand why so few are available today.

In 1953 the Albertype Company was purchased by the Artvue Post Card Company of New York. Artvue continued to issue Hall of Fame black and white plaque postcards until about 1963. The front of the Artvue postcards varied slightly from their Albertype predecessors, a different type style below the plaque was moved up to allow greater space below the plaque for autographing. The back of the card centered the word POST CARD over the acknowledgement line that appeared in the middle of the card, and the name ARTVUE was decoratively added in a half-elliptical format centered at the bottom. It is likely that only 48 out of a field of 94 inducted to this point could have signed an Artvue postcard. Again contrary to previously published information, Rabbit Maranville, who died weeks before his induction, could have never signed an Artvue postcard. Also inconceivable are autographed Artvue postcards of Ed Barrow, who died Dec. 15, 1953, just a few months following his election and Eppa Rixey who was elected on Jan. 27, 1963, and died a month later on Feb. 28; the time needed to complete their plaques, the photography necessary along with the printing and distribution by Artvue, makes the feasibility unlikely if not impossible. The scarcer Artvue autographed postcards are those of Jesse Burkett, Kid Nichols and Chief Bender. Also highly sought-after, due to a limited signing period, are those of Hugh Duffy, Clark Griffith, Honus Wagner and Cy Young. The last two players to sign Artvue postcards are Bill Dickey and Bob Feller.

The two primary suppliers of the now common yellow and brown plaque cards since 1964 have been those produced first by "Curteichcolor — 3-D Natural Color Reproduction," followed by "Mike Roberts Color Productions" of Oakland, Calif. The postcards are produced on an as-needed basis and each manufacturer has shown significant production variations. The Curteichcolor postcards have varied most notably in image and stock quality, ink color, text placement and information printed on the back. Variations include the use of black or green ink on the back of the card, the inclusion of "Printed in Ireland" within the stamp box, the inconsistent placement variation of "National Baseball Hall of Fame & Museum, Cooperstown, New York" text on the front and the brightness of the printing stock. The Mike Roberts Color Productions have varied primarily in the corporation's logo design centered on the bottom of the back of the post card, capitalization, and titles. Recently they have added the "Made in USA" logo to the inside of the stamp box and gone through another logo revision. To date the overall quality of the yellow and gold reproductions by both manufacturers has shown significant variation in exposure and other elements of the color printing process. Both Curteichcolor (limited to few players) and Mike Roberts Color Productions postcards are still available through the Baseball Hall of Fame Gift Shop; manufacturer will depend on the specific player. Since numerous variations have been and still are available, it has been difficult to assess which inductee could have signed each variation. Those signatures highly sought-after by collectors are Dave Bancroft, George Weiss, Cal Hubbard, Walter Alston, Paul Waner and Bill McKechnie.

Around 1980, Dexter Press of West Nyack, N.Y., was employed to develop a new design for the plaque postcard. Bright colored backgrounds of orange, green, blue and red were added to the traditional plaque front. Underneath the plaque was added a decorative border to house the "National Baseball Hall Of Fame & Museum, Cooperstown, New York" which also had a typography change. The backs were simplified by excluding the information regarding when and what committee elected the inductee. These plaques soon became unpopular with collectors due to the lack of the useful information that was commonly included on the back by both of the yellow and brown plaque manufacturers, not to mention that the colored backgrounds detracted from the autographing capability. Dexter Press plaques are sought by those collectors wishing to have a full set of autographed plaques available from every manufacturer. Since they were available for such a limited amount of time, their value is generally greater than the plaque postcards of the yellow and brown predecessors, depending upon variation.

Collecting autographed plaque postcards will forever be a favorite among baseball hobbyists, despite the fact that a collection including every member of the Baseball Hall of Fame is impossible. For collectors it remains economical in cost and for the members autographing these cards, they realize that they are signing the ultimate salute that will forever immortalize their baseball accomplishments.

A useful group of checklists have been provided to accommodate your collecting needs.

Autographed Albertype plaque postcard checklist

☐ Ty Cobb (1961)
☐ Walter Johnson (1946)
☐ Babe Ruth (1948)
☐ Honus Wagner (1955)
☐ Larry Lajoie (1959)
☐ Connie Mack (1956)
☐ Tris Speaker (1958)
☐ Cy Young (1955)
☐ Grover Alexander (1950)
☐ Eddie Collins (1951)
☐ Lou Gehring (1941)
☐ George Sisler (1973)
☐ Rogers Hornsby (1963)
☐ Fred Clarke (1960)
☐ Hugh Duffy (1954)
☐ Jesse Burkett (1953)

☐ John Evers (1947) **
☐ Clark Griffith (1955)

☐ Joe Tinker (1948)
☐ Ed Walsh (1959)
☐ Mickey Cochrane (1962)
☐ Frankie Frisch (1973)
☐ Lefty Grove (1975)
☐ Carl Hubbell (1988)
☐ Pie Traynor (1972)
☐ Charlie Gehringer (*)
☐ Kid Nichols (1953)
☐ Jimmie Foxx (1967)
☐ Mel Ott (1958)
☐ Paul Waner (1965) **

** = Rare
( ) = Year Deceased
* = Living

Autographed Artvue plaque postcard checklist

☐ Ty Cobb (1961)
☐ Honus Wagner (1955)
☐ Larry Lajoie (1959)
☐ Connie Mack (1956)
☐ Tris Speaker (1958)
☐ Cy Young (1955)
☐ George Sisler (1973)
☐ Rogers Hornsby (1963)
☐ Fred Clarke (1960)
☐ Hugh Duffy (1954) **
☐ Jesse Burkett (1953) **
☐ Clark Griffith (1955)
☐ Ed Walsh (1959)
☐ Mickey Cochrane (1962)
☐ Frankie Frisch (1973)
☐ Lefty Grove (1975)
☐ Carl Hubbell (1988)
☐ Pie Traynor (1972)
☐ Charlie Gehringer (*)
☐ Kid Nichols (1953) **
☐ JImmie Foxx (1967)
☐ Mel Ott (1958)

☐ Paul Waner (1965)
☐ Chief Bender (1954) **
☐ Tom Connolly (1961)
☐ Dizzy Dean (1974)

☐ Al Simmons (1956)
☐ Rod Wallace (1960)
☐ Bill Dickey (*)
☐ Bill Terry (1989)
☐ Frank Baker (1963)
☐ Joe DiMaggio (*)
☐ Gabby Hartnett (1972)
☐ Ted Lyons (1986)
☐ Ray Schalk (1970)
☐ Dazzy Vance (1961)
☐ Joe Cronin (1984)
☐ Hank Greenberg (1986)
☐ Sam Crawford (1969)
☐ Joe McCarthy (1978)
☐ Zack Wheat (1972)
☐ Max Carey (1976)
☐ Bob Feller (*)
☐ Bill McKechnie (1965)
☐ Jackie Robinson (1972)
☐ Edd Roush (1988)
☐ Elmer Flick (1971)
☐ Sam Rice (1974)

Note:
The names of Ed Barrow (1953) and Eppa Rixey (1963) have not been included, due to the improbability that they, just weeks after election, could have signed an Artvue plaque post-card prior to their deaths.

Autographed Dexter Press plaque postcard checklist

☐ Lou Boudreau (*) (green)
☐ Stanley Coveleski (1984) (red)
☐ Joe DiMaggio (*) (orange)
☐ Waite Hoyt (1984) (blue)
☐ Judy Johnson (1989) (green)
☐ George Kelly (1984) (orange)
☐ Sandy Koufax (*) (red)
☐ Mickey Mantle (*) (orange)
☐ Eddie Mathews (*) (red)
☐ Willie Mays (*) (orange)

☐ Stan Musial (*) (orange)
☐ Edd Roush (1988) (red)
☐ Lloyd Waner (1982)
   (blue) **
☐ Ted Williams (*) (orange)

** = Rare
( ) = Year Deceased
* = Living

Note:

Some confusion still surrounds the players issued, however all the above have been confirmed. Color of postcard background indicated next to each player. These postcards were difficult for players to sign. Often, like the yellow and brown version, they were first rubbed with a pencil eraser prior to the player signing in ink pen. Some players even placed transparent tape over their signatures so they wouldn't smear.

Autographed Curteichcolor & Mike Roberts
plaque postcard checklist

☐ George Sisler (1973)
☐ Frankie Frisch (1973)
☐ Lefty Grove (1975)
☐ Carl Hubbell (1988)
☐ Pie Traynor (1972)
☐ Jimmie Foxx (1967) **
☐ Paul Waner (1965) **
☐ Dizzy Dean (1975)
☐ Bill Dickey (*)
☐ Bill Terry (1989)
☐ Joe DiMaggio (*)
☐ Gabby Hartnett (1972)
☐ Ted Lyons (1986)
☐ Ray Schalk (1970)
☐ Joe Cronin (1984)
☐ Hank Greenberg (1986)
☐ Sam Crawford (1968)
☐ Joe McCarthy (1978)
☐ Zack Wheat (1972)
☐ Max Carey (1976)
☐ Bob Feller (*)
☐ Bill McKechnie (1965) **

☐ Jackie Robinson (1972)
☐ Edd Roush (1988)
☐ Elmer Flick (1971)
☐ Sam Rice (1974)

☐ Urban Faber (1976)
☐ Burleigh Grimes (1985)
☐ Heinie Manush (1971)
☐ Luke Appling (*)
☐ Ted Williams (*)
☐ Casey Stengel (1975)
☐ Red Ruffing (1986)
☐ Lloyd Waner (1982)
☐ Goose Goslin (1971)
☐ Joe Medwick (1975)
☐ Roy Campenella (*)
☐ Stan Coveleski (1984)
☐ Waite Hoyt (1984)
☐ Stan Musial (*)
☐ Lou Boudreau (*)
☐ Earl Combs (1976)
☐ Ford Frick (1978)
☐ Jesse Haines (1978)
☐ Dave Bancroft (1972) **
☐ Chick Hafey (1973)
☐ Harry Hooper (1974)
☐ Rube Marquard (1980)

□ Satchel Paige (1982)
□ George Weiss (1972) **
□ Yogi Berra (*)
□ Lefty Gomez (1989)
□ Sandy Koufax (*)
□ Buck Leonard (*)
□ Early Wynn (*)
□ Monte Irvin (*)

□ George Kelly (1984)
□ Warren Spahn (*)
□ Cool Papa Bell (*)
□ Jocko Conlan (1989)
□ Whitey Ford (*)
□ Mickey Mantle (*)
□ Earl Averill (1983)
□ Bucky Harris (1977)

□ Billy Herman (*)
□ Judy Johnson (1989)
□ Ralph Kiner (*)
□ Cal Hubbard (1977) **
□ Bob Lemon (*)
□ Freddie Lindstrom (1981)
□ Robin Roberts (*)

Majority of above postcards will be Curteichcolor.

Majority of below postcards will be Mike Roberts.

□ Ernie Banks (*)
□ Al Lopez (*)
□ Joe Sewell (*)
□ Eddie Mathews (*)
□ Willie Mays (*)
□ Al Kaline (*)
□ Duke Snider (*)
□ Bob Gibson (*)
□ John Mize (*)
□ Hank Aaron (*)
□ Happy Chandler (*)
□ Travis Jackson (1987)
□ Frank Robinson (*)
□ Walter Alston (1984) **
□ George Kell (*)
□ Juan Marichal (*)
□ Brooks Robinson (*)
□ Luis Aparicio (*)
□ Don Drysdale (*)

□ Rick Ferrell (*)
□ Harmon Killebrew (*)
□ Pee Wee Reese (*)
□ Lou Brock (*)
□ Hoyt Wilhelm (*)
□ Enos Slaughter (*)
□ Willie McCovey (*)
□ Bobby Doerr (*)
□ Catfish Hunter (*)
□ Billy Williams (*)
□ Ray Dandridge (*)
□ Carl Yastrzemski (*)
□ Johnny Bench (*)
□ Red Schoendienst (*)
□ Al Barlick (*)

** = Rare
( ) = Year Deceased
* = Living

Note: Both Paul Waner and Bill McKechnie signed few, if any at all.

Collecting Perez-Steele postcards

One of the most popular autograph collectibles of the 1980s has been the postcards of Perez-Steele Galleries of Ft. Washington, Pa.

Perez-Steele Galleries was founded by designer/illustrator Dick Perez and Frank Steele, a successful financial consultant. Perez met Steele at a meeting to discuss the creation of artwork for a National Football League coloring book. At that time Perez had been associated with the Philadelphia Eagles through a variety of projects including consulting on their 1976 yearbook. Through a mutual interest in baseball they became good friends.

Steele, an avid baseball memorabilia collector, had Perez visiting one evening, when the latter began marveling over the artwork on vintage tobacco cards. Perez' thought of resurrecting the old-style art, combined with Steele's vision for a limited edition offering to collectors gave birth to Perez-Steele Galleries.

Their first project was to issue a set of baseball Hall of Fame postcards officially sanctioned by the Cooperstown institution. The gallery began issuing the postcards in series, about every six to 12 months, beginning in 1980. The entire set was finally offered in a limited edition (10,000) numbered set in 1983. Since that time, the set has been updated every two years to include the most recent inductees or to honor a particular individual associated with the Hall of Fame or the Perez-Steele Galleries.

In 1982, Dick Perez's artwork expanded into the baseball card arena when Donruss utilized his services to produce the hallmark of their set — "The Diamond Kings". This sub-set became enormously popular among autograph collectors.

The size, however, became an issue. The cards were simply too small to accommodate a legible signature. Listening carefully to collectors' concerns Donruss and Perez-Steele Galleries opted for a 5x7" expanded size version. The increased size has proven especially effective as an autograph medium.

Perez' work also extends beyond these issues to a variety of commission assignments and freelance projects for companies such as Nabisco and the National Olympic Committee.

As the Hall of Fame's lead licensee, Perez-Steele Galleries works with the institution to procure the approval for each player's likeness. Perez-Steele, therefore has no agreements with the individual players. Dependent upon which set bears his inclusion, each inductee is given his own postcard set or sets. Distribution of the sets has only been through the Perez-Steele Galleries or the Baseball Hall of Fame gift shop.

The sets begin as a labor of love and can take, as was the case with the "Celebration" set, as long as three years for the artist to complete. Particular attention is paid to every detail; the elaborate packaging for the "Celebration" set took one year to design. The "Celebration" set is the Perez-Steele Galleries latest release honoring the Baseball Hall of Fame's 50th anniversay, as well as the Gallery's 10th year. The set includes 45 cards at 3½x5¼", including 44 Hall of Famers and one checklist card. Originally intended to represent living members of the Cooperstown shrine, the set was not completed before the deaths of "Lefty" Gomez and Bill Terry.

Not illustrated in the set, due to lack of an agreement or response, are Joe DiMaggio, Early Wynn, Luke Appling, Don Drysdale, Hoyt Wilhelm, Willie Mays, Whitey Ford, Frank Robinson, Robin Roberts, Sandy Koufax, Lou Brock, Bob Feller and Bob Gibson.

Inspired by W.S. Kimball & Company's 1880s release of "Champions of Games & Sports," each full color card features a portrait of the player, accompanied with a scene of him in action. The card set comes housed in a brass-hinged box, with a 12-page album. On the inside back lid is a painting featuring a depiction of a baseball game in the 1880s entitled by Dick Perez, "A Casual Game." The set originally sold for $200.

Perez-Steele Galleries
postcard set overview

Set I — Hall of Fame Art postcards

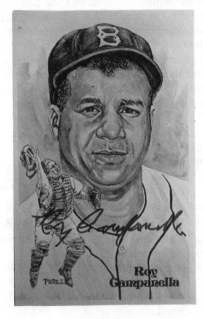

Series	Year released
1	1980
2	1980
3	1980
4	1981
5	1981
6	1981
7	1983
8	1985
9	1987
10	1989

Number of cards in set: 204 primary

Number of sets issued: 10,000

Original selling price: $124

Elapsed time to sell out: seven years

Set II — Great Moments

Series	Year released
1	1985
2	1987
3	1988
4	1988

Number of cards in set: 48 primary

Number of sets issued: 5,000

Original selling price: $100

Elapsed time to sell out: 2½ years

Set III — Celebration

Series	Year released
1 (Initial)	1989

Number of cards in set: 44 primary

Number of sets issued: 10,000

Original selling price: $200

Elapsed time to sell out: 11 weeks

Source: Perez-Steele Galleries

A tradition follows with the release of each Perez-Steele Galleries card set, of offering it first to owners of previous sets, then to the public. The Perez-Steele following now numbers

7,000 strong, represented by all 50 states and eight foreign countries. A computer data base records each set number and its owner. A registered owner establishes "rights" to future updates of each card set. The Perez-Steele family of owners is so loyal a following that only 2-3% have given up their rights to future updates.

The Galleries had humble beginnings a decade ago, a far cry from today being a household word among collectors. The team of Dick Perez and Peggy and Frank Steele was determined to offer a quality product, regardless of its revenue impact. Opportunities were secondary to quality, and as collectors themselves, paramount was each individual hobbyist's concerns. "We are only trustees to a loyal family of 7,000, acting to maintain the quality and integrity of our gallery," said Frank Steele. "We have built up an intimacy with our following, being treated mutually with courtesy and respect. Collectors are great people and decent human beings, they own this company," said Steele.

As for the decade that lies ahead, the Perez-Steele Galleries will continue to update its established sets, work with a variety of corporations, such as Donruss, and continue to establish Dick Perez as a fine artist. In the fall of 1989, "Dick Perez; The Masterpieces," an exhibit of original artwork was featured at the Bianco Gallery in Lahaska, Pa. Perez-Steele has also announced plans to publish a limited edition trilogy of books featuring Perez' artwork, available in 1990. Additionally, the gallery will continue to offer for sale Perez' original artwork, currently commanding between $1,000 to $3,500, depending upon the piece.

There is not a baseball autograph collector today that does not appreciate the level of professionalism and personal pride brought to the hobby by the Perez-Steele Galleries. Through Dick Perez' eyes all of us have seen a sensitive, yet compelling view of our baseball idols, magically drawn closer.

Perez-Steele Hall of Fame art postcards checklist

First Series - (Brown)
1 - Ty Cobb
2 - Walter Johnson
3 - Babe Ruth
4 - Honus Wagner
5 - Morgan Bulkeley
6 - Ban Johnson
7 - Nap Lajoie
9 - Connie Mack
10 - John McGraw
11 - Tris Speaker
12 - George Wright
13 - Cy Young
14 - Grover Alexander
15 - Alexander Cartwright
16 - Henry Chadwick
17 - Cap Anson
18 - Eddie Collins
19 - Candy Cummings
20 - Charles Comiskey
21 - Buck Ewing
22 - Lou Gehrig
23 - Willie Keeler
24 - Hoss Radbourne
25 - George Sisler
26 - A.G. Spalding
27 - Rogers Hornsby

28 - Kenesaw Landis
29 - Roger Bresnahan
30 - Dan Brouthers

Second Series - (Green)
31 - Fred Clarke
32 - Jimmy Collins
33 - Ed Delahanty
34 - Hugh Duffy
35 - Hugh Jennings
36 - King Kelly
37 - Jim O'Rourke
38 - Wilbert Robinson
39 - Jesse Burkett
40 - Frank Chance
41 - Jack Chesbro
42 - Johnny Evers
43 - Clark Griffith
44 - Thomas McCarthy
45 - Joe McGinnity
46 - Eddie Plank
47 - Joe Tinker
48 - Rube Waddell
49 - Ed Walsh
50 - Mickey Cochrane
51 - Frankie Frisch
52 - Lefty Grove

53 - Carl Hubbell [ ]
54 - Herb Pennock
55 - Pie Traynor
56 - Mordecai Brown
57 - Charlie Gehringer [ ]
58 - Kid Nichols
59 - Jimmie Foxx
60 - Mel Ott

Third Series - (Blue)
61 - Harry Heilmann
62 - Paul Waner
63 - Ed Barrow
64 - Chief Bender
65 - Tom Connolly
66 - Dizzy Dean
67 - Bill Klem
68 - Al Simmons
69 - Bobby Wallace
70 - Harry Wright
71 - Bill Dickey [ ]
72 - Rabbit Maranville
73 - Bill Terry [ ]
74 - Frank Baker
75 - Joe DiMaggio [ ]
76 - Gabby Hartnett
77 - Ted Lyons [ ]

78 - Ray Schalk
79 - Dazzy Vance
80 - Joe Cronin [ ]
81 - Hank Greenberg [ ]
82 - Sam Crawford
83 - Joe McCarthy
84 - Zack Wheat
85 - Max Carey
86 - Billy Hamilton
87 - Bob Feller [ ]
88 - Bill McKechnie
89 - Jackie Robinson
90 - Edd Roush [ ]

Fourth Series - (Red)

91 - John Clarkson
92 - Elmer Flick
93 - Sam Rice
94 - Eppa Rixey
95 - Luke Appling [ ]
96 - Red Faber
97 - Burleigh Grimes [ ]
98 - Miller Huggins
99 - Tim Keefe
100 - Heinie Manush
101 - John Ward
102 - Pud Galvin
103 - Casey Stengel
104 - Ted Williams [ ]
105 - Branch Rickey
106 - Red Ruffing [ ]
107 - Lloyd Waner [ ]*
108 - KiKi Cuyler
109 - Goose Goslin
110 - Joe Medwick
111 - Roy Campanella [ ]
112 - Stan Coveleski [ ]
113 - Waite Hoyt [ ]
114 - Stan Musial [ ]
115 - Lou Boudreau [ ]
116 - Earl Combs
117 - Ford Frick
118 - Jesse Haines
119 - David Bancroft
120 - Jake Beckley

Fifth Series - (Yellow)

121 - Chick Hafey
122 - Harry Hooper

123 - Joe Kelley
124 - Rube Marquard
125 - Satchel Paige [ ]*
126 - George Weiss
127 - Yogi Berra [ ]
128 - Josh Gibson
129 - Lefty Gomez [ ]
130 - William Harridge
131 - Sandy Koufax [ ]
132 - Buck Leonard [ ]
133 - Early Wynn [ ]
134 - Ross Youngs
135 - Roberto Clemente
136 - Billy Evans
137 - Monte Irvin [ ]
138 - George Kelly [ ]
139 - Warren Spahn [ ]
140 - Mickey Welch
141 - Cool Papa Bell [ ]
142 - Jim Bottomley
143 - Jocko Conlan [ ]
144 - Whitey Ford [ ]
145 - Mickey Mantle [ ]
146 - Sam Thompson
147 - Earl Averill [ ]
148 - Bucky Harris
149 - Billy Herman [ ]
150 - Judy Johnson [ ]

Sixth Series - (Orange)

151 - Ralph Kiner [ ]
152 - Oscar Charleston
153 - Roger Connor
154 - Cal Hubbard
155 - Bob Lemon [ ]
156 - Freddie Lindstrom
157 - Robin Roberts [ ]
158 - Ernie Banks [ ]
159 - Martin DiHigo
160 - John Lloyd
161 - Al Lopez [ ]
162 - Amos Rusie
163 - Joe Sewell [ ]
164 - Addie Joss
165 - Larry MacPhail
166 - Eddie Mathews [ ]
167 - Warren Giles
168 - Willie Mays [ ]
169 - Hack Wilson

170 - Al Kaline [ ]
171 - Chuck Klein
172 - Duke Snider [ ]
173 - Tom Yawkey
174 - Rube Foster
175 - Bob Gibson [ ]
176 - Johnny Mize [ ]
  A - Abner Doubleday
  B - Stephen C. Clark [ ]
  C - Paul S. Kerr [ ]
  D - Edward D. Stack [ ]

Seventh Series - (Brown)

177 - Hank Aaron [ ]
178 - Happy Chandler [ ]
179 - Travis Jackson [ ]
180 - Frank Robins [ ]
181 - Walter Alston [ ]*
182 - George Kell [ ]
183 - Juan Marichal [ ]
184 - Brooks Robinson [ ]

Eighth Series - (Green)

185 - Luis Aparicio [ ]
186 - Don Drysdale [ ]
187 - Rick Ferrell [ ]
188 - Harmon Killebrew [ ]
189 - Pee Wee Reese [ ]
190 - Lou Brock [ ]
191 - Enos Slaughter [ ]
192 - Arky Vaughan
193 - Hoyt Wilhelm [ ]

Ninth Series - (Blue)

194 - Bobby Doerr [ ]
195 - Ernie Lombardi
196 - Willie McCovey [ ]
197 - Ray Dandridge [ ]
198 - Catfish Hunter [ ]
199 - Billy Williams [ ]
  E - Perez-Steele Galleries [ ]

Tenth Series - (Red)

200 - Willie Stargell [ ]
201 - Al Barlick [ ]
202 - Johnny Bench [ ]
203 - Red Schoendienst[ ]
204 - Carl Yastrzemski [ ]

[ ] = Possible for player or individual(s) to have autographed postcard.
* = Scarce in autographed form.

Perez-Steele Great Moments checklist

First Series

1 - Babe Ruth
2 - Al Kaline [ ]
3 - Jackie Robinson
4 - Lou Gehrig
5 - Whitey Ford [ ]
6 - Christy Mathewson
7 - Roy Campanella [ ]
8 - Walter Johnson
9 - Hank Aaron [ ]
10 - Cy Young
11 - Stan Musial [ ]
12 - Ty Cobb

Second Series

13 - Ted Williams [ ]
14 - Warren Spahn [ ]
15 - The Waner Brothers
16 - Sandy Koufax [ ]
17 - Robin Roberts [ ]
18 - Dizzy Dean
19 - Mickey Mantle [ ]
20 - Satchel Paige
21 - Ernie Banks [ ]
22 - Willie McCovey [ ]
23 - Johnny Mize [ ]
24 - Honus Wagner

Third Series

25 - Willie Keeler
26 - Pee Wee Reese [ ]
27 - Monte Irvin [ ]
28 - Eddie Mathews [ ]
29 - Enos Slaughter [ ]
30 - Rube Marquard
31 - Charlie Gehringer [ ]
32 - Roberto Clemente
33 - Duke Snider [ ]
34 - Ray Dandridge [ ]
35 - Carl Hubbell [ ]*
36 - Bobby Doerr [ ]

Fourth Series

37 - Bill Dickey [ ]
38 - Willie Stargell [ ]
39 - Brooks Robinson [ ]
40 - Tinker-Evers-Chance
41 - Billy Herman [ ]
42 - Grover Alexander
43 - Luis Aparicio [ ]
44 - Lefty Gomez [ ]
45 - Eddie Collins
46 - Judy Johnson [ ]
47 - Harry Heilmann
48 - Harmon Killebrew [ ]

BROOKS ROBINSON

[ ] = Possible for player to have autographed postcard.
* = Scarce in autographed form.

68

Perez-Steele Celebration checklist

1 - Hank Aaron [ ]

2 - Luis Aparicio [ ]

3 - Ernie Banks [ ]

4 - Cool Papa Bell [ ]

5 - Yogi Berra [ ]

6 - Lou Boudreau [ ]

7 - Roy Campanella [ ]

8 - Happy Chandler [ ]

9 - Jocko Conlan [ ]*

10 - Ray Dandridge [ ]

11 - Bill Dickey [ ]

12 - Bobby Doerr [ ]

13 - Rick Ferrell [ ]

14 - Charlie Gehringer [ ]

16 - Lefty Gomez

17 - Billy Herman [ ]

18 - Catfish Hunter [ ]

19 - Monte Irvin [ ]

20 - Judy Johnson [ ]

21 - Al Kaline [ ]

22 - George Kell [ ]

23 - Harmon Killebrew [ ]

24 - Ralph Kiner [ ]

25 - Bob Lemon [ ]

26 - Buck Leonard [ ]

27 - Al Lopez [ ]

28 - Mickey Mantle [ ]

29 - Juan Marichal [ ]

30 - Eddie Mathews [ ]

31 - Willie McCovey [ ]

32 - Johnny Mize [ ]

33 - Stan Musial [ ]

34 - Pee Wee Reese [ ]

35 - Brooks Robinson [ ]

36 - Joe Sewell [ ]

37 - Enos Slaughter [ ]

38 - Duke Snider [ ]

39 - Warren Spahn [ ]

40 - Willie Stargell [ ]

41 - Bill Terry

42 - Billy Williams [ ]

43 - Ted Williams [ ]

44 - Carl Yastrzemski [ ]

RAY DANDRIDGE

[ ] = Possible for player to have autographed postcard.

* = Scarce in autographed form.

Collecting autographed baseballs

Collecting autographed official major league baseballs has never been so popular. Though many cards, equipment and photographs are also signed, it is the autographed baseball that remains the most popular showpiece for a player's signature. To understand the popularity of this sphere, one should first appreciate its history and evolution.

The early manufacturing of baseballs

During the late 1850s the National Association of Baseball Players (NABP) required the baseball to be 6¼ ounces in weight and 10¼" in circumference. Compare that to the game's current standards of 5-5¼ ounces and 9-9¼".

Although assorted manufacturers made baseballs during the late 1800s, the dominant firm was the A.J. Reach Company of Philadelphia. Former second baseman Al Reach was highly acclaimed by the turn of the century for his advancement in machinery dedicated to the manufacturing of baseballs. Each baseball was so perfectly created that the Reach ball made the astounding claim for that period of being able to retain its shape over a nine-inning game.

In the late 1800s the average number of baseballs put into play during a professional game was four to six. In that era, baseballs hit out of play were returned, rather than kept as souvenirs. Baseballs were removed from play only when they were severely damaged. Often the damaged professional balls were re-stitched for amateur use. The Reach factory was in production year-round producing an estimated three to four million baseballs a year by 1900, a far cry from their estimated 1870s production of only 24 a day.

Today each major league game uses between 30 to 50 baseballs, with some researchers stating that the average game-life of a ball is about five minutes.

Reach's success was attributed to the machinery invented by Benjamin F. Shibe, who was Reach's partner in the enterprise. This machinery would wind wool threads, or cut and punch covers, or even compress the fillings with absolute uniformity which was virtually impossible by hand. Shibe's success enabled the A.J. Reach company to virtually dominate production of baseballs for professional use.

Professional baseballs during the turn of the century were composed of a round rubber ball, one inch in diameter, layered with a half-inch of wound woolen yarn, covered by a thin coating of glue. Two more layers were then added of half-inch woolen yarn, coated again by cement and covered by horsehide, stitched by hand with cotton thread of either red or black.

The alum-tanned horsehide, made as white and soft as possible, provided the outer coating of the baseball. One stretched horsehide during the early years was good for between 18 and 20 covers. Perfectly formed covers were then adhered manually by men astride a bench that incorporated a clamping device tightly grasping the ball. Upon the cover's completion, an additional machine process rolled the ball guaranteeing roundness and smoothness. Once determined smooth, the ball was stamped with the official league designation and trademark, wrapped in tinfoil and tissue paper and sealed in a box. In 1910 a dozen Official American League baseballs manufactured by Reach would cost a club $15.

The cork-centered baseball was invented by Ben Shibe in 1909 and marketed by the A.J. Reach Co. When the ball was adopted by the American League, Reach's major competitor, A.G. Spalding Brothers, quickly countered with a version for the National League. This dramatic change in the manufacture of baseballs improved runs scored per game and contributed to point gains in batting average.

Though rubber seemed to give life to the bounce of a ball, most experts claimed it did not add to its traveling capability. The end of the 1910 season yielded praises for the new cork-centered ball that possessed the necessary qualities to last throughout a game. Baseballs without the cork center had a tendency to become soggy and void of the elasticity required for a team to rally from behind in the later innings of a game.

The cork-centered ball began with the cork core surrounded by a layer of rubber cover, then three layers of wool yarn — blue, white and blue — which was finally covered by horsehide. The Official American League Ball produced by the A.J. Reach Co. was patented on April 6, 1909, while the Official National League Ball produced by A.G. Spalding & Brothers was patented on Aug. 31, 1909.

A.G. Spalding & Brother's National League baseball was adopted by 28 out of a possible 41 professional baseball leagues in 1908. Both official baseballs were double stitched, the Spalding National League ball in red and black until 1933, and the A.J. Reach American League ball in red and blue until 1934. Following the 1933-1934 seasons the stitching colors changed to the present color of red.

Official league baseball manufacturers

American Association - Mahn (1882), Reach (1883-91)

American League - Reach (1901-74), Spalding (1975-76), Rawlings (1977-present)

Federal League - Victor

National League - Spalding (1876-1977), Rawlings (1978-to present)

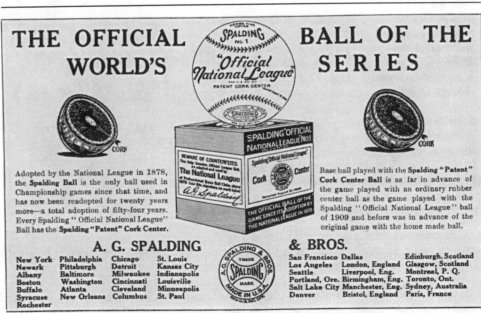

An early ad for an A.G. Spalding cork-centered ball.

By 1973 the bulk of the baseballs being used professionally were made in Haiti, due to growing production costs. In 1972, Spalding's manufacturing costs were about $23 a dozen, while teams were actually paying a dollar below cost. In 1971, major league baseball production was estimated at about 350,000 annually or an average of about 1,200 to 1,300 dozen per team. In the 1970s horsehide became so costly that most manufacturers had to import it from France. The result was substituting cowhide for the baseball's cover around 1974.

Spalding eventually acquired Reach, though the name Reach remained on the American League ball for years to follow. In 1970 Spalding became a subsidiary of the Toledo-based Questor Corporation. Spalding, in an effort to ward off competition, acquired Rawlings, but lost an antitrust suit, forcing them to sell the newly acquired firm.

Rawlings is now the exclusive manufacturer of major league baseballs under an agreement that will last until 1996. Few realize that Rawlings made baseballs under the Spalding trademark from 1968 to 1974. Rawlings produces baseballs to very demanding specifications, winding 300 yards of wool yarn and poly-cotton thread around the "pill" or cushioned cork center. Precise measurements of weight and circumference are attained prior to the application of the two pieces of cow-hide manually sewn together with 108 stitches.

Following a final inspection, the balls are stamped with the manufacturer's name, registered trademark, patented type — "cushioned cork center," patent number "17200" and the signature of the league president.

The most prominent identifier used to determine the age of modern day baseballs is the signature of the league president stamped on one of the two "sweet spots." The first signature of the National League president to appear on a baseball was in 1934 — John A. Heydler. National League baseballs with Heydler's name upon them were used briefly and are considered very rare. The signature of the American League president followed in 1935, that of William Harridge.

League presidents' names on official baseballs

National

John A. Heydler	Dec. 10, 1918-Dec. 11, 1934	
Ford C. Frick	Dec. 11, 1934-Oct. 8, 1951	
Warren C. Giles	Oct. 8, 1951-Dec. 31-1969	
Charles S. Feeney	Jan. 1, 1970-Dec. 11, 1986	
A. Bartlett Giamatti	Dec. 12, 1986-March 31, 1989	
William D. White	April 1, 1989-present	

American

William Harridge	May 27, 1931-Jan. 31, 1959
Joseph E. Cronin	Feb. 1, 1959-Dec. 31, 1973
Leland S. MacPhail, Jr.	Jan. 1, 1974-Dec. 31, 1983
Robert W. Brown	Jan. 1, 1984-present

Collectors can determine from the list of league presidents which deceased players could have signed a particular ball. Upon the departure of any league president, it is usually months before any official league baseballs appear with the new president's signature.

Also worth noting is that over the past decade Rawlings has manufactured exclusive official league baseballs for many major events including the All-Star Game, World Series and Olympics. These special-events baseballs include additional identifying stamps and decorative logos, making them outstanding collectible pieces.

Tools for autographing baseballs

The best tool for autographing baseballs is a good basic ink pen. The characteristics of the ink make it less susceptible to signature damage over time.

In 1884 fountain pens were introduced in the United States, therefore it is conceivable, though unlikely, that every member of the Baseball Hall of Fame could have autographed a baseball with this type of pen (See the chapter on the History of Writing Materials). In 1937 the ballpoint pen became commercially available, though versions had been available as far back as 1888. The ballpoint pen remains a valuable tool for autographing baseballs, but be certain to use the most permanent based inks you can find to avoid deterioration. Fiber-tip markers are not recommended for autographing baseballs due to their deterioration characteristics.

The mid-1970s found collectors purchasing the highly water-resistant, permanent, large fiber-tip "Sharpie" manufactured by Sanford. Extremely easy to use on a variety of surfaces, including baseballs, this writing instrument has turned out to be a real concern to the collector, often deteriorating autographed materials. This instrument is not recommended for use on baseballs, nor are any other similar decorative colored inks now being manufactured. Additionally, many collectors are not using the larger fiber-tipped markers because it is difficult to distinguish the characteristics (individual letters) of the autograph for authentication purposes.

Suggested ideas for collecting autographed baseballs

There are so many different ways to collect autographed baseballs, that one chapter alone could not cover all the possibilities. Mentioned below, however, are some of the most popular types.

Team baseballs

Collecting the signatures of an entire team on a single baseball has always been a popular form of autograph collecting. The difficulty involved with acquiring each player's signature at the ballpark has only added to the demand. Fortunately for collectors, ballclubs will often sign dozens of team baseballs over the season to use in promotions or as giveaways. Eventually these treasured collectibles find their way into the market. Another source for autographed team baseballs has been the "theme" baseball card shows that have reunited many outstanding teams such as the "Miracle Mets" of 1969 and the 1984 USA Olympic team. It is through these shows that many collectors will have a chance to revisit a portion of baseball's history and commemorate it with the unique combination of signatures placed on a team baseball. Though there is a price associated with acquiring team baseballs at these types of events, most collectors feel it is easily cost justified, because few had the chance to acquire these signatures during the teams' rise to fame.

What qualifies a ball as a legitimate autographed team baseball? The answer is obvious, yet dubious in its interpretation; simply the signatures of every member of that team written upon the baseball. In the early 1900s this could mean as few as 10 to 15 signatures. However, since the 1940s this number has increased to between 18 and 25 autographs on a single baseball. It is fair to assume that the greater the number of signatures, the greater the value, especially if the baseball includes every player on the roster, or every player who played during that particular season. The later situation is highly unlikely due to the recalling, optioning, releasing, and trading of so many players during a single season.

Lacking key players or the more popular players on a team baseball will also affect value. Certain individuals on a team often personify the team's legacy for that era. For example, Mickey Mantle is not a particularly valuable or difficult signature to obtain. Nevertheless, his image is so distinct that any Yankee team baseball from that era without his signature would be extremely devalued. This same analogy holds true for an Oakland A's World Series team ball without Reggie Jackson or a Cub autographed team ball without Ernie Banks. Collectors are encouraged to assess the signatures included on the team baseball, compared to those missing, to determine the historical significance and thus the value of the item.

Collectors are also encouraged to obtain only official American or National League autographed team baseballs. In addition to better preservation characteristics due to better materials, these baseballs can also be easily dated. The condition of the team baseball should also be a concern to the collector. Faded signatures, shellacked or scuffed surfaces will dramatically reduce the value of an autographed team baseball.

Collectors should suggest to key players or coaches where to sign, to avoid lesser known players signing in prominent postions on the baseball. Autographed team baseballs signed by players who played only a small portion of a season would naturally add value to the collectible. Collectors should avoid adding non-team players, such as broadcasters, umpires, and guests, to an autographed team baseball as they detract from the value. Personalization or miscellaneous quotes should also be avoided for the same reasons.

For several decades, machine-printed "autographed" team baseballs have been available in the market. Experts can easily spot these facsimiles by the characteristic equal pen pressure of each signature, uncommon beginning and end strokes, small autograph sizes, lack of signature variation from baseball to baseball, and often outdated versions of the player autographs. Collectors should be aware of these anomalies to avoid confusion with authentic autographed team baseballs.

Members of the Hall of Fame — single signature

Extremely popular are single signature versions on official league baseballs. Though complete collections are rare, the baseball is one of the few materials collected that every member of the Hall of Fame could have autographed during their lifetime. Collectors are encouraged to purchase only the signatures autographed in ink and on the "sweet spot." Multiple signatures seem to have little interest unless a particular theme underlies the combination, such as "Yankee Hall of Famers."

Autographed baseballs with a single signature of a Hall of Famer are among the most desirable in this field of collecting.

Commemoratives/theme/significant events

Some collectors only choose to acquire baseballs commemorating a special or significant event in the game's history. From career milestones to extraordinary events, these baseballs run the gamut of variation. For example: "500 home run hitters," "300 game winning pitchers," "Don Larsen dated 10-8-56," and "Pete Rose dated 9-11-85." Unique combinations could include John Roseboro and Juan Marichal, Roger Maris and Tracy Stallard, Pete Rose and Eric Show and the DiMaggio brothers.

Individual players

There is little interest among collectors to acquire signatures of individual players on a baseball unless the player is All-Star caliber. Demand for certain players with Hall of Fame potential is strong but cyclic. Examples of current players who fall in this category include: Wade Boggs, Daryl Strawberry, Don Mattingly, Jose Canseco, Roger Clemens, Eddie Murray, Jim Rice, etc.

Game baseballs

This type of collectible appeals to a specialized collector. Authentication becomes an issue as there is generally no way to prove a specific baseball was used during a certain portion of any game. Game baseballs of greatest demand are usually donated to the Hall of Fame by the specific player the feat salutes. There have been rare occasions, however, where a fan or player sells a baseball from an historic game.

Miscellaneous

Some collectors will acquire signatures of celebrities on baseballs. I must admit as a collector I have never had a celebrity turn down my request. There seems to be some type of fascination around autographing a baseball that appeals to the non-player. From rock bands to U.S. presidents, everyone loves to sign a baseball.

With so many ways to collect autographed baseballs, this element of the hobby should provide any collector with significant challenges and endless hours of fun.

Though many cards, equipment items and photographs are signed, it is the autographed baseball that remains the most popular showpiece for a player's signature.

Collecting autographed bats

The mighty stick, the mace, the powerful war club, all synonymous for the most prized possession of any ballplayer — his bat. From Edd Roush's three pounder to fictional Roy Hobbs' "Wonderboy," the bat has taken on an almost mythical role in baseball.

During baseball's infancy, bats could be found in a wide variety of shapes and sizes. From ornate hand-carved sticks to spokes from wagon wheels, baseball players experimented in search of the ultimate bat. Timbers of ash, spruce, pine, maple, willow and hickory all found their way in one shape or another onto the baseball diamond. Handles were commonly experimented with being wound or even plated with various materials. Numerous manufacturers advertised their offerings, but it was A.G. Spalding & Bros., prior to the turn of the century, who clearly established itself in a leadership position in the bat market. Spalding's most popular models were the "Wagon Tongue," appropriately named commemorating its predecessors, and their "Trade-Marked" bats introduced in 1877 and used by the most prominent players of the time.

The patented Spalding "Mushroom" bat, invented by one of the finest bat markers of the times, Jack Pickett, soon surpassed the Trade-Marked bats in popularity. It was believed that the unique knob at the end of the bat contributed to a more even weight distribution. Pickett's days at Spalding also led to the introduction of the "Gold Medal" bats, which included a successful line of autographed bats modeled after those used by Fred Clarke, Sam Crawford, John Evers and Willie Keeler. Pickett was a fanatic about bats and was instrumental in the creation of many specially designed models for players. Most noteworthy of his designs was Cap Anson's bat that was so heavy most of his teamates couldn't even swing it. Anson used a core of hickory surrounded by bamboo or even ash. Pickett's death in 1922 was the turning point in Spalding's fall from dominance in the bat market.

The A.J. Reach Company was also a prominent manufacturer of bats at the beginning of the century. The "Reach Burley" professional model bats were the most popular. These bats were made primarily in three finishes: white finish, plain handle; white finish, taped handle; and burnt and burnished oil finish with plain handle. All bats were of white ash and hand-turned for some of the leading players of the day including Frank Baker. The bats ranged in length from 32 to 35 inches, and weight from 34 to 44 ounces. Reach's bat manufacturing grew in the 1920s-1930s, yielding many popular models including the "Special Pro-Finish" bat and the "Frankie Frisch Model."

Hillerich & Bradsby and baseball's second era

The legacy of Hillerich & Bradsby began one day in 1884, when 18-year-old John A. "Bud" Hillerich played hooky from his father's woodworking shop to attend a game played by the Louisville Eclipses of the American Association. Their star, Pete Browning, was in a deep slump, which deepened even more when he broke his favorite bat. Following the game Bud Hillerich invited the despondent Browning to the shop where he began to create a new bat. Young Hillerich began forming a bat out of a piece of white ash selected by Browning, a feat that would end up taking all night to complete. Finally Browning pronounced the bat complete, and after a few practice swings returned home.

The next day Browning used the Hillerich bat to hit three-for-three, pulling himself out of a slump and the Hillerichs into a new business. The elder Hillerich, J. Frederick Hillerich, found little value in producing bats and in comparison to his daily work of shaping bed posts, bowling balls and even roller skates, a bit trivial.

Browning's success persuaded Bud to continue, and along with a few fellow workers, he was soon memorizing the weight, length and style of bats to be used by some of the greatest names in baseball.

By the turn of the century, block letter bats were being turned for Hugh Duffy, Hugh Jennings, Honus Wagner and the Delahanty brothers. Hillerich even shaped bats for a few of Spalding's endorsees — Willie Keeler and John McGraw.

In 1897, the company's name changed to "J.F. Hillerich and Son" thanks to Bud's efforts in heading up the expanding bat department of his father's business.

One of the most historical dates in the history of bat production was Sept. 1, 1905, the day Honus Wagner signed a contract giving Hillerich and Son permission to use his autograph on Louisville Slugger bats (Trademarked in 1894). This practice is still employed today at Hillerich & Bradsby.

Honus Wagner's contract was soon followed by Napoleon Lajoie, Ty Cobb, Eddie Collins and Frank Baker. Hillerich was soon so busy with production and meeting players demands that little attention was being paid to his products' distribution.

The Simmons Hardware Company of St. Louis signed an agreement with the Hillerichs to handle all bat sales, except those for professional baseball players and a few chosen outlets. Working for Simmons as a sporting goods buyer at the time was Frank W. Bradsby.

In 1910 a disastrous fire damaged the Hillerich bat factory. While rebuilding, Bradsby was asked to join the company and assumed responsibility for the firm's sales. In 1911 the company's name lengthened to "J.F. Hillerich & Son Co." and the relationship with the Simmons Hardware Company was ended.

In 1916 the company made its last name change and became "Hillerich & Bradsby Company."

Weight and sizes

With baseball's rules limiting bats to no more than 42 inches long and 2¾" wide, endless possibilities for variation exist. Bats came in sizes as long as Al Simmons' 38-incher and as small as High Duffy's 30½-inch stick. There are heavy bats, like Edd Roush's 50-ounce war club and sticks as light as Joe Morgan's 30-ouncer. Major league bats indeed come in all shapes and sizes.

Each bat is precisely tailored to detailed specifications. Master craftmen using calipers record each precise measurement. Players are particular about their bats. Ted Williams once sent back an order because he felt the handles weren't right. After careful measurement they were found to be 5/1,000ths of an inch off. Players such as Ted Williams would even visit the plant and climb through the seasoned timber to choose which pieces would make the best bats.

In the Twenties and Thirties heavier bats were in vogue, those of 40 ouncers or better. The popular Rogers Hornsby model was 35 inches long, 2⅝" in diameter, and weighed 37-39 ounces.

The now famous Heinie Groh bottle bat measured 34 inches long, with a diameter just under 2¾" and a weight of 39 ounces. Groh's bat was half an inch longer than Roush's legendary 50-ouncer. In the early years few players modified their selections, Cobb went 20 seasons with his choice, while Roush never changed.

Babe Ruth in 1930 was using a 35-incher, with a diameter of 2-9/32 of an inch and a weight of 41 ounces. Ruth bats were not confined to just him, many players simply chose to use the popular models of the time. The Hornsby model was used by Bill Terry, Chuck Klein and Jim Bottomley.

The Bambino also preferred bats with knots in the barrel, and average grain, not too wide or narrow. Ruth attended to every detail in his bats. He would order 20 bats while in spring training and after careful inspection choose one or two to become his prized possessions. Following a squirt of tobacco juice, the Babe would use a bottle to "bone" the bat, rolling it back and forth. "Boning" is a process that smooths and tightens the surface of the bat and helps to prevent the wood from chipping. Honus Wagner carried around a bone from a prime rib of beef that he used to modify his lumber. Eventually a chemical lacquering process was added to achieve this process synthetically, though some players still prefer the old-fashioned way.

Babe Ruth went through as many as 170 bats a season, including his mammoth 52-ounce model. Ruth broke relatively few bats, most were given away to his many fans. Prominent among some Ruth bats are notches made in his bats that represented home runs. One of Babe's bats enshrined in Cooperstown has 27 such distinguishing marks.

Many players used few bats in their career; Lou Gehrig used only six a season, Bill Terry used just two for his record breaking .401 season of 1930, and Jimmie Foxx used seven the year he won an American League batting title.

Bats commonly break when the ball inadvertently hits on the handle, on the label or off the end of the stick. A player is taught at an early age not to hit the ball with the label. The label indicates which way the grain runs in the wood. The trademark is placed with the grain and the batter hits against the grain.

Good wood will add driving power to the ball. The grain is the key; the straighter it is, the better the wood. A heavier bat often has better wood than a lighter bat. The older and harder bats get, the heavier they become. Cap Anson stored bats for years in his cellar, curing them to just the right weight.

Not all players were particular in the early years. Paul Waner would often reach into a bat pile and use whatever he picked up.

Often players would have both lighter and heavier style bats made. Most used the heavier bats in the spring, before pitchers reached their peak, then switched to lighter bats near the middle or last part of the season, when players who play regularly often become tired.

Another trick is to use a different bat depending on what type pitcher you are facing. Edd Roush, for example used a longer bat when pitchers would try to curve him outside.

Players often cared for their bats in unique ways. At the end of the season Ty Cobb would take his sticks home with him and oil them down numerous times before hanging them up in his barn to dry.

When the Babe broke into baseball, bats were changing to a style of small handles, longer tapers and larger barrels. Prior to Ruth, bats were shorter, 34 or 34½ inches long with smaller barrels and larger handles.

With the Forties and Fifties came shorter and lighter bats. Hank Aaron used a 32- or 33-ounce bat, and Eddie Mathews also used a 32-ouncer. These bats had even smaller handles with dramatically shorter tapers that seemed to begin and end over a small distance. Hitters had to be extremely accurate to take advantage of the limited "meat" or "sweet spot" on these bats and breakage became commonplace. Stan Musial's bat reflected the times with a 30/32" handle, 34½" long and the largest part of the barrel at 2-17/32". Players believed the small slender handles aided in "whip action" not possible with thicker handled bats.

Most professional players today prefer the thinner handles, and smaller barrels. The smaller handles allow hitters to bring the bat around more quickly. Marty Barrett supposedly uses one of the lightest bats in the game at 30 ounces. Today, average length is 34-35 inches with weight only about 30-34 ounces. The most popular models of today are Chuck Klein's K55 and Eddie Malone's M110. Since about 1945 Hillerich & Bradsby labels each bat with the initials of the players name and a number. The number is called a "turn number" or identifier for each individual style. Names are burned into bats in autograph form if the player is under contract with the manufacturer, or block letters.

Bat color

Some players also have become particular about the color of their bats. National League star Harry "The Hat" Walker was touring the Hillerich & Bradsby plant when he noticed a bat propped up in a vat of brown stain. He took it out, carefully inspected it, then ordered some bats half-stained, and half-unfinished. The style caught on and the "Walker Finish" is now a standard with the company.

In the Seventies, George Foster used a black stained bat. Many hitters followed, claiming the bat's advantage to be the difficulty in seeing the ball come off the bat during a night game.

Bat production

Due to the decreasing size requests by players, bats seem to be breaking during games at an increasing rate. Some players are even proclaiming that they average one hit per bat, a great contrast to Joe Sewell's proclamation of using only one bat for all 14 seasons from 1920 to 1933. Thinner handles and lighter weights aren't conducive to longevity.

Despite the number of bats being broken in professional baseball, overall demand for wood bats is declining, as the use of aluminum in the amateur ranks has caught on in the past decade. Today, wooden bats represent only 20 percent of Hillerich & Bradsby sales, and the company has seen production drop to around one million bats per year from six million in 1972. Rawlings-Adirondack has seen the demand also fall to around 500,000 from one and a half million bats per year.

The most popular model bat to date has been Hillerich & Bradsby's "Louisville Slugger" which has sold an estimated 22 million.

Hillerich & Bradsby has seen the Louisville Slugger slip to an estimated 60 percent market share, due to heavy competition from Rawlings-Adirondack, Worth Sports Company, Cooper and Mizuno. Most of the big league bat producers actually lose money supplying the major leagues ($10 to $13 per bat), but do so as a prestige builder for the company.

Collecting autographed bats

During the last few years, the hobby has seen an increased interest in collecting auto-

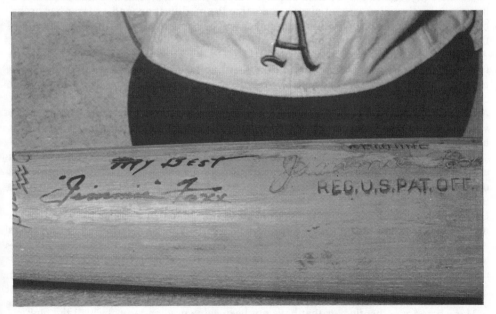

Jimmie Foxx's autographed 38-ounce Louisville Slugger.

graphed bats. Though not as difficult for collectors to obtain as uniforms, game-used authentic player bats are not readily available. Most make their way slowly to collectors through various team sources or are given away by the players themselves

Lack of accurate information to identify particular bats, along with sources to purchase them from, have been the two greatest obstacles for beginning collectors. Also complicating the hobbyist's acquisition is the lack of the proper terminology to describe a bat. Novice collectors often incorrectly mistake store-bought or retail bats for authentic game used models. Both collectors and dealers simply do not take enough time to research the background of their acquisitions, often resulting in the false advertising of the bat and a worthless acquisition by a novice collector.

Classes of bats

There are thousands of bat styles, but only four classes of bats:

Authentic cracked or uncracked game-used bats

This class of bat refers to bats owned and used by the particular player whose name appears on the bat. Granted, there is no way to guarantee or prove that a particular player used the bat. If his name appears on the bat, however, it is likely that the stick was at least ordered by the player's team. Collectors should be aware of the fact that some players commonly use a variety of bats including those of other players and team bats. In fact, Mickey Mantle's legendary 565-foot homer was hit with Loren Babe's Louisville Slugger.

Team bats are also classified under this class of bat. In addition to ordering player-specific models in a variety of styles, ballclubs will also order team bats. Team bats are simply popular styles, such as Hillerich & Bradsby's U1, M110, S2 or T85. Instead of bearing the player's name or signature on the barrel of the bat, the team's name is branded on the stick. Typically, these bats are used as back-ups should a player accidently deplete his personal supply. Additionally, many pitchers will often use team bats.

Game-used bats will show indications of wear depending upon the amount of use. Scuffs, dents, tape and pine tar are all indications of bat use. All players prepare and care for their bats differently. Knobs may be filed off, tape may be wrapped around a handle in a particular way uniquely suited for that player; you name the modification, and a player has probably tried it. Often the player's uniform number will be painted on, or written on, the end of the knob or barrel of the bat for quick identification.

Authentic bats are either cracked or uncracked. Cracking or breaking is the most common form of damage to a bat, ranging from small hairline separations to large chunks of wood removed from the timber. The value of a bat decreases depending upon the severity of the crack. Some bats actually break into two pieces, rendering them virtually worthless. Attempts at tastefully piecing a bat back together are often futile. Collectors who intend to sell bats should take particular care in adequately describing an authentic bat. If a piece is missing from a bat, it should be properly described as such to avoid buyer confusion.

Game-used uncracked bats are difficult to obtain. They are often gifts from players that eventually find there way into the hobby market. Collectors should be cautious of mint bats offered for sale that have been treated or prepared to resemble game-used by unscrupulous individuals. Often the only way to determine game use is to have witnessed the feat directly. Careful inspection of the bat for the traditional physical anomalies associated with use is a must. Collectors can avoid acquisition problems by dealing only with reputable dealers who obtain material through reliable sources and guarantee authenticity. Additionally, collectors should familiarize themselves with the peculiarities indicative of use by certain players.

Mint or authentic non-game-used bats

Many bats are authentic bats that have not been game used and thus lack all the physical characteristics indicative of such. Mint bats are often ordered by teams or other businesses for resale or promotional giveaways. They typically never find their way into a player's possession. They are, however, considered authentic, as they are made to exact specifications. Lumber grades and manufacturing techniques may or may not vary with mint bats, depending upon how the particular order was placed.

Collectors should be aware that value varies significantly with mint bats. Some dealers place the value between an authentic cracked and uncracked bat, others price them dramatically lower than either of the authentic styles previously mentioned. A mint bat's primary purpose often is for autographing or as a gift, few end up being used due to the cost associated with them.

Model or retail bats

Store-bought bats are commonly referred to as model or retail bats. Players who are under contract with the manufacturers typically allow their name to be placed on these bats in one form or another as a promotional tool to sell the bat. Most model bats carry additional or different markings that indicate them as such. Model bats typically do not meet the specifications of the player whose name is on it. Often retail bats vary in dimension to appeal to the particular market they are targeted at — from youth to semi-pro styles.

In recent years the term "authentic model bat" has been used to describe a retail bat. This term confuses the collector and in no way lends itself to a correct description. The proper descriptive terminology is simply a model or retail bat. Few hobbyists choose to collect this class of bat, however vintage model bats of star players playing before 1950 typically sell well.

Although there have been instances where a player has resorted to a model or retail bat during a game, the appearance of this class of bat in the major leagues is a rarity. Collectors are urged to visit local sporting goods shops to familiarize themselves with retail bat markings.

Commemorative bats

The last class of bat is the "commemorative" bat, appropriately named because its manufacture is in rememberance of a particular person, place or event. Commemorative bats come in a wide variety of styles, from "World Series," "Hall of Fame Induction," and "Stadium" bats to "Personalized," custom created bats. Commemorative bats make nice collectibles, as their decorative style lends itself to autographing and display. The most popular among the commemorative bats have been those saluting the annual Hall of Fame inductees and World Series Champions.

Identification markings of commemorative bats vary significantly depending upon their style and manufacturer. Collectors wishing to collect this class of bat should familiarize themselves with the appropriate issue.

Bat manufacturers and markings

All the major manufacturers who have produced professional model bats since the game's origin, have chosen to mark their products differently for identification purposes. Typically this procedure is done to differentiate between product styles. A collector must remember that not all styles were manufactured for and used by major league players. Also, variations in the procedures for bat markings over the history of the game have existed. A brief summary of the major manufacturers not covered thus far, and their marking procedure should be beneficial.

Hillerich & Bradsby

Hillerich & Bradsby has traditionally marked their professional model 125 bats with a four-inch diameter oval trademark (there are different size stamps), branded into the bat approximately 10-11 inches from the end of the barrel. Contained inside the oval trademark are the following variations:
* Louisville Slugger
* 125

* J.F. Hillerich (before 1897)
  J.F. Hillerich & Son (1897-1911)
  J.F. Hillerich & Son Co. (1911-1916)
  Hillerich & Bradsby (1916-removed from bat in 1979 and replaced by current "Louisville Slugger" label).
* Made in the U.S.A.
* Louisville, Kentucky
* Reg. U.S. Pat. Off. (Removed from bat circa 1970)

Additional Markings:

* "Powerized" — outside of trademark label (Some early models do not have it added)
* Name — Autographed (player under contract with H&B), block letters if not. Signature may be by itself on the barrel, or appear between the words "Trademark" and "REG. U.S. PAT. OFF." or between the words "Genuine" and "Louisville Slugger." Variations exist where only the word "Trademark" or "REG. U.S. PAT. OFF." have appeared below the signature. Block lettered variations also exist: "Musial Model", for example, on authentic bats.
* Turning Number or Model Number — Commonly found on the end of the knob on early models, became a practice in 1945. "J19" would indicate the turning number for a Joe Cronin model, for example. This procedure stopped circa 1980, when most model numbers were moved to the barrel.

Collectors should be aware that some variations do exist, but are rare in comparison to normal production. Common among retail bats are the words "Flame Tempered" or "Flame Treated". Also a single-digit number such as a "4", an abbreviation for 34 inches, is found on the knob. Additionally, older models without the 125 style number, replaced by "40 W.J." for example, are indicators of a store-bought bat.

McLaughlin - Millard, Inc. / Adirondack / Rawlings

McLaughlin-Millard, Inc., began turning bats at their Dolgeville, N.Y., plant in 1946. They soon gained professional prominence by signing players such as Willie Mays, Hank

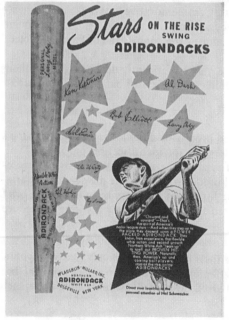

An early ad for Spalding bats.

A late 1940s ad for Adirondack bats.

Bauer, Vic Wertz, Gil Hodges and Joe Adcock to bat contracts. McLaughlin-Millard evolved into Adirondack Bats, Inc., and eventually was purchased by Rawlings. The Adirondack Pro Ring-Big Stick is now Rawling's answer to H&B's Louisville Slugger in the professional bat market. The 302 style has by far been the mainstay in their product line. Collectors should be aware that "302" and "P302" styles are for professional use, while "302F" styles are indications of a retail model bat. In recent years it has been easy to identify Adirondack bats because of the single colored ring painted around the neck of the bat.

Many label variations exist with this manufacturer, making dating a bat particularly difficult. Information contained in the diamond shaped trademark stamped at the beginning of the barrel includes:

* REG. U.S. PAT. OFF. — found on McLaughlin-Millard, Inc. version.
* Name:
  > McLaughlin-Millard, Inc. (Removed and replaced by Adirondack Bats, Inc.)
  > ADIRONDACK BATS, INC. — removed on later versions.
* Northern White Ash — removed on later versions.
* ADIRONDACK — name appears on all bats over the years in different typography.
* 302 or P302
* Dolgeville, New York — removed on later versions and replaced with Pro-Ring.
* Made In U.S.A. — removed on later versions.

Additional Markings:

* "Flexible Whip Action" or "Whip Action"
* Name — In signature form on the barrel (those under contract), or if not under contract, block letters. The name on the barrel falls between the words "Personal" and "Model", or between "Adirondack" and "Personal Model", or between "Big Stick" and "Flame Treated", just to name a few variations.
* Turning Number or Model Number — commonly found on the end of the knob. For example, "DD 26" — Fred Lynn, "300 A" — Greg Luzinski. Another smaller identification number can also be found on most models.

Collectors should be aware that many variations do exist of this manufacturer's product, making authentication and dating difficult.

Worth Sports Company

The Worth Sports Company began in 1912, when George Sharp Lannom, Jr., purchased a tannery in Tullahoma, Tenn., and began the Lannom Manufacturing Company. The company originally manufactured harnesses and horse collars, until a declining market forced the company to shift its interest to the production of leather coverd baseballs and softballs.

The company thrived for over six decades on its outstanding reputation for the manufacture of sporting goods. In 1975 the Worth Sports Company was formally organized as the sales and marketing team for all sporting goods products and divisions of Lannom.

Worth formally entered the bat business in 1970. They soon established wood mills in New York and Pennsylvania to provide the necessary northern white ash for their production. All the selected wood pieces are shipped to Tullahoma where they are turned into one of over 300 Worth patterns.

Worth's reputation has grown fast. Players such as Jose Canseco, Andre Dawson, Glenn Davis, Alan Trammell and Kirk Gibson have all turned to using the company's bats. Worth's hand-turned bats are now being used by over 100 players. Some Worth bats have even found their way to Cooperstown: Alan Trammell's 1984 World Series MVP bat, Andre Dawson's 1987 MVP bat, and Darrell Evans' stick saluting the only 40-year-old to hit more than 30 home runs in a season.

Worth's premier challenge to the major league bat market is the "Tennessee Thumper," model 500T. Worth's professional grade models are labeled as follows:

* WORTH — trademark screened on bat about nine inches from the end of the barrel
* Model Number — screened above trademark — "Model 500T"
* Tullahoma, Tennessee, Made In U.S.A. - screened below trademark
* Tennessee Thumper — screened to right of trademark

Additional Markings:

* Name — in block letters is stamped between "Hand Crafted" and "Model."
* Turning Number of Model Number — three numbers appear on the end of the Knob — players initials, size, and identification number. For example, Kirk Gibson's bat reads — KG, 5, WC137. The "5" stands for 35" in length.

Cooper Canada Limited

Founded in 1905 as General Leathergoods Company, the company was sold to Jack Cooper and Cecil Weeks in 1945. Prior to 1945 the company offered a limited line of sports equipment concentrating mainly on fine leather products. Weeks sold his interest in 1954 to Cooper who later renamed the company Cooper Canada Limited in 1969. The company went public in 1970 with the Cooper family retaining 60% ownership. During the Seventies and into the Eighties the company continued to diversify its product offerings, while expanding to meet increased production needs. In May, 1987, the company was sold to Charan Industries, a privately held firm, which operates Cooper as a subsidiary.

Cooper's first full season providing major league baseball with bats began in 1986. In a three-year time frame, the Toronto-based company claims it has grabbed a 30% market share of the professional bat market. Due to capacity restrictions Cooper believes that they can only adequately supply 130 professional players a year with bats. Players such as Tim Raines, Tony Fernandez and Jody Reed have turned to Cooper products.

Cooper offers to the major leagues the "Cooper Pro 100," which is one of their six major wooden bats styles. Cooper's white ash offering is marked as follows:

* COOPER — Made in Canada oval trademark screened at the beginning of the barrel.
* Model — Cooper Pro 100 screened on barrel above player name.
* Identification — "Professional" — then turning or identification number, such as C235.
  * Cooper's distinctive blue, orange and yellow ring is placed about 15 inches from the end of the knob.

Additional Markings:

* Name — placed between model and identification line in script.
* Knob — has length and weight designation stamped on it. For example, 33½", 31 oz

Major league baseball has also seen an influx of new companies providing bats to selected players; companies such as Mizuno of Japan. The reason is pure economics. Professional teams spend between $60,000-$100,000 a year for bats; a mere pittance compared to the United States 1989 recreational baseball equipment market valued at $500 million plus. No doubt in the years to come we will see more manufacturers.

Some companies such as Worth believe the bat of the future will be made out of graphite. With the durability of aluminum and all the traditional features of wood, a player who now uses 20 or 30 bats a season, will need only two graphite bats. The big question is, how does a player autograph a graphite bat?

Typically, collectors utilize the popular "Sharpie" by Sanford for use in autographing wooden bats; an application better suited for this type of writing device because of its ink permanence and easy application. Additionally, a number of manufacturers produce a variety of gold and silver opaque oil-based inks, which when used for autographing on darker finished bats, exhibit a signature quite nicely. Commonly bats are autographed near the name of the player on the barrel of the bat.

Hall of Fame autograph gallery

This section provides an overview of each inductee's career, signing habits, signature availability and autograph demand. Authentic signature samples — to the best of the author's ability to so determine — have been provided for reference. In addition to the samples included in this section, collectors are encouraged to use the photographs provided in other chapters for comparison. Some samples were excluded due to authentication concerns, since so few samples were available for comparison, or because the signature would not reproduce due to condition.

Many of the samples provided reflect specific periods during an inductee's lifetime, therefore are not exemplary of every signature style an individual may have used.

Both availability and demand are in constant flux due to market conditions. A variation in either of these characteristics could have an enormous impact on the value of a signature. The signature's status in terms of availability and demand is understood to be in comparison to the other inductees. Popular among many collectors is to possess at least one authentic signature from each inductee, explaining why often a relatively obscure inductee may be labeled "Strong" in demand due to the limited availability of the autograph. Both these characteristics could vary significantly depending upon the specific item the signature adorns. Guidelines for value, as of the date of this book's printing, have been provided for: Cut signatures — those cut from letters, documents or autograph books; 3x5" index cards — a common and inexpensive media popular with collectors in past decades; ball — a single signature on an official league baseball (where applicable); photo (where available) — generally an 8x10" print, less popular sizes may have somewhat lower value; Hall of Fame plaque postcards — also a popular and inexpensive media, and, Perez-Steele Hall of Fame postcard, where applicable. It should be remembered that not all Hall of Famers could have, or are known to have, signed items in each of these categories.

These values are included only as a guideline, collectors are urged to read the chapter in this book on "Baseball Autograph and Memorabilia Values" to better understand what factors impact an item's worth. The values reflected in this section are a result of an independent survey conducted by Krause Publications. "Unknown" in the value guide indicates that while an item could possibly exist, it is not currently known in any collection.

Key

Availability
- Plentiful: Living inductees or inductees deceased during the last decade.
- Above Average: Prolific deceased inductees.
- Average: Inductees deceased between 1940 and 1960.
- Limited: Inductees deceased between 1900 and 1939.
- Scarce: Pioneers of the game, or players deceased before 1900.

Demand

- Little: A living inductee or an inductee deceased during the last decade.
- Average: An inductee deceased between 1940 and 1979, or a popular nonprolific living inductee.
- Above Average: An inductee deceased between 1900 and 1939, or a popular living or deceased player.
- Strong: An extremely popular player, baseball pioneer or a signature with limited availability.

TERMINOLOGY KEY

Arm   Serif   Ascender   Arm

Loop

Superscript

Capitalization Height

x - height or lower case height

Signature Base Line   Stem   Decender   Leg

Degree of Slant
90°

Loop of Letter Left Open

Signature Break

Stylized

Traditional

Double Backed Stroke

Henry Aaron

Henry Louis Aaron
(Feb. 5, 1934-   )

Known primarily for his conquest of Babe Ruth's all-time home run record, which he achieved on April 8, 1974, at 9:07 pm, on a pitch thrown by Al Downing, Aaron compiled 2,771 hits during his 23 years of major league play. Additionally, his lifetime 755 home runs contributed extensively to another all-time record, 2,297 runs batted in.

This lifetime .305 hitter began his career in Milwaukee in 1954. His autograph in the 1950s was far less flamboyant and more block formatted than is the case today. Signing typically "Henry" instead of "Hank," early examples will show inconsistencies in all elements, except the "ar" in Aaron. Capitalization and signature slant will also commonly vary.

During the 1960s and 1970s, as Aaron's popularity grew, his flamboyance in signature capitalization also became more evident, specifically the "A" in Aaron which changed from a block formatted, minimal slant "A," to an almost 45-degree angle slant capitalization. Additionally, the height of the "A" in Aaron grew about 30% larger than the "H" capitalization in Henry. The break between the capital "A" and the "aron" in Aaron became more common. Some early samples may, however, not have this signature break.

By the late 1970s Aaron's signature became exemplary of his modern day style. Signing "Hank" instead of "Henry," his first name slant became more evident, resembling the "A" in Aaron. The "a" in Hank also commonly appears larger, almost twice the size of the "n". The "A" in Aaron is commonly closed in modern day samples, though during his playing days the beginning stroke of the letter varied. During the 1970s his popularity soared forcing him to seek alternative methods to answering his volumes of mail. Facsimile and ghost signature samples can be found that originated during this period. Ghost signature samples from this period will vary considerably from authentic authographs, making identification fairly easy.

Since Aaron's 1982 Hall of Fame induction and involvement in major league baseball management, he has been somewhat more accessible to collectors. A very undervalued autograph considering his career accomplishments.

Availability: Plentiful
Demand: Average

Cut signature	$3
Single-signature baseball	$20
3x5" index card	$6
Photograph/baseball card	$13
HOF plaque postcard	$11
Perez-Steele postcard	$35

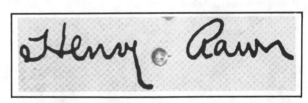

Grover Cleveland Alexander

Grover Cleveland Alexander
(Feb. 26, 1887-Nov. 4, 1950)

"Ol' Pete" compiled a lifetime 373 wins at an ERA of 2.56 over his 20-year career. He set a modern major league rookie record in 1911 by winning 28 games.

Alexander joined the Army in 1918. It was an event that would dramatically change his life. Upon his return home, he began to suffer epileptic fits that haunted him throughout the remainder of his life. Not only did his career dramatically change, but his signature habits became equally erratic.

Signing either "GC Alexander" or "Grover C Alexander" his signature varied in flamboyance, specifically in the capitalization in Alexander. Size also varied. Early samples will show the "l" in Alexander extending above the capital "A" versus later samples (post 1918) that exhibit a "l" about 80% of the height of the "A". Later examples vary erratically in the angle of "Grover", as well.

Consistent in "Ol' Pete's" signature was a break between in the "x" and the "a" in Alexander, a capital "A" in Alexander that didn't close and the character formation of "a" in Alexander.

Additionally, his middle initial of "C" often varied in style and slant, as did the "d" in Alexander.

Alexander was a popular player and though erratic in behavior, a frequent signer. His excessive drinking habits after the war no doubt contributed to many unpredictable signatures. Some of his later signature samples may be difficult to authenticate.

Availability: Limited
Demand: Average

Cut signature	$200
Single-signature baseball	$1,850
3x5" index card	$275
Photograph/baseball card	$500
HOF plaque postcard	$775
Perez-Steele postcard	Impossible

Walt Alston

Walter Emmons Alston
(Dec. 1, 1911-Oct. 1, 1984)

A strong, unemotional man, Alston spoke little, but was highly admired by both his players and the public. During his 23 years as Brooklyn and Los Angeles Dodgers manager he won seven pennants and four World Series titles.

During the 1950s Alston commonly signed "Walter" instead of "Walt." Capitalization in "Walter", though fairly consistent in form throughout his lifetime, varied slightly with the beginning stroke starting at the top of the "W" instead of the bottom. The "l" in Walter was much larger in size, about twice the height of the "a". A signature trait that remained characteristic throughout his lifetime was the crossing of the letter "t" almost at the top of the stem of the letter. Capitalization in "Alston" also varied from later samples, with the letter "A" rounder in form and either closed or open, but not connected to any letter in his first name.

Later samples, in the 1970s and 1980s, exhibit many changes in Alston's signature style. The flamboyance of the signature had clearly been enhanced by a larger signature with greater style in the capitalization. The "t" in Walt was now crossed by a flamboyant stroke that stretched to capitalization height and began the "A" in Alston. The "lston" in Alston showed significant variation in character formation, with the only consistency being the high crossing of the letter "t" and short ending stroke of the "n".

Alston was a dedicated signer, who usually responded quickly to requests. Despite failing health during the final months before his death, he continued to answer collectors with a noticeably deteriorating signature. A signature recognizable only by the "W" and unique crossing of the "t" in Walt, and the high crossed "t" and short ending stroke of the "n" in Alston. Autographed Hall of Fame plaque postcards are highly sought after by collectors, due to the limited time Alston had to sign them prior to his death.

Availability: Above average
Demand: Average

Cut signature	$6
Single-signature baseball	$75
3x5" index card	$18
Photograph/baseball card	$35
HOF plaque postcard	$50
Perez-Steele postcard	$500

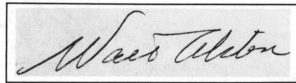

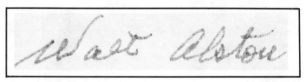

Cap Anson

Adrian Constantine Anson
(April 11, 1852-April 14, 1922)

Extremely popular during his playing days, Anson was the first player to reach the 3,000 hit pinnacle. The winner of three batting championships, Anson remained in baseball from 1876 until 1898 when he quit during a brief managerial stint with the Giants.

A well educated man and a Notre Dame graduate, Anson was a prolific writer. His handwriting was particularily notable in style due to many unique character formations, such as the letters "a", "d", "g", "c" and, "T". The "a", "g" and "d" when beginning a word would be double stroked at the start of the character. The letter "C" or "c" were identical in formation with a loop at the beginning of the beak of the letter. His capitalized letter "T" often had a beginning stroke starting at the capital height that resembled a lower case "s."

An Anson autograph was commonly signed "AC Anson". Unique was the closeness between both the "A" and the "C", varying little in character formation, but sometimes in slant. The "nson" in Anson could vary in character formation and style, leaving only the "A" as a relatively consistent factor.

Anson handwriting is very easy to authenticate, but some signature samples alone could be a bit more difficult. Anson hoarded his equipment and stored hundreds of bats in his basement for years. There have been many stories written about his outrage if he found anyone in possession of his equipment.

Availability: Limited
Demand: Strong

Cut signature	$1,200
Single-signature baseball	$4,850
3x5" index card	$1,000
Photograph/baseball card	$2,750
HOF plaque postcard	Impossible
Perez-Steele postcard	Impossible

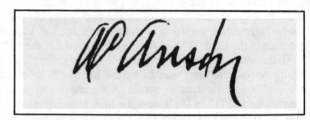

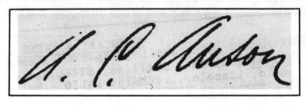

Luis Aparicio

Luis Ernesto Montiel Aparicio
(April 29, 1934-   )

His outstanding career spanned 18 years with a variety of American League clubs including Chicago, Baltimore and Boston. Aparicio was the American League Rookie of the Year in 1956. During his career he compiled 2,677 hits at a batting average of .262.

Early Aparicio signature examples vary radically compared to his modern day autograph. During the 1950s his signature was far more compact, yet each letter was distinqishable. Flying starts and finishes were common, with the "o" in Aparicio ending with a dynamic finishing loop that stretched above his entire last name. The only feature that has remained consistent has been the break between the "p" and the "a" in Aparicio.

By 1959 his signature had become elongated with greater space between each individual character. Capitalization was more distinct, the "L" taking on a traditional look, while the "A" exhibited a more printed simplified style. A break between the "A" and the "p" in Aparicio occurred on occasion. Other than slight occasional modifications, Aparicio's signature remained fairly consistent until the later 1970s.

Aparicio's signature of today is far more flamboyant, with the capitalization, especially the "A", being dramatically altered to a more artistic design. The break between the "p" and the "a" in Aparicio remains, however a break between the "r" and the "i" has also become common. The "L" in Luis can vary in character width, as can the "p", "o" and "c" in Aparicio.

Aparicio's residency in Venezuela has made his appearances in the United States very rare. When he has appeared in this country he has been obliging and congenial to autograph requests.

Availability: Plentiful
Demand: Little

Cut signature	$3
Single-signature baseball	$20
3x5" index card	$7
Photograph/baseball card	$13
HOF plaque postcard	$13
Perez-Steele postcard	$25

Luke Appling

Lucius Benjamin Appling
(April 2, 1909-   )

Appling compiled a lifetime batting average of .310 that included 2,749 hits. Appling hit over .300 in 16 seasons and in 1936 hit a career high .388.

Still active in the Braves organization during spring training, his love for baseball is only surpassed by his popularity with the players he teaches and his adoring fans.

Early Appling examples are far more fluent than his signature of today. Character definition, particularily the lower case letters, are easier to distinguish.

Later samples, circa 1970s and 1980s, show typical aging characteristics. Most character formations are not smooth, with numerous minor variations. Appling's general style has remained consistent in character height, slant, etc. The "pp" in Appling is a good reference point for authentication. Comparing slant, character formation, and descender length should help in determining an authentic Appling autograph.

Availability: Plentiful
Demand: Little

Cut signature	$3
Single-signature baseball	$18
3x5" index card	$6
Photograph/baseball card	$12
HOF plaque postcard	$10
Perez-Steele postcard	$60

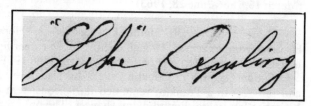

Earl Averill

Howard Earl Averill
(May 21, 1902-Aug. 16, 1983)

Averill ended his career with a .318 batting average that included 2,020 hits and 238 home runs. A five time All-Star game participant, Earl hit over .300 eight times.

Averill's signature style was fairly consistent throughout his life. Earlier examples will show smoother strokes and improved character formation.

Averill's signature exhibited typical aging characteristics. Autograph samples from the 1980s should show little or no smooth strokes. Averill signed very slowly during the last three years of his life, thus excess ink absorption is common with later examples. Characteristic of Averill signatures has been the break between the "E" and the "arl" in Earl, capitalization style of the "A" in Averill and the double stroked beginning of the "a" in Earl.

Earl was a prolific signer and always accessible to his fans during the induction ceremonies that he attended in Cooperstown.

Availability: Plentiful
Demand: Little

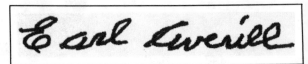

Cut signature	$7
Single-signature baseball	$70
3x5" index card	$15
Photograph/baseball card	$30
HOF plaque postcard	$20
Perez-Steele postcard	$650

Frank Baker

John Franklin Baker
(March 13, 1886-June 28, 1963)

With an impressive .307 lifetime batting average, "Home Run" Baker was known most fo his fierce competiveness. Though he hit only 96 career home runs, his nickname stuck with him due to his roundtripper performance during the 1911 World Series.

Commonly signing "J Franklin Baker," his signature exhibited few consistencies. The "J" and the "F" in J Franklin remained fairly consistent throughout his lifetime, howeve his entire last name showed many changes. The only common break was between the "F" and "ranklin" in Franklin. Some authentic samples will also show a break between the "B" and "aker" in Baker. Capitalization, slant and character formation all commonly varied in his last name. The best reference point for authentication is the Franklin portion of his sig nature. The bowl formation of the letter "k" in Franklin forms what appears to be a lowe case "c". Additionally, the "r" always joins the "a" on the top loop of the character forma tion in Franklin.

During the last years of his life he suffered a series of strokes that hampered his signature capabilities. Samples from this time period, the 1960s, may be difficult to authenticate.

Availability: Average
Demand: Average

Cut signature	$50
Single-signature baseball	$675
3x5" index card	$100
Photograph/baseball card	$195
HOF plaque postcard	$275
Perez-Steele postcard	Impossible

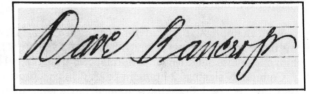

Dave Bancroft

David James Bancroft
(April 20, 1891-Oct. 9, 1972)

Known primarily for his fielding ability, "Beauty" was a favorite of John McGraw's Giants in the early Twenties. Dave batted over .300 five times, and finished his career with 2,004 hits.

Bancroft's signature varied over the years in character formation and slant, particularily in capitalization. Common breaks in his signature occurred between the "D" and the "a", also the "v" and the "e" in Dave. Additionally, between the "B" and the "a", also the "n" and the "c" in Bancroft. A good character pair to reference for authentication is the "cr" in Bancroft which commonly exhibits two distinguishing loop formations in the letters. The unique ending character stroke of the "ft" has also become a hallmark of his signature. During his playing days and retirement, Bancroft was responsive to autograph requests.

Availability: Average
Demand: Average

Cut signature	$30
Single-signature baseball	$400
3x5" index card	$50
Photograph/baseball card	$160
HOF plaque postcard	$375
Perez-Steele postcard	Impossible

Ernie Banks

Ernest Banks
(Jan. 31, 1931-   )

An outstanding 19 years in the major leagues, culminated on May 12, 1970, when "Mr. Cub" blasted his 500th home run. Though he never played in a World Series, his hitting and fielding prowess gained him baseball immortality. Ernie came to the Cubs from the Kansas City Monarchs of the Negro National League in Spetember of 1953.

Other than the "s" in Banks, early signature samples bear little resemblance to his modern day autograph. Most samples will show breaks between the "E" and "rnie" or "rnest", also between the "B" and the "anks". Capitalization of both the "E" and the "B" is single stroked and far more formal in appearance.

By the late 1970s Banks signature had evolved to a less formal format with greater emphasis on capitalization. The "E" and the "B" were now about three times the height of the lower case letters, with a different character formation. "Ernie" became all one stroke and "Banks" became four strokes. The "k", which in earlier samples was about twice the lower case character height, was now smaller than the "a" in Banks. A good authentication reference is the "nks" in Banks, paying particular attention to the formation of the "k" and the ending stroke of the "s".

Banks signature is best obtained at a baseball card show. Most alternative acquisition methods usually prove unsuccessful.

Availability: Plentiful
Demand: Little

Cut signature	$3
Single-signature baseball	$20
3x5" index card	$5
Photograph/baseball card	$12
HOF plaque postcard	$13
Perez-Steele postcard	$25

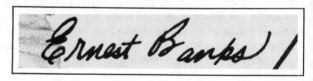

Al Barlick

Albert Joseph Barlick
(April 2, 1915-   )

Barlick began umpiring in 1936 in the Northeast Arkansas League. After a tour of duty in the U.S. Coast Guard which ended in 1946, he rejoined the National League staff that he had joined in 1940. During the 1956-1957 seasons, Barlick was out of the game due to illlness. His career included umpiring many fall classics and All-Star contests.

Commonly signing "Al Barlick", his signature has varied only slightly in character formation, size and slant. The only consistent break in his signature fell between the "B" and the "a" in Barlick. The capitalized "A" began at the top of the letter and may or may not be closed. The "l" varied in size, often equalling or exceeding the height of the "A" in Al. His signature has gradually increased in degree of right slant over the years, while his last name has gradually decreased in size.

The "B" is often a two-stroke construction, however I have seen a single-stroke variation. The slant of the stem of both the "A" in Al and "B" in Barlick should be similar. Both loops that make up the major portion of the "B" can vary in size and the "B" is left open at the bottom. The "a" can vary in size and begins at the top of the letter. The "l" typically exceeds the height of the "B" in later examples, but is typically smaller than the "k". The "i" can vary in size and the "c" can resemble an "e" in later examples. The ascender of the "k" is typically wider than that of the "l" and is usually the highest point in his signature. The loop of the "k" often does not intersect the stem of the letter.

Barlick's contribution to baseball has been obscured for many years, until his recent induction to the shrine at Cooperstown. He is a responsive signer and his autograph should be an easy acquisition for the collector.

Availability: Plentiful
Demand: Little

Cut signature	$4
Single-signature baseball	$20
3x5" index card	$5
Photograph/baseball card	$15
HOF plaque postcard	$16
Perez-Steele postcard	$35

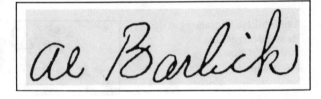

Edward Barrow

Edward Grant Barrow
(May 10, 1868-Dec. 15, 1953)

It was Ed Barrow who successfully established the New York Yankees as the most powerful team during the Twenties and Thirties. When Barrow retired in 1945 the Yankees had captured 14 pennants and an astounding 10 World Series championships. Barrow, like most executives, signed numerous documents.

Barrow's signature varied considerably, primarily because of the expediency needed to respond to his correspondence. He commonly signed "EG. Barrow", though I have seen examples signed as both "Ed" and "Edward". Capitalization in Barrow's signature was very inconsistent. The capital "E" in early signature samples was easy to read, formal in structure and began with an almost decorative beginning stroke that began just below the base line of the letter. The "E" evolved into an extended top loop version that consisted of three recognizable loops. When signing "EG Barrow" there were no breaks in the capitaliztion of the "EGB," however when signing "Ed" or "Edward" there was often a break after the "E". Of all the capitalizaion, the "G" remained most consistent in form. The "B" in Barrow was inconsistent and is not recommended for authentication comparison.

In Barrow a break may or may not exist between the "B" and the "arrow". This break is common on earlier samples. The "arrow" can vary in slant, character height and formation. Additionally, the ending stroke after the "w" can vary, being looped or curled, but always ending at the top of the character formation.

With little signature consistency, collectors should acquire Barrow material in document form. Barrow was elected to the Hall of Fame on Sept. 28, 1953 a mere three months before his death. A highly sought collectible would be an autographed Hall of Fame plaque post card, as none are believed to exist.

Availability: Average
Demand: Average

Cut signature	$40
Single-signature baseball	$800
3x5" index card	$80
Photograph/baseball card	$175
HOF plaque postcard	Impossible
Perez-Steele postcard	Impossible

Jake Beckley

Jacob Peter Beckley
(Aug. 4, 1867-June 25, 1918)

During "Old Eagle Eye's" 20 years in the major leagues he posted over 2,900 hits at an average of .308. A popular player, he was notorious for his erratic throwing and fans often witnessed the strangest fielding plays of the day from Beckley.

Typically signing "Jacob P. Beckley", or "J. Beckley", his signature varied primarily in character formation during his lifetime. Consistent signature breaks fell between the "J" and the "a" in Jacob, also between the "B", and the "e" in Beckley. The "J" began with a left upward stroke that could originate from below the signature's base line or at lower case height. The stem of the "J" may or may not close at the bottom. The "a" may or may not close at the top where it originates, and the "c" can resemble an "e" due to the lack of definition in its loop. The "b" could vary in size and was often equal in height to the beginning stroke of the "B" in Beckley. The finishing stroke of the "b" was often a small loop. His middle initial of "P" began with an opening formation that resembled a number "7" and the loop may vary in size but should be very similar in slant to that of the "B". The loop of the "P" may or may not be closed.

The "B" begins with an opening formation similar to that of the "P", which resembles a number "7". The loop of the "B" may vary in its degree of right slant and the letter is typically left open at the bottom. The "e" can vary a bit in slant and the "c" in Beckley has the same characteristics as the "c" in Jacob. The unique "k" formation can vary in size and often resembles the letters "u" or "h". The ascenders of Beckley's lower case letters are typically small and may or may not extend only to the height of the bottom loop of the "B". The "l" may vary a bit in size and the flamboyant right slanted descender of the "y" often curves slightly before creating a looped formation which transforms into an underline for this signature. The slant of the stem on the "k" and the descender of the "y" should be very similar.

Like may other baseball pioneers, Beckley signatures are are often found in pencil. Details on Beckley's life remain uncertain following his retirement from baseball, however he was reported to have lived it up a bit, and eventually died broke. Collectors are advised to cautiously acquire his signatures as I have seen a few fake Beckley autographs adorning material that was printed after his death.

Availability: Scarce
Demand: Strong

Cut signature	$1,375
Single-signature baseball	$3,250
3x5" index card	$1,850
Photograph/baseball card	$3,500
HOF plaque postcard	Impossible
Perez-Steele postcard	Impossible

Cool Papa Bell

James Thomas Bell
(May 17, 1903-   )

A sensational player with over 27 years in the Negro Leagues, "Cool Papa" was perhaps the fastest player to ever play the game. Since his induction into the shrine at Cooperstown, his recognition among fans and collectors has soared.

Bell was inducted in 1974. Up to that point in time his signature was sought primarily by collectors trying to reconstruct the history of the Negro Leagues. His signature stayed fairly consistent from 1974 until the mid 1980s, when failing health began impacting his ability to respond to the numerous mail requests. With his signature deteriorating and sight failing, he began returning collector's mail requests with a note documenting his condition. During this period Bell did however sign items for some collectors with whom he had established a good relationship.

By the late 1980s his signature, almost printed in format, had deteriorated to a point that made it almost indistinguishable as an authentic example. In the future, these later signature samples will become a nightmare to authenticate due to the numerous inconsistencies.

Prior to the late 1980s, he commonly signed "James 'Cool Papa' Bell". Most notable perhaps, was the signature's unusually small size. Capitalization, specifically the "J", was very consistent in character formation. Additionally worth noting for authentication purposes is Bell's consistency in slant and the lack of signature breaks. Character formations such as the "B", "P", "p" and "s" can vary a bit, but not radically. The descender of the letter "J" is always the lowest point in his signature and the quotation marks before the word Cool, will always be directly above the "s" in James or between the "s" and the "C".

Collectors are advised to seek samples of Bell's signature prior to the late 1980s to avoid future authentication issues.

Availability: Above average
Demand: Average

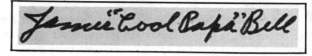

Cut signature	$6
Single-signature baseball	$50
3x5" index card	$12
Photograph/baseball card	$30
HOF plaque postcard	$18
Perez-Steele postcard	$75

Johnny Bench

Johnny Bench
(Dec. 7, 1947-   )

A catalyst for the "Big Red Machine" of the 1970s, Bench is the first, but not the last, of a dynasty to enter the walls of Cooperstown. Bench established numerous records for catchers, however it was for his post-season play which he is often most remembered. He was named Most Valuable Player of the 1976 World Series. Bench, always a popular player, has remained a favorite among collectors.

Earlier signature examples, late 1960s and 1970s, bear little resemblance to his autograph of today. Notable signature breaks exist between the "J" and the "o" in Johnny and the "B" and the "e" in Bench. One consistent characteristic has been the size relationship between the capitalization and the lower case letters, typically the "J" and the "B" are three times larger. The ascender and descender of the "J" in Johnny are usually about equal in size, in stark contrast to later examples where the descender is very small in comparison. The "B" in Bench is much wider in earlier signature samples.

By the mid 1970s Bench's signature had become more flamboyant, particularily the "J" in Johnny, and began to resemble his modern day autograph. His entire signature seemed to compress in size and the "ohnn" began to take on the consistent looped appearance. Inconsistentcies in capitalization can be found, specifically during the last few years of his career.

During the last decade Bench's signature has remained fairly consistent. For years, Bench commonly responded to mail requests with a rubber stamped version of his signature that is easily recognizable as a facsimile.

Availability: Plentiful
Demand: Above average

Cut signature	$4
Single-signature baseball	$20
3x5" index card	$5
Photograph/baseball card	$16
HOF plaque postcard	$18
Perez-Steele postcard	$65

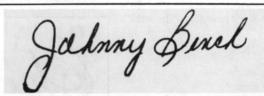

Chief Bender

Charles Albert Bender
(May 5, 1884-May 22, 1954)

Bender began pitching at the age of 19 for the Philadelphia A's, under Connie Mack. He compiled a lifetime record of 210 wins and pitched in five World Series contests.

Early authentic Bender autographs can be found in the form of "Charles Albert", though they are extremely rare in this format. Bender's signature style was very legible, commonly signing "'Chief' Bender". Examples in the form of "Charles Bender" or "Charles A. Bender" are usually restricted to formal documents.

Early signature examples usually have no breaks, while those signed later in his life commonly show a break between the "B" and the "e" in Bender. Inconsistencies exist in slant and the character formation of the "f" in Chief. The "B" in Bender also varies in character formation and even size. The "ender" in Bender remained relatively consistent as did the flamboyant looped ending after the "r".

Bender often complied with signature requests from collectors.

Availability: Average
Demand: Average

Cut signature	$110
Single-signature baseball	$1,075
3x5" index card	$155
Photograph/baseball card	$400
HOF plaque postcard	$900
Perez-Steele postcard	Impossible

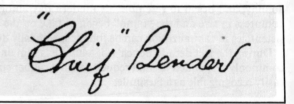

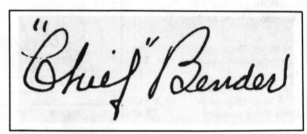

Yogi Berra

Lawrence Peter Berra
(May 12, 1925-   )

Popular indeed is "Yogi" Berra, the catcher who propelled the Yankees into 14 World Series contests. Berra has long been established with the game of baseball, holding a variety of positons since he hung up his gear in 1965.

Early Berra examples, late 1940s and early 1950s, show a signature not radically different from his autograph of today, but less flamboyant. The "Y" in particular is less dramatic and the "o" in Yogi is clearly distinguishable. The "B" on Berra is a departure from current examples in character formation, much stiffer in appearance. The "g" in Yogi had a straight descender and lacked the now characteristic large loop.

Later Berra examples can vary in capitalization and character formation. Most consistent has been the "erra" with the traditional back looped ending after the letter "a". The formation of the "rr" can vary, usually depending upon the expedience of the signature. Typically the "o" and sometimes the "g" fall beneath the "Y" in Yogi. Not worth basing an authentication decision upon is the "B" in Berra which can vary dramatically. The "i" in Yogi can also connect to the "B" in Berra in authentic samples, though typically it does not.

In addition to catching him at the ballpark, or occasionally through the mail request, collectors may find Yogi on the baseball card show circuit.

Availability: Plentiful
Demand: Little

Cut signature	$3
Single-signature baseball	$18
3x5" index card	$7
Photograph/baseball card	$13
HOF plaque postcard	$14
Perez-Steele postcard	$50

Jim Bottomley

James Leroy Bottomley
(April 23, 1900-Dec. 11, 1959)

A popular player during his years with the Cardinals, "Sunny Jim" ended his career with a lifetime batting average of .310. His best season came in 1925 when he led the National League in hits (227) and doubles (44), while batting .367.

Commonly signing "Jim Bottomley" or "James L. Bottomley", his signature varied in character formation, size and slant. The flamboyant "J", in James or Jim, was often more than 10 times the size of his lower case letters. The "J" varied in slant and flamboyance, with the ascender's loop stroke extending as far as the "m" in James. The descender of the "J" exhibited greater variation, from a rounded loop formation, to a double-pointed looped style. The "a" could vary a bit in size and may or may not be left open at the top of the letter.

The "im" combination can resemble a "uuu" formation and the "e" can also vary in size. Bottomley's ending stroke in his first name can vary from a simple curl, to a looped extending line. When he signed his middle initial, the top loop of the two-looped "L" was usually much larger in size and could extend above the bottom loop of the "B" because of its degree of right slant.

The "B" in Bottomley can be either a single- or double-stroke formation. The single-stroke formation is more traditional in appearance and begins from the signature's base line and includes a flamboyant bottom loop. The two-stroke variation includes an extended top loop that may extend backward as far as the last letter of his first name. The "ott" combination has been the most consistent element in his signature, showing only moderate variation in size. An occasional break can fall between the "t" and the "o" in Bottomley. The second "o" in Bottomley often bears little resemblance to the first "o" and is usually much larger in size. The second "o" in his last name can resemble an "a" and may or may not be left open at the top. The "l" can vary in size, however its height typically exceeds that of both "t"s in his last name. The "y" can vary from a long simple downward stroke to a much shorter version that may include a loop or hook. The slant of the "l" and the slant of the stem of the "y" should be similar.

Bottomley was troubled by arthritis in his later years, making his signatures generated during this period inconsistent with earlier examples. He was a responsive signer, although ironically, few examples of his signture surface in the autograph market.

Availability: Limited
Demand: Average

Cut signature	$100
Single-signature baseball	$900
3x5" index card	$200
Photograph/baseball card	$200
HOF plaque postcard	Impossible
Perez-Steele postcard	Impossible

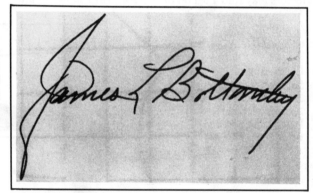

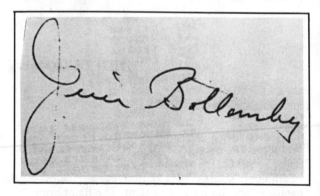

Lou Boudreau

Louis Boudreau
(July 17, 1917-   )

A crafty ballplayer and a keen manager, Boudreau became one of the most popular players to ever put on a Cleveland Indians uniform. At the age of 24 he became one of the youngest managers to head a team from the beginning of a season.

Changes to Boudreau's signature over his lifetime have been minimal. Earlier examples tend to have better character formation and less flamboyance. Capitalization, particularily the "B" has varied consistently in character width.

Later samples, show a consistency in slant (about 45 degrees), and character formation of the lower case letters. Capitalization will be the most inconsistent element of Boudreau's autograph. A break exists only between the "L" and the "o" in Lou. The "o" in Lou has a consistent straight line segment prior to the formation of the letter that is usually half the character height of the "L". The "o" and sometimes the "u" typically fall underneath the top loop of the capitalized "L".

Boudreau has been a consistent signer throughout his career in baseball. In addition to catching Lou on the baseball card show circuit or through mail requests, he can also be found behind the microphone for the Chicago Cubs.

Availability: Plentiful
Demand: Little

Cut signature	$3
Single-signature baseball	$18
3x5" index card	$5
Photograph/baseball card	$8
HOF plaque postcard	$10
Perez-Steele postcard	$25

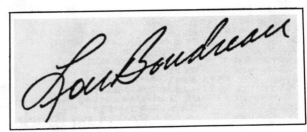

Roger Bresnahan

Roger Phillip Bresnahan
(June 11, 1879-Dec. 4, 1944)

Bresnahan was best known as Christy Mathewson's battery mate. His popularity climaxed during his years with New York, specifically 1905 when he hit .313 in the World Series.

Early Bresnahan samples have a tendency to be less flamboyant with easier character identification. Missing in early examples is the flamboyant finishing stroke that underlined almost his entire name. Consistent throughout his lifetime has been no signature breaks, in fact his entire name — "Roger P. Bresnahan" consists of one stroke.

Bresnahan was a fairly prolific writer. Voluminous correspondence exists from his years with the Toledo minor league baseball club, where he was president and manager.

Capitalization, specifically the "R", varied in character formation, with earlier versions showing the loop of the letter, and later samples commonly omitting it. A good reference point for the authenticator is the unique "rPB" letter connection. The second connection between the "P" and the "B" is generally equal or above the height of the first connection between the "r" and the "P". Occasionally the "n" in Bresnahan is omitted in authentic examples and the "r" in Roger commonly looks like an "o."

Bresnahan's handwriting is very easy to identify by the characteristic slant and unique character formations, such as the letter "I."

Availability: Average
Demand: Average

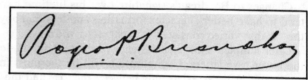

Cut signature	$350
Single-signature baseball	$2,250
3x5" index card	$450
Photograph/baseball card	$1,250
HOF plaque postcard	Impossible
Perez-Steele postcard	Impossible

Lou Brock

Louis Clark Brock
(June 18, 1939-   )

One of baseball's fastest all-time players swiping a record 938 stolen bases. Brock became the 14th player to achieve the 3,000 hit mark on Aug. 13, 1979.

Commonly signing "Louis Brock" or "Lou Brock", earlier Brock samples (circa 1960s) tend to be less flamboyant. Variations in character formation, particularly the "B" in Brock, were typical in samples from both the 1960s and 1970s. Earlier signatures exhibit breaks between the "L" and the "o" in Lou and the "B" and the "r" in Brock. By the late 1970s he had added another common break between the "o" and "c" in Brock. The most consistent characters have been the "u" in Lou and the "r" in Brock. The two-looped "L" formation in Lou has varied in size, while increasing both in slant and flamboyance with age. The degree of right slant exhibited by the "L" often allows the character's top loop to extend beyond the "u" in Lou. The "L" in later versions is often five or six times the height of his lower case letters. The "o" may begin from inside the letter or with a small stroke originating from the signature's base line.

The "B" in Brock has varied considerably in character formation and size. Later versions of the "B" (circa 1970s), may be three to four times wider than in his earlier signatures (circa 1960s), while originating from inside of the character versus outside. The "r" has varied in character formation, however typically exceeds the height of the "o" in later examples. By the late 1970s his signature began to resemble his autograph of today. The "k" in Brock now typically shows no loop in the ascender, only a line. The slant of the "k" should be very similar to that of the "L" in Lou. The ending stroke of the "k" is commonly a simple upward curl.

Brock has been a difficult signature to obtain by mail, forcing many collectors to pursue acquisition via the baseball card show circuit. Collectors should, however, find the acquisition of his signature fairly easy.

Availability: Plentiful
Demand: Little

Cut signature	$3
Single-signature baseball	$18
3x5" index card	$4
Photograph/baseball card	$13
HOF plaque postcard	$10
Perez-Steele postcard	$40

Dan Brouthers

Dennis Joseph Brouthers
(May 8, 1858-Aug. 2, 1932)

Dan Brouthers was one of the greatest players in the 19th Century game of baseball. He consistently hit above the .300 mark and was a natural hitter. His career ended in 1904 and in 1907 he became a scout for the Giants.

Like so many pioneers of the game, few Brouthers autographs ever surface in the collector's market. The few I have seen have been in pencil and are notably legible. Consistent signature breaks occur between the "D" and the "a" in Dan, also between the "B" and the "r" in Brouthers. His signature varied a bit throughout his life in slant and character formation. Later signature samples have a very slight slant right primarily notable in the lower case letters. The capitalization, near vertical in slant, can vary in character formation. The "D" is very recognizable, due to character width, resembling a "Jl" formation. The "D" in later examples does not close. The "an" remained relatively consistent. The "B" in Brouthers can vary in slant and character formation a bit, but primarily begins with a downward stroke that doubles back to form the main letter. The "B" typically loops on the bottom and may or may not close the letter, however is often left slightly open. The "rou" remained fairly consistent and the "t" and the "h" could vary in ascender width and slant. Brouthers' "s" formation at the end of words is a bit unusual, resembling a simple closing stroke, rather than a letter. I have seen no flamboyant ending strokes in his autograph. Authenticators should concentrate on the "D" and the "s" as good reference letters. Again, these noted characteristics appear to be indicative of later signature examples, post 1900; they may vary considerably with earlier authentic autographed Brouthers material.

Brouthers loved baseball and spent many years as a night watchman and custodian at the Polo Grounds. Sample signatures of "Big Dan" on dated Giant memorabilia would no doubt be of great interest to collectors.

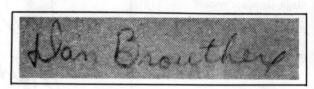

Availability: Scarce
Demand: Strong

Cut signature	$1,600
Single-signature baseball	$4,000
3x5" index card	$2,850
Photograph/baseball card	$3,750
HOF plaque postcard	Impossible
Perez-Steele postcard	Impossible

Mordecai Brown

Mordecai Peter Centennial Brown
(Oct. 19, 1876-Feb. 14, 1948)

"Three-Fingered" Brown made his professional debut in 1901. Brown helped Chicago to National League Championships in 1906, 1907, 1908 and 1910. He also became the first major leaguer to pitch four consecutive shutouts in 1908.

Early Brown examples exhibit breaks between the "M" and the "o", "e" and the "c" and the "c" and the "a" in Mordecai, and none in Brown. Variations in capitalization were common, with the signature slant being relatively consistent. Brown commonly didn't close the letter "o" and "a" in his signature.

Later Brown examples exhibited radical departures in captialization, especially the character formation. Common breaks were between the "M" and the "o", "r" and the "d", "d" and the "e", "e" and the "c" and "c" and the "a" in Mordecai. A break developed between the "B" and the "r" in Brown.

Consistent in all samples in the ascender of the "d" being the highest point in the signature and the lack of closing the lower case letter "o" and "a". Authentication of later samples of Brown's signature can be a bit difficult due to the variations from his earlier styles.

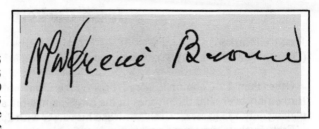

Availability: Limited
Demand: Average

Cut signature	$265
Single-signature baseball	$2,675
3x5" index card	$400
Photograph/baseball card	$425
HOF plaque postcard	Impossible
Perez-Steele postcard	Impossible

Morgan Bulkeley

Morgan G. Bulkeley
(Dec. 26, 1837-Nov. 6, 1922)

A gentleman of high regard in his day, Bulkeley served in many prestigious positions including Governor of Connecticut and as a member of the United States Senate. He was the National League's first president in 1876, a position he held for one year.

Bulkeley's signature frequently adorned official correspondence associated with the particular office he held. Common characteristics of Bulkeley's signature include not closing the letter "o" in Morgan, a gradual decrease in the letter size in the lower case letters of Morgan, and the descender of the letter "G" in his middle initial seldom crossing significantly below the base line of his signature. Variation in capitalization is common, though his signature slant remained relatively consistent. The "ulkele" in Bulkeley had a tendency to vary in character formation, probably due to signature speed.

A prolific writer, Bulkeley's signature should prove fairly accessible to collectors through many autograph houses or auctions.

Availability: Average
Demand: Average

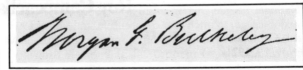

Cut signature	$1,450
Single-signature baseball	$4,000
3x5" index card	$2,350
Photograph/baseball card	$3,500
HOF plaque postcard	Impossible
Perez-Steele postcard	Impossible

Jesse Burkett

Jesse Cail Burkett
(Dec. 4, 1868-May 27, 1953)

Other than Ty Cobb or Rogers Hornsby, there was no better a hitter than Jesse Burkett. Burkett hit over .400 three times in his career, amassing an amazing 240 hits in 1896 while playing only 133 games. "Crab" finished his career with 2,873 lifetime hits.

Early Burkett signatures are easily identified by the unique capitalization of letter "J" in Jesse, almost appearing like a printed capital "C" with a capital "J" attached. The only break in his signature was between the "B" and the "u" in Burkett and it remained consistent throughout his lifetime. His middle initial "C" had a tendency to look like a capitalized "L". The character formation of the "B" in Burkett remained fairly consistent, however became more upright in later versions.

Later Burkett examples change slightly in slant and primarily differed in the construction of the "J" in Jesse. The "e" in Burkett remained consistently the smallest letter in his last name. He commonly used a single stroke crossing of the "tt" in Burkett.

Availability: Average
Demand: Average

Cut signature	$350
Single-signature baseball	$3,300
3x5" index card	$750
Photograph/baseball card	$1,300
HOF plaque postcard	$835
Perez-Steele postcard	Impossible

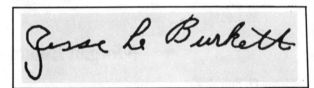

Roy Campenella

Roy Campanella
(Nov. 19, 1921-   )

A three-time Most Valuable Player, Campy's career was cut short in Janury of 1958 by an automobile accident that left him paralyzed below the waist. In his 10 seasons with the Brooklyn Dodgers he set numerous records for catchers, most home runs in a season (41), most runs batted in (142), and many others.

Early signature examples, prior to Campanella's accident, typically show breaks between the "R" and the "o" in Roy, also between the "C" and the "a" and occasionally between the "p" and the "a" in Campanella. Capitalization was somewhat consistent, primarily varying in width. Good reference points for authentication are the character formation of the letters "R" and "p". Campanella's signature slant was also consistent and is a good comparison characteristic. Signature size and letter spacing were generally inconsistent. The lower case letter "a"s in Campanella may or may not be closed, and the loops in the "ll" may or may not be recognizable.

Over the years he has typically answered mail requests with stamped signatures, however, on rare occassions he has answered with an autograph utilizing a device that aids him in the task. These signatures bear a close resemblance to his pre-accident signature, in particular the character formation of the "oy" in Roy and the "ampanella" in Campanella. Closer inspection of these signatures will show some roughness and ink accumulation, primarily due to the writing device and the nature of its use. In time, these device-aided signatures could prove difficult to authenticate due to the anomalies associated with its use.

Availability: Limited
Demand: Strong

Cut signature	$120
Single-signature baseball	$1,200
3x5" index card	$225
Photograph/baseball card	$425
HOF plaque postcard	$600
Perez-Steele postcard	$300

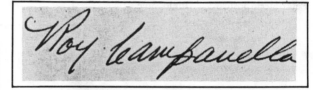

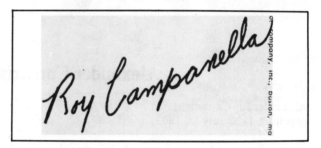

Max Carey

Max Carey
(Jan. 11, 1890-May 30, 1976)

"Scoops" was an outstanding all-around ballplayer whose impressive fielding performance was equaled by his batting. His National League fielding records are numerous, and he also held the record for most years leading the league in stolen bases — 10.

Carey's signature remained incredibly consistent throughout his lifetime. Early examples show minimal variation when compared to those signed later in his life. Common breaks in his signature were between the "C" and the "a" in Carey and occasionally between the "m" and the "a" in Max. Variations occur in the crossing of the "x", or a separate short downward stroke. The "M" in Max may show two loops, one loop, or no loops at the beginning of

109

the character formation. Early examples will not slash the descender of the "y" in Carey, but will instead usually include an underline beneath his signature.

Carey was most responsive to autograph requests by mail and generally a prolific signer.

Availability: Plentiful
Demand: Average

Cut signature	$7
Single-signature baseball	$75
3x5" index card	$13
Photograph/baseball card	$40
HOF plaque postcard	$35
Perez-Steele postcard	Impossible

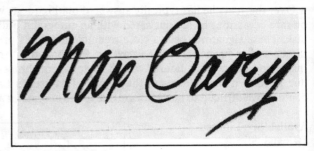

Alexander Cartwright

Alexander Joy Cartwright
(April 17, 1820-July 12, 1892)

The "Father of Modern Base Ball," Cartwright shares his game's creation with the "Doubleday Myth." He formulated the game while still in his twenties, and by 1846 his team, the New York Knickerbockers, was the team to beat.

Early Cartwright examples, circa 1840, exhibited a writing flamboyancy characteristic of that time. Typically signing "Alex J. Cartwright", common signature breaks were between the "A" and "l" in Alex, also between the "C" and the "a", "t" and the "w", and the "i" and the "g" in Cartwright. Capitalization varied a bit in early examples, by far the most prominent being the unusually large "C" in Cartwright. The "C" usually was about one and a half times the size of the other capitalized letters. The slant of the "C" allowed the top loop to extend above the "artw" in Cartwright. The crossing of the "t" typically varied in length and was commonly a separate line. The "J" in early examples does not usually have a complete descender loop.

Cartwright utilized two capital "A" letter formations, a traditional (for that time period) style "A" and a capital "a" that was an enlarged lower case style letter. By the 1860s, the "J" in his middle initial became double-looped, with a well extended descender; variations of dropping either of the two loops were occasional.

As Cartwright got older, his capital "C" became smaller and less flamboyant. By the 1880s the "C" was almost the same height as the other capitalized letters — "A" and "J". A break developed in older examples between the "g" and "h" in Cartwright. Character formations appeared to get wider with letters such as "a" not completely closing. Capitalization became more upright in slant in later signatures. The letter "g" in Cartwright remained fairly consistent during the last four decades of his life and is a good authentication reference point. On earlier examples the "C" in Cartwright would be a good choice for signature comparisons, looking for slant, flamboyance and size.

Signatures of the prolific Cartwright are usually found on receipts, many of which have found there way into the autograph market.

Availability: Limited)
Demand: Strong

Cut signature	$700
Single-signature baseball	Unknown
3x5" index card	$850
Photograph/baseball card	$2,500
HOF plaque postcard	Impossible
Perez-Steele postcard	Impossible

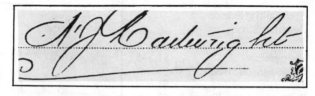

Henry Chadwick

Henry Chadwick
(Oct. 6, 1824-April 20, 1908)

The founder of the box score, Chadwick fell in love with the game of baseball upon his migration to this country from the United Kingdom. He authored the first rule book in 1858, however it was as the editor of the *Spalding Base Ball Guide* that brought him greatest prominence.

The few early Chadwick examples I have seen show greater character definition and flamboyance than his later signatures. Only one consistent break in early examples exists and that is between the "d" and the "w" in Chadwick. Descender length in letters such as the "y" in Henry will be much longer in earlier examples. Greater character formation in the lower case letters is evident in earlier versions, and the top loop of the "d" is far more conservative in flamboyance. Chadwick samples from later in his life typically have breaks between the "C" and the "h", "h" and the "a", and "a" and the "d" in Chadwick. The finishing stroke of the "k" is usually a flamboyant ending that can resemble an "E" attached to an "l" and it was common for Chadwick to add an occasional underline beneath his name. Some variation in capitalization exists, usually just an alteration to the beginning stroke. The "h" in Chadwick decreased a bit in size with age. Earlier examples will show the ascender of the letter rising above the "C" in Chadwick. Chadwick's handwriting is easily identified by its slant, numerous character breaks and certain distinct character formations, such as the letters "G", "I" and "H."

Authenticators should concentrate on the character formations of the "H" in Henry, also the "d" and "k" in Chadwick for comparison purposes. The "d" in Chadwick is without doubt the most notable characteristic of his signature, with the evolved flamboyant looped ascender. His later signature samples have a tendency to show little character definition in the "enry" of Henry.

In spite of the fact that he was a prolific writer, few examples of Chadwick's signature have found there way to the collector's market.

Availability: Scarce
Demand: Strong

Cut signature	$1,575
Single-signature baseball	Unknown
3x5" index card	$1,600
Photograph/baseball card	$3,500
HOF plaque postcard	Impossible
Perez-Steele postcard	Impossible

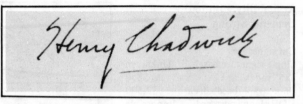

Frank Chance

Frank Leroy Chance
(Sept. 9, 1877-Sept. 14, 1924)

"Husk," of "Tinker to Evers to Chance" fame, was the leadership behind the Chicago Cubs pennant drives at the turn of the century. Most notable of his baseball skills was his speed on the base paths, and in 1903 while batting .327, Chance led the league in stolen bases with 67.

Common signature breaks in Husk's autograph are between the "F" and the "r", and "r" and the "a" in Frank, also between the "h" and the "a" in Chance. Capitalization varied a bit in character formation, usually showing more or less flamboyance. The most prominent letter in Chance's autograph is no doubt the large capital "F" in Frank. The arm or extension on the letter "F" commonly covered the "ran" in Frank. The ascender of the "h" in chance was typically the high point in his last name and the "c" had a tendency to be a bit larger than the "an" or "e."

Availability: Average
Demand: Average

Cut signature	$725
Single-signature baseball	$3,575
3x5" index card	$1,050
Photograph/baseball card	$1,850
HOF plaque postcard	Impossible
Perez-Steele postcard	Impossible

Happy Chandler

Albert Benjamin Chandler
(July 14, 1898-   )

Following the death of Kenesaw Landis, "Happy" Chandler was voted in as baseball's second commissioner, a position he held from 1945 to 1951. Chandler was a controversial commissioner, often siding against team management on his decisions. In retrospect, he brought a lot to baseball during his short term. Particularly worth noting was his approval for Jackie Robinson to play in the major leagues.

Not unlike most executives, Chandler signed numerous correspondences from the many offices he held which included Senator and Governor for the state of Kentucky. He typically signed "A.B. Chandler", a signature that had no breaks. On occasions where he has signed "Albert Chandler", a break can fall between the "A" and the "l" in Albert. The "A.B." capitalization connection is consistent, with the bottom of the "A" connecting to the top of the "B". The capitalized "A", which resembles an enlarged lower case "a" in style, closes only about 10% of the time. The "B" in certain instances, primarily dependent upon the writing material, may exhibit no top loop and look much like a capitalized "D" in formation. The "C" in Chandler generally varies in width, with the top loop being very tight to the stem and sometimes indistinguishable. The "andler" in Chandler can vary in character formation, often making specifically the "a" unrecognizable. A notable characteristic is the larger spacing, compared to the related lower case letters, between the "n" and the "d" in Chandler. The finishing stroke following the "r" in Chandler resembles a "v" and is always stroked upward. The connection between the "d" and the "l" often resemble an enlarged "u" character formation.

Chandler has always been an avid signer and his wonderful personality has alway made him a favorite among baseball fans.

Availability: Plentiful
Demand: Little

Cut signature	$4
Single-signature baseball	$30
3x5" index card	$10
Photograph/baseball card	$20
HOF plaque postcard	$13
Perez-Steele postcard	$70

Oscar Charleston

Oscar McKinley Charleston
(Oct. 14, 1896-Oct. 11, 1954)

Typically signing "Oscar Charleston" or "Oscar M Charleston", his signature varied primarily in character formation and size. An occasional break fell between the "O" and the "s" in Oscar. The "O" in Oscar was often the largest letter in his signature, typically twice the height of the surrounding lower case letters. The "s" can vary in size and may or may not close at the bottom of the letter. The "c" can vary in width, but typically includes a well formed loop at the top of the letter, particularly noticeable in earlier examples. The "a" may or may not close at the top of the letter and the bottom loop of the character, in earlier examples, is often sharply formed. The "r" often shows little formation to the top of the letter and thus can resemble an undotted "i".

The "C" in Charleston, like the lower case version in Oscar, usually includes a well formed loop at the top of the letter. The width of the "h" can vary and it is common for the ascender of the letter to exceed the height of the "C". The right slant of the letters "h" and "t" should be nearly identical. The "l" can vary in width but is often exceeded in height by the ascender of the "h" and the stem of the "t". The "t" extends in height to that of the "h" and is usually crossed by a simple short stroke through the letter's stem. The "o" has a tendency to be the smallest letter in his signature, but equal in height to the "n". The finishing stroke following the "n" is often a simple upward curl to lower case height. Perhaps the best authentication reference lies with his consistent right slant, particularly noticeable in the letters "h", "l" and "t". If the slant of these letters are not very similar, pass on the purchase of the signature. Additionally worth noting is Charleston's tight letter spacing between the letters "l" and "e". Later signature examples show a decrease in capitalization height and an increase in character width.

Material surrounding his life in Cuba seems to occasionally surface in the form of receipts or contracts. Charleston was managing the Indianapolis Clowns when he suffered a sudden and fatal heart attack. Charleston signature samples are not abundant and collectors wishing to add his autograph to their collection may find acquisition a real challenge.

Availability: Scarce
Demand: Above average

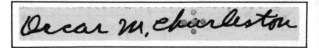

Cut signature	$1,050
Single-signature baseball	$4,675
3x5" index card	$1,700
Photograph/baseball card	$2,150
HOF plaque postcard	Impossible
Perez-Steele postcard	Impossible

Jack Chesbro

John Dwight Chesbro
(June 5, 1874-Nov. 6, 1931)

"Happy Jack" was a popular pitcher during his years in both leagues. Chesbro won 41 games in 1904 while playing for the New York Yankees. Chesbro had an outgoing personality, however he was often hot and cold with his fans, depending on his daily pitching performance. He had brief stints with Amherst College and the Washington Senators during his final years in baseball.

Chesbro's signature varied considerably during his lifetime. Early samples show a flamboyant style with breaks between the "J" and "a" in Jack, also between the "C" and "h", and "s" and "b", and "r" and "o" in Chesbro. Earlier signature slant was left, with clear character definition. The descender in the "J" was unusually large, about three times the size of the ascender. The capitalized "C" in Chesbro varied in width with the bottom loop typically falling beneath the baseline of his signature.

Chesbro's signature evolved with age to a less compact, more upright format with less flamboyance. The "J" in Jack showed little slant, with a descender of reduced size compared to its predecessor. Another break developed between the "a" and the "c" in Jack, while the breaks in his last name, characteristic in older samples, had disappeared. A unique characteristic that remained relatively consistent was a small loop extending from the stem in the letter "k" in Jack. On occassion this loop would grow in size and begin to resemble an "e" at the end of his name. Character formation, though variable, remained identifiable. The "r" in Chesbro has a tendency to be a bit larger than the other lower case letters of his last name. Additionally, I have seen Chesbro's autograph in a printed format with each letter an individual stroke. Typically this format has appeared on baseballs, rather than flat items.

Chesbro's autograph can be a real challenge to authenticate due to the numerous signature variations exhibited during his lifetime. Collectors are advised to approach the acquisition of his material cautiously.

Availability: Limited
Demand: Above average

Cut signature	$1,150
Single-signature baseball	$5,250
3x5" index card	$1,800
Photograph/baseball card	$2,500
HOF plaque postcard	Impossible
Perez-Steele postcard	Impossible

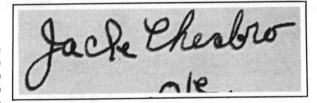

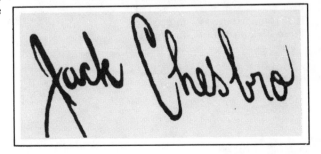

Fred Clarke

Fred Clifford Clarke
(Oct. 3, 1872-Aug. 14, 1960)

Clarke finished his career with over 2,700 hits and a batting average of .315. He helped take Pittsburgh to four pennants and a World Championship in 1909.

Clarke's signature varied little over his lifetime. Notable signature breaks exist between the "F" and the "r" in Fred, also between the "C" and the "l" in Clarke. The "k" in Clarke makes an excellent reference point for authenticators, because of the unique break in the middle of the letter between the stem and the arms. Capitalization may vary in size, specifically the "F" in Fred. His middle initial "C" and the "C" in Clarke will almost be identical in size. In some instances the "CC" will be connected together, though it typically is not, and may even be connected to the "l" in Clarke. The connection between the "r" and the stem stroke of the letter "k" is also a unique formation, however often the "r" will look more like an "o". The ending stroke of Clark's signature was usually simplistic in nature, though he often added an underline beneath this name. The capitalization of the "F" in Fred typically had a long extended bottom loop that doubled back almost to the stem of the letter.

Clarke corresponded regularly during his retirement from his "Little Pirate Ranch" in Winfield, Kansas.

Availability: Average
Demand: Average

Cut signature	$85
Single-signature baseball	$650
3x5" index card	$125
Photograph/baseball card	$260
HOF plaque postcard	$300
Perez-Steele postcard	Impossible

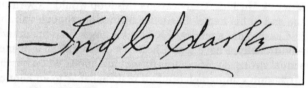

John Clarkson

John Gibson Clarkson
(July 1, 1861-Feb. 4, 1909)

Clarkson was a temperamental pitcher who had an outstanding career that totaled 326 wins. In 1885 he won 53 games, 10 of which were shutouts. During the last seasons of his 12-year career, a severe accident to a personal friend had a profound mental impact on Clarkson.

Typically signing "John Clarkson" or "J.G. Clarkson", his signature varied in character formation and size. Common, however somewhat unpredictable, signature breaks occurred between the "J" and the "o" in John, also between the "l" and the "a", and "k" and the "s" in Clarkson. The flamboyant capitalization of the "J" became a hallmark of his signature. The descender of the "J" could vary in width, while the character's ascender, which resembled a stylized "E", could vary in both size and formation. Occasionally, the "J" will connect to the "o" in John. The "o" will vary significantly in size, but typically is closed at the top of the letter. The ascender of the "h" commonly extends to about two-thirds of the height of his capitalization and should be nearly identical in right slant to both the "J" and the "C".

The flamboyant formation of the "C" begins from the signature's base line, extends upwards to form the top loop of the letter, then intersects the initial stroke twice before finishing with a two-loop configuration that completes the character. The "C" typically connects to the top of the "l" in Clarkson. The single stroke "l" should also be nearly identical in right slant to that of the "C". The "a" can vary in size and often resembles the letter "r". The "r" in Clarkson is typically the smallest letter in his signature and shows little character formation. The "k" in Clarkson is a two-stroked stylized variation that typically extends to the height of the "l". The "son" configuration is the most consistent element to his signature and shows only moderate variation.

Clarkson's unpredictability in temperament could alter his signature dramatically in character formation and slant, making authentication of many examples fairly difficult. Additionally, from 1905 to his death in 1909, he suffered from general paralysis that also contributed significantly to signature variations. Clarkson samples are common in pencil, but characteristic of baseball pioneers, very limited in supply. Collectors should find the acquisition of his signature a considerable challenge.

Availability: Scarce
Demand: Strong

Cut signature	$2,000
Single-signature baseball	Unknown
3x5" index card	$3,250
Photograph/baseball card	$4,000
HOF plaque postcard	Impossible
Perez-Steele postcard	Impossible

Roberto Clemente

Roberto Walker Clemente
(Aug. 18, 1934-Dec. 31, 1972)

Clemente led the National League in batting four times, and picked up his 3,000th hit on Sep. 30, 1972. Easily one of basball's most underrated players, this 1966 Most Valuable Player, was killed in a plane crash during a Nicaraguan earthquake relief effort.

Early signature samples exhibit signature breaks between the "R" and "o" in Roberto, also between the "C" and the "l", "e" and the "m", and the "t" and the "e" in Clemente. The character formation of the capitalized "R" was unique and consisted typically of two distinct strokes. The capitalized "C" in Clemente varied little and consisted of two well defined loops on the top and bottom of the character. Character formations in the lower case letters of Roberto could vary a bit, with the most distinguishing element being a crossed "t" that typically would include a loop in the slash. The lower case letters in Clemente could vary with the "ente" being illegible at times.

Clemente handwriting is easily recognized by his capitalization of the Letters "J", "S" and "T" that carry unique looped descenders, also by the circles that dot his "i"s and by the similarities of characters relating in form, such as a "P" or a "R".

Later Clemente signatures show variations in capitalization, primarily due to what appears to be signature speed. By the late 1960s Clemente's popularity had grown enormously, and with it his fan mail. Common breaks in his later signature were between the "R" and the "o", the "b" and "e", the "a" and "t" and "t" and "o" in Roberto. Additionally, each letter of his last name could be separate, most common breaks being between the "C" and "l", "l" and "e", and "m" and "e" in Clemente. Capitalization of the "R" in Roberto also had a tendency to vary in character formation.

Clemente's popularity continues, as new fans realize the significance of his contribution to baseball. There is no doubt that his legacy will forever make him one of the most popular players in the Hall of Fame.

Availability: Average
Demand: Strong

Cut signature	$75
Single-signature baseball	$800
3x5" index card	$110
Photograph/baseball card	$260
HOF plaque postcard	Impossible
Perez-Steele postcard	Impossible

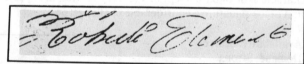

Ty Cobb

Tyrus Raymond Cobb
(Dec. 18, 1886-July 17, 1961)

Cobb was a outspoken man who led the American League in batting 12 times. Most consider him the greatest hitter to ever play the game. Second all-time in career hits with 4,191, "The Georgia Peach" was known for his fierce competitiveness. He was a prolific writer, particularly after he had retired from the game, with many of his letters being priceless in content.

Early examples of Cobb's signature typically show no breaks, unless he signed "Tyrus" instead of "Ty", when a break was found betwen the "y" and the "r". Cobb used two "T" character formations, a two-stroked capitalized version or a single-stroked letter. In earlier examples, a tighter looped formation of the "bb" in Cobb is common. The flamboyant ending following the last "b" in Cobb was to become a hallmark of his signature.

Comparing Cobb's signature in 1925, to that of 1960, shows marginal variation. Later signatures will show a bit more slant, less roundness in the capitalized "C" in Cobb, and less flamboyance in the beginning loop of the capital "C".

Cobb's handwriting is easily recognized by its slant and character formation of the letters "D", "g" and "A". Additionally, Cobb's writing has a tendency to use long run on sentences, separated only by commas. He appeared to have a fascination with using green ink, as many examples of such have surfaced in the market.

Cobb was never afraid to state his opinion on a variety of topics, making most of his letters filled with interesting content. As an investment, a Cobb letter of profound content should forever be an outstanding acquisition. Collectors should be aware, however, of a recent rash of forged Cobb postcards, bearing genuine dates in the early 1900s, which have surfaced. Caution is urged.

Availability: Average
Demand: Strong

Cut signature	$130
Single-signature baseball	$1,700
3x5" index card	$200
Photograph/baseball card	$500
HOF plaque postcard	$800
Perez-Steele postcard	Impossible

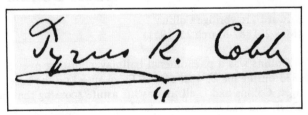

Mickey Cochrane

Gordon Stanley Cochrane
(April 6, 1903-June 28, 1962)

Cochrane was considered one of the best catchers during the Twenties and early Thirties. He led the Athletics to championships in 1929, 1930 and 1931. His career was cut short when he was struck in the temple, fracturing his skull on May 25, 1937.

Early Cochrane examples appear stiffer, with less slant and greater character definition. His signature had no notable signature breaks. On the occasions where he has signed "Gordon Cochrane", instead of "Mickey Cochrane", there were also no breaks present. A characteristic that remained consistent in his signature throughout his lifetime was a looped beginning to the "M" in Mickey.

Later signature samples show a significant departure from his earlier style, notably the increased slant, tightness in character formation, and greater flamboyance.

Mickey's wife Mary had a signature that resembled his own and on occasion she may have signed for him. Her signature of his name will show no slant and may have a small stroke added to the "y" in Mickey.

Availability: Average
Demand: Average

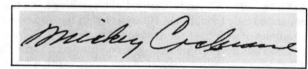

Cut signature	$60
Single-signature baseball	$475
3x5" index card	$100
Photograph/baseball card	$230
HOF plaque postcard	$350
Perez-Steele postcard	Impossible

Eddie Collins

Edward Trowbridge Collins
(May 2, 1887-March 25, 1951)

Collins was a phenomenal ballplayer posting over 3,000 hits and a batting average of .333 during his 25-year career. From speed on the base paths to insights as a general manager, Collins had it all. It was his astute scouting that helped the Red Sox acquire Bobby Doerr and Ted Williams.

Eddie's flamboyant signature varied little throughout his lifetime. Exhibiting no signature breaks, Collins typically signed very large. Early signature samples will have tighter letter formations than later versions. Capitalization may vary a bit in slant or character formation, but not radically. Both "d"s in Eddie will not typically be identical, varying in loop thickness, with the second "d" usually equal to or smaller in height than the first "d". The last "e" in Eddie is always larger in size than its predecessor letter "i", which often resembles an "e".

The most unique trait of a Collins signature is the flamboyant "C" in his last name. Typically, the beginning looped stroke will stretch to the first "l" in Collins, however I have seen samples where it extends as far as the "n". The unusually large "s" at the end of Collins is a good reference point for authenticators. This "s" always extends above or equal to the top loop of the capitalized "C", and may vary a bit in character formation.

The very popular Collins was a prolific signer during his lifetime.

Availability: Average
Demand: Above average

Cut signature	$90
Single-signature baseball	$1,700
3x5" index card	$150
Photograph/baseball card	$350
HOF plaque postcard	$500
Perez-Steele postcard	Impossible

Jimmy Collins

James Joseph Collins
(Jan. 16, 1870-March 6, 1943)

Considered one of the finest third baseman to ever play the game, Collins developed some of the widely accepted defensive strategies used today. Collins' keen play and leadership helped the Red Sox win their first World Series in 1903.

Typically signing "Jimmy Collins", his signature varied in character definition, size and slant. A consistent signature break fell between the "C" and the "o" in Collins. The large "J" in Jimmy usually originated from slightly to the left of the letter's top loop at about lower case height. The "J"'s beginning stroke looped inward before creating the letter's top loop. The descending loop of the "J" extended well below the signature's base line and outward at about twice the width of the top loop. The "J" in Jimmy can often be six to seven times larger than his lower case letters. The "i" can vary in slant and often exceeds the height of the "mmy" in Jimmy. The "mm" combination can vary in width and the "y" is usually a simple downward line. It is common for the "J" to descend twice the length of the "y".

The "C" typically begins from inside the letter, with a loop that may or may not close at the top of the letter. The "C" typically rests on the signature's base line, with both the top and bottom loop of the letter often aligned on the right side. The "o" begins from the top of the letter and may or may not close at the top. Both "l"s can vary in size, however should be similar in slant. The "i" in Collins is often noticeably smaller than the "i" in Jimmy. Collins often dotted each "i" above the letter which followed it. The "n" can vary in size, as can the letter "s". The "s" in Collins commonly ends with a simple inward stroke. Collins had a tendency to vary the height of his lower case letters, some of which may not rest on the signature's base line.

Collins signed many real estate documents following his career in baseball. Autographs signed following 1930 seem to be less abundant than his earlier signatures. Suprisingly few examples of his signature have surfaced in the autograph market.

Availability: Scarce
Demand: Strong

Cut signature	$725
Single-signature baseball	$4,000
3x5" index card	$1,000
Photograph/baseball card	$1,750
HOF plaque postcard	Impossible
Perez-Steele postcard	Impossible

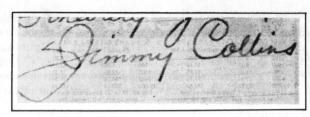

Earle Combs

Earle Bryan Combs
(May 14, 1899-July 21, 1976)

Earle was the pivotal lead-off hitter for "Murderers' Row," and helped lead the Yankees to championships in 1926, 1927, 1928, and 1932. Earle ended his career with a .325 lifetime batting average and 1,866 hits.

"The Kentucky Colonel" had a signature which varied little throughout his life. Early autograph examples show a signature break typically between the "E" and the "a" in Earle with Combs usually being a single stroke. The most significant variation in early examples, as compared to his autograph later in life, was the capitalized "C" in Combs which varied significantly in character formation. The beginning loop of the letter "C", that began usually on the top, was much wider than later versions which began the character stroke from the bottom.

Later versions of Combs' signature show a change to a different style "C" in Combs, and a break in his last name between "C" and the "o". The lower case letter "e" is typically the smallest letter in his signature and the ending stroke of the letter "s" may vary in direction and style.

Combs was always responsive to autograph requests, and a fairly prolific signer. When his health began to fail, some ghost-signed responses became common. Collectors should be cautious of acquiring any autographed later material that appears uncharacteristic.

Availability: Plentiful
Demand: Average

Cut signature	$17
Single-signature baseball	$275
3x5" index card	$35
Photograph/baseball card	$65
HOF plaque postcard	$55
Perez-Steele postcard	Impossible

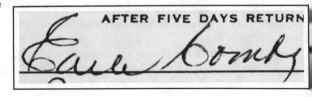

Charles Comiskey

Charles Albert Comiskey
(Aug. 15, 1859-Oct. 26, 1931)

"The Old Roman" spent 50 years in baseball, beginning in 1882 with the St. Louis Browns, where he was a manager, captain and player. His guidance enabled the Browns to win four straight pennants from 1885 to 1888. He is best remembered, however, as the owner and president of the Chicago White Sox from 1900 to 1931.

Comiskey's flamboyant signature style is easily recognizable. His autograph varied primarily in capitalization, particularly the letter "C" in Charles. He typically signed "Chas.a. Comiskey", with his middle initial "a" resembling a lower case letter. The only common break in his signature came between the "s" and "k" in Comiskey.

The capitalized "C" in Comiskey was always the dominant letter in his signature, with the beginning loop of the "C" usually extending to the letter "i". The "o" in Comiskey commonly varied and could resemble an undotted "i"or a "u". The ascender loops in the "h" and the "k" could also vary in thickness. The ending stroke of Comiskey usually had some flamboyance in style exhibited. Authenticators should concentrate on the "C" in Comiskey as a good reference point.

As an executive Comiskey signed numerous correspondences, contracts and receipts. Collectors should find his signature fairly accessible in the market.

Availability: Average
Demand: Average

Cut signature	$350
Single-signature baseball	$2,750
3x5" index card	$365
Photograph/baseball card	$675
HOF plaque postcard	Impossible
Perez-Steele postcard	Impossible

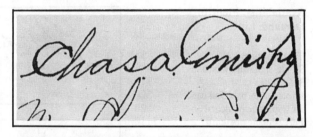

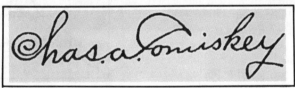

Jocko Conlan

John Bertrand Conlan
(Dec. 6, 1899-April 16, 1989)

"Jocko" umpired in the National League from 1941-1965. His warm disposition and accuracy brought him great respect from his peers. Few realize that "Jocko" also had a respectable career as a ballplayer from 1920-1935, racking up some impressive minor league numbers, and playing 128 games with the Chicago White Sox in 1934 and 1935.

Jocko's signature varied little during his lifetime. His signature exhibited consistent breaks between the "J" and the "o" in Jocko, also between the "C" and the "o" in Conlan. Variation in his signature is most evident in the capitalized "J" in Jocko which can vary in ascender and descender stroke width. The descending loop in the "J" can be rounded, flattened or even sharp edged at the bottom. The top loop in the "J", also commonly varied in size. The capitalized "C" in Conlan could also vary slightly in character formation. The "onlan" of his last name remained fairly consistent, though it seemed to become slightly compressed with age. The ascender of the "k" in Jocko and the "l" in Conlan often varied in width.

During the later years of his life his signature showed many common aging characteristics such as rough strokes, ink acumulation and lack of character definition. Conlan was a prolific signer and a favorite of many collectors.

Availability: Plentiful
Demand: Little

Cut signature	$5
Single-signature baseball	$40
3x5" index card	$10
Photograph/baseball card	$20
HOF plaque postcard	$20
Perez-Steele postcard	$110

JOHN BERTRAND (JOCKO) CONLAN

Thomas Connolly

Thomas Henry Connolly
(Dec. 31, 1870-April 28, 1961)

Connolly was a native of England and began his professional umpiring career in 1895. He had the honor of umpiring in the first American League game held in Chicago (1901) and the first World Series (1903).

Connolly's signature varied in capitalization and character formation during his lifetime. The most consistent break in his signature came between the "C" and he "o" in Connolly. Commonly signing "Tommy Connolly", the most distinctive feature of his signature is the increased size of his last name in comparison to his first name. The capitalized "T" in Tommy was about half the size of the capitalized "C" in Connolly. Additionally, the character spacing in his first name seemed compressed in comparison to his last name. Though the letters in his name were always identifiable, Connolly's signature did exhibit many common aging charcteristics. The letter "o" in his name varied in size and character formation. The "y" in Connolly was always larger in size, with a greater descender length, than its predecessor in Tommy. The width and flamboyance in the descender of the "y" could vary.

Connolly was fairly responsive to signature requests, and samples of his autograph should be accessible for acquisition by collectors through numerous auction houses and autograph dealers.

Availability: Average
Demand: Average

Cut signature	$200
Single-signature baseball	$1,250
3x5" index card	$250
Photograph/baseball card	$700
HOF plaque postcard	$775
Perez-Steele postcard	Impossible

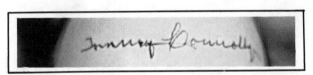

Roger Connor

Roger Connor
(July 1, 1857-Jan. 4, 1931)

Connor was the premier power hitter of the 19th Century, finishing his 18-year career with a batting average of .318, while compiling over 10 seasons of hitting above the .300 mark.

Connor's signature exhibits breaks between the "R" and the "o", "o" and the "g" and "g" and the "e" in Roger, also between the "C" and the "o" and the "n" and the "o" in Connor. A good letter for authentication purposes is the capitalized "R" in Roger, which is somewhat unique in style with its sharp upward stroke at the beginning of the letter. Connor's signature slant is consistent, with any variation in capitalization being primarily in width. Both the lower case "r"s in his name will be nearly identical in character formation.

Connor's capitalization size is typically three times that of his lower case letters and seldom dips below the base line of his signature.

Connor was an obliging signer in his day and samples of his signature do surface on occasion in the market.

Availability: Limited
Demand: Above average

Cut signature	$1,250
Single-signature baseball	$4,750
3x5" index card	$2,500
Photograph/baseball card	$3,300
HOF plaque postcard	Impossible
Perez-Steele postcard	Impossible

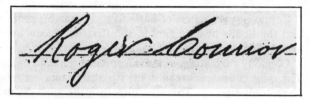

Stan Coveleski

Stanley Anthony Coveleski
(July 13, 1889-March 20, 1984)

Born Stanislaus Kowalewski, Coveleski compiled a record of over 210 wins with four different American League clubs — Philadelphia, Cleveland, Washington and New York. Winning 20 or more games in five seasons, Stanley's lifetime ERA was 2.88.

Coveleski's signature varied moderately throughout his lifetime. Early examples will show greater definition in characters and their formation. Consistent signature breaks common in his autograph exist between the "S" and the "t" in Stanley and the "C" and the "o" in Coveleski. Capitalization could vary in size and in slant, with the "C" in Coveleski the most dominant and recognizable feature of his signature. The capitalized "C" in early examples was often four times larger than lower case letters such as the "o" and the "v". the crossing of the "t" in Stanley was typically a single long stroke that would usually extend to the "n" or "l" in Stanley.

Covelseki's signature gradually deteriorated, due to his health, and showed many common aging characteristics. By the late 1970s his signature had dropped the "e" in Stanley and the "i" in Coveleski. The "C" in Coveleski was gradually reduced in size, until it was equal to or smaller than the "S" in Stanley. The "C" that was elongated in earlier autographs had also become circular in format in later renditions. The "S" in Stanley could vary in slant, size and character formation. A consistent element of Coveleski's signature was that he almost never closed the "a" in Stanley. It may appear closed on older examples due to ink absorption, however there was no conscious attempt to do so. The beginning upward stroke of the "C" in Coveleski was always intersected by the loop of the letter. The "ovelsk" varied in later examples, making character definition between the letters "v" and "e" very difficult.

When Coveleski used an ink marker to sign his Hall of Fame plaque postcards he would often apply clear tape over them to avoid smudging.

Stanely Coveleski was a quiet and polite man who answered all autograph requests. He was exemplary of what every baseball fan wants his hero to be.

Availability: Plentiful
Demand: Little

Cut signature	$10
Single-signature baseball	$130
3x5" index card	$15
Photograph/baseball card	$25
HOF plaque postcard	$25
Perez-Steele postcard	$450

Sam Crawford

Samuel Earl Crawford
(April 18, 1880-June 15, 1968)

"Wahoo Sam" posted a lifetime .309 batting average with 2,964 hits. He was a superb extra-base hitter, setting league and season records for triples and doubles.

Crawford's signature remained fairly consistent throughout his lifetime, typically signing "Samuel E. Crawford" or "Wahoo Sam Crawford". Signature breaks were inconsistent, with early samples showing a break between the stem of the "f" and the beginning stroke leading to the "o" in Crawford. However the "f" did vary in character formation on occasion, negating this characteristic. A break between the "S" and "a" in Sam is common and the ending stroke of the "m" may end, or continue if his middle initial is used. The "am" in Sam or "amuel" in Samuel remained fairly consistent. His middle initial of "E" could have a bottom loop added prior to the upward stroke to the letter "C". The capitalized "C" varied significantly in character formation and is not a good authentication reference. The "f" in Crawford also varied significantly in character formation between a single-stroke version and a two-stroke rendition. The "d" in Crawford may or may not have a flamboyant ending stroke.

Crawford was a regular signer and samples of his signature should be fairly easy to acquire.

Availability: Average
Demand: Average

Cut signature	$35
Single-signature baseball	$1,175
3x5" index card	$65
Photograph/baseball card	$200
HOF plaque postcard	$220
Perez-Steele postcard	Impossible

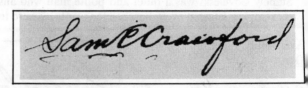

Joe Cronin

Joseph Edward Cronin
(Oct. 12, 1906-Sept. 7, 1984)

Cronin, seven-time All-Star shortstop, was voted the Most Valuable Player in the American League during the 1930 season. He exhibited outstanding fielding prowess, only overshadowed by his hitting ability, posting a lifetime batting average of over .300. Not content to be only a star player and field manager, Joe pursued baseball front office management, gaining recognition as a team general manager and president, and as chairman of the American League.

Typically signing "Joe Cronin" or "Joseph E. Cronin", he signed many correspondences from his many positions in baseball management. Early Cronin examples typically show no signature breaks, or on occasion a break between the "J" and the "o" in Joe. His signature was commonly a single stroke. Capitalization was the most prominent and recognizable feature of his signature, with the unusually large "J" in Joe often seven or eight times the size of the succeeding letter "o". The "C" in Cronin had a unique style that added a loop to the ending stroke to begin the upward motion to the letter "r". The "J" in Joe evolved into a two-stroke formation eliminating the bottom loop of the "J" in later examples. The top of the "C" in earlier versions began with a double backed stroke, versus beginning with a loop common in later versions. The "ronin" varied in character formation and slant with age. Often when signed with ink marker, this letter configuration would lack recognizable character definition.

Authentication of his signature should concentrate on slant and capitalization characteristics to determine an autograph's legitimacy. Cronin was irregular in responding to autograph requests by mail, but in person he was generally obliging. He commonly responded to mail with a stamped facsimile of his signature that is easily recognizable as such.

Candy Cummings

William Arthur Cummings
(Oct. 18, 1848-May 16, 1924)

Cummings is remembered most for his invention of the curve ball in 1867. He was a pitching standout during baseball's early days, ending his career as a pitcher in the National League in 1877. He became president of the first minor league, the International Association that same year.

Cummings' autographs, like so many early baseball pioneers, can be difficult to find. The few I have seen have been signed "W.A. Cummings" and "Arthur Cummings". I have never seen a "Candy Cummings" or "William Cummings" version of his signature. The samples I have seen have been in pencil and signed later in his life. The breaks I have witnessed have been between the "A" and the "r" in Arthur, also between the "C" and the "u" in Cummings. His middle initial of "A" had a unique formation that crossed the letter with a looped stroke. The middle point of the "W" also commonly extended above the beginning and last stroke of the letter. The "mmin" typically resembled a series of lower case "v"'s in format. The "s" in Cummings looked more like an "e" with a downward stroked ending.

Some receipts from the paint and wallpaper store that he owned for about 18 years have surfaced, however, in general he remains a difficult signature to acquire.

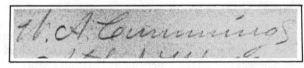

Ki Ki Cuyler

Hazen Shirley Cuyler
(Aug. 30, 1899-Feb. 11, 1950)

Cuyler was an outstanding fielder and a speed demon on the base paths, often leading the National League in stolen bases. He ended his career with 2,299 hits at a lifetime batting average of .321.

Cuyler's very legible signature varied little throughout his lifetime. Commonly signing "Hazen KiKi Cuyler" or just "KiKi Cuyler", his signature varied only slightly in character formation, character width and flamboyance. The two-stroked "H" in Hazen was always the most distinct of the capitalized letters, typically five or six times the height of the succeeding letter "a". The "K"s in "KiKi" are good comparison letters for authenticators; they will be nearly identical except for some slight differences in rounding at the center of the letter, or the possible lacking of a small serif-like stroke on the top of the letter formation. The descender of the letter "y" in Cuyler is always the lowest point of his signature.

Cuyler was generally obliging to signature requests and his autograph should be fairly easy to acquire through many dealers.

Availability: Average
Demand: Average

Cut signature	$90
Single-signature baseball	$900
3x5" index card	$170
Photograph/baseball card	$400
HOF plaque postcard	Impossible
Perez-Steele postcard	Impossible

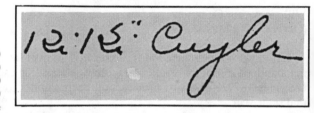

Ray Dandridge

Raymond Dandridge
(Aug. 31, 1913-   )

Dandridge began his professional career with the Detroit Stars of the Negro Leagues in 1933. He was a sleek third baseman with great defensive skills. Ray was 37 years of age when he was named the American Association's Most Valuable Player in 1950, while playing for the Minneapolis Millers.

Dandridge's signature has varied moderately during his lifetime, primarily in capitalization and character formation. Common breaks in his signature fall between the "D" and the "a" and the "g" and the "e" in Dandridge. Earlier signature examples are more compressed in format exhibiting less flamboyance in stroke. The capitalized "R" in Ray has a long extended stroke beginning the letter, that is intersected by the stroke that begins the top loop, making the "R" probably the best comparison point in his signature for authentication purposes. The ending letters of Dandridge have a tendency to increase a bit in size with each succeeding letter. The lower case "a" or "g" in Dandridge may or may not close on the top loop and the ascenders of the letter "d" tend to vary in thickness. The capitalized "D" in Dandridge has a tendency to be inconsistent in character formation.

Dandridge has been a good signer, and since his induction his popularity has grown significantly among baseball enthusiasts.

Availability: Plentiful
Demand: Little

Cut signature	$3
Single-signature baseball	$25
3x5" index card	$5
Photograph/baseball card	$12
HOF plaque postcard	$9
Perez-Steele postcard	$25

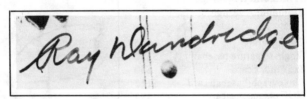

Dizzy Dean

Jay Hanna Dean
(Jan. 16, 1911-July 17, 1974)

"Dizzy" was a good old-fashioned story teller, fans loved him for his down to earth broadcasts of the St. Louis Browns, but most of all Dean was a great pitcher. One of four modern pitchers to win 30 or more games in a season, Dizzy compiled a lifetime record of 150 wins and 83 losses, at an E.R.A. of just over 3.00. His outstanding 1934 season earned him the Most Valuable Player award for the National League.

Dean's earlier signatures showed less flamboyance and character definition.

The capitalization in his signature grew with Dean's popularity, to about four or five times the size of the lower case letters. The flamboyant finishing stroke of the "D" in Dizzy commonly intersected his entire autograph and ended well after the "n" in Dean. This characteristic was not common in earlier Dean samples that exhibited a short finishing stroke at the end of the "D". The most consistent signature break was between the "D" and the "i" in Dizzy, later examples will show the development of a break between the "D" and the "e" in Dean. The "izzy" in Dizzy was unpredictable in character formation, with descenders varying in length and width. The ending stroke of the "y" in Dizzy consistently connected to the "D" in Dean. The finishing stroke of the "D" in Dean connected to the "e" in early autograph examples, however became disconnected in his later signatures. The formation of the "a" in Dean consisted of two loops that may or may not join together at the top to form the letter. The finishing stroke of the letter "n" in Dean was generally inconsistent.

Dean employed the services of a ghost-signer for many years. These examples were outstanding in their reproduction quality and commonly on black and white photographs. Collectors should acquire only samples obtained in person, such as cuts from autograph albums, and team baseballs. The reproductions will be easy for an expert to spot, but will prove very difficult for a novice to identify. The ghost signatures primarily will differ in character size and formation.

Availability: Average
Demand: Average

Cut signature	$25
Single-signature baseball	$550
3x5" index card	$50
Photograph/baseball card	$115
HOF plaque postcard	$95
Perez-Steele postcard	Impossible

Ed Delahanty

Edward James Delahanty
(Oct. 30, 1867-July 2, 1903)

Delahanty compiled 2,591 hits in his career, with a lifetime average of .345. Considered one of the game's finest hitters in his day, Delahanty was an elite member of the ".400 Club," batting .408 in 1899. "Big Ed" is the only man in major league history to lead both the American and National Leagues in hitting. Delahanty, apparently discontent over various attempts by teams to have him jump leagues, disappeared early in the month of July, never to be seen alive again. His body was pulled from the Niagara River on July 9, 1903, having fallen from the International Bridge. Mystery still surrounds his death to this day. Some say suicide, others believe he was mugged and thrown from the bridge.

Delahanty's sudden death contributes to the scarcity of his signature. The relatively few I have seen make it extremely difficult to draw conclusions about his early writing habits, so I will concentrate on traits of his post-1900 signature. The pencil examples I have seen were signed "Ed J. Delahanty" or "Edward J. Delahanty". A consistent break occurred between the "D" and the "e" in Delahanty. Capitalization varied in character formation and size. The "E" in Ed began at the top of the letter and exhibited Delahanty's characteristic slant right. The "d" on most of the samples I have seen has been left open, with the ascenders showing some variation in width. His middle initial of "J" often had a descender consisting only of a simple downward stroke and the ascender was typically a thin loop. The "D" in Delahanty had a character all its own, making it a fairly good reference point for authenticators. The "D" formation resembled two different size backward letter "C"s connected on the bottom and typically didn't close atop the letter. The "l" and the "h" could vary in ascender width and height, but typically were consistent in slant. The stem of the "t" was unusually large and typically the same height as the "l". The "y" had a simple looped close, with a descender length equal to that of the "J".

Delahanty's signature is considered to be one of the toughest to obtain of all the Cooperstown inductees. Due to the limited availability of his signature, authentication can be a considerable task for a collector.

Availability: Scarce
Demand: Strong

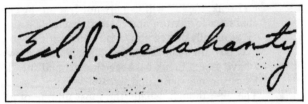

Cut signature	$1,650
Single-signature baseball	Unknown
3x5" index card	$2,150
Photograph/baseball card	$4,250
HOF plaque postcard	Impossible
Perez-Steele postcard	Impossible

Bill Dickey

William Malcolm Dickey
(June 6, 1907-   )

Dickey was perhaps the greatest catcher of this century. Incredibly durable, he caught over 100 games for 13 successive seasons. Dickey finished his career with a batting average of .313 and a defensive reputation equally as impressive. A member of eight All-Star teams, he helped guide the New York Yankees to seven World Series titles.

Though he may have shown consistency in his athletic prowess, it didn't carry over to his penmanship. He is one of the few inductees who has shown no consistency in a single letter of his name throughout his entire lifetime. To make it easier to follow the variations I will deal with each letter separately:

Letter   Variation

B   Varied in character formation slant and size. May exhibit a break between the "B" and the "i". Could begin character stroke at the top of the letter or at the bottom and could begin with a downward stroked line or loop or the reverse. The bottom loop of the "B" may or may not cross the stem of the letter. The middle of the letter, where the two loops meet, may or may not be looped. The top loop of the letter could be flat, sharp, or rounded. The beginning stroke of the letter will vary radically. The top loop in his angled style, commonly extends beyond the "il" in Bill.

i   May be a line or looped formation, usually dotted above the character, however the dot could also fall above the first "l" in Bill. May or may not break with the letter "B".

ll   Generally minimal variation, only in ascender width, slight slant alteration and maybe size. Ending stroke following the last stroke will not be flamboyant.

D   Will exhibit radical changes in character formation. Can be a single-stroke version or a two-stroke configuration. The first stroke of the "D" commonly starts at the top of the letter. The bottom of the first stroke may or may not loop, prior to beginning the top of the letter. On a single-stroked version the top of the letter will usually loop, while on a two-stroke version it will be crossed like a "t". The crossed "D" stroke will extend to the "c" in Dickey. Instead of a top loop, the stroke may simply cross the stem at an angle, stop, then stretch to the "i" in Dickey with a flat extension. The "D" is usually smaller in height than the capital "B" in Bill.

i   There may or may not be a break between the "D" and the "i" in Dickey. If there is no break, the "i" will usually not rest on the signature base line. The "i" may lack character formation and instead resemble a simple upward stroke to the "c". The "i" is usually dotted above the letter, or if a two-stroke version of the "D" is used, it may be dotted above the "c". The "i" may show a break with the "c".

c   I have seen a break between the "c" and the "k", but it is rare. The "c" can often have minimal definition.

k   The "k", though usually the most unique of all the letter formations, can change radically in character formation. It can range from a simplified traditional "k", to Dickey's prominent two-looped stroke. The double looped style can be found on signatures dating back into the 1930s, and has shown limited alteration. The large loop usually extends beyond the end of his signature and may intersect with the first smaller loop.

e   May or may not exhibit the loop in the "e".

y   Can vary radically in descender formation, from a single downward stroke to a large finishing loop.

Dickey has been an obliging signer throughout his career, however mail requests can have unpredictable results. He has appeared at private signings allowing collectors more access to his autograph. In the future, his signature will prove to be very difficult to authenticate due to all his variations.

Availability: Plentiful
Demand: Little

Cut signature	$4
Single-signature baseball	$35
3x5" index card	$11
Photograph/baseball card	$25
HOF plaque postcard	$18
Perez-Steele postcard	$85

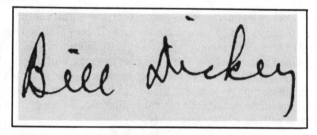

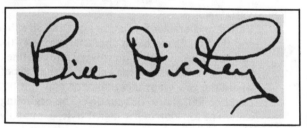

Martin Dihigo

Martin Dihigo
(May 25, 1905-May 22, 1971)

"El Maestro" was a versatile star of the Negro Leagues, considered by some to be the game's greatest natural player. Dihigo compiled over 260 wins as a pitcher, and batted consistently over .300. He spent his winters playing ball in Cuba and later began an extended career in Mexico.

Typically signing "Martin Dihigo", his signature varied in character formation, size and slant. Consistent signature breaks fell between the "M" and the "a" in Martin, also between the "D" and the "i" in Dihigo. The "M" often began with a flamboyant large opening loop that could span the entire height of the character. The loops of the "M" could vary in size, however were very similar in slant. The flamboyant opening loop often exceeded both of the character's loops in height. The "M" can occasionally connect to the "a". The "r" could vary in character formation and the large ascender of his "t" was often the highest point in his signature. The slant of the "t" is typically crossed by a separate stroke. The "i" could vary in slant and the "n" typically exhibited no flamboyant ending stroke.

The flamboyant "D" in Dihigo was commonly the largest letter in his name. The "D" began from the top of the letter with a sharp right-slanted downward stroke that looped to change direction before creating the major formation of the character. The beginning stroke of the "D" is often intersected at least once by the flamboyant major loop of the character. The "i" usually began with an upward extended line which originated from the signature's base line. Both the "i"'s in Dihigo could vary in size, however their slant was typically similar. The "h" could vary in size, with its ascender often extending to the beginning stroke of the "D", however the letter's slant should be similar to both the "i"'s and the "D". The "g" may or may not close at the top and its descender can vary in size. The "o", which occasionally separated from the "g", can vary in size and may or may not be left open at the top of the letter.

Dihigo spent his final days in Cuba, where mystery still surrounds his death. He was an obliging but not prolific signer and collectors could find his signature a greater challenge than one might expect. Dihigo samples have occasionally surfaced in the autograph market.

Availability: Limited
Demand: Strong

Cut signature	$725
Single-signature baseball	$3,500
3x5" index card	$1,150
Photograph/baseball card	$2,000
HOF plaque postcard	Impossible
Perez-Steele postcard	Impossible

Joe DiMaggio

Joseph Paul DiMaggio
(Nov. 25, 1914-   )

"The Yankee Clipper" is by far one of the most popular players ever to play the game of baseball. The man who hit safely in 56 consecutive games in 1941 holds numerous batting records. An 11-time All-Star and three-time Most Valuable Player, he participated in 10 World Series contests. DiMaggio finished his career with 2,214 hits, 361 of them home runs for an average of .325.

Like Dickey, DiMaggio's signature has varied dramatically throughout his lifetime. Dickey, however, was always inconsistent and could revert to different signature styles during the same signature session. DiMaggio's signature styles were more evolutionary in nature. Commonly signing "Joe DiMaggio", earlier signatures are common as "J. DiMaggio". His earlier signature was a departure from his modern day autograph, showing variation in capitalization, flamboyance, slant and character formation. Common breaks were between the "J" and the "o" in Joe, also between the "D" and the "i", and the "i" and the "M" in DiMaggio. The large capitalized "J" in Joe was usually twice the size of the capitalized "D" and "M" in DiMaggio. The stroke under the ascender loop of the "J" crossed the stem of the letter and commonly extended as far as the "i" in DiMaggio. The "oe" in Joe has remained the most consistent portion of his signature during his lifetime. The traditional, for that time period, letter "D" varied most in the formation of the top loop. Often it would cross the stem of the letter "D", or it could simply just curl and never make it far enough to finish the loop. The early examples of the "i" in DiMaggio looked more like a slanted number 5 with a serif on the loop. The ending stroke of the "i" may or may not connect to the "M". The "M" in DiMaggio varied in size and flamboyance, particularily the opening loop to the letter. The "aggio" varied in character formation and letter spacing. The descender of the "g" routinely varied in length and formation. The "o" may or may not have a loop formation on top and the ending stroke could be flamboyant or simply close the letter "o". I have seen, though they are extremly rare, a sample with a break between the second "g" and the "i" in DiMaggio.

Later examples, near the end of his career and following his playing days, typically show the following variations:

Letter	Variation
J	Both loops of the "J" can vary in size, with both the opening and ending stroke of the letter possibly crossing the stem. Commonly it is the top loop that usually crosses the stem of the letter and extends to the "o" or "e". The loops can vary in roundness.
oe	Little variation compared to the other letters in his signature. Both letters are always legible with the "o" occasionally a bit larger.
D	The "D" normally begins with a downward stroke that loops to change direction at the signature's base line, then curves and extends upward to form the loop on the top of the letter. I have seen samples where the "e" in Joe has connected to the "D", primarily to facilitate writing speed. The ending stroke of the "D" usually ends at the same height of the beginning stroke of the "M".
i	Usually a separate letter, however it can connect to the "M" or even be left out all together. The character formation varies often and the dot on the top of the "i" can fall under or over the beginning stroke of the "M".
M	The "M" varies often, but typically begins with a stroke level to the last stroke of the "D". The first loop in the character is usually larger than the second, with the

second having a tendency to curve inward toward the middle stem of the letter. The beginning loop of the "M" can even be connected to the "i" and form the letter as part of the same stroke.

a   Varies in character formation, often looking more like an "o" than an "a".

gg   The descenders of the "g" can vary in slant and width. Early DiMaggio samples have large flamboyant descenders in the "g", the later examples are much smaller. The top loop of the second "g" is usually open, due to the descender not extending vertically enough to meet it.

io   The "i" shows little variation, while the "o" typically closes neatly at the top of the letter formation. A mysterious slash, probably left over from his earlier flamboyant ending strokes, typically fails beneath the "io".

DiMaggio has used a ghost signer, supposedly his sister, to autograph his many requests in the late 1970s. These signatures are fairly easy to identify due to their many inconsistencies. Because of his many signature styles, authentic DiMaggio samples are often mistaken for forgeries. His signature has been inflated in price over the past few years, considering the sheer number of autographs he has signed during his lifetime. Collectors may have to pay a lot to add a DiMaggio to their collection, however in time the acquisition should prove to be a worthwhile investment.

Availability: Plentiful
Demand: Strong

Cut signature	$12
Single-signature baseball	$120
3x5" index card	$20
Photograph/baseball card	$35
HOF plaque postcard	$40
Perez-Steele postcard	$300

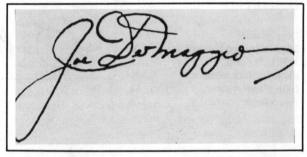

Bobby Doerr

Robert Pershing Doerr
(April 7, 1918-   )

Renowned for his fielding, this Red Sox second baseman held numerous records for defensive prowess. He finished his career with a lifetime batting average of .288 that included six seasons of 100 or more RBIs. Additionally, Doerr slammed 223 home runs and batted an impressive .409 in the 1946 World Series.

Doerr's signature has varied only slightly throughout the years in capitalization and character formation. The "B" in Bob can vary in width, as can the "D" in Doerr. The beginning stroke of the "B" may or may not intersect the first loop of the character. The ascender of the "b" in Bob can vary in height and width. Common signature breaks are between the "B" and the "o" in Bob, also between the "D" and the "o" in Doerr. The stem of the "D" in Doerr can be a single stroke or a loop. The "oerr" is consistent, with the ending stroke looping above the last letters of his name.

Doerr has responded quickly to autograph requests, and remains one of the few players who doesn't typically charge for a response.

Availability: Plentiful
Demand: Little

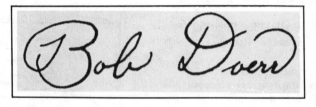

Cut signature	$5
Single-signature baseball	$20
3x5" index card	$5
Photograph/baseball card	$11
HOF plaque postcard	$9
Perez-Steele postcard	$25

Don Drysdale

Donald Scott Drysdale
(July 23, 1936-   )

Well over six feet tall, the "Big D" was an intimidating pitcher and wasn't hesitant to show a batter who was in charge. He ended his career with a record of 209 wins and 166 loses at an ERA of 2.95. Hurling 49 shutouts and 2,486 strikouts, Don led the National League in strikeouts three times.

Earlier signature samples will commonly show breaks between the "D" and the "o" in Donald, also between the "D" and the "r", "y" and the "s" and the "s" and the "d" in Drysdale. The "D" in Drysdale will be typically closed by the finishing downward stroke. The capitalized "D" in Donald has always been the largest character in his signature.

Later examples, following his retirement from baseball can exhibit a break between the "s"and the "d" in Drysdale, or no breaks at all. Character slant is consistent and the capitalized "D"s in his name have changed in character formation to resemble a "W" with a loop on the end. The "D"s don't close, and typically neither does the "a" in Drysdale, that consists of two small loops resembling an "ee" formation. The descender of the "y" has become shorter and will connect to the "s" in Drysdale. The "d" in Drysdale doesn't close and the "r" has changed from earlier examples to a stroke that resembles an "e".

Drysdale was a good signer throughout his career, however, like so many other inductees may now request a signing fee.

Availability: Plentiful
Demand: Little

Cut signature	$3
Single-signature baseball	$20
3x5" index card	$5
Photograph/baseball card	$11
HOF plaque postcard	$9
Perez-Steele postcard	$35

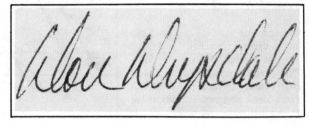

Hugh Duffy

Hugh Duffy
(Nov. 26, 1866-Oct. 19, 1954)

Duffy finished his career with over 2,300 hits and a lifetime batting average of .328. Most remembered for his record .438 season in 1894 while playing with the Boston Nationals, Duffy was also an excellent defensive fielder.

Duffy's signature varied primarily in slant and character formation. Early samples, around the turn of the century, will show a slight left slant easily noticed in capitalization. The only common signature break occurred between the "D" and the "u" in Duffy. On occasion a break may occur between the "u" and the "g" in Hugh. The ascender of the "h" in Hugh was the highest point in his signature, while the descender of the "g" the lowest. The capitalized "D" in Duffy resembled a style of "D" used by Bill Dickey. The "f's in Duffy could vary in size, however were usually identical in character formation. Duffy's handwriting is easily recognizable by his unique character formations of letters such as "F", "B", and "P".

Later Duffy signatures (circa late 1930s), showed a signature slant change to a right direction. The only consistent break remained between the "D" and the "u" in Duffy. The "H" in Hugh remained a two-stroke version, however the "g" changed to a rougher version showing less character formation. The "D" varied radically and was unpredictable in character formation. The "uff" was altered in slant, but character formation was relatively the same. The descender of the "y" became much larger and more flamboyant.

Duffy's variance in slant in later examples can be deceiving to authenticators. As a scout for the Boston Red Sox organization in his later years, he corresponded often with fans and other baseball management. Letters on Boston American League Baseball Company letterhead surface occasionally in the autograph market.

Availability: Average
Demand: Average

Cut signature	$250
Single-signature baseball	$1,150
3x5" index card	$275
Photograph/baseball card	$400
HOF plaque postcard	$1,150
Perez-Steele postcard	Impossible

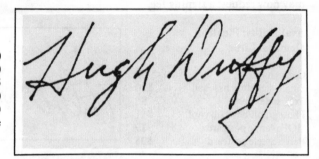

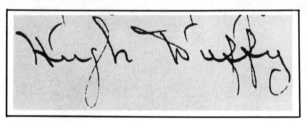

Billy Evans

William George Evans
(Feb. 10, 1884-Jan. 23, 1956)

Evans was the youngest umpire to ever serve major league baseball. He was just 22 when he began employment with the American League. He worked in six World Series contests, and was instrumental in making many decisions for the future of umpiring.

Commonly signing "Billy Evans" or "William G. Evans", his signature showed moderate variation throughout his lifetime. Typically his signature exhibited no breaks. The capitalized "B" in Billy was about three times larger in size that he lower case letters in his name. The "B" in Billy could vary a bit in width, but generally remained thin in formation. Quotation marks around Billy were common, with the second set of marks falling usually above the second "l", rather than after the "y". The "E" in Evans was unique in character formation and is a good comparison letter for authenticators. The slant of the "B" and the "E" were usually identical. The "v" in Evans could resemble an "o" in character formation, with the ending stroke always connecting to the top of the "a" in Evans. The "ns" was inconsistent at times, with the "s" being unrecognizable in certain instances. The descender of the "y" in Billy was always the lowest point in his signature and could vary in flamboyance.

Though he began as a sportswriter, and grew into an umpire, he ended his years associated with the game, in baseball management — general manager of the Detroit Tigers. As a baseball executive he signed numerous correspondences, some of which have surfaced in the autograph market.

Availability: Limited
Demand: Above average

Cut signature	$125
Single-signature baseball	$1,400
3x5" index card	$180
Photograph/baseball card	$500
HOF plaque postcard	Impossible
Perez-Steele postcard	Impossible

Johnny Evers

John Joseph Evers
(July 21, 1883-March 28, 1947)

"The Trojan" was part of the "Tinker to Evers to Chance" infield that brought the Chicago Cubs pennants in 1906, 1908, and 1910. Evers was named the National League's Most Valuable Player in 1914 and was a true competitor in every phase of the game. In 1942 Evers was stricken by a paralytic stroke that left him relatively confined, however John did make it to Cooperstown in 1946 when the famous trio was inducted into the Hall of Fame.

Variations in capitalization were characteristic of Evers' signature. The "J" in John, or his middle initial, commonly exhibited changes in size and the construction of the letter. Samples of his earlier signatures had a tendency to be more flamboyant, with greater attention to character detail. An Evers signature usually displayed no breaks, however on occasion one could be exhibited between the "J" and the "o" in John. The "ohn" in John could vary slightly in slant and the ascender of the "h" could vary in width. The "E" in Evers varied in character formation and doesn't make a good authentication reference. Variations in the "vers" were less radical, with the finishing stroke of the "s" unpredictable in style. Some Evers autograph samples can be a single-stroke format, exhibiting characteristics of an accelerated signature speed. This characteristic is more common today with players than in the early days of baseball, because of the sheer volume of autograph requests.

Evers was an obliging signer until his health deteriorated later in his life.

Availability: Limited
Demand: Average

Cut signature	$225
Single-signature baseball	$2,675
3x5" index card	$300
Photograph/baseball card	$900
HOF plaque postcard	$1,250
Perez-Steele postcard	Impossible

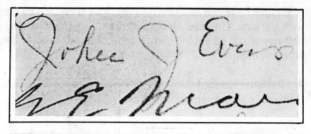

Buck Ewing

William Buckingham Ewing
(Oct. 17, 1859-Oct. 20, 1906)

Ewing was considered one of the greatest catchers to play baseball during the turn of the century. With a lifetime batting average over .300, he helped lead the New York Giants to championships in 1888 and 1889.

Commonly signing "Wm. Ewing", his signature varied in character formation, size and slant. A consistent signature break fell between the "E" and the "w" in Ewing. The "W" began from capitalization height at a point that was often directly above its second loop (common in early examples), and extended at a significant right slant downward to the base line to form the first loop. The last loop in the "W" can resemble an "O" formation. The ending stroke of the "W" commonly looped, particularly in early examples, and intersected the middle of the letter. The "W" was connected to the superscript "m" via its looped ending stroke. Ewing's lower case letters gradually increased in size with age, however early examples are typically small and elongated. The "m" often resembled a "uu" formation and is typically underlined.

The flamboyant large letter "E" was the hallmark of his signature. The significant degree of right slant, found in early examples, allowed the beginning loop, or the opening stroke of the letter, to extend above the "w" in Ewing. The middle and bottom loops of the "E" often were aligned on their right side. the flamboyant bottom loop of the "E" often closed with a double stroke. The "E" typically rested on, or slightly below, the signature's base line. The elongated "w" often looped at the end of the letter before creating the "e", which could resemble a letter "r". The "n" can resemble a "u" and the "g" may or may not close at the top of the letter. The character spacing between the "n" and the "g" varies, particularly in early examples (those signed during his playing days). The descender of the "g" is usually well extended below his signature and is often a simple line exhibiting little flamboyance (early examples) or a shortened looped version (later examples). The slant of the first stroke of the "W" and the descender of the "g" is often similar.

Ewing samples are common in pencil and, characteristic of baseball pioneers, limited in supply. Collectors should find the acquisition of his signature a challenge, however they do occasionally surface in the autograph market.

Availability: Scarce
Demand: Strong

Cut signature	$1,675
Single-signature baseball	Unknown
3x5" index card	$3,250
Photograph/baseball card	$4,750
HOF plaque postcard	Impossible
Perez-Steele postcard	Impossible

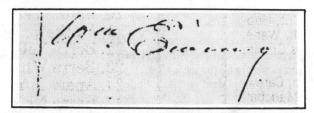

Red Faber

Urban Clarence Faber
(Sept. 6, 1888-Sept. 25, 1976)

Faber won 254 games during his career with a 3.15 ERA. A classic spitball pitcher, he was one of the few select players who was not denied the opportunity to continue to throw his favorite pitch when it was outlawed in 1920.

Commonly signing "U.C. Faber" or "U.C. "Red" Faber", his signature varied primarily in the capitalization of the "F" in Faber and slant. The "F" in Faber could be a two- or three-stroke version in various configurations. The top of "F" could be a single stroke or part of a loop from the stem of the letter. Of all the capitalized letters the "C" was most consistent, typically constructed with three identifiable loops. The "F" in Faber was usually the largest letter in both height and width. On the occasions where Faber has signed "Red", the capitalized "R" typically shows no loop formation on the top of the letter. The "aber" has been relatively consistent, changing from a right slant in older examples, to a more vertical format in later signatures. Earlier examples will show a little flamboyance in the ending stroke, where later autographs will not.

Faber, at one point in time, had resorted to a ghost signer due to health reasons. These signatures tend to show little of the detailed characteristics of his autograph, particularly in capitalization, and should be easily recognizable after careful examination.

Availability: Above average
Demand: Average

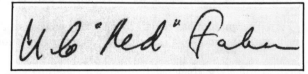

Cut signature	$10
Single-signature baseball	$325
3x5" index card	$25
Photograph/baseball card	$55
HOF plaque postcard	$60
Perez-Steele postcard	Impossible

Bob Feller

Robert William Andrew Feller
(Nov. 3, 1918-   )

Considered by some to be the fastest pitcher of all time, Feller ended his career with a lifetime record of 266 wins and only 162 losses, at an ERA of 3.25. A natural, Feller won 107 games before he turned 24.

Commonly signing "Bob Feller", his signature has shown only one consistent break, between the "F" and the "e" in Feller. Capitalization has varied in character formation and slant. The beginning downward stroke of the "B" in Bob can be a line or a loop. The "b" in Bob can vary in style, often resembling a letter "j" or "t". The "F" in Feller commonly has two forms, one looks like a number 7 with a slash through the middle, the other resembles a number 2 with a slash through the stem. The "eller" can vary in slant and letter spacing, but remain fairly consistent in character formation.

Feller has been a prolific signer throughout his life and his enthusiastic response to the fans he greets has made him a favorite at baseball card shows.

Availability: Plentiful
Demand: Little

Cut signature	$3
Single-signature baseball	$15
3x5" index card	$4
Photograph/baseball card	$12
HOF plaque postcard	$9
Perez-Steele postcard	$30

Rick Ferrell

Richard Benjamin Ferrell
(Oct. 12, 1905-   )

Considered one of the games most durable players, Ferrell caught over 1,800 games in the American League. He ended his career with a batting average of .281 that included 1,692 hits.

Ferrell's signature has remained relatively consistent throughout hs lifetime with only a slight variation in capitalization and character formation. Common signature breaks fall between the "R" and the "i" in Rick and between the "F" and the "e" in Ferrell. Earlier samples will show greater definition and smoother strokes. The "R" in Rick can vary in width and character formation. Generally the "R" begins with a curve, then a downward doubled back stroke that forms the main loop which then intersects the stem with a smaller loop before forming the leg of the letter. All letters in his name appear legible, with the "k" in

Rick having the most unique lower case letter formation. The "F" in Ferrell resembles a "C" with a number 7, with a slash through the middle, attached to the top loop. The "errell" is fairly consistent, with the last "l" being slightly larger than the preceding "l". The "R" in Rick exhibits the greatest variation in his signature.

Ferrell has always been very obliging to signature requests and collectors should find his autograph an easy acquisition.

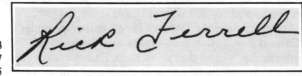

Availability: Plentiful
Demand: Little

Cut signature	$3
Single-signature baseball	$17
3x5" index card	$5
Photograph/baseball card	$12
HOF plaque postcard	$9
Perez-Steele postcard	$35

Elmer Flick

Elmer Harrison Flick
(Jan. 11, 1876-Jan. 9, 1971)

Flick batted .315 during his 13 major league seasons. The "Bedford Sheriff" hit a career high .378 in 1900 while playing for Philadelphia.

Flick's signature varied moderately, until the later years of his life when deteriorating health radically altered certain elements of his autograph. Consistent throughout his lifetime were breaks between the "E" and the "l" in Elmer, also between the "F" and the "l", and "i" and the "c" in Flick. Earlier examples were smoother in formation with slight variations in character width. The ascender of the "l" in Elmer was often the highest point in his signature and was commonly larger than the "l" in Flick. The capitalized "F" in Flick looked like a number 7 with a slash through the middle of the stem.

Later examples (circa late 1960s), showed many significant aging characteristics such as rough strokes, inconsistent letter spacing and ink accumulation. The capitalized "F" in Flick evolved into a three-stroke character formation. The ascender of the "k" was typically looped instead of a single line, as found in earlier examples. Because of the impact of the aging characteristics on his signature, autographs signed later in his life could prove difficult to authenticate. Later examples, via mail requests, were typically responded to with the words "Base Ball Hall of Fame" under his name and dated. Worth noting was his older style spelling of baseball, now common in a single-word format. Flick was generally responsive to signature requests.

Availability: Above average
Demand: Average

Cut signature	$15
Single-signature baseball	$175
3x5" index card	$25
Photograph/baseball card	$100
HOF plaque postcard	$195
Perez-Steele postcard	Impossible

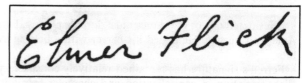

Whitey Ford

Edward Charles Ford
(Oct. 21, 1926-   )

During his career Ford collected 236 wins and 106 loses at an ERA of 2.75. With 11 World Series appearances as a Yankee, totaling 146 innings of post-season play, he set marks for games pitched (22), wins (10), and strikeouts (94).

Commonly signing "Whitey Ford", earlier examples (circa 1950s), may be signed simply "Edward Ford". Common breaks exist between the "E" and the "d" in Edward and also between the "r" and the "d" in Ford. Earlier examples will show a greater slant in his signature and greater flamboyance in the capitalization. The "E" in Edward will typically have a long stroke extending from the base line of the signature to the top loop of the letter.

Later examples of Ford's signature will show a break between the "W" and the "h" in Whitey, and a consistent break between the "r" and the "d" in Ford. The capitalization may vary a bit in size and character formation, in particular the "W". The bottom loops of the "W" may not be symmetrical. The "h" in Whitey usually has a sharpness to the bottom loop and the "t" is characteristically larger with an extended ascender that can be twice or three times the size of the "i". The "y" in Whitey will commonly have a loop before the downward stroke that forms the descender. The bottom finishing stroke of the "y" is typically an oval loop that extends below his signature to the "h" in Whitey. The ascender of the "F" in Ford can be looped and the descender is a downward stroke that angles left to form the bottom of the letter. The slash of the "F" is a separate stroke that intersects the stem of the letter to form the "or". The "d" is formed as an individual letter, with a wide ascender.

Ford has been a good signer, though mail requests at times have been erratic. He regularly attends baseball card shows, where he remains an extremely popular guest.

Availability: Plentiful
Demand: Little

Cut signature	$3
Single-signature baseball	$18
3x5" index card	$5
Photograph/baseball card	$20
HOF plaque postcard	$11
Perez-Steele postcard	$40

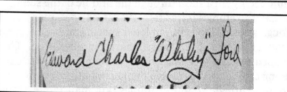

Rube Foster

Andrew Foster
(Sept. 17, 1879-Dec. 9, 1930)

Foster was considered the "father of black baseball." Although he was an outstanding pitcher during his day, he is most remembered for the teams he owned and managed. Foster in 1919 organized the Negro National League and through his showmanship the league flourished.

Commonly signing "Rube Foster", his signature varied in character formation, slant and size. A consistent signature break fell between the "F" and the "o" in Foster. The flamboyant "R" originated from below the signature's base line with a long upward stroke to capitalization height, before changing direction to curve downward, then above the previous stroke to form the major loop of the letter. The leg of the "R" was formed from the letter's middle loop, which may or may not intersect the stem, that changed the stroke's direction at lower case height. The "R" was often four to five times the height of his lower case letters. The degree of right slant in the "R" typically allowed the loop to extend above the "u" in Rube. The "u" varied a bit in size, as did the "b". The ascender of the "b" commonly equalled the height of the "t" in Foster. The "e" could vary slightly in slant, with the ending stroke usually a small simple curl upward. Foster typically added quotation marks around his nickname.

The "F" was a two-stroke formation, with the first stroke resembling a number "7" with a "J" added to the bottom, and the second stroke a slash through the stem of the letter. The "F" rested on the signature's base line and was equal in height to the "R". The typically upward slash of the "F" usually originated just slightly above the loop at the bottom of the first stroke, and often ended as far as the "s" in Foster. The "o" varied slightly in slant and the "s", which originated from the top of the "o", may or may not be left open at the bottom. The formation at the bottom of the "s" was either a curved looped formation or a double backed single line. The large ascender of the "t" usually extended to the height of the "b" and could vary in width. The "t" was often crossed with an upward slash, similar to that of the "F" in Foster, that originated from nearly lower case height and extended to the "r". The formation of the "r" resembled a "v", with its curled outward finishing stroke. The "r" could vary in both formation and size. Foster's lower case letters didn't always rest neatly on the base line, and as a result may angle a bit upward.

Like so many of the pioneers of the Negro Leagues, Foster's signature is highly sought-after. Foster was an obliging signer, however few samples of his signature have surfaced in the autograph market.

Availability: Limited
Demand: Above average

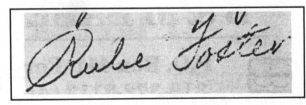

Cut signature	$2,600
Single-signature baseball	$4,500
3x5" index card	$4,200
Photograph/baseball card	$6,500
HOF plaque postcard	Impossible
Perez-Steele postcard	Impossible

Jimmie Foxx

James Emory Foxx
(Oct. 22, 1907-July 21, 1967)

Jimmie Foxx hit the ball harder than any player to play the game. Scouted by Frank "Home Run" Baker, Foxx soon became one of the game's premier sluggers, swatting 534 home runs with a career average of .325.

Foxx's signature varied considerably throughout his lifetime in capitalization and character formation. His right signature slant, however, remained consistent (around 55 degrees). Earlier examples will show greater flamboyance in character formation, particularily in capitalization. The unique formation of the "J" and the "F" became easily recognizable. Common early signature breaks were between the "J" and the "i" in Jimmie, also between the "F" and the "o", and between the "x"'s in Foxx. The "J" was the largest character in his signature, often five or six times larger than the lower case letters in Jimmie. The "F" in Foxx commonly consisted of two strokes resembling a number 2 with a seperate slash that could extend to the last "x" in Foxx.

Later Foxx samples exhibit rougher strokes and a dramatic variation in the character formation of the letter "J", which became more traditional in style. The "F" in Foxx could be a single- or double-stroked version. The "oxx" varied in signature breaks, often consisting of individual letter construction. The "immie" in Jimmie grew to about twice the size of earlier versions.

During his retirement he suffered some physical setbacks which left him partially paralyzed. Signature inconsistencies are common in autographs signed during his later years, making these a bit challenging to authenicate.

Availability: Average
Demand: Average

Cut signature	$65
Single-signature baseball	$425
3x5" index card	$125
Photograph/baseball card	$250
HOF plaque postcard	$550
Perez-Steele postcard	Impossible

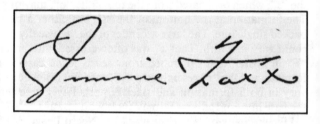

Ford Frick

Ford Christopher Frick
(Dec. 19, 1894-April 8, 1978)

Frick's contribution to the game he loved included 14 years as its commissioner, 17 years as the National League's president and the Baseball Hall of Fame and Museum.

Commonly signing "Ford Frick" or "Ford C. Frick", his signature exhibited some variation, primarily in capitalization, during his lifetime. Signature breaks existed between the "F" and the "o" in Ford, also between the "F" and the "r" in Frick. Characteristic in his signature was a break between the stem and the arms of the letter "k". The "F" in Ford was a two-stroke character formation consisting of a top and bottom looped stroke to form the letter's stem, crossed by a seperate stroke. Earlier versions of the capitalized letter "F" in Frick could also have no top formation to the letter, instead choosing only a downward stroke with a bottom loop. The crossing slash of the "F" in earlier versions tends to be much longer. The "or" remained consistent, but the "d" in Ford could vary in ascender length. The "c" in Frick could also vary and occasionally resembled an "e". The unique break in the "k" letter formation was consistent throughout his life and a good authentication reference.

During his many years as an executive he signed numerous documents and letters, many of which have surfaced in the autograph market. Collectors should find his signature fairly easy to acquire.

Availability: Average
Demand: Average

Cut signature	$20
Single-signature baseball	$125
3x5" index card	$25
Photograph/baseball card	$50
HOF plaque postcard	$55
Perez-Steele postcard	Impossible

Frankie Frisch

Frank Francis Frisch
(Sept. 9, 1898-March 12, 1973)

"The Fordham Flash" spent 19 years in the major leagues posting a .316 batting average that included 2,880 hits. Frankie was the spark behind the Giants pennant-winning seasons of 1921 through 1924 and the Cardinals 1928 through 1931 seasons. Being ritually tossed out of many games, manager Frisch was renowned for his escapades with the game's umpires.

Commonly signing, ""The Old Flash" Frank Frisch", his signature showed moderate variation throughout his life. Signature breaks were consistent, falling between the "F" and the "r" in Frank, also between the "F" and the "r" in Frisch. Early examples showed a more flamboyant character formation in the "F" in Frank, with the "F"in Frisch bearing little resemblance to its predecessor. The "rank" remained fairly consistent, as did the "risch". The ascender of the "h" occasionally varied in height and width. A good signature authentication reference is the character formation of the letter "r". Both of the letters have an extended stroke upward, beginning below the signature's base line, that starts the formation of the "r". The extension of the first "r" is usually the lowest point in his signature.

Later examples are easily identified by a different character formation for the letter "F", which resembled a number 7 with an upside down check mark connected to it. In older examples, both "F"s will look very similar. The finishing stroke of the first "F" can extend to the "n" in Frank, and the second as far as the "s" in Frisch. The spacing between the capitalization and lower case letters is greater in later autographs. The "a" in Frank may or may not close.

Frisch was generally responsive to signature requests and collectors should be able to acquire his autograph through hobby dealers or auction houses.

Availability: Above average
Demand: Average

Cut signature	$18
Single-signature baseball	$225
3x5" index card	$45
Photograph/baseball card	$85
HOF plaque postcard	$110
Perez-Steele postcard	Impossible

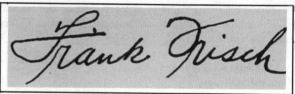

Pud Galvin

James Francis Galvin
(Dec. 25, 1856-March 7, 1902)

Galvin hurled over 5,900 innings, winning 361 games over his 14-year career. For two seasons in a row Galvin won a career high 46 games for Buffalo in the National League. Posting only a .538 winning percentage, Galvin's election to the Baseball Hall of Fame was 63 years after his death.

Commonly signing "Jas. F. Galvin" the few signatures I have seen exhibit signature breaks between the "J" and the "a", also between the "G" and the "a" and on occasion between the "l" and the "v". The capitalized "J" has been unusually large, four to five times larger than the lower case letters of "a" or "s". His middle initial of "F" was a three-stroked configuration with a large curve loop formation on top. The descender of the "J" was about twice the height of the ascender. The generally large top loop of the "G" in Galvin, could vary a bit in size. The formation of the "G", typically didn't close on the bottom of the letter. The ascender of the "l" often extended to the height of the "G" and the "alvin" typically exhibited an increased signature slant compared to the rest of the signature.

A father of 11 children, Galvin passed away in 1902 at the early age of 45. He was so poor at the time that a group of his friends had to hold a benefit to raise money for his funeral expenses. Galvin signatures are rare and collectors should find the acquisition of his signature a real challenge.

Availability: Scarce
Demand: Strong

Cut signature	$1,825
Single-signature baseball	$4,250
3x5" index card	$3,050
Photograph/baseball card	$3,500
HOF plaque postcard	Impossible
Perez-Steele postcard	Impossible

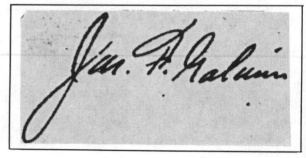

Lou Gehrig

Henry Louis Gehrig
(June 19, 1903-June 6, 1941)

The "Iron Horse," Lou Gehrig is known most for playing in 2,130 consecutive games, a major league record unlikely to ever be broken. This durable first basemen finished his career with a .340 lifetime batting average that included 2,721 hits. Gehrig was a gentlemen who epitomized every thing positive about the game of baseball. He was stricken by lateral sclerosis, now known as "Lou Gehrig's disease," which took his life in 1941.

Commonly signing "Lou Gehrig" his signature exhibited numerous variations during his lifetime. Variations that primarily occurred were in slant, size and character formation. To thoroughly understand Gehrig's signature, a letter by letter analysis is necessary.

Letter	Variation
L	The "L"is typically equal to or slightly smaller in size than the "G" in Gehrig. A break is more common in earlier examples between the "L" and the "o" in Lou, while later versions (circa 1930s), do not usually include it. The right slant of the "L" can vary significantly, with most falling between the 50-65 degree mark. The top loop of the "L" commonly extended to the "u" in Lou, or slightly beyond the letter. The finishing stroke of the top loop always ended in an upward direction.
ou	This combination remained relatively consistent. The "o" was typically closed, although earlier versions I have seen have had it open.
G	The "G" can vary in character formation and width, yet remain consistent in slant with the "L". A break is consistent between the "G" and the "e" in Gehrig. The descender of the "G" is typically equal to or smaller in height than the top loop of the same letter. The top loop of the letter can extend above the "e" in Gehrig. I have also seen samples where the "u" in Lou has connected to the "G" in Gehrig.
e	The "e" remained relatively consistent.
h	The ascender of the "h" can vary in width and height. The angle of the slant of he "h" should be similar (within 10 degrees), to that of the "L" in Lou.
ri	The "r" can change in character formation, being sharper (pointed) on the top in older examples. The "i" has remained fairly consistent.
g	The loop of the "g" typically resembles the loop of the "G" in Gehrig, both in formation and slant. The descender of the "g" can vary in formation, but the slant should be similar to the capitalized version. If the variation is greater than 10 degrees in slant, I would reconsider purchasing the item.

Gehrig's handwriting is recognizable by certain characteristics, such as the loop in a capitalized "C" that will be nearly identical in formation to the top loop of the "L" in Lou. The slant in his lower case letters usually (circa 1930s) falls around a 60 to 65 degree angle, with capitalization slant around 65 to 70 degrees. The range may vary plus or minus 10 degrees. Unique letter formations such as an "I", "F" and "p" are good comparisons for authenticators. The bottom loop of the "G" in Gehrig and the "L" in Lou, should always lie on the base line of his signature.

Complicating matters for authenticators have been numerous ghost-signed autographs, most of which appear on photographs. The ghost-signed versions are typically larger with little attention paid to the detailed characterisitics of his signature. Additionally, the ghost-signed materials typically have short and generic salutations. Gehrig typically enscribed photos with more then "Best Wishes", and friends characteristically received a 10- to 15-word greeting.

Unfortunately, his popularity and increased signature demand has led to a flood of forgeries in the market. In my opinion his signature is forged more than any other inductee. A factor worth noting is Eleanor Gehrig's signature resemblance to her husband's autograph. In certain instances where she has signed his name, collectors have been fooled by the signature's true identity.

Gehrig's signature can be an authentictor's nightmare and is not a recommended purchase for the novice. Being a prolific signer in his day has led to numerous samples finding their way to the collector's market.

Availability: Average
Demand: Strong

Cut signature	$575
Single-signature baseball	$3,625
3x5" index card	$775
Photograph/baseball card	$1,750
HOF plaque postcard	Unknown
Perez-Steele postcard	Impossible

Charlie Gehringer

Charles Leonard Gehringer
(May 11, 1903-   )

Gehringer was a lifetime .320 hitter who stroked 2,839 hits before his retirement in 1942. A consumate performer he was considered by many to be the premier second basemen of the Thirties and Forties.

Commonly signing "Chas. Gehringer", his signature has shown moderate variation throughout his life. Common signature breaks in earlier examples fall between the "C and the "h", also between the "g" and the "e" in Gehringer. Later samples added a break between the "h" and the "a" and between the "G" and the "e". Earlier Gehringer samples will also show an increased right slant, less character definition and smoother strokes.

The "C" has changed only slightly in character formation over the years, later examples (1970s & 1980s) will be larger with the top loop formation wider and more defined. The "C" has always begun with a long extended stroke from the signture's base line that curves backward and intersects the line twice during the major loop's formation. The ending of the stroke is always a bottom loop that curls downward. The ascender of the "h" was much smaller in later versions, about half the character's size compared to earlier versions where it was twice as large. The "a" will commonly close in earlier versions and be left open a bit in later autographs. The "G" in earlier versions had a larger and more pronounced top loop, with the finishing stroke making a small loop before connecting to the "e". Later versions of the "G" will intersect the upward stroke of the letter with a dramatic finishing curl. The "rin" will be much more defined in later samples, with the "i" displaying the separation between both the upward and downward strokes. The "g" in earlier examples may show some flamboyance in the descender with a finishing loop, yet later examples will show a simplified single-stroke descender. "The Mechanical Man" on the field was just as mechanical with his penmanship. His signature is easily identified by the precision character formations and consistency in letter slants. Gehringer's slow meticulous signature during the last two decades exhibits many common aging characteristics.

Gehringer has been generally responsive to autograph requests and collectors should have many alternatives for the acquisition of his signature.

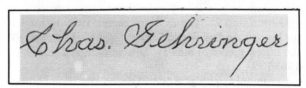

Availability: Plentiful
Demand: Little

Cut signature	$3
Single-signature baseball	$30
3x5" index card	$5
Photograph/baseball card	$15
HOF plaque postcard	$13
Perez-Steele postcard	$85

Josh Gibson

Joshua Gibson
(Dec. 21, 1911-Jan. 20, 1947)

Gibson displayed awesome power during his career in the Negro Leagues, swatting, by some estimates, about 800 home runs. Playing for two of the greatest black teams of all time, the Homestead Grays and the Pittsburgh Crawfords, Josh hit consistently over .300 every season.

Commonly signing "Joshua Gibson" or "Josh Gibson", his signature showed a common break between the "G" and the "i" in Gibson. Variations in capitalization were common, particularily the "J" in Josh, which resembled a "g" in later versions of his autograph. His signature slant in early examples was consistent, with each letter of his signature clearly identifiable. Remaining fairly consistent throughout his lifetime, the "G" in Gibson was also the most unique character formation in his signature. The ending of the letter formation in the "G" varied in length and may or may not intersect the stem of the letter. The "s"s in Joshua or in Gibson commonly were open a bit on the bottom of the letter. The ascenders in the "h" and the "b" could vary in width, however similar slant in both letters is common. Deteriorating health contributed to varitions in his signature during the last few years of his life.

In 1942 medical examinations diagnosed a presence of a brain tumor, after Gibson had been suffering severe headaches. His life was cut short just five years later at the early age of 35. He was an extremely popular player and reportedly responsive to autograph requests. Not unlike many of the great Negro League ball players, Gibson's signature can be a real challenge to find and perhaps a greater challenge to authenticate.

Availability: Limited
Demand: Strong

Cut signature	$1,000
Single-signature baseball	$3,500
3x5" index card	$2,000
Photograph/baseball card	$2,000
HOF plaque postcard	Impossible
Perez-Steele postcard	Impossible

Bob Gibson

Robert Gibson
(Nov. 9, 1935-   )

Gibson won 251 games in his career, striking out 3,117 at an ERA of 2.91. Known most for his outstanding World Series play, he achieved an ERA of 1.89 in 89 innings. Considered the fastest picher of his day, Gibson fanned a record 17 batters during the first game of the 1968 Fall Classic.

Commonly signing "Robert Gibson" or "Bob Gibson", his earlier signatures showed considerable variation from his autograph of today. Early examples (circa 1959 and the early 1960s), varied in character formation and size, with no signature breaks. On rare occasions, however, I have seen a break between the "R" and the "o" in Robert. His signature has always shown a slight left slant and dotting of the "i" close to the letter's stem. The "b" in Robert and the "b" in Gibson could vary in size or ascender width. When he signed Robert his "R" was flamboyant in style with the beginning stroke of the letter resembling a number 7, before the traditional formation of the character was made. The "t" in Robert typically had a large ascender that was crossed by the same stroke that doubled back across the stem. The capitalized "G" in Gibson was a wider formation and typically showed two pinnacles atop the character, the first a loop, the second either a point or a loop. The bottom of the "G" may or may not close the letter formation.

Later examples, typically signed "Bob Gibson", show a more circular appearance to the autograph, with letters showing a final outward hook on ending strokes. The "ob" in Bob exhibited changes in character formation, with the "o" consisting of two loops that may or may not close. The end of the second loop, beginning the upward stroke of the "G", was now much wider and circular in appearance. The "B" could vary in style and may be a single- or two-stroke formation. Some samples may show a break between the "B" and the "o" in Bob. The top two pinnacles of the "G" became a closed double looped formation. The closing of the "G" may be a separate stroke leading to the "i". The "i" occasionally will be dotted with a circle instead of a dot. The "b" in Gibson is usually much wider than earlier examples but commonly varying in width. The "son" was fairly consistent, though the "o" may or may not close, and the "n" tends to vary in roundness.

Gibson's signature has never been an easy acquisition. Often unpredictable via mail requests, collectors are urged to pursue his autograph at local baseball card shows.

Availability: Plentiful
Demand: Little

Cut signature	$4
Single-signature baseball	$20
3x5" index card	$5
Photograph/baseball card	$15
HOF plaque postcard	$11
Perez-Steele postcard	$35

Warren Giles

Warren Christopher Giles
May 28, 1896-Feb. 7, 1979)

Giles commanded the National League for 18 years as president. A gentle uncontroversial figure, Giles had a lengthy illness claim his life just weeks before his induction to the Hall of Fame.

Commonly signing "Warren Giles" or "Warren C. Giles", his autograph varied moderately throughout his life. The only consistent break in his signature was between the "W" and the "a" in Warren. His entire signature could be a single stroke following the "W", with the possibility of a break developing after the "n" in Warren. When his middle initial was used it was part of the same stroke as his last name. The "W" in Warren was consistent in character formation, resembling a large number 2 with a serif attached. The major large loop in the "W" could vary in width, and the "arren" seemed to decrease in size with each subsequent letter (more noticeable in later examples). His middle initial of "C" decreased in size with age and the "e" in Giles became less defined, often resembling a letter "r". Characteristic of older samples are two slashes below his name (under the "C" & the "G"), with a third added in later examples under the "y".

Giles was a responsive signer and like all baseball executives a prolific signer of correspondences or contracts. Collectors should find his signature fairly easy to acquire.

Availability: Above average
Demand: Average

Cut signature	$15
Single-signature baseball	$110
3x5" index card	$35
Photograph/baseball card	$45
HOF plaque postcard	Impossible
Perez-Steele postcard	Impossible

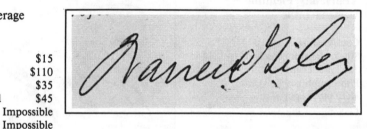

Lefty Gomez

Vernon Louis Gomez
(Nov. 26, 1908-Feb. 17, 1989)

Gomez established himself as one of the finest pitchers of the Thirties with seasons like that of 1934, where he won 26 games while losing only five with an ERA of 2.33. An outspoken prankster, Gomez's wit became a constant source of entertainment for his teammates.

Commonly signing "Lefty Gomez", his signature varied considerably throughout his lifetime. Earlier signatures, during his playing days in the 1930s, exhibited no signature breaks. The "L" in Lefty resembled a large "S" and the capitalization style in Gomez looked like an enlarged "g". The "f" in Lefty was a wider character formation and the ascender of the "t" was typically extended almost to the height of the "G"in Gomez. The "ey" in Lefty and the "ez" in Gomez, with the exception of the finishing strokes, looked nearly identical. The "o" in Gomez was typically closer to the "G" and in a closed formation. The crossing of the

155

"t" in Lefty was a single stroke that could begin at the "f" and extend as far as the "G" in Gomez. The descender of the "G", in earlier examples, was the lowest point in his signature.

Signature variation continued throughout his retirement from baseball and later examples are a radical departure from his earlier style. The "L" in Lefty took on a traditional look in character formation, with a large loop atop the stem of the latter that could extend as far as the "y". The "efty" condensed a little in character spacing during the 1960s and 1970s, but by the 1980s was spread out once again. Later examples (circa 1980s), may show the top loop of the "L" not closing and only extending to the "f" in Lefty. The "f" became thinner and during the 1960s and 1970s was commonly the lowest point in his signature.

The "t" in later examples seems to be crossed higher in the letter than in earlier examples. The descender of the "y" varied in length and width. In 1960s or 1970s examples the "y" may connect to the "G", however it would often not connect in examples from the 1980s. The "G" in Gomez varied in size and character formation. Samples from the 1960s or 1970s, show a flamboyant exended loop beginning the top of the letter "G" in Gomez, that slowly during the 1980s decreased in size. The "omez" in Gomez grew in character spacing over time, however was fairly consistent in formation. The "e" in Gomez often appeared unusually larger than either the "o" or the "m".

Gomez was a fairly responsive signer throughout his life, however mail requests were often unpredictble. He did spend some time on the show circuit and collectors should have little difficulty acquiring his signature.

Availability: Plentiful
Demand: Little

Cut signature	$7
Single-signature baseball	$55
3x5" index card	$10
Photograph/baseball card	$30
HOF plaque postcard	$20
Perez-Steele postcard	$125

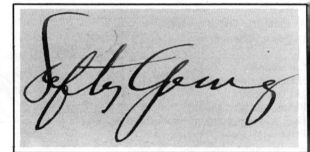

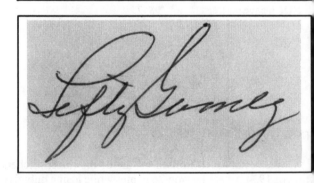

Goose Goslin

Leon Allen Goslin
(Oct. 16, 1900-May 15, 1971)

Goslin ended his career with 2,735 hits for an average of .316. He feared no pitcher and routinely crowded the plate during his at bats. He led the American League in batting in 1928 with an average of .379. Goslin hit three home runs in one game three times, while compiling a lifetime total of 248.

Commonly signing "L. Goslin" or "Goose Goslin", his signature varied in size, slant and character formation during his lifetime. A common signature break in early examples was consistent between the "G" and the "o" in Goslin. Later signature samples typically exhibit no breaks. His first initial of "L" could vary from a traditional style, with a larger loop on both the top and bottom of the letter. The slant of the "G" in Goslin was gradually reduced, while the first loop of the letter grew in size. Early samples of Goslin's signature will have two conservative loops atop the "G", while the later versions eliminate the second loop and construct the first loop two to three times larger. Consistent throughout his lifetime was not closing the "G" on the bottom of the letter. In later examples the ascender of the "l" will increase in height and may vary a bit in width. The "s" will commonly not close on the bottom and may show a slight loop at the base line. Later examples of Goslin's handwriting are easily recognized by the unusual height of his characters' ascenders, which typically are three to four times the height of surrounding lower case letters.

Goslin was fairly responsive to signature requests and collectors should be able to acquire his autograph through major auction houses or dealers.

Availability: Average
Demand: Average

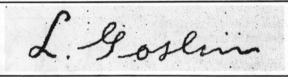

Cut signature	$40
Single-signature baseball	$290
3x5" index card	$50
Photograph/baseball card	$135
HOF plaque postcard	$475
Perez-Steele postcard	Impossible

Hank Greenberg

Henry Benjamin Greenberg
(Jan. 1, 1911-Sept. 4, 1986)

Greenberg finished his career with a .313 average that included 331 home runs, 58 which were during the 1938 season. Greenberg batted over .300 nine times and drove in over 100 runs seven times. In four World Series contests he smacked 27 hits while batting a respectable .318.

Commonly signing "Hank Greenberg", his signature varied primarily in capitalization and character formation during his lifetime. Common signature breaks occur between the "H" and the "a", and the "n" and the "k" in Hank, also between the "r" and the "e", "e" and the "e", and the "b" and the "e" in Greenberg. Characteristic of his signature was a slight left slant, an extended ascender formation of the first stroke of the capitalized "H", and the flamboyant looped finishing stroke in Greenberg. The two-stroked "H", with the top looped ascender in the first stroke, usually extended three times the height of the lower case "a" in Hank. The "an" remained relatively consistent, however the "k" can be a single- or two-stroke formation. The "G" in Greenberg can vary in size, with the opening loop of the character also varying in width. The "ee" formation may be connected in later examples and the "n" can often be unidentifiable in Greenberg. The ascender of the "b" in Greenberg can vary a bit in height and width. The "erg" has remained fairly consistent with the flamboyant ending hooked stroke typically extending to about the capitalization height of the "G". The ending stroke should not extend above any letter in his last name. Greenberg was a responsive signer, but often unpredictable via mail request. Collectors should find his signature fairly easy to acquire.

Availability: Above average
Demand: Average

Cut signature	$10
Single-signature baseball	$65
3x5" index card	$18
Photograph/baseball card	$45
HOF plaque postcard	$40
Perez-Steele postcard	$450

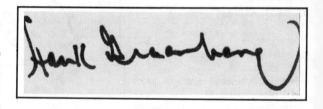

Clark Griffith

Clark Calvin Griffith
(Nov. 20, 1869-Oct. 27, 1955)

The "Old Fox" compiled 240 victories during his career at a winning percentage above .630. His .774 winning percentage (24-7) in 1901 led the league. He was a cunning pitcher who learned many secrets on the art from Hoss Radbourn. Griffith's love for the game extended into management (Cincinnati and Washington) and eventually team ownership (Washington Senators).

Giffith's signature varied moderately during his lifetime. Early examples exhibit breaks between the "C" and the "l" in Clark, also between the "G" and the "r", and the "f" and the "f" in Griffith. The capitalized "C" was a traditional formation with a loop on the top and bottom of the letter. The "G" had an extended loop atop the letter, similar to a Lefty Gomez "G" of the 1970s. The "f"'s in Griffith can vary in character formation from each other, however the descenders of the letters were usually identical in slant. Griffith typically crossed the "t" with an extended flat stroke that often intersected the "h". The "k" can have a separate stroke for the arms of the letter. The bottoms of the capitalized letters always rested on the signature's base line.

During the 1920s, Griffith's signature made some changes in character formation. The "C" became far less flamboyant and began with a stroke that didn't intersect the loop of the letter. The "C" could also connect to the "l", with a break in Clark between the "l" and the "a". The "k" grew in height, with some samples I have seen equal the size of the "C" in Clark. The "k" remained a two-stroke version, with the break a bit more evident. His entire signature appeared larger in size. The "G" had a longer upward stroke to the top loop, that was a little smaller in comparison to earlier examples. The character formation of the "f"'s became more traditional, however typically varied in ascender and descender width. His bold crossing of the "t" in Griffith was erratic and sometimes never even intersected the stem of the letter.

In his later years Griffith's signature showed many common aging characteristics: rough strokes, ink deposition and altered character formations. The "G" in Griffith decreased in size and often the descenders of the letter "f" were only a straight line. A new break betwen the "f" and the "i" was also not uncommon. The "t" in Griffith often crossed the very top of the character stem, sometimes missing it all together. The "C" in Clark can be a single- or two-looped style and the first stroke of the "k" had become much smaller. The second stroke of the "k" often was the lowest point in his signature.

As a baseball executive he signed numerous correspondences, some of which have gradually surfaced in the autograph market. Later examples of his signature can be a challenge to authenticate, with many authentic signatures often mistaken for forgeries.

Availability: Average
Demand: Average

Cut signature	$100
Single-signature baseball	$450
3x5" index card	$135
Photograph/baseball card	$350
HOF plaque postcard	$450
Perez-Steele postcard	Impossible

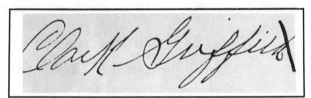

Burleigh Grimes

Burleigh Arland Grimes
(Aug. 9, 1893-Dec. 6, 1985)

"Old Stubblebeard" won 270 games during his major league career. A tough competitor with a difficult disposition, Grimes was one of the select (17) spitball pitchers in 1921, to not have the pitch disallowed in his repertoire.

Commonly signing "Burleigh A Grimes", his signature exhibited moderate variation during his lifetime. A consistent break existed between the "i" and the "g" in Burleigh. Capitalization often varied in character formation and slant. The "B" in Burleigh began with a downward stroke that could double back in either direction to form the top loop of the letter. The right slant of the "B" was inconsistent, ranging from a 50 to 90 degree position. The descender of the "g" in Burleigh varied often from a vertical downward stroke to that of a traditional form. The "h", which was always connected to the "g", varied from a straight lined ascender to a looped variation. The "l" in Burleigh varied in height, width and slant. Both his middle initial of "A" and the "G" in Grimes were unpredictable in character formation. The extended top loop of the "G" in Grimes commonly varied in size, while the "A" often changed styles in the beginning stroke. The "rimes" varied only slightly in character formation and spacing, however for the most part it was consistent.

Grimes was very responsive to autograph requests and always a favorite among collectors.

Availability: Plentiful
Demand: Little

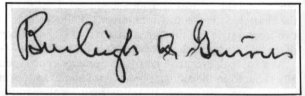

Cut signature	$6
Single-signature baseball	$60
3x5" index card	$18
Photograph/baseball card	$30
HOF plaque postcard	$22
Perez-Steele postcard	$375

Lefty Grove

Robert Moses Grove
(March 6, 1900-May 23, 1975)

During 3,940 innings pitched, Grove won 300 games at an ERA of 3.06. In 1931 he led the American League with 31 wins at a victory percentage of .886. Grove had eight seasons winning 20 or more games and compiled 35 career shutouts.

Commonly signing "Lefty Grove", his signature varied considerably during his lifetime in size and character formation. Early samples, during Grove's playing days, typically exhibited no consistent signature breaks. The "L" in Lefty looked like an enlarged "y" with a long hooked stroke leading to a descender that shared the same slant as the "t" and the "y" in Lefty. The descender of the "y" was commonly the lowest point in his earlier signatures, although the finishing stroke of the "L" in Lefty would gradually surpass the ending letter. The "t" was crossed by the finishing stroke of the "y", with earlier examples being much more flamboyant in style. The descender of the "y" could vary in length and in form, but commonly was at the same slant as the "f" and "t" in Lefty. Early examples of the "G" in Grove, commonly didn't close on the bottom of the letter and may even break with the "r". The "ove" was the most consistent configuration in his signature during his lifetime, although it could vary slightly in character formation and spacing. Early Grove examples may show a finishing stroke that extends beneath the length of his last name.

In later examples, Grove altered the "G" in Grove by eliminating the two loops atop the letter. The break between the "G" and the "r" became more consistent, as did the break between the "L" and the "e" in Lefty. Later examples also exhibited many typical aging characteristics. The "e" in Lefty remained consistent in character formation throughout his life.

Grove was generally responsive to autograph requests and collectors should be able to acquire his signature through auction houses or dealers. Because of his variance in signature style and the deterioration with age, Grove's later signatures can be a challenge to authenticate.

Availability: Above average
Demand: Average

Cut signature	$17
Single-signature baseball	$170
3x5" index card	$30
Photograph/baseball card	$50
HOF plaque postcard	$55
Perez-Steele postcard	Impossible

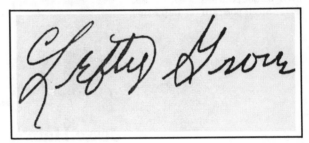

Chick Hafey

Charles James Hafey
(Feb. 12, 1903-July 2, 1973)

Hafey achieved a .317 career average and in 1931 won the batting title at .349. Despite being constantly hampered by physical problems, Hafey's strength was often compared to that of Rogers Hornsby. In 13 professional seasons he smacked 164 home runs and batted over .300 nine times.

Commonly signing "Chick Hafey", his signature exhibited moderate variation during his lifetime. A consistent signature break occurs between the "C" and the "h" in Chick, and occasionally a break may fall between the "H" and the "a" in Hafey, or the "h" and the "i" in Chick. Character formation changes are common in capitalization, particularily in certain circumstances such as return addresses on an envelope. Hafey could use an almost printed formation for both the "C" and the "H" during these occasions. The right slant of his signature was fairly consistent (between 50 to 60 degrees on a 3x5"), depending on the particular sample. The slant of the "h" and the "k" in Chick are often identical. The ascender of the "h", "k" and "f" in his signature can vary both in height and width. The "H" in Hafey is typically a two-stroke version, where the middle loop may or may not intersect the first stroke. The "i" in Chick can be dotted simply or with a circle. The "f" in Hafey, although it could vary in both ascender and descender size, did not typically vary in formation. The "k" was often a single-stroke version, however Hafey did use a two-stroke version as well. The "ic" in Chick remained relatively consistent throughout his life. The formation of the "f" in Hafey, and the similarity in slant of the letters "h" and "k" in Chick, make good reference points for authentication.

Hafey was obliging to signature requests and his autograph should be accesible through the many autograph houses or dealers.

Availability: Above average
Demand: Average

Cut signature	$18
Single-signature baseball	$160
3x5" index card	$25
Photograph/baseball card	$55
HOF plaque postcard	$65
Perez-Steele postcard	Impossible

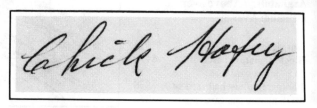

Jesse Haines

Jesse Joseph Haines
(July 22, 1893-Aug. 5, 1978)

"Pop" Haines won 210 games in his career at an ERA of 3.64. A knuckleball pitcher with a good fastball, he helped take the "Gas House Gang" of 1934 to a world championship.

During his lifetime Haines' signature exhibited variations in slant, character size and formation. the only consistent signature break was between the "J" and the "e" in Jesse. The beginning and ending strokes of the "J" could vary in size, as could the loops of both the ascenders and descenders. The "J" did always close with either a beginning or ending stroke extending to either the "e" or the "s" in Jesse. The beginning stroke of the "e" in Jesse typically extended about a quarter of an inch before the letter formation. Each "s" in Jesse could vary in size and may or may not be closed on the bottom of the letter. The "e" in Jesse could vary in width and the extension of the ending stroke. The "H" in Haines was consistently a two-stroke formation that could vary a bit in the size of the middle double looped configuration. Haines generally left a full letter spacing between the "H" and the "a" in Haines. The "a" may or may not close, and the "i" could be dotted above either the letter, or above the "n" or the "e". The "nes" varied little, however the "s" could be either open or closed. The "J" could extend to an inch or better on a 3x5" index card, and was typically seven or eight times larger than the "e" that followed it. The first stroke of the "H" commonly originated at between a 30 to 40 degree left slant.

He retired at the age of 44, and suffered ill health during the years prior to is death in 1978. Haines was obliging to autograph reguests and collectors should find the acquisition of his signature fairly easy.

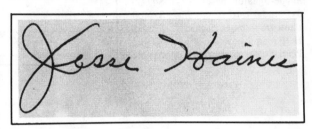

Availability: Above average
Demand: Average

Cut signature	$12
Single-signature baseball	$225
3x5" index card	$20
Photograph/baseball card	$55
HOF plaque postcard	$60
Perez-Steele postcard	Impossible

Billy Hamilton

William Robert Hamilton
(Feb. 16, 1866-Dec. 15, 1940)

"Sliding Billy" was a real distraction on the base paths, leading the league seven times in stolen bases. Hamilton batted .344 during his career with 2,163 hits.

Commonly signing "Billy Hamilton" or "Sliding Billy Hamilton", his signature exhibited some variation in character formation, slant and size. The "B" in Billy showed variation in the beginning stroke by being either a small stroke downward which then doubled back to form the character's stem, or simply an upward line. The "B" was typically the largest letter in his signature and didn't close on the bottom. A two-character lower case spacing between the stem of the "B" and the bottom loop was common. The "illy" varied slightly in both ascender width and height. The descender of the "y" was typically a single downward stroke. The "H" was a two-stroke construction with the middle loop usually crossing through the first stroke to form the middle of the letter. The "a" in Hamilton may or may not close and the ascender of the "l" can vary in width. Often the highest point in Hamilton, the "t" commonly extends above the "l" and makes a nice reference point for authenticators. The "n" can resemble an "ie" at times with the ending stroke showing minimal flamboyance. Hamilton's handwriting is easily identifiable by his unique character formations of the letters "I" and "S".

He was fairly obliging to autograph requests and often very outspoken in his responses. Samples of his signature have appeared periodically in the market.

Availability: Limited
Demand: Strong

Cut signature	$1,200
Single-signature baseball	$4,000
3x5" index card	$2,400
Photograph/baseball card	$2,875
HOF plaque postcard	Impossible
Perez-Steele postcard	Impossible

Will Harridge

William Harridge
(Oct. 16, 1883-April 9, 1971)

Harridge was the American League's president from 1931 to 1958. Following his presidency he became chairman of the American League Board of Directors from 1958 to 1971. He was a dignified man who ruled with a stiff hand when needed.

Harridge's signature varied primarily in character formation and size during his lifetime. Signature breaks were common between the "W" and the "i" in Will, and between the "H" and the "a" in Harridge. Although the "W" could vary in slant and size, it commonly had a shortened last stroke, similar to the signature of W.A. Cummmings. The "l"s in Will could differ in size and ascender width, but commonly extended to capitalization height. The "H" was a two-stroke construction with the second stroke flamboyantly crossing the first. The "a" may or may not close and the "r"s in Harridge could vary both in height and width. The desender of the "g" was typically wide and looped to form the unusually large "e" in Harridge. The "e" often looked like an "l" with the character extending nearly to capitalization height. The uniqueness of the size of the "e" makes it a useful reference point.

As a baseball executive he signed numerous contracts and letters, some of which have found their way into the autograph collector's market.

Availability: Above average
Demand: Average

Cut signature	$35
Single-signature baseball	$550
3x5" index card	$65
Photograph/baseball card	$125
HOF plaque postcard	Impossible
Perez-Steele postcard	Impossible

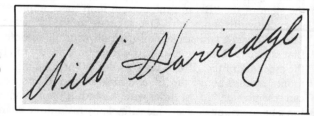

Bucky Harris

Stanley Raymond Harris
(Nov. 8, 1896-Nov. 8, 1977)

Although he was a major league player for 12 seasons, Harris is most remembered for his strength and leadership as a manager. From 1924 to 1955 he recorded over 2,000 wins and took Washington twice and New York once to the World Series.

Commonly signing "Bucky Harris" his signature exhibited variation in slant, size and character formation during his lifetime. The only consistent break was between the first and second stroke of his two-stroke "H" character formation. The "B" in Bucky began with a downward stroke that doubled back to form the main character formation of the letter. The upward stroke of the "B" was often inconsistent in slant, with the bottom of the letter left open. The "uck" could vary in size and character spacing, however was relatively consistent in character formation. The ascender of the "k" could vary in both height and width, with the loop of the letter never touching its stem. The "y" resembled in appearance a "r7" configuration, with a variable length descender. The descender of the "y" was typically connected to the first stroke of the "H" in Harris and could vary in slant. The second stroke of the "H" commonly varied in slant, with the crossing of the letter being a loop that typically did not make contact with the first stroke. The "arri" varied slightly in character formation and letter spacing. The ending stroke in Harris was typically not flamboyant, but often varied in length and direction.

Harris was an obliging signer in person, however mail requests were often unanswered.

Availability: Above average
Demand: Average

Cut signature	$20
Single-signature baseball	$225
3x5" index card	$30
Photograph/baseball card	$75
HOF plaque postcard	$130
Perez-Steele postcard	Impossible

Gabby Hartnett

Charles Leo Hartnett
(Dec. 20, 1900-Dec. 20, 1972)

Hartnett was an outstanding catcher who had a natural gift for fielding. He caught 100 or more games per season for 12 years, and was the National League's catcher in the first five All-Star games.

Commonly signing "Leo Gabby Hartnett" or "Gabby Hartnett", his signature exhibited consistent breaks between the "L" and the "e" in Leo, also between the "G" and the "a" in Gabby. Capitalization often varied in size and slant, with the "L" and the "G" also showing changes in flamboyance. The "L" in Leo was traditional in formation and commonly the largest letter in his signature. The ending stroke of the "L" could extend well below the base line and is often the lowest point of his signature. The loop of the "L" typically extends above both the "e" and the "o" in Leo. The "G" in Gabby has an unusually large extended first loop, similar to that of "Goose" Goslin. The descender of the "y" in Gabby commonly connected to the "H" in Hartnett. It was common for the second stroke of the "H" to extend well above the first, equal to the height of the "L". The first "t" in Hartnett was usually much larger in width than the final two "t"s. Hartnett typically crossed his "t"s with a long extended stroke that intersected all three letters.

Hartnett was generally responsive to autograph requests and collectors should find his signature fairly easy to acquire.

Availability: Above average
Demand: Average

Cut signature	$30
Single-signature baseball	$450
3x5" index card	$50
Photograph/baseball card	$115
HOF plaque postcard	$185
Perez-Steele postcard	Impossible

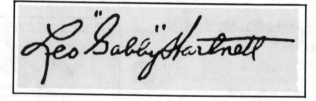

Harry Heilmann

Harry Edwin Heilmann
(Aug. 3, 1894-July 9, 1951)

Heilmann played 17 years in the major leagues and ended his career with a lifetime batting average of .342. Heilmann had 2,660 lifetime hits, won four batting titles and in 1923 hit a career high .403.

Typically signing "Harry Heilmann", his signature exhibited consistent breaks between the "H" and the "a" in Harry, also between the "H" and the "e" in Heilmann. Both capitalized "H"s typically were seven or eight times larger than his lower case "a" or "r". The right slant of his capitalization remained very consistent. The beginning formation of the "H" resembled an angled number 2, with the second half of the letter forming a loop that could vary both in width and length. The "a" in Harry always began at the top of the letter and may show some space between the loop and the stem. The descender of the "y" could vary in length, often extending to the end of the finishing strokes of the capitalized "H"s. The "a" in Heilmann typically didn't close, and occasionally could vary in formation from the "a" in Harry by becoming a two-looped construction. The capitalized "H"s, the descender of the "y" and the letter "l", should all be similar in slant.

Heilmann was obliging to signature requests and examples of his signature have periodically surfaced in the market.

Availability: Average
Demand: Above average

Cut signature	$175
Single-signature baseball	$1,400
3x5" index card	$250
Photograph/baseball card	$400
HOF plaque postcard	Impossible
Perez-Steele postcard	Impossible

Billy Herman

William Jennings Bryan Herman
(July 7, 1909-   )

Herman ended his career with a lifetime batting average of .304 that included 2,345 hits. Considered one of the smartest men to play the game, his baseball knowledge was instinctive.

Commonly signing "Billy Herman", his signature has varied in character formation and size throughout his life. Characteristic signature breaks fall between the "B" and the "i" in Billy, also between the "m" and the "a" in Herman. Herman uses a distinct two-stroke construction for the letter "B" in Billy that resembles a "13" configuration. The second stroke of the "B" may or may not connect to the first. The "ill" can vary in slant, and the second "l" will typically be a bit larger than the first in height. The "y" remained fairly consistent with only a straight line as a descender. The "H" in Herman is typically a two-stroke construction, however it can occasionally exhibit a third stroke. The "erm" will vary a bit in size, with the "e" typically the largest of the three. The "an" configuration has been fairly consistent, with the "a" commonly open on the top.

Herman has been a gracious signer for years, and as a result remains very popular among collectors.

Availability: Plentiful
Demand: Little

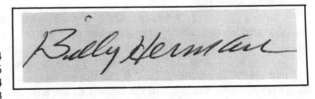

Cut signature	$4
Single-signature baseball	$16
3x5" index card	$4
Photograph/baseball card	$13
HOF plaque postcard	$9
Perez-Steele postcard	$35

Harry Hooper

Harry Bartholomew Hooper
(Aug. 24, 1887-Dec. 18, 1974)

Hooper batted .281 over his lifetime that included 2,466 hits. As their lead-off hitter, he helped the Red Sox to the World Series four times — 1912, 1915, 1916 and 1918.

Commonly signing "Harry Hooper", his signature varied significantly in character formation and letter spacing. A consistent signature break fell between the "H" and the "a" in Harry. The "H"in Harry was typically a two-stroke formation, but did occasionally alter to a single stroke. The "arry" varied in letter spacing and the descender of the "y" could vary in size. The "H" in Hooper was typically a single-stroke version which could resemble a capitalized "A". The "o"s could differ in both size and character formation. The descender of the "p" varied in formation and the loop of the letter was typically open. The "er" remained relatively consistent with little flamboyance in the ending stroke. Hooper's later signatures often exhibited typical aging characteristics.

Hooper was obliging to autograph requests and collectors should find his signature fairly accessible through autograph dealers.

Availability: Above average
Demand: Average

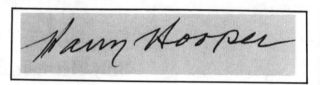

Cut signature	$12
Single-signature baseball	$300
3x5" index card	$25
Photograph/baseball card	$45
HOF plaque postcard	$55
Perez-Steele postcard	Impossible

Rogers Hornsby

Rogers Hornsby
(April 27, 1896-Jan. 5, 1963)

"Rajah" ended his career with a lifetime batting average of .358, that included 2,930 hits. A seven-time National League batting champion, he hit over .400 three full seasons. Often considered the greatest right-handed hitter of all-time, "Rog" could also hit for power with 301 lifetime home runs.

Hornsby's signature varied in character formation, size and slant during his lifetime. Additionally, his signature breaks were also inconsistent, particularily in his last name which could vary between two breaks or none. The more consistent breaks were between the "R" and the "o" or "o" and the "g" in Rogers, also occasionally between the "H" and the "o" or "n" and the "s" in Hornsby. The "R" in Rogers was relatively consistent in character formation, only showing variation in the ending stroke and the size of the letter. The "g" may be open or closed at the top loop of the letter and the descender could vary in length. The flamboyant ending stroke of the "s" could vary in length and in some cases may even reach the height of the "R" in Rogers. The "H" was common in two character formations. In older examples the first stroke of the letter could resemble an "F", while in later versions it was simplified to resemble a formation similar to the number 7. The second stroke of the "H" remained relatively consistent in formation, and always exceeded the first stroke in height. It was common for the ascender of the second stroke of the "H" to extend as far as the "r" in Hornsby. The "orn" appeared slightly more condensed in earlier versions of his signature with some modification in character form. The "sby" remained consistent, except for the flamboyant ending stroke of the "y"s descender that could extent below his entire last name.

Hornsby was generally obliging to autograph requests and samples of his signature surface periodically in the market.

Availability: Average
Demand: Above average

Cut signature	$75
Single-signature baseball	$800
3x5" index card	$110
Photograph/baseball card	$250
HOF plaque postcard	$450
Perez-Steele postcard	Impossible

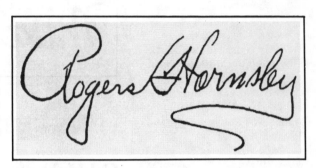

Waite Hoyt

Waite Charles Hoyt
(Sept. 9, 1899-Aug. 25, 1984)

Hoyt ended his career with 237 wins at an ERA of 3.59. In seven World Series appearances he pitched 83⅔ innings at an ERA of 1.83. In 1927 he compiled a record of 22 wins and only seven loses at an ERA of 2.63.

Commonly signing "Waite C. Hoyt", his signature varied only slightly during his career. Minor alterations in both size and flamboyance were exhibited by his autograph. Common signature breaks were between the "W" and the "a" in Waite, also between the "y" and the "t" in Hoyt. Both of these signature breaks were inconsistent, particularly the "W" and the "a" separation. Older examples will exhibit a larger bottom loop construction in the "W", an unusually large middle initial that could be twice the size of the "W", and greater flamboyance to the character formation in the "H" in Hoyt. The "a" in Waite increased in size over the years until it was equal to the height of the "t". Hoyt's large middle initial, was the most prominent feature of his early signature. His middle initial of "C", did however become much more compact with age. The "H" was always a two-stroke formation, with the second stroke exceeding the height of the first. The second stroke of the "H" could show a slight right curvature on the top, that disappeared with age. The "o" may or may not close on the top and the "t" could vary in size and character formation.

Hoyt was a gracious and prolific signer. Collectors were often thrilled to receive a lengthy response from their autograph requests. Always a gentleman, his courtesy toward collectors is missed by everyone who had an opportunity to correspond with him.

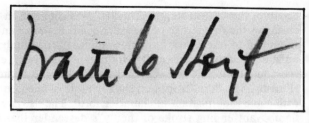

Cut signature	$6
Single-signature baseball	$115
3x5" index card	$16
Photograph/baseball card	$40
HOF plaque postcard	$30
Perez-Steele postcard	$550

Cal Hubbard

Robert Cal Hubbard
(Oct. 31, 1900-Oct. 16, 1977)

Big Cal stood 6'2½" and 268 pounds, an authoritative figure who is the only man to be inducted into both the football and baseball Hall of Fame. He umpired three All-Star games and four World Series, during his American League service fom 1936-1951.

Commonly signing "Cal Hubbard" or "Robert Cal Hubbard", his signature varied moderately during his lifetime. The only consistent signature break was between the "C" and the "a" in Cal. The "R" varied only slightly in character formation and formation and size. The "o" in Robert may or may not be closed on the top of the letter. The "b"s in both Robert and Hubbard commonly varied in slant, height or width. The "t" in Robert was typically crossed by the finishing stroke of the letter. The "C" varied both in size and formation, although it was always the smallest of the capitalized letters. The "a" may or may not close on the top of the letter and the "l" could vary in size, at time resembling an "e". The formation of the "H" was unique, often looking more like and "A", and was typically the largest letter in his signature. The "d" could change in size, with the finishing stroke variable in flamboyance.

Hubbard was very responsive to autograph requests and collectors should find his signature accessible through autograph dealers or auction houses.

Availability: Above average
Demand: Average

Cut signature	$22
Single-signature baseball	$370
3x5" index card	$45
Photograph/baseball card	$100
HOF plaque postcard	$300
Perez-Steele postcard	Impossible

Carl Hubbell

Carl Owen Hubbell
(June 22, 1903-Nov. 21, 1988)

"King Carl" won 253 games during his career while posting an ERA of 2.97 and a winning percentage of .622. During his 16 years with the Giants he led the National League three times in both wins and ERA. In three World Series performances with the Giants he pitched 50⅓ innings at an ERA of 1.79.

Commonly signing "Carl Hubbell", his signature varied dramatically during his lifetime, primarily due to deteriorating health. In early signature samples breaks were common between the "C" and the "a" in Carl, also between the "H" and the "u", and "b" and the "e" in Hubbell. The "C" could vary radically in character formation, in earlier examples often even resembling an "L" at times. Compressed in appearance, his signature's ascenders were often three or four times the height of the other lower case letters. The "a" in Carl may or may not be closed, also the "l" typically was larger in height than the two main strokes of the "H" in Hubbell. The "H" was a three-stroke formation with the middle slash cutting through his signature at a steep left slant. Both the "b"s and the "l"s in Hubbell will typically vary in size, however maintaining similar slants. His earlier signature samples will have a characteristic right slant.

By the end of the 1970s deteriorating health had dramatically altered his signature. A now left-slanted signature began to exhibit numerous aging characteristics, such as rough strokes, ink deposition and altered character formations. The "C" was most unpredictable in formation showing various degrees of roundness. The "a" could often resemble a "u", with the "rl"'s downward formation commonly not level with the signature's base line. The only two consistent breaks that were notable in later versions of his signature were between the "C" and the "a" in Carl and between the "H", and the "u" in Hubbell. The "H" was consistent as a three-stroke formation, but unpredictable in slant and size. The "b"s and "l"s varied in slant and character formation. The ending stroke of Hubbell was usually a simple downward continuation from the "l".

Hubbell signatures generated during the final years of his life can be difficult to authenticate. Collectors should be wary of any older style Hubbell signatures adorning material printed after 1980. Early Hubbell autographs will be far easier to authenticate because of the lack of aging characteristics. Fortunately, Hubbell was a prolific signer and collectors should have little trouble acquiring a genuine example.

Availability: Plentiful
Demand: Little

Cut signature	$5
Single-signature baseball	$60
3x5" index card	$9
Photograph/baseball card	$20
HOF plaque postcard	$20
Perez-Steele postcard	$135

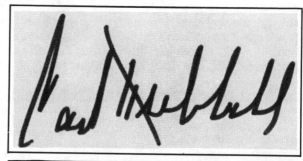

Miller Huggins

Miller James Huggins
(March 27, 1879-Sept. 25, 1929)

Huggins played 13 years in the National League establishing himself as a good second basemen, however it is his managerial skills that brought him greatest acclaim. Huggins took the New York Yankees to the World Series six times during the Twenties.

Commonly signing "Miller J. Huggins" or "M.J. Huggins", his signature varied in slant, capitalization and character formation during his lifetime. There were no consistent signature breaks exhibited in his autograph. The "M" in Miller could vary at the beginning of the letter formation, occasionally creating a small loop or hook prior to the first part of the letter. The "M" often varied in size, however the slant was usually consistent with the other letters. Character formation in both the "l"s and the "g"s was fairly consistent. The "H" in Huggins could vary from a single-stroke style, similar to that of Cal Hubbard, to a two-stroke, more traditional, style. The "u" and the "ins" remained relatively consistent. The "J" may or may not connect to the "H" in Huggins. The "uggins" is a good comparison point for authenticators as it exhibited no radical variations.

Huggins was generally a good signer, his sudden illness and death from blood poisoning shocked the entire baseball community. Death at such an early age certainly contributes to the scarcity of his signature, however examples do occasionally surface in the market.

Availability: Limited
Demand: Above average

Cut signature	$800
Single-signature baseball	$3,250
3x5" index card	$950
Photograph/baseball card	$1,500
HOF plaque postcard	Impossible
Perez-Steele postcard	Impossible

172

Catfish Hunter

James Augustus Hunter
(April 18, 1946-   )

"Catfish" won 224 games, struckout 2,012, posted 42 shutouts at an ERA of 3.26 and retired at the age of 33. The 1974 Cy Young award winner posted a 5-3 record in 12 World Series games.

Commonly signing "Jim Catfish Hunter", his signature has varied in both size and character formation. The only consistent signature break has been between the "J" and the "i" in Jim. The "J" in Jim has always been the dominant character in his signature with both the ascender and the descender commonly varying in size. The top of the "J" will typically be the highest point of his signature and the descender of the letter will be the lowest. The "im" can vary in character spacing, but has remained relatively consistent in character formation. The "C" in Catfish can vary in character formation, particularly in the beginning of the letter that may open with a loop or hooked stroke. The ascender of the "t" is unusually large, often equal to the height of the "h". The crossing of the "t" is a single stroke that can begin at the "a" and extend to the "h" in Catfish. The "fis" remained relatively consistent with only the descender of the "f" varying in width. The "h", which typically resembles an "l", can vary in character formation and the "i" can be dotted above the "s". Earlier examples of his signature will show greater character definition in his entire last name, in great contrast to his current autograph where only the "H", "t" and "e" are recognizable. The "H" has always been a two-stroke formation, however earlier examples show variation in the opening of the first stroke, which may begin with a loop or an additional line. The loop that crosses the "H" formation shows greater flamboyance in later signature examples. The ascender of the "t" can vary in both height and width, with the "n" often an unrecognizable formation. Hunter is generally a good signer, however mail requests can have unpredictable results.

Availability: Plentiful
Demand: Little

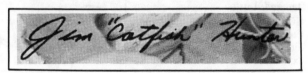

Cut signature	$3
Single-signature baseball	$18
3x5" index card	$5
Photograph/baseball card	$11
HOF plaque postcard	$10
Perez-Steele postcard	$30

Monte Irvin

Monford Merrill Irvin
(Feb. 25, 1919-   )

Irvin spent 11 years in the Negro Leagues where he maintained star status as a slugger. While with the Newark Eagles in 1946, he won the league's batting title. From 1949 to 1956 he played 764 major league games, primarily with the New York Giants, but also with the Chicago Cubs, contributing to two Giants World Series contests.

Commonly signing "Monte Irvin" his signature has shown variation in capitalization, size and character formation. His signature breaks are inconsistent in frequency, however consistent in placement, falling between the "M" and the "o" in Monte, also between the "I" and the "r" in Irvin. During his playing days he commonly signed "Monford Monty Irvin", before eventually dropping the Monford and modifying the spelling of Monte. The "M" has remained relatively consistent in character formation, except for the addition of a hooked portion before the first downward stroke. The first downward stroke of the "M" in earlier examples did not loop, and the "t" in Monty was much larger in both height and width. The "I" in Irvin has always been inconsistent in character formation, and should not be considered as a good comparison point for judgement in authenticity. The "r" in Irvin can also vary, however the "vin" has been relatively consistent throughout his life. The ending stroke in Irvin can vary, but typically it is a short simple line. The capitalization in later examples his signature is usually much larger, often two or three times the height of the lower case letters.

Irvin has been a responsive signer and collectors should find the acquisition of his autograph fairly easy.

Availability: Plentiful
Demand: Little

Cut signature	$3
Single-signature baseball	$18
3x5" index card	$5
Photograph/baseball card	$13
HOF plaque postcard	$9
Perez-Steele postcard	$25

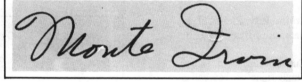

Travis Jackson

Travis Calvin Jackson
(Nov. 2, 1903-July 27, 1987)

"Stonewall" was an exceptional fielder who showed great depth in the Giant infield from 1933 to 1936. Travis batted .291 during a career which included six years of .300-plus baseball.

Typically signing "Travis Jackson" or "Travis C. Jackson", his signature varied in character size, slant and formation during his lifetime. Signature breaks were common between the "T" and the "r" in Travis, also between the "J" and the "a" in Jackson. Earlier examples, those signed during his playing days, will also exhibit a break between the "r" and the "a" in Travis, and the "J" may connect to the "a" in Jackson. The "T" has commonly been a two-stroke formation, with the top of the letter usually consisting of a single loop crossing that could include a smaller loop at the end of the stroke. The "r" character formation in Travis was unique, and makes a good comparison point for authenticators. The first stroke of the "r" may or may not intersect the stem of the "T". The "r" can vary in width and the "a" in Travis may or may not close on the top of the letter. The "v" often resembled a "u" and the "is" could vary in both slant and size. The "s" may or may not close on the bottom. His middle initial of "C" could vary a bit in formation, however was commonly small in size, equal in height to the "r" in Travis. The "J" could vary in size with some samples being four to five times larger than the "a" in Jackson. The "J" may also vary in slant and character formation, with both the beginning and ending strokes possibly intersecting each other or the stem of the letter. The "ack" remained fairly consistent, although both the height and width of the "k" could vary. The "k" had a unique looped formation that makes a good comparison point for authenticators. Some samples of his signature may have the "s" excluded from Jackson, however it is typically intertwined with the "o". The "o" can change in formation and may or may not close at the top of the letter.

Jackson was a prolific signer and collectors should find the acquisition of his signature fairly easy.

Availability: Plentiful
Demand: Little

Cut signature	$7
Single-signature baseball	$70
3x5" index card	$15
Photograph/baseball card	$25
HOF plaque postcard	$20
Perez-Steele postcard	$200

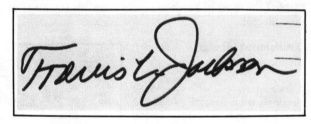

Hugh Jennings

Hugh Ambrose Jennings
(April 2, 1869-Feb. 1, 1928)

Jennings ended his career with a batting average over .310 which included over 1,500 hits, most of which came with the old Baltimore Orioles who dominated the National League in the 1890s. Following his playing days, Jennings established himself as a good manager and coach with both Detroit and the New York Giants. Upon his retirement he took advantage of his Cornell law degree and went into practice.

Commonly signing "H.A. Jennings" or "Hugh Jennings", his signature varied in slant, size and character formation during his lifetime. The relatively few samples I have seen exhibit a break between the "H" and the "u" in Hugh, also between the "J" and the "e" in Jennings. The "H" typically began from the top of the letter with a small loop which then descended to construct a formation similar to the number "2", before ascending and forming a "C" configuration. At times the uniquely formed "H" resembled a "W". The "u" began with a small upward stroke from the signature's base line and the "g" was often unpredictable in it's formation. The "g" is often left open at the top and will vary in the size of its descender. The ascender of the "h" often equalled or exceeded capitalization height and the loop of the letter was typically pointed. On rare occasions Jennings may have connected the "h" in Hugh to the "J" in his last name, however typically a break existed.

The flamboyant "J" in Jennings often had a descending loop that was twice the size of its ascender. The right slant of the stem of the "h" and the "J" should be nearly identical. Jennings used a stylized "e" that could vary in size and was often twice the size of the "n"s in Jennings. The "n"s in Jennings were not very well defined and often nearly identical in formation to the "i". The "g" in Jennings was typically larger than the "g" in Hugh and showed much greater flamboyance. The flamboyant finishing stroke following the "g" was unpredictable in formation.

The well-educated Jennings was a responsive signer and a fairly prolific writer. Jennings commonly authorized secretarial signatures which can be mistaken for his authentic autograph. Like most of baseball's early stars, his signature remains a challenging acquisition for the collector.

Availability: Limited
Demand: Strong

Cut signature	$850
Single-signature baseball	$3,250
3x5" index card	$1,550
Photograph/baseball card	$2,100
HOF plaque postcard	Impossible
Perez-Steele postcard	Impossible

Ban Johnson

Byron Bancroft Johnson
(Jan. 6, 1865-March 28, 1931)

Johnson organized the American League and was its first president from its inception in 1900 until 1927. He was instrumental in eliminating unethical behavior and supported strict jurisdiction by his umpires. Johnson helped drive the National Agreement that brought both the American and National Leagues together.

Commonly signing "Ban Johnson" or "B.B. Johnson", his signature varied considerably in character formation and size. Johson's signature typically exhibited no signature breaks. Prior to 1910, signature examples signed "Ban Johnson", were in a style that was traditional in appearance with normal character spacing. The rounded "B" in Ban was wider than later versions, equivalent to about four lower case letter spaces. The shape of the "B" also made a rather large loop in the middle of the character. The "a" may or may not be closed on the top of the letter and the "n" could resemble a "w", because of an extended ending stroke that connected to the "J". The "J" was inconsistent in both ascender and descender size, however the formation remained relatively the same. The "o" seldom closed and the "h" usually had a large ascender that could equal or exceed the height of the "B" in Ban. The right slant of the "h" usually allowed the ascender of the letter to extend above the "n" in Johnson. The "son" could vary a bit in size and formation.

Post-1910 signatures are typically his condensed "B.B. Johnson" format. The capitalization in this style signature is so intertwined that it is often difficult to recognize the individual letters. His entire signature was a single stroke, with letters such as the "J" only being recognizable by its descender. The "o" varied considerably in formation and the ascender of the "h" was often so flamboyant that it would extend well beyond the character height of both the "B"s. The "on" commonly slanted downward at the end of his signatures, probably attributable to the laborious task of signing so much documentation.

Illness prompted Johnson to resign on Oct. 17, 1927. He never seemed to fully recover and during the final years of his life his health had deteriorated so significantly that he was almost blind. As a baseball executive he signed numerous pieces of documentation, some of which has found its way to the autograph market.

Availability: Average
Demand: Average

Cut signature	$160
Single-signature baseball	$1,375
3x5" index card	$235
Photograph/baseball card	$535
HOF plaque postcard	Impossible
Perez-Steele postcard	Impossible

Walter Johnson

Walter Perry Johnson
(Nov. 6, 1887-Dec. 10, 1946)

The "Big Train" played for 21 years in the major leagues, all with the Washington Senators, compiling 416 wins, 3,508 strikeouts and 110 shutouts. In 1913 he went 36-7, with an ERA of 1.09 and hurled 11 shutouts.

Commonly signing "Walter Johnson", his signature varied in character formation, slant and size. The only consistent signature break was between the "W" and the "a" in Walter. The "W" could vary in size, and was not always symmetrical in formation. The "alter" was fairly consistent throughout his lifetime only showing slight variation in character width. The "t" was unusually large, often equaling or exceeding the height of the "l". The crossing of the "t" could vary in length and may extend as far as the "r" in Walter. Ironically, I have rarely seen the crossing of the "t" intersect any other letter. The "a", "e" and "r" could all vary in size. The "J" in Johnson exhibited the greatest degree of change in character formation. The descender of the "J" was typically smaller in both height and width when compared to the ascender. The beginning stroke of the "J" in Johnson typically began below the base line of the signature. The "o" may have a slight opening to it, and the ascender of the "h" was often the highest point in his signature. The "nson" varied in size, with the ending stroke unpredictable in direction.

Johnson was extremely popular and considered the fastest pitcher of his day. He was a responsive signer until a near fatal stroke left him partially paralyzed months before his death in 1946. Samples of his signature do surface periodically in the market.

Availability: Limited
Demand: Strong

Cut signature	$260
Single-signature baseball	$2,000
3x5" index card	$425
Photograph/baseball card	$900
HOF plaque postcard	Unknown
Perez-Steele postcard	Impossible

Judy Johnson

William Julius Johnson
(Oct. 26, 1899-June 13, 1989)

Johnson played third base in the Negro Leagues from 1923-1937, and was considered an exceptional fielder, as well as keen hitter. Batting over .300 most of his career, he helped Hilldale capture three pennants in a row (1923-1925) and the 1935 Pittsburgh Crawfords win the championship. Following his playing days he became a scout and instructor for the Philadelphia A's.

Commonly signing "Judy Johnson", his signature varied in character formation and size during his lifetime. Common signature breaks occurred between the "J" and the "u" in Judy, also between the "J" and the "o", and the "s" and the "o" in Johnson. The capitalized "J" was typically a two-stroke formation in later examples, and a single-stroke construction in earlier autographs. Occasionally, in later examples, he would revert back to the single-stroke "J". The construction of the "J" was typically unique in character formation, thus a good reference point for authenticators. Both the ascender and the descender of the "J" could vary in size, with finishing strokes often at different lengths. The "u" traditionally began with an extended upward stroke from below the signature's base line, that may or may not intersect the stem of the "J". The "d" may or may not be closed at the loop and I have seen a two-stroke variation of this character, although it was not common in this form. The descender of the "y" was typically a single line that could extend to the level of the descender of the capitalized letter "J". The "o" may or may not close at the top and always connects to the top loop of the "h". Worth noting is an occasional two-stroke variation in the "h", typically not noticeable without magnification. The ascender of the "h" can vary in both slant and width. The "ns" in Johnson could slightly vary in character formation, with the "s" either opened or closed on the bottom. The last "o" in Johnson was often a bit larger in height than the preceding "s", with the ending stroke varying in flamboyance.

Despite deteriorating health during the last few years of his life, Johnson was still relatively responsive to autograph requests. Autographs signed during the late 1980s can vary radically and will, in time, no doubt be difficult to authenticate. He was a prolific signer and collectors should find his autograph an easy acquisition. He was always a quiet and well respected gentleman and a favorite among collectors.

Availability: Plentiful
Demand: Little

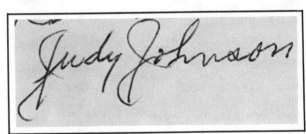

Cut signature	$7
Single-signature baseball	$35
3x5" index card	$8
Photograph/baseball card	$18
HOF plaque postcard	$15
Perez-Steele postcard	$70

Addie Joss

Adrian Joss
(April 12, 1880-April 14, 1911)

Joss pitched for the Cleveland Indians from 1902-1910, posting 160 career victories and 46 shutouts. He won 20 or more games four seasons in a row and in 1907 his 27 victories led the American League.

Commonly signing "Adrian Joss", "A. Joss" and "Addie Joss", his signature showed variation in character formation, size, and slant. The few samples I have seen exhibit a break between the "A" and the "d" in Adrian or Addie. The "A" in Addie typically began with a long upward stroke which originated from the signature's base line, before forming an enlarged lower case capitalized version of the letter. The "J" typically begins slightly above the signature's base line and often exceeds the height of the "A". The ascender of the "J" varies in size, however is typically smaller than the letter's descender. The "o" is typically closed and due to the significant right slant of the "J", may fall completely beneath the capitalized letter's ascender. The "s" can vary in size and may or may not be closed at the bottom of the letter. It is difficult, based on such a limited sampling, to determine the consistency of these characteristics throughout Joss' short life. Little is known about his signature habits during the last few years of his life, however it is speculated that variations of his autograph occurred due to his failing health.

Joss was taken ill while in training camp in 1911, and asked to return to his home in Toledo. He died of tubercular meningitis at the young age of 31. His early death contributes greatly to the scarcity of his signature, and few have turned up over the years in the market. A highly sought autograph, collectors should find the acquisiton of his signature a significant challenge.

Availability: Scarce
Demand: Strong

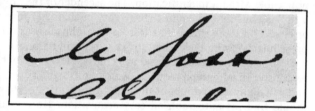

Cut signature	$1,925
Single-signature baseball	$4,500
3x5" index card	$2,700
Photograph/baseball card	$4,000
HOF plaque postcard	Impossible
Perez-Steele postcard	Impossible

Al Kaline

Albert William Kaline
(Dec. 19, 1934-   )

On Sept. 24, 1974, Al Kaline hit his 3,000th hit. He played his entire career in Detroit from 1953-1974, and became the youngest player, at the age of 20, to win a batting title. He socked 399 home runs, and had 242 consecutive errorless games in the outfield from 1970-1972.

Commonly signing "Al Kaline", his signature has exhibited variation in character formation and size. Later examples of his signature typically have no breaks, however earlier versions will break between the "K" and the "a" in Kaline. The "A" has been consistent, with only the "l" in Al showing variation in size. With age the "K" has varied in character formation, showing greater flamboyance in the second stroke of the letter. Kaline will typically show a rounded change in direction, at the middle of the stem, while making the second stroke of the "k". The "l" can vary in both height and width. Later Kaline examples seem to show greater space between the "n" and the "e" in Kaline, in comparison to earlier examples. Generally speaking his signature has shown only minor variation.

Kaline is an obliging signer, however mail requests have typically been unpredictable. Collectors may find the best form of acquisition is via his attendance at a local baseball card show.

Availability: Plentiful
Demand: Little

Cut signature	$3
Single-signature baseball	$18
3x5" index card	$6
Photograph/baseball card	$11
HOF plaque postcard	$9
Perez-Steele postcard	$30

Tim Keefe

Timothy John Keefe
(Jan. 1, 1857-April 23, 1933)

Keefe was a star during the evolution of the game, pitching over 5,000 innings and winning over 340 games at a percentage above .605. This right-hander who pioneered the change of pace delivery, had a career 40 shutouts. Keefe recorded 19 straight victories in 1888 to lead the Giants to the pennant.

Commonly signing "Tim Keefe", his signature varied in character formation, slant and size during his lifetime. The only consistent break in his signature was between the "T" and the "i" in Tim. The "T" was a two-stroke formation with the stem varying in height. The top of the "T" could vary in the length of the stroke, with earlier examples having it extending past the "m" in Tim. The loop at the beginning of the top of the stroke of the "T", may or may not close. The "im" could vary in roundness of the character formation and may show a slight hook to the beginning or ending of the stroke. The "K" was a two-stroke formation that varied in flamboyance with age, becoming much more conservative. The first stroke of the "K" could extend from the highest to the lowest point in his signature. The right slant of the first stroke of the "K" decreased with age, as did the letter's size. The second stroke of the "K" was flamboyant in earlier versions and much stiffer with later examples. The "f" could vary in both the length and width of the descender, but typically did not close the bottom loop. The final "e" in Keefe could also vary in size. Keefe's handwriting is recognizable by the unique formations of some of his lower case letters, "p" for example, that typically had extended ascender formations.

Keefe was an obliging signer in his day, but remains a fairly difficult signature to acquire. Autographs signed later in his life show typical aging characteristics and may be a bit more difficult to authenticate.

Availability: Scarce
Demand: Strong

Cut signature	$1,275
Single-signature baseball	$4,000
3x5" index card	$2,200
Photograph/baseball card	$3,000
HOF plaque postcard	Impossible
Perez-Steele postcard	Impossible

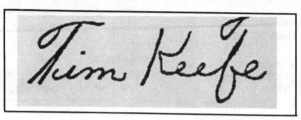

Wee Willie Keeler

Willaim Henry Keeler
(March 3, 1872-Jan. 1, 1923)

Keeler, famed for his "Hit'em where they ain't" style, was perhaps baseball's most skilled batsman, finishing his career with over 2,900 hits in over 8,500 at bats, for an average of .345. In 1897, he hit a career milestone of .432 that included 243 hits and over 60 stolen bases. This two-time batting champion played for a number of teams before his retirement in 1911.

Commonly signing "Willie Keeler" or "Wm. H. Keeler", his signature varied primarily in character formation. A consistent signature break falls between the "W" and the "i" in Willie, also occasionally between the "K" and the "e" in Keeler. The "W" varied in formation from a rounded, traditionally constructed letter, to a configuration that resembled a "JV". The "illie" varied in both slant and size, with the ascenders of the "l"s typically reaching the height of the "W" in Willie. Keeler's middle intial of "H" was typically connected to the first stroke of the "K", which was a two-stroke construction. The second stroke of the "K", particularilly in earlier examples, was very flamboyant. This stroke could extend above the second "e" and below the "l" in Keeler. The "eeler" remained relatively consistent, however the "r" could vary in character formation and usually included an extended ending stroke.

Keeler was obliging to autograph requests, but like so many of basball's pioneer has had few samples of his signature ever surface in the autograph market. Collectors should find the acquisition of his signature a real challenge.

Availability: Limited
Demand: Strong

Cut signature	$1,350
Single-signature baseball	$3,875
3x5" index card	$2,650
Photograph/baseball card	$3,350
HOF plaque postcard	Impossible
Perez-Steele postcard	Impossible

George Kell

George Clyde Kell
(Aug. 23, 1922-   )

During his career of 15 years Kell stroked 2,054 hits for an average of .306. He batted over .300 nine times and won the American League batting title in 1949. The game's premier third baseman of the 1940s and 1950s, he led the American League in fielding percentage seven times, assists four times and putouts and double plays twice.

Commonly signing "George Kell", his signature has varied in slant and character formation. Signature breaks occur between the "G" and the "e" in George, also between the "K" and the "e" in Kell. The "G" is typically very large, about five or six times the size of the "e" in George. Earlier examples will show an increased right slant to his signature. The "g" can vary in both descender length and width, with earlier versions typically smaller. The "K" is a two-stroke construction that consists of a short first stroke, intersected by a separate flamboyant stroke that forms the rest of the character. In earlier examples the first loop of the second stroke in the "K" can extend as far as the second "l" in Kell. Later Kell signatures seem to show less flamboyance in the "K". The "ell" typically shows only slight variation in size. In comparison to his fellow inductees, his signature has shown little variation.

Kell's responsiveness to autograph requests has made him very poular with baseball fans. He has always been a prolific signer and collectors should have little trouble acquiring his autograph.

Availability: Plentiful
Demand: Little

Cut signature	$3
Single-signature baseball	$17
3x5" index card	$5
Photograph/baseball card	$11
HOF plaque postcard	$9
Perez-Steele postcard	$25

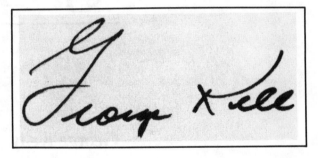

Joe Kelley

Joseph James Kelley
(Dec. 9, 1871-Aug. 14, 1943)

Kelley compiled over 2,240 hits, over 440 stolen bases and batted well above .300 during his 17-year career. In 1896 he stole over 80 bases while hitting above .360 for Baltimore. Kelley batted over .300 for 11 consecutive years with a career high .393 in 1894. Following his playing years he scouted and coached for a number of ballclubs, including Toronto and the New York Yankees.

Commonly signing "Joe Kelley" or "Joe J. Kelley", his signature exhibited changes in character formation and flamboyance during his lifetime. A consistent signature break occurred between the "l" and the "e" in Kelley and on occasion between the "J" and the "o" in Joe. His slightly left-slanted signature could vary in flamboyance. The "J" in Joe could vary in size, however the descender was typically larger than the looped ascender. The "e" is very notable in character formation and is an excellent reference point for authenticators. The last "e" in Kelley will typically vary in formation from the preceding "e"s. The "e" at the end of Joe typically connects to the next capitalized letter and forms another noteworthy reference point for authenticators. The second stroke of the two-stroke "K" formation, typically extends far enough to be the highest point in his signature. The "l"s will vary a bit in slant with the finishing stroke of the second "l" possibly intersecting the character's stem. The "y" can vary both in flamboyance and size.

Joe was the last survivor of the old Orioles, and a responsive signer. Unfortuantely for collectors, few of his signatures ever surface in the autograph market.

Availability: Limited
Demand: Strong

Cut signature	$1,025
Single-signature baseball	$4,675
3x5" index card	$1,900
Photograph/baseball card	$2,875
HOF plaque postcard	Impossible
Perez-Steele postcard	Impossible

George Kelly

George Lange Kelly
(Sept. 10, 1895-Oct. 13, 1984)

"Highpockets" batted a career .297 with 1,778 hits and over 1,000 RBIs. Kelly hit seven home runs in six consecutive games in 1924, and swatted homers in three consecutive innings in 1923. He set numerous league records for first baseman and played on four different National League teams.

Commonly signing "George L. Kelly", his signature varied in character formation during his lifetime. There were no consistent signature breaks exhibited in his autograph. The "G" commonly varied in size, with earlier examples showing a slight increase in slant. Kelly's lower case letters had a tendency to be large in size, and the "e" in George could often reach the second pinnacle of the "G" in George. The "o" was a two-looped formation that typically closed. The "g" in George could often looked like a "y", showing little formation in the top loop. The "g" could vary in descender width, but not significantly in length. The "L" was fairly consistent, with only slight variation in the size of the character's loops. The "K" was a two-stroke construction that showed little variation. Characteristic of the second stroke of the "K" was a small loop that joined the arms of the letter. This stroke does not typically intersect the first stroke of the "K". The "ell" could vary a bit in both height and width. The top formation of the "y" may or may not be recognizable, with the descender varying a bit in width. Kelly commonly placed a period after the "L" and also after the "y" in Kelly.

Kelly was very responsive to autograph requests and collectors were often treated to congenial personalized responses. Collectors who had an opportunity to correspond with George Kelly were never disappointed. A prolific signer, his autograph should be a fairly easy acquisition.

Availability: Plentiful
Demand: Little

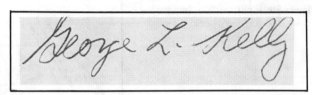

Cut signature	$7
Single-signature baseball	$80
3x5" index card	$13
Photograph/baseball card	$20
HOF plaque postcard	$25
Perez-Steele postcard	$325

Mike Kelly

Michael Joseph Kelly
(Dec. 31, 1857-Nov. 8, 1894)

"King" Kelly stroked over 1,800 hits while compiling a lifetime batting average of over .300. An extremely popular individual with a variety of talents, Kelly was an actor, author, and a ballplayer. Off the field the flamboyant Kelly lived it up, and had a reputation as a free spender. Kelly was one of baseball's first idols, so popular in fact that he was made the subject of a song, "Slide, Kelly, Slide!".

Commonly signing "M. J. Kelly" or "Mike Kelly", his signature varied considerably throughout his lifetime in both character formation and slant. A consistent signature break can be fond between the "K" and the "e" in Kelly. The capitalization in his signature varied from a condensed elongated variation to a wider, more rounded appearance. When he signed "M.J. Kelly", the "M" may or may not attach to the "J". The "J" varied in flamboyance, with earlier signatures having descenders of great length. The beginning stroke of the letter "J", which commonly intersected the stem, was fairly consistent in formation. The "K" was unpredictable in style, but was typically a two-stroke construction. The second stroke of the "K" could exhibit an elaborate formation that resembled an "E" in style. The "K" will commonly break with the "e", however I have seen examples where they have been connected. The "ell" will vary in both height and width, with the "y" variable in flamboyance.

His popularity made him subject to numerous autograph requests, and although he died at the young age of 36, his signatures do occasionally surface in the market. Improvidence led to poverty during the final years of his life and signatures originating during this time period have a tendency to be a bit erratic in formation.

Availability: Scarce
Demand: Strong

Cut signature	$2,100
Single-signature baseball	$3,000
3x5" index card	$3,500
Photograph/baseball card	$5,250
HOF plaque postcard	Impossible
Perez-Steele postcard	Impossible

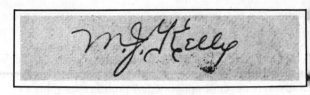

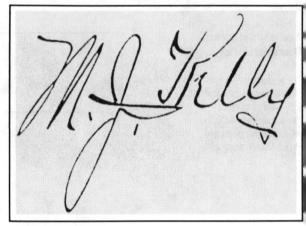

Harmon Killebrew

Harmon Clayton Killebrew
(June 29, 1936-   )

Killebrew clouted 573 home runs and batted .256 during his 22 seasons in the major leagues. Known most for his power, Killebrew won or shared six American League home run titles and belted 40 or more homers in eight seasons. The 1969 Most Valuable Player appeared in 11 All-Star games.

Commonly signing "Harmon Killebrew", his signature has slightly varied in character formation and size. Consistent signature breaks fall between the "H" and the "a" in Harmon, also between the "K" and the "i" in Killebrew. The two-stroke construction of the "H" can vary slightly in the formation of the top loop of the first stroke and the bottom loop which crosses the letter, and the "r" can resemble a "u". Both the "m" and the "n" in Harmon can occasionally be illegible as letters. The two-stroke formation of the "K" has increased in flamboyance over the years, with the long top arm of the second stroke commonly extending to the "b" or possibly the "w" in Killebrew. The "l"s vary in both height and width, and seem to have decreased in size over the years. The ascender of the "b" is typically larger in height than the "l"s in Killebrew. The "rew" is somewhat unpredictable in formation, particularly in older examples where only one of the three letters may be distinguishable.

Killebrew has been an obliging signer, however mail requests can be a bit inconsistent. Collectors should find his signature an easy acquisition.

Availability: Plentiful
Demand: Little

Cut signature	$3
Single-signature baseball	$20
3x5" index card	$5
Photograph/baseball card	$14
HOF plaque postcard	$11
Perez-Steele postcard	$25

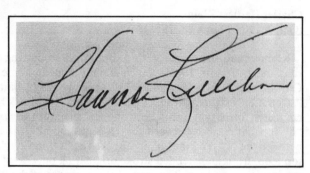

Ralph Kiner

Ralph McPherran Kiner
(Oct. 27, 1922-   )

Kiner swatted 369 career home runs in 5,205 at bats. Only Babe Ruth had a better lifetime home run percentage. In 1946, Kiner's rookie season, he led the National League in home runs with 23 — and continued to lead the league in that category for the next six years.

Commonly signing "Ralph Kiner", his signature has varied in character formation, slant and flamboyance. No consistent breaks are exhibited in his signature. The looped formation of the "R" can vary in size and roundness, with the top loop of the letter typically extending as far as the "p" or "h" in Ralph. The "a" can vary in size and may resemble an "o" on occasion. The "l" can vary in both height and width, commonly extending to the loop of the "R". The "p" can vary in size and the loop may or may not be closed. The "h" varies in height and may even intersect the extended loop of the "R". The "K" is typically a two-stroke construction, with the top of the second stroke extending well above the height of the capitalized "R". The "K" has a looped bottom formation as part of the second stroke, which can vary in size. The "iner" has remained relatively consistent, with the exception of the "r", which varies in character formation. The ending stroke in Kiner typically curls above the "r" at a variety of heights.

Despite a busy schedule, Kiner has been generally responsive to signature requests. His popularity with the fans is attributable to both his congenial responses and exposure as a television announcer for the New York Mets.

Availability: Plentiful
Demand: Little

Cut signature	$3
Single-signature baseball	$20
3x5" index card	$5
Photograph/baseball card	$14
HOF plaque postcard	$10
Perez-Steele postcard	$35

Chuck Klein

Charles Herbert Klein
(Oct. 7, 1904-March 28, 1958)

Klein ended his career with a lifetime .320 batting average that included 300 home runs and 2,076 hits. He led the National League in home runs four times and had a "Triple Crown" season in 1933, leading the league in homers, batting average and runs batted in.

Commonly signing "Charles Chuck Klein" or "Chuck Klein", his signature varied both in character formation and size. Common signature breaks were between the "C" and the "h" in Charles, also between the "K" and the "l" in Klein. Only an occasional break fell between the "C" and the "h" in Chuck. The "C" in Chuck could vary in the formation of the top loop, from an extended stroke originating outside of the letter, to a hook beginning on the inside of the loop. The loop of the ascender of the "h" may be large enough to extend above the "u" in Chuck. the "uc" remained relatively consistent, and the "k" may or may not close the top of the letter. The two-stroke "K" formation in Klein could vary in size and flamboyance. The end of the second stroke in the "K" typically extended below the signature's base line. The "lein" could vary in slant and size, with the ending stroke usually showing little flamboyance.

Klein was an obliging signer and although he was not overly prolific, his signatures do surface on occasion in the autograph market.

Availability: Average
Demand: Average

Cut signature	$95
Single-signature baseball	$600
3x5" index card	$115
Photograph/baseball card	$325
HOF plaque postcard	Impossible
Perez-Steele postcard	Impossible

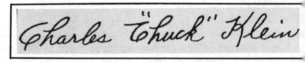

Bill Klem

William Joseph Klem
(Feb. 22, 1874-Sept. 16, 1951)

Klem spent 37 years umpiring in the National League, with a decade of additional service as its chief of staff. "The Old Arbitrator's" legendary accuracy led to accolades of being the best umpire to ever serve the National League. He is often credited with being the first umpire to use arm signals to indicate the status of a pitch.

Commonly signing "W. J. Klem" or "William J. Klem", his signature varied in size, slant and character formation. Consistent signature breaks were between the "W" and the "i" in William, also between the "K" and the l" in Klem. The "W" could vary slightly in character formation, however it typically exhibited flamboyance in both the beginning and ending strokes of the letter. The "illiam" could vary in both character height and width, but gen erally remained consistent in formation. A notable formation was his middle initial of "J". The descender of the "J" extended well below the base line, making the letter about twice the size of the capitalized "W". The two-stroke "K" formation could vary in both size and flamboyance. The top of the second stroke of the "K" typically rose well above the height of any other letter in his signature, with the ending stroke dipping slightly below the base line. The "em" remained somewhat consistent and typically included a flamboyant ending stroke.

Klem was a good signer, however like so many of the game's early arbitrators, his accomplishments went unrecognized for years. Samples of his signature do surface on occasion in the market, however are not as abundant as one might think.

Availability: Average
Demand: Average

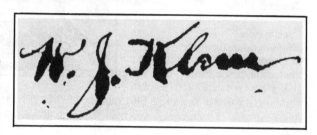

Cut signature	$200
Single-signature baseball	$1,450
3x5" index card	$290
Photograph/baseball card	$775
HOF plaque postcard	Impossible
Perez-Steele postcard	Impossible

Sandy Koufax

Sanford Koufax
(Dec. 30, 1935-   )

During his short career, Koufax won 165 games, struck out 2,396 and posted an ERA of 2.76. A popular player whose World Series performances became legendary, Koufax pitched 57 innings during the fall classic at an ERA of 0.95. An arthritic elbow forced Koufax to an early retirement at the age of 30 following the 1966 season.

Commonly signing "Sandy Koufax" or "Sanford Koufax", his signature has varied primarily in character formation and flamboyance. Consistent signature breaks fall between the "S" and the "a" in Sandy or Sanford, also between the "K" and the "o" in Koufax. The "S" has decreased in width over the years, but remained consistent in character formation when he used a traditional letter style. During the late 1950s, Koufax could also use a stylized "S", resembling a printed rather than script letter. The "a" in Sandy is typically left a bit open on the top of the letter. The "d" could vary in size and the height of the ascender was typically equal to the height of the "S". The loop of the "d" may or may not close and the "f" in Sanford was usually very similar in character formation to the "f" in Koufax. The descender of the "y" can vary in length and formation, from a simple downward stroke to a looped finish. The two-stroke "K" has varied significantly in character formation, with the major changes being exhibited primarily by the second stroke of the letter. The second stroke of the "K" may vary from resembling a letter "C", to a stroke that intersects the stem with a variable sized loop. The slant in his last name has a tendency to vary, as does the formation of

189

the descender of the "f". The "a" typically resembles an "o" and may or may not close at the top. The "x" is commonly crossed by the ending stroke doubling back, forming a loop, and intersecting the first piece of the letter. The size of the ending loop and the ascender of the "f" in Koufax are usually similar in height. Koufax has occasionally used a separate stroke to cross the "x", but this was common primarily during his playing days.

A quiet person who values his privacy, Koufax has been an obliging signer in person, however mail requests seldom prove to be a worthwhile effort.

Availability: Plentiful
Demand: Little

Cut signature	$5
Single-signature baseball	$25
3x5" index card	$11
Photograph/baseball card	$14
HOF plaque postcard	$16
Perez-Steele postcard	$40

Nap Lajoie

Napoleon Lajoie
(Sept. 5, 1874-Feb. 7, 1959)

Larry Lajoie recorded 3,251 hits for a career batting average of .339. Posting a Triple Crown season in 1901, Lajoie hit .422 with 229 hits, 145 runs, 125 RBIs and 14 homers. Lajoie won three batting titles and was considered by most to be the best second baseman of his era.

Typically signing "Napoleon Lajoie" or "Larry Lajoie", his signature varied in character formation and size during his lifetime. Consistent signature breaks fell between the "L" and the "a" in Larry. A break between the "L" and the "a", and between the "j" and the "o" in Lajoie was consistent. Occasionally a break could fall between the "i" and the "e" in Lajoie. The "N" in Napoleon had a notable formation that often hooked in the ending stroke. Both the "a" and the "o" in Napoleon may be open or closed and the "l" could vary in both height and width. The "p" formation had an extended ascender, with a descender that clearly exemplified Lajoie's right signature slant. The "e" could vary in style (a traditional lower case "e", or a reduced "E" formation), but whichever was used, was typically consistent in his entire name. His "L"s began with a long extended upward stroke, with the bottom loops of the letters varying in style. The "j" typically had a flamboyant descender, which because of its right slant usually extended below the entire "L" in Lajoie. Lajoie would typically dot the top of the "j" as well as the "i".

An extremely popular player and a prolific signer, his autographs do surface regularly in the autograph market. Collectors should be able to acquire his signature through major dealers or auction houses.

Availability: Average
Demand: Strong

Cut signature	$120
Single-signature baseball	$1,775
3x5" index card	$175
Photograph/baseball card	$550
HOF plaque postcard	$575
Perez-Steele postcard	Impossible

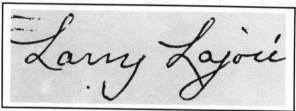

Kenesaw Landis

Kenesaw Mountain Landis
(Nov. 20, 1866-Nov. 25, 1944)

Judge Landis was an authoritative figure hired as major league baseball's first commissioner after the 1919 "Black Sox" World Series scandal. "Kenesaw," named after Kennesaw Mountain in Georgia, was strictly opposed to gambling and made it a personal goal to re-establish integrity to the game of baseball.

Commonly signing "K.M. Landis", "Kenesaw M. Landis", or "Kenesaw Landis", his generally illegible signature varied considerably during his lifetime. Typically his signature exhibited no breaks. Samples signed before 1930 will show greater character formation in his first name. The most consistent element in his signature was the slant and character spacing. The "K" was unpredictable in format and seldom resembled any letter. The first "e" in Kenesaw was occasionally discernable, as was the "n". The "saw" was often nothing more than a rough stroke. When the "s" was discernable it may or may not close on the bottom of the letter and it connected to the top of the "a" in Kenesaw. The ending upward stroke of the "w" was flamboyant and may or may not connect to the top of the "M". The "M" is recognizable in earlier examples, but typically disappears in later versions. The "La" was unpredictable in formation, but consistent in slant. I have never seen samples where the "n" was distinguishable, with the only exception being the many secretarial signature versions of Landis. His secretarial signatures are initialed and easily recognizable by their legibility. The "dis" could vary in both character formation and size. The slant and formation of Landis remained relatively consistent. The "an" in Landis was simply an extended stroke between the "L" and the "d". A "K.M. Landis" format is common in later examples and will typically appear very large.

A Landis signature can be a nightmare to authenticate. Fortunately, he commonly generated his numerous correspondences on official letterhead. Landis was an outspoken individual and like Ty Cobb, his letters are typically priceless in content.

Availability: Above average
Demand: Average

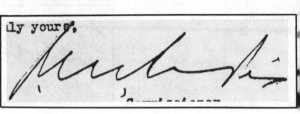

Cut signature	$135
Single-signature baseball	$1,275
3x5" index card	$200
Photograph/baseball card	$400
HOF plaque postcard	Impossible
Perez-Steele postcard	Impossible

Bob Lemon

Robert Granville Lemon
(Sept. 22, 1920-   )

Lemon won 207 games, at a winning percentage of .618, and posted an impressive 3.23 ERA during his career. In 1954 he helped guide the Indians to the World Series with a 23-7 record at an ERA of 2.72. One of the more versatile players to play the game, having begun his major league career as a third baseman and outfielder, Bob was also a proficient hitter and managed numerous teams, including the 1978 World Champion New York Yankees.

Commonly signing "Bob Lemon", his signature has varied slightly in size, slant and character formation. There are no consistent signature breaks exhibited in his autograph. The "B" commonly varies in slant and the size of the loops that are included in the character's formation. The "o" may be open or closed and the ascender of the "b" can vary in size, often exceeding the height of the "B" in Bob. The width of the ascender of the "b" can vary, as can the formation of the ending stroke of the letter. The "L" can vary in size or slant and typically is the largest letter in his signature. The "em" can vary in size with the "on" commonly changing in character formation.

Lemon has always been a responsive signer and a favorite among collectors. Collectors should find his signature an easy acquisition.

Availability: Plentiful
Demand: Little

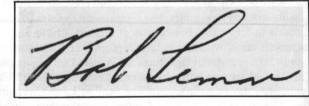

Cut signature	$3
Single-signature baseball	$17
3x5" index card	$5
Photograph/baseball card	$13
HOF plaque postcard	$9
Perez-Steele postcard	$30

Buck Leonard

Walter Fenner Leonard
(Sept. 8, 1907-   )

Leonard was consistently one of the Negro Leagues' top hitters, belting 42 homers in 1942 and hitting .391 in 1948. He spent 17 productive years with the Homestead Grays, dominating the league from 1937 to 1945. A 12-time All-Star, Buck closed out his career in the Mexican Leagues.

Commonly signing "Buck Leonard" or "Walter Leonard", his signature exhibited significant variation in character formation, size and slant. Consistent signature breaks fall between the "B" and the "u" in Buck, also betwen the "L" and the "e" in Leonard. The "B" could vary in size, particularly in the formation of the beginning and ending strokes. The "u" begins with an extended stroke upward before the character formation. The "k" was a two-stroke construction, with the first stroke typically showing a slight hook at the end. The "L" was a traditional two-loop formation with the top loop occasionally extending above the "e" or the "o" in Leonard. The "e", like the "u", began with an extended stroke upward before the character formation. The "o" may or may not close at the top and I have witnessed a break between the loop and the top formation of the letter. The "a" could vary in formation and the ending stroke of the "d" varied in length.

In 1986, Leonard suffered a stroke that dramatically altered his signature style. The major signature breaks remained relatively consistent, however most of the character formations were altered. Numerous variations are common and some autographs following his stroke may prove difficult to authenticate. Despite his physical setbacks, Leonard has remained responsive to autograph requests and a real favorite among collectors.

Availability: Plentiful
Demand: Little

Cut signature	$5
Single-signature baseball	$30
3x5" index card	$10
Photograph/baseball card	$18
HOF plaque postcard	$17
Perez-Steele postcard	$50

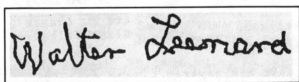

Freddie Lindstrom

Frederick Charles Lindstrom
(Nov. 21, 1905-Oct. 4, 1981)

"Lindy" hit .311 during his career with 1,747 lifetime hits. During his 1928 season with the Giants he batted .358 and led the National League in hits with 231. Lindstrom batted over .300 in seven of his 13 seasons.

Commonly signing "Freddie Lindstrom" or "Fred Lindstrom", his signature exhibited only slight variation in both size and character formation during his lifetime. Common signature breaks fell between the "L" and the "i" and the "d" and the "s" in Lindstrom. The "F" could vary in both height and width of the bottom loop formation. The "e" was typically larger than the "r" and the ascender of the "d" could extend above the "F" in Fred. His middle initial of "C" was a two-looped formation that could vary a bit in size. The "L" was the largest letter in his signature, with the ending stroke typically extending below his signature's base line. The "ind" showed only slight variation in size, with the ascender of the "d" equal or above the height of the unusually large "t" in Lindstrom. The "s" appeared slightly more rounded in later examples, and the "o" may or may not close on the top of the letter. The flamboyant ending stroke in Lindstrom typically looped back to cross the "t" and may even extend the length of his entire signature, although earlier examples will show the "t" crossed by a simple separate stroke.

A warm person with a good sense of humor, Lindstrom was always popular with collectors. He was a prolific signer and collectors should find his autograph an easy acquisition.

Availability: Plentiful
Demand: Average

Cut signature	$7
Single-signature baseball	$135
3x5" index card	$16
Photograph/baseball card	$45
HOF plaque postcard	$25
Perez-Steele postcard	Impossible

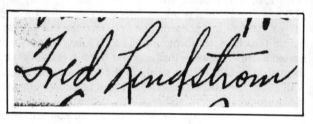

John Lloyd

John Henry Lloyd
(April 25, 1884-March 19, 1964)

"Pop" Lloyd played on numerous Negro League teams during his career from 1906 to 1932. Lloyd broke the .400 barrier three times in batting and in 1911 recorded an astounding .475 for the Lincoln Giants.

Commonly signing "John Henry Lloyd" or "John Lloyd", his signature varied in character formation, size and slant. A common signature break fell between the "J" and the "o" in John and occasionally between the "o" and the "h". The capitized "J" in John was a traditional formation that could vary in slant. His "o"s commonly varied in size and formation. The ascender of the "h" in John could vary in width, but typically equalled or exceeded the height of the "J". The "H" in Henry was either a two- or, occasionally, a three-stroke construction, with the middle stroke or loop connected to the "e". The "y" in Henry could vary in size and ending stroke flamboyance, when compared to the same letter in Lloyd. The length of the "y"'s descender typically was equal to the descender of the "J". The "L" in Lloyd was a two-looped construction, with the top loop typically larger in size than that of the bottom. The "o" in Lloyd may or may not close and the "y" can vary in right slant from "y" in Henry. Lloyd's "d"s commonly had wide ascenders. All examples I have seen of his handwriting have showed many inconsistencies in slant.

A great competitor and a good signer, Lloyd's signature varied during the last few years of his life due to failing health. Collectors may find the acquisition of his signature a challenge, as few seem to surface in the autograph market.

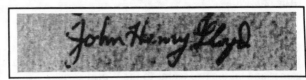

Availability: Limited
Demand: Above average

Cut signature	$765
Single-signature baseball	$4,650
3x5" index card	$1,550
Photograph/baseball card	$3,000
HOF plaque postcard	Impossible
Perez-Steele postcard	Impossible

Ernie Lombardi

Ernest Natali Lombardi
(April 6, 1908-Sept. 26, 1977)

Never known for his speed, Lombardi managed to bat .306 over 17 seasons in the National League. Batting over .300 ten times, he was also able to win two batting titles, in 1938 and in 1942. He was a skilled catcher who was awarded the National League's Most Valuable Player award in 1938.

Commonly signing "Ernie Lomabrdi" or "Ernest Lombardi", his signature varied in character formation and size during his lifetime. Consistent signature breaks occurred between the "E" and the "r" in Ernie, also between the "L" and the "o", the "b" and the "a", and the "r" and the "d" in Lombardi. The "E" varies slightly in the size of the beginning and ending character loops. The "rni" remained relatively consistent, with the ending "e" typically a bit larger than the preceeding lower case letters. The two-loop formation of the "L" could vary in size, however the slant remained relatively consistent. The "omb" could vary slightly in character formation, and the ascender of the "d" could vary in both height and width. The "a" may or may not be closed on the top and he typically added no ending stroke.

Lombardi was generally responsive to autograph requests and collectors should have little trouble acquiring his signature through dealers and auction houses.

Availability: Above average
Demand: Average

Cut signature	$25
Single-signature baseball	$400
3x5" index card	$40
Photograph/baseball card	$125
HOF plaque postcard	Impossible
Perez-Steele postcard	Impossible

Al Lopez

Alfonso Raymond Lopez
(Aug. 20, 1908-   )

As a player "Senor" compiled a lifetime batting average of .261 on 1,547 hits. Lopez spent over 1,900 games behind the plate before closing his career in 1947 with the Cleveland Indians. It was as a manager, however, that he gained his greatest acclaim, winning 1,422 games and taking two teams to the World Series.

Commonly signing "Al Lopez", his signature has varied primarily in size. No consistent signature breaks are exhibited in his autograph. The loops in the "A" can vary a bit in size, as can the "l", which can occasionally resemble an "e". The "L" can vary in flamboyance, with a top loop that can extend above his signature as far as the "z" in Lopez. The "o" seems to be a bit smaller in later examples, with an ending stroke that has decreased slightly in flamboyance with age.

Lopez has been a responsive signer over the years, however mail requests can have unpredictable results.

Availability: Plentiful
Demand: Little

Cut signature	$7
Single-signature baseball	$45
3x5" index card	$10
Photograph/baseball card	$25
HOF plaque postcard	$25
Perez-Steele postcard	$70

Ted Lyons

Theodore Amar Lyons
(Dec. 28, 1900-July 25, 1986)

A popular member of the Chicago White Sox, Lyons played from 1923 to 1946, winning 260 games at an ERA of 3.67. At the age of 41, and in his last full season (1942), Ted led the American League with an ERA of 2.10.

Typically signing "Ted Lyons", his signature varied in both size and character formation. Consistent breaks were between the "T" and the "e" in Ted, also between the "L" and the "y" in Lyons. An occasional break also occurred between the "y" and the "o" in Lyons, and between the "e" and the "d" in Ted. The two-stroke "T" formation could vary in size, but was typically smaller than the "L" in Lyons. The top stroke of the "T" in Ted may or may not intersect the stem of the letter. The "d" varied often in character formation, with an ascender that showed little consistency in height. The "d" was typically open at the loop of the letter. The traditional two-looped "L" formation varied in size, with the top loop of the letter possibly extending above the "y" in Lyons. The "y" may or may not connect to the "o" via an additional backward stroke off the descender. The descender of the "y" did not extend far below the base line. The "o" may or may not close and the "n" typically resembled a "u". The "s" could vary in width and often resembled an "e".

Lyons was vary responsive to autograph requests and collectors should find his signature an easy acquisition.

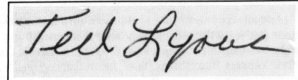

Availability: Plentiful	
Demand: Little	
Cut signature	$7
Single-signature baseball	$85
3x5" index card	$16
Photograph/baseball card	$30
HOF plaque postcard	$20
Perez-Steele postcard	$300

Connie Mack

Cornelius Alexander McGillicuddy
(Dec. 22, 1862-Feb. 8, 1956)

"The Grand Old Man of Baseball," Connie Mack managed for half a century with the Philadelphia A's. Both Mack and Ben Shibe, a prominent sporting goods manufacturer, built a baseball legacy in Philadelphia with players like Cochrane, Grove, Baker, Collins and Plank. Mack took nine pennants and five world championships as one of the game's greatest managers.

Commonly signing "Connie Mack", his signature varied both in slant and character formation. Consistent signature breaks fall between the "C" and the "o" in Connie, also occasionally between the "M" and the "a" in Mack. The two-looped "C" was fairly consistent and often was the largest letter in his signature. The "o" varied in the close of the letter, either being a loop or a horizontal line that connected to the "n". The "nni" varies in both slant and width. The character formation of the "e" could be in two styles, either a traditional lower case "e" or a reduced rounded "E" formation. The "M" in Mack changed in slant and size, particularly noticeable in the peaks of the letter. The capitalized "M" commonly began from the top of the letter with a hook formation that led to a downward stroke that doubled back to form both the loops of the letter. The "ac" could vary in degree of right slant and the ascender of the "k" could vary in size. The lower case letters in Connie are typically larger than those in Mack, often the peaks of the "M" in Mack may only reach the height of the "n"s in Connie. The ending stroke of the "k" typically extended below his signature's base line.

Mack was a responsive and prolific signer. Collectors should be able to acquire his signature through autograph dealers or auction houses.

Availability: Average	
Demand: Average	
Cut signature	$65
Single-signature baseball	$525
3x5" index card	$125
Photograph/baseball card	$275
HOF plaque postcard	$365
Perez-Steele postcard	Impossible

Larry MacPhail

Leland Stanford MacPhail
(Feb. 3, 1890-Oct. 1, 1975)

McPhail was known for his ability to turn a club around; teams such as the Cincinnati Reds (1939, 1940) and the Brooklyn Dodgers (1941). It was MacPhail who introduced night baseball to the major leagues in 1935. His final conquest was purchasing the New York Yankees from the estate of Jacob Ruppert in 1942, and establishing the team as a modern contender.

Commonly signing "Larry MacPhail", his signature has varied in size, slant and character formation. His signature often exhibits no breaks, however an occasional break can be found between the "L" and the "a" in Larry. The "L" could vary radically in style, from a traditional two-looped "L" to a condensed version that resembled a "W". The "arry" can slightly decrease in size with each subsequent letter, with the descender of the "y" typically a simple single downward stroke. The beginning stroke of the "M" often appears as if an additional loop has been added to the letter. Both "a"s in MacPhail may or may not close on the top and the "c" had little formation to the top of the character. The "c" could resemble a "u" in appearance and a single-stroke underline typically was added beneath the "ac" formation. The "p" could vary in width, with the descender typically resting on the signature's base line. The loop of the "p" connected to the "h" to form the character's ascender. The ending stroke of the "l" was commonly a sharp downward finish. McPhail occasionally added an underline beneath his name and also typically varied the slant of his entire signature.

MacPhail, like most baseball executives, was a prolific signer. Collectors should find the acquisition of his signature fairly easy.

Availability: Above average
Demand: Average

Cut signature	$55
Single-signature baseball	$525
3x5" index card	$100
Photograph/baseball card	$215
HOF plaque postcard	Impossible
Perez-Steele postcard	Impossible

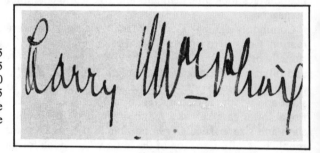

Mickey Mantle

Mickey Charles Mantle
(Oct. 20, 1931-   )

"The Mick" is by far one of the most popular players to ever play the game of baseball. Known during his playing days for legendary tape measure home runs, some carried 550 feet or better. Home runs were routine for Mantle who blasted 536 and led the American League in "round trippers" four times. A "Triple Crown" winner and three time Most Valuable Player, Mantle smacked 18 home runs in 12 World Series contests.

Commonly signing "Mickey Mantle", his signature has varied significantly in character formation, slant and size. Mantle's signature breaks have also been inconsistent. Signatures originating during the 1950s exhibit breaks between the "M" and the "i", the "c" and the "k" in Mickey, also between the first and second stroke of the letter "k" in Mickey. His last name typically had just one break, which fell between the "M" and the "a" in Mantle. During the last two decades his signature was reduced to two consistent breaks, between the first and second stroke of the "k", and between the "M" and the "a" in Mantle. An occasional break also falls between the "M" and the "i" in Mickey. The right slant of his signature has gradually been reduced with age, while the flamboyance in his stroke has increased. Like DiMaggio and Dickey, the variations exhibited by his signature necessitate a character-by-character analysis.

Letter	Variation
M	Early examples (1950s) are traditional in character formation, with a heavier right slant. The beginning stroke, during the 1950s, began at the top of the letter with a small hook before the first loop. The stroke that formed the character began to incorporate loops which gradually increased in size and flamboyance. By the 1960s, the character had become much rounder in appearance, with the opening stroke beginning to exhibit a large loop formation. The late 1960s saw the loop gradually beginning to dip below the signature's base line, and by the 1970s the formation became established as a distinct characteristic of his autograph. The opening of the loop now commonly extends below the base line and as far as the "i" in Mickey. The width of the descending loop is inconsistent and the "M" may or may not connect to the "i".
i	The "i" has varied in width and may or may not connect to the "M". The "i" can be dotted with a circle instead of a dot. The beginning stroke leading to the character's formation can vary in length.
c	The "c" may break with the "k", particularly in 1950s examples. The "c"'s finishing stroke may form the stem of the "k" (circa 1960) or the letter's top arm (circa 1970 to present). The upward finishing stroke, exhibited by later signatures, may extend above the "e" in Mickey.
k	During the 1950s the "k" could break with the "c" in Mickey. The "k"'s formation has traditionally consisted of two strokes, a base (stem) stroke and a stroke for the letter's arm formation. Earlier examples may have the "k"'s ascender extending to the height of the "M". The stem's stroke can be formed by the ending stroke of the "c", or may begin an entirely new stroke which then completes his first name. The stem's formation does vary, particularly if it is the beginning of an entirely new stroke. The top arm of the "k" can also vary in size.
e	The "e" has remained relatively consistent in character formation.
y	The "y" can vary in definition, with earlier examples showing greater attention paid to the character's formation. The descender of the "y" can extend well below the base line in earlier examples, however later examples typically show a reduced

descender, only extending as far as the bottom loop of the "M" in Mickey.

M   The "M" is typically identical in formation to the "M" in Mickey, however can vary slightly in size. The "M" commonly breaks with the "a" in Mantle. The opening loop of the letter typically is smaller than its predecessor's loop (The "M" in Mickey).

an   The "an" has shown little variation.

t   The "t" in earlier examples will have an ascender that can extend to or exceed the height of the "M" in Mantle. The ascender can also vary in width. Later examples show a simplified stem structure that has been reduced in size. The crossing of the "t" is typically a single stroke that extends the length of the character's space. The "t" may break with the "l" in earlier examples.

l   Similar to the "t", its ascender has varied in size, becoming smaller and wider with age. Earlier examples will typically have the "l" extending well above any letter in his signature. The "l" can vary slightly in slant.

e   The "e" has shown little variation, with the ending stroke typically being a simple ending to the letter. During the 1960s, on rare occasions, he may have added a flamboyant ending that doubled back above his signature to cross the "t".

Mantle has utilized the services of a ghost signer. These signatures, although challenging to recognize, typically are a bit larger with less attention paid to detail. The ghost signatures can adorn both black and white photographs and baseballs. Mantle facsimiles are also common, however are easily distinguished as such because of the identical appearance of each signature. Like Babe Ruth, complicating the authentication of his signature are allegations of other New York Yankee personnel signing material on his behalf. Although these stories are just allegations, they remain a source of concern and discomfort to collectors.

Although mail requests typically go unanswered, Mantle has frequented the baseball card show circuit, allowing collectors easy access to his signature. Authentication of older material such as photographs or team baseballs may prove to be a challenge for the collector.

Availability: Plentiful
Demand: Average

Cut signature	$8
Single-signature baseball	$45
3x5" index card	$16
Photograph/baseball card	$30
HOF plaque postcard	$35
Perez-Steele postcard	$195

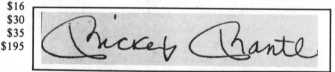

Heinie Manush

Henry Emmett Manush
(July 20, 1901-May 12, 1971)

Manush hit .330 during his career that included 2,524 hits. His slugging prowess won him the American League batting title in 1926 (.378). Manush was elected to one All-Star team, in 1934, while playing with the Senators. He batted over .300 11 times during his 17-year career.

Commonly signing "Heinie Manush", his signature varied in character formation, size and slant. Consistent signature breaks fell between the "H" and the "e" in Heinie, also between the "M" and the "a" in Manush. The "H" varied in formation and often resembled a "VC" letter configuration. The loop at the beginning and ending stroke of the "H" could vary in size. His capitalization was typically four to five times larger than his lower case letters. The "e"s could vary in size and the "ini" formation resembled a "w" with two dots above it. Most notable was his signature's steep right slant (30 to 40 degrees) and the formation of his capitalized letters. The "M" in Manush was seldom distinguishable as such, often resembling a slanted "cuc" or "ne" configuration. The "M" began from the top of the letter with a downward stroke that doubled back at lower case letter height, then created two other similar formations before looping the ending of the line. The "a" may or may not close at the top of the letter and the "nu" configuration resembled a "uu" in appearance. The "s" varied in size and may or may not close at the bottom. The ascender of the "h" varied in width, and extended almost to capitalization height.

Manush was a responsive signer and collectors should have little trouble acquiring his signature.

Availability: Average
Demand: Average

Cut signature	$18
Single-signature baseball	$385
3x5" index card	$35
Photograph/baseball card	$95
HOF plaque postcard	$215
Perez-Steele postcard	Impossible

Rabbit Maranville

Walter James Vincent Maranville
(Nov. 11, 1891-Jan. 5, 1954)

Maranville played in the National League from 1912 to 1935, recording 2,605 hits at an average of .258. Maranville helped guide two teams to the World Series, batting .308 in both contests. A zany personality both on and off the field, Maranville would always go out of his way for a laugh. He played more games at shortstop than any other National Leaguer — 2,153.

Commonly signing "Rabbit Maranville", his signature varied in character formation and size during his lifetime. Consistent signature breaks fell between the "R" and the "a" in Rabbit, also between the "M" and the "a" in Maranville. The "R" could vary in size, however was typically the largest letter in his signature (six or seven times the height of his lower case letters). The "R" resembled a "JR" formation, with a flamboyant opening loop. The ending stroke of the "R" extended well below the signature's base line and was typically the lowest point of his signature. Both the "a"s and the "s"s could vary in size, but were similar in slant. The ascender of the "t" could equal in height, or extend above, the "b"s in Rabbit. The beginning stroke of the "M" could resemble a "JM" formation and the letter typically did not extend below the signature's base line. The "nv" was often unidentifiable and both "l"s could vary in size. The ending stroke of the "e" was generally simple and showed no flamboyance.

Maranville was a colorful character and a responsive signer. He died less than month before his election into the Baseball Hall of Fame at the age of 62.

Availability: Average
Demand: Average

Cut signature	$125
Single-signature baseball	$1,025
3x5" index card	$150
Photoggaph/baseball card	$450
HOF plaque postcard	Impossible
Perez-Steele postcard	Impossible

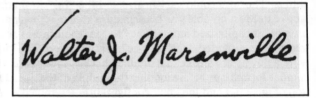

Juan Marichal

Juan Antonio Sanchez Marichal
(Oct. 20, 1937-   )

"The Dominican Dandy" debuted on July 19, 1960, throwing a one-hit shutout against the Phillies. It was the beginning of a career that recorded 243 wins, 2,303 strikeouts, and an ERA of 2.89. This high-kicking right hander was named to eight All-Star Teams and chosen as the 1965 Most Valuable Player.

Commonly signing "Juan Marichal", his signature has varied significantly in character formation, slant and size. Samples from earlier in his career (1960s), show signature breaks between the "u" and the "a" in Juan, also between the "M" and the "a", "c" and the "h", and the "h" and the "a" in Marichal. Near the end of his career (1970s) breaks were common between the "J" and the "u" in Juan, also between the "M" and the "a", and the "h" and the "a" in Marichal. During the 1980s his signature exhibited breaks between the J and the "u", and the "u" and the "a" in Juan, also between the "M" and the "a", and the "h" and the "a" in Marichal. During his career, Marichal's signature became more condensed with a distinctly greater right slant. Following his active departure from the game, his signature has become more flamboyant with increased character spacing. Additionally, changes to a slightly left slant are evident in some of his characters. The "J" in Juan exhibited radical character formation changes, from a traditional styled "J" to a formation that could resemble a large number 2. In later years the "J" has gone back to a more traditional style that shows greater consistency in character formation. The "u" varied in slant and in later examples may break from both the "J" and the "a". The beginning stroke of the "a" may have an extended top loop in later examples, compared to earlier versions where the loop and the stem meet neatly togther. With age, the "n" has shown less definition in character formation and greater flamboyance in the ending stroke from the "n" to the capitalized "M".

The "M" has increased in width over the years and can often resemble a "u" in later examples. Earlier examples of his signature will have a more traditional look to the "M", which exhibits a greater right slant and less flamboyance. The "r" shows less definition in later samples and resembles an undotted "i". The "i" can be dotted with a circle, particularly in samples from the 1970s. Over the years the "c" has gradually lost character definition and in later versions can be indistinguishable from the "r" or the "i". The "h" has shown a decrease in ascender height and significantly less right slant in later examples. The "a"s may or may not close at the top and all three in his name will be similar in character formation. The "l" can vary in slant and width, with later examples exhibiting a wider, more upright, style. The ending stroke in Marichal is typically a simple downward storke from the "l". Signature samples from the 1960s and the 1980s look very similar; it is Marichal's autographs originating during the 1970s that depict the greatest departure from his traditional style.

Marichal has never been an easy autograph to acquire and mail requests generally remain unanswered. Collectors should find his signature easiest to acquire during his occasional attendance at baseball card shows.

Availability: Plentiful
Demand: Little

Cut signature	$4
Single-signature baseball	$17
3x5" index card	$8
Photograph/baseball card	$13
HOF plaque postcard	$12
Perez-Steele postcard	$30

Rube Marquard

Richard William Marquard
(Oct. 9, 1889-June 1, 1980)

Marquard won 201 games during his career at an ERA of 3.13. In 1912, Marquard peaked winning 26 games at an ERA of 2.57. He became as popular off the field as on, when he teamed up with his wife to perform dance routines during the off seasons.

Commonly signing "Rube Marquard", his signature varied in character formation and slant during his lifetime. Marquard's signature typically exhibited no breaks, however careful examination can show an occasional break between the "q" and the "u". His condensed right slant signature can obscure a break, possibly requiring magnification to confirm its existence. The "R" remained fairly consistent in formation, but could vary in size. The ascender of the "b" can vary in both height and width. The "b" can be the highest point of his signature. The "e" can vary in size and may resemble the letter "l". The "M" can resemble a "y", with the second loop of the letter extending below the signature's base line, similar to a descender. The "a"s may or may not close on top and the descender of the "q" can vary in length. The last "ar" combination in Marquard is generally smaller than the first. The "d" may or may not be closed at the loop and the flamboyant ending stroke can extend well beneath the signature's base line, even as far as the "u".

Marquard was a very responsive signer and collectors should find the acquisition of his autograph fairly easy.

Availability: Plentiful
Demand: Little

Cut signature	$8
Single-signature baseball	$235
3x5" index card	$14
Photograph/baseball card	$40
HOF plaque postcard	$25
Perez-Steele postcard	Impossible

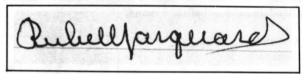

Eddie Mathews

Edwin Lee Mathews
(Oct. 13, 1931-   )

Mathews was a born slugger and a natural athlete, smashing 512 career home runs while batting .271. He led the National League twice in home runs, first in 1953, then again in 1959. Mathews played in three World Series contests and set a rookie record of 25 home runs in 1952.

Commonly signing "Eddie Mathews" or "Ed Mathews", his signature has primarily varied in size and slant. Earlier examples of his signature (during his playing days) exhibit a break between the "M" and the "a" in Mathews, while later examples typically show none. On occasions where he has signed Edwin instead of Ed, a break may fall between the "E" and the "d". The "E" in Eddie is a unique character formation which begins with a long upward stroke from below the signature's base line to form the first loop of the letter. A smaller loop, before the first loop of the letter, is common and can vary in size. The "d" may or may not close and will vary in ascender size. The "M" in Mathews has varied slightly in size and slant. The beginning stroke of the letter "M" may vary in style and flamboyance. The "a" may or may not close and the ascender of the "t" can vary in both height or width. The ascender of the "h" is commonly the highest point in his signature, and like the "t", can exceed the height of the "M" in Mathews. The "t" can be crossed by a separate stroke or by the ending stroke and typically has an unusually large width to the stem of the letter. The "s" commonly varies in character formation and often can even be unrecognizable.

Mathews has been an obliging signer, however mail requests may have unpredictable results. Collectors should find the acquisition of his signature fairly easy.

Availability: Plentiful
Demand: Little

Cut signature	$3
Single-signature baseball	$20
3x5" index card	$6
Photograph/baseball card	$12
HOF plaque postcard	$11
Perez-Steele postcard	$25

Christy Mathewson

Christopher Mathewson
(Aug. 12, 1878-Oct. 7, 1925)

The "Big Six" established himself as the game's premier pitcher in the National League during the beginning of the century. Matty won 373 games and lost only 188, while leading the league in wins four times. Mathewson was an extremely popular player with great control and pioneered the fadeaway (screwball) pitch.

Commonly signing "Christy Mathewson", his signature varied in character formation, size and slant. Typically his signature exhibited no consistent breaks. On some occasions breaks did fall between the "i" and the "s" in Christy, and between the "s" and the "o" in Mathewson. When Mathewson autographed baseballs he often exhibited breaks between the "C" and the "h" in Christy, also between the "M" and the "a" in Mathewson. The "C" is notable because of its long upward beginning stroke which originates from well below the signature's base line and extends to the top of the character to form a distinct top loop formation to the letter. The ascender of the "h" could vary in slant, however typically was the same height as the "C" in Christy. The "r" could vary in width and the "s" may or may not close on the bottom. The "t" in Christy consisted of just a stem which was typically crossed by the flamboyant beginning stroke of the "M" in Mathewson, or occasionally by a separate stroke. The descender of the "y" was typically a simple downward stroke. The "M" varied in the formation and flamboyance of its beginning stroke, as well as in size. The "a" could resemble an "o" and the "o" and the "t" in Mathewson was crossed by a separate stroke, usually downward in slant. The "hew" varied primarily in slant, with the ascender of the "h" often exceeding in height both loops of the "M" in Mathewson. The unusually large "s" in Mathewson has become a hallmark of his signature. The "s" will vary in flamboyance, and may or may not close on the bottom of the letter. The "s" was typically equivalent in height to the "t" in Christy.

Mathewson was a responsive signer and served as president of the Boston Braves from 1923 until his death. He generated numerous correspondences from his post in Boston, though few have turned up in the autograph market. He had been attacked by tuberculosis for five years until it finally took his life at the young age of 45. Collectors may find the acquisition of his signature a bit of a challenge.

Availability: Limited
Demand: Strong

Cut signature	$700
Single-signature baseball	$4,900
3x5" index card	$800
Photograph/baseball card	$2,000
HOF plaque postcard	Impossible
Perez-Steele postcard	Impossible

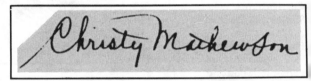

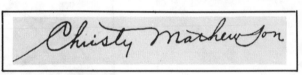

Willie Mays

Willie Howard Mays
(May 6, 1931-   )

The "Say Hey Kid" was one of the legendary power hitters of the game. Mays clouted 660 home runs and 3,283 hits while batting a career average of .302. Willie was a gifted athlete whose achievements with his bat were often overshadowed by his fielding prowess. This two-time National League Most Valuable Player appeared in 24 All-Star games.

Commonly signing "Willie Mays", his signature has varied in size, character formation and breaks. Early signatures (1950s) exhibit breaks between the "W" and the "i" in Willie, also between the "M" and the "a", and "y" and the "s" in Mays. Later examples (1980s), although unpredictable, exhibit breaks between the "W" and the "i" in Willie, also between the "a" and the "y" in Mays. Capitalization has been the most inconsistent element of his signature. The "W" in early examples (1950s) looked like a "y", then evolved to a more traditional "W" format (circa 1960s), and by the 1970s resembled a "U" formation. The beginning stroke of the "W" has consistently showed variation in formation and flamboyance. The ending stroke of the "W" seldom completes the second loop of the character, with the exception being the style he used in the early 1960s. By the mid 1960s his signature began to mature in style, more exemplary of his current autograph. The "illie" in Willie became very consistent in formation, only varying slightly in character width. It is common to have the "i"s in Willie dotted with a circle. The "M" evolved from a form that resembled a "gn" or "2n" (1950s and early 1960s) combination to its current style (circa mid to late 1960s). Similar to the "W", the opening stroke of the "M" has consistently shown variation in size and flamboyance. The "y" during the 1950s and 1960s had a longer descender that extended well below the signature's base line. By the late 1970s the descender of the "y" was shortened to a length that typically extends only slightly below the signature's base line. The "s" varied radically from a separate character that resembled an "E" in the 1950s to a letter that is now reduced in size and connected to the "y". The ending stroke in his last name transformed from a simple close to the "s" during the 1960s and early 1970s, to a flamboyant backward stroke that can extend upward as far as the "M" in Mays. The "ys" combination has shown variation in size and flamboyance during the 1980s. The "illie" has been the most consistent element of his signature, and probably makes the best comparison point for authenticators. Variations in size and character formation are commonplace, making a Mays signature often difficult to authenticate.

Mays has been a responsive signer and like may other Hall of Fame inductees, has used his autograph to generate contributions to various foundations. His frequency on the baseball card show circuit make his signature an easy acquisition for collectors.

Availability: Plentiful
Demand: Little

Cut signature	$6
Single-signature baseball	$30
3x5" index card	$10
Photograph/baseball card	$17
HOF plaque postcard	$16
Perez-Steele postcard	$75

Joe McCarthy

Joseph Vincent McCarthy
(April 21, 1887-Jan. 3, 1978)

McCarthy won 2,126 games as a manager and took nine teams to the World Series. Although he managed both in Chicago and Boston during his career, it was his 16 years in New York that gained him greatest prominence. During his 24 years of service, McCarthy became the first manager to win championships in both leagues.

Commonly signing "Joe McCarthy", his signature varied in both character formation and size during his lifetime. Consistent signature breaks fell between the "J" and the "o" in Joe, also between the "Mc" and the "C", and the "C" and the "a" in McCarthy. The "J" was commonly a two-stroke construction. The ascender of the "J" resembled an "e" at times, with the second stroke usually a simple line segment intersecting the first. The stroke which formed the ascender of the "J" extended below the base line to form half of the descender. Occasionally the second stroke of the "J" could extend as far as the "o" in Joe. The "o" may or may not close at the top and the "e" resembled a stylized "E" that was reduced in size. The "M" could vary in the flamboyance of the opening stroke of the letter, with the ending stroke connecting to the superscript "c" in McCarthy. The superscript "c" was underlined and the "C" in McCarthy varied in both character formation and size. The "C" could have an elaborate beginning (hook) and ending (loop or hook) stroke, particularly in earlier examples. The "thy" varied in both ascender and character width. The descender of the "y" was usually a simple downward single stroke with a separate line intersecting it. The "y" did vary in the length of the descender but was consistent in slant. McCarthy's later signature samples exhibit typical aging characteristics.

McCarthy was a very responsive signer and collectors should be able to acquire his signature through dealers and auction houses.

Availability: Average
Demand: Average

Cut signature	$11
Single-signature baseball	$265
3x5" index card	$25
Photograph/baseball card	$40
HOF plaque postcard	$45
Perez-Steele postcard	Impossible

208

Tom McCarthy

Thomas Francis Michael McCarthy
(July 24, 1863-Aug. 5, 1922)

In Boston, Hugh Duffy and Tom McCarthy were known as the "Heavenly Twins" pioneering infield plays and posting significant batting performances. Tommy hit over .290 with 1,496 hits during a career that lasted for over a decade. Master of the "trap play" that led to the infield fly rule, McCarthy exhibited strong fielding skills.

Typically signing "Thomas F. McCarthy", his signature varied in character formation, size and slant. Consistent signature breaks fell between the superscript "c" and the "C", and the "C" and the "a" in McCarthy. A less consistent break could also occur between the "T" and the "h" in Thomas. The "T" was a two-stroke formation, with the stem stroke resembling a "J" in appearance, and the other stroke forming the traditional top to the letter. The top stroke may or may not intersect the stem and could connect to the ascender of the "h". The "h" could vary in slant and ascender width. the "oma" remained fairly consistent, with the unique "s" formation hooking below his first name and extending as far as the "m" in Thomas. The "F" was typically a three-stroke construction that could vary in flamboyance. The "Mc" remained fairly consistent throughout his life. The "M" could resemble a "y" on occasion and was connected to the "c" superscript which may or may not be underlined. The "C" in McCarthy varied in size and flamboyance. The "art" remained fairly consistent, with the ascender of the "t" varying a bit in height. The "h" could vary in size, with the "y" exhibiting some size changes in the descender. The single-stroke crossing of the "t" was unpredictable in both style and length.

McCarthy was a very popular player in Boston and responsive to autograph requests. Collectors should find the acquisition of his signature a challenge, although they do occasionally surface in the autograph market.

Availability: Limited
Demand: Above average

Cut signature	$1,850
Single-signature baseball	$3,000
3x5" index card	$2,650
Photograph/baseball card	$4,500
HOF plaque postcard	Impossible
Perez-Steele postcard	Impossible

Willie McCovey

Wille Lee McCovey
(Jan. 10, 1938-   )

"Stretch" was the Rookie of the Year in 1959 and soon became one of baseball's most feared left-handed home run hitters, accumulating 521 during his career. This 1969 Most Valuable Player is second all-time in career grand slams with 18. In combination with Willie Mays, they became one of the game's greatest slugging duos.

Typically signing "Willie McCovey", his signature has exhibited variation in character formation and size. Consistent signature breaks have fallen between the "W" and the "i" in Willie, also between the "M" and the superscript "c", the superscript "c" and the "C", and occasionally between the "C" and the "o" in McCovey (common in early examples). The "W" was more ornate in appearance during the 1960s, often adding an elaborate loop configuration to the beginning stroke. The first "i" in Willie has been reduced in size with age, and in some instances is nonexistent in his autograph. The "l"'s show a greater left slant in earlier examples, however have remained generally consistent. Both "l"'s commonly vary in size and width. The "M" in McCovey has varied considerably from what once resembled an enlarged "nl" configuration (circa 1960s), to a more traditional style (1970s). The downward beginning stroke of the "M" can vary in length and may be twice the size of either loop in the letter. The second loop of the "M" commonly hooks upward underneath the superscript "c". The "c" superscript varies in size and character formation, and may or may not be underlined. The "C" has condensed over the years and lost its break with the "o", due to the addition of a bottom hook formation that makes the letter resemble a "G". The "ey" combination seems to have also condensed in space with age, with the "e" nonexistent in some signatures. The slant of the first downward stroke in the "W" and the "M" has been identical in recent examples.

McCovey has been a responsive signer and collectors should have little difficulty adding his signature to their collections.

Availability: Plentiful
Demand: Little

Cut signature	$3
Single-signature baseball	$20
3x5" index card	$7
Photograph/baseball card	$13
HOF plaque postcard	$12
Perez-Steele postcard	$25

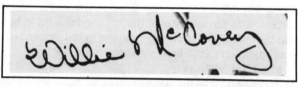

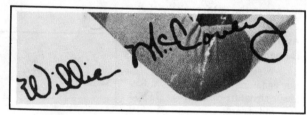

Joe McGinnity

Joseph Jerome McGinnity
(March 19, 1871-Nov. 14, 1929)

"Iron Man" won 247 games and lost 144 for a career winning percentage of .632. McGinnity led or shared the league title in wins five times, innings pitched five times and games seven times. His best season came in 1904 for the Giants, when he posted a 35-8 record that included nine shutouts while appearing in 51 games. He pitched until the age of 54 in 1925.

Commonly signing "J.J. McGinnity", his signature varied in character formation, slant and size. Signature breaks fell between the "M" and the superscript "c", also between the "G" and the "i" in McGinnity. Both the "J"'s can vary in size, however the top loop is always smaller than the descending bottom loop. The formation of the "J" allows the stem to be intersected at almost the same location by both the beginning and ending strokes. Both the "J"s should be nearly identical in slant and typically extend to the height of the "M" in McGinnity.

The "M" begins with a formation that can resemble a "J" at times, with the stroke originating from near the signature's base line. The opening loop of the "M" often rises above both pinnacles of the letter. The "M" can vary a bit in size and its right slant should resemble that of the stem of the "G". The "c" superscript can vary in size and may even be a bit larger than his other lower case letters. The "c" superscript is often underlined and may ascend higher than the "M" in McGinnity. The "G" begins from lower case height with an extended stroke upward to create the looped first pinnacle of the letter. The second pinnacle of the "G" is often pointed rather than looped and is often exceeded in height by the letter's first pinnacle. The stem of the "G" extends slightly below the signature's base line and often forms a triangular ending stroke formation. The "G" is typically left open at the bottom. The "inn" is often just five identical loops that begin with a stroke upward from the base line. The last "i" in McGinnity may differ in size and formation from the first "i". Both "i"s are typically dotted. The unusually large ascender of the "t" is often the highest point in his signature. The ascender of the "t" can vary in width, however its slant should be nearly identical to that of the "y". The "t" is crossed by a separate stroke that is somewhat haphazard in placement and may or may not even intersect the stem of the letter. The loop of the "y" is usually well defined and at lower case height. The descender of the "y", which is typically the lower point in his signature, often ends with a triangular stroke formation that can vary in size and flamboyance.

McGinnity was an obliging signer, however few examples of his signature have surfaced in the autograph market. Collectors should find the acquisition of his signature a bit of a challenge.

Availability: Scarce
Demand: Above average

Cut signature	$1,250
Single-signature baseball	$3,500
3x5" index card	$1,700
Photograph/baseball card	$3,250
HOF plaque postcard	Impossible
Perez-Steele postcard	Impossible

John McGraw

John Joseph McGraw
(April 7, 1873-Feb. 25, 1934)

"Little Napoleon" won 2,840 games as a manager, primarily for the New York Giants, and took nine teams to the World Series. During his 30 years with the Giants he gained the respect of everyone affiliated with the game. Due to failing health he ended his career in June of 1932, less than two years before his death.

Commonly signing "John J. McGraw" or "John McGraw", his signature varied primarily in character formation during his lifetime. The only consistent break was between the superscript "c" and the "G" in McGraw. Occasional breaks were also between the "M" and the superscript "c", also between the "G" and the "r" in McGraw. The "J" could be either a single- or two-stroke formation. The "J" in John was identical in slant to his middle initial, but may vary slightly in the length of its beginning and ending strokes. The "J" typically connected to the "o", which was often left open on the top of the letter. The "h" varied slightly in ascender width, but was consistent in slant. The "n" in John often resembled a "u" because of its formation. The "M" could vary in size and flamboyance, but typically began at the top of the letter. The "M" may connect to the superscript "c", which occasionally resembled an "o". The superscript was typically underlined. The "G" varied in size and may or may not be closed on the bottom of the character.

The "raw" was relatively consistent, with the "a" often left slightly open on the top. The ending stroke in his last name was typically short and simple. The "oh" combination was the most consistent element in his signature and makes a good reference point for authenticators.

McGraw was an obliging signer, but few samples of his signature surface in the autograph market. Collectors may find the acquisition of his signature a bit challenging.

Availability: Limited
Demand: Strong

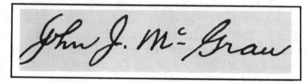

Cut signature	$425
Single-signature baseball	$2,875
3x5" index card	$475
Photograph/baseball card	$1,175
HOF plaque postcard	Impossible
Perez-Steele postcard	Impossible

Bill McKechnie

William Boyd McKechnie
(Aug. 7, 1886-Oct. 29, 1965)

A keen manager, "Deacon Bill" won well over 1,800 games and took three different clubs — Pittsburgh, St. Louis, and Cincinnati — to the World Series. In 1940 his Cincinnati team posted a record of 100 wins and only 53 defeats.

Typically signing "W.B. McKechnie" or "Bill McKechnie", his signature varied in character formation, size and slant during his lifetime. Consistent signature breaks fell between the "M" and the superscript "c", also between the "K" and the "e" in McKechnie. The "B" in Bill, or his middle initial, was typically two or three times the size of the "M" in McKechnie. Older examples of his signature will show a more ornate formation to the "B", adding larger loops to the top and bottom of the letter. The "M" could vary in size and the beginning stroke of the letter could resemble a "2" on occasion. The "c" could also vary in size, but was typically connected to the top of the letter "K". The distinct single-stroke formation of the letter "K" resembled an "n" in appearance and ended typically with a long extended descending stroke. The "e" and the "c" often looked alike, with the "e" beginning with an upward stroke from below the signature's base line. The ascender of the "h" varied in height, but was typically larger than the "M" or the "K" in McKechnie. The last "e" in McKechnie varied in size, and may not rest even with the signature's base line. The "i" in McKechnie may be dotted with a circle. The opening formation to the "W" in William and the "M" in McKechnie are often identical. The "McK" combination, because of its uniqueness in character formation makes a good authentication reference point.

McKechnie was an obliging signer and collectors should have little trouble acquiring his autograph through dealers or auction houses.

Availability: Above average
Demand: Average

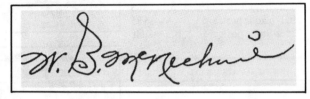

Cut signature	$55
Single-signature baseball	$625
3x5" index card	$100
Photograph/baseball card	$275
HOF plaque postcard	$375
Perez-Steele postcard	Impossible

Ducky Medwick

Joseph Michael Medwick
(Nov. 24, 1911-March 21, 1975)

Medwick cracked 2,471 hits and 205 homers during a career that ended at a batting average of .324. In one of the greatest individual performances of the game, Medwick led the National League in at-bats (633), runs (111), hits (237), doubles (56), home runs (31), RBIs (154), slugging average (.641) and batting average (.374) during the 1937 season.

Commonly signing "Joe Medwick", his signature varied in character formation, slant and size during his lifetime. The only consistent signature break fell between the "J" and the "o" in Joe. Occasional breaks fell also between the "M" and the "e" and the "e" and the "d" in Medwick. The "J" in Joe is always larger than the "M" in Medwick. The ascender of the "J" is always larger than the descender of the letter. The descender of the "J" typically falls slightly below the signature's base line. The "oe" in Joe varies in size and appeared to decrease with age. The formation of the "M" remained relatively consistent and his entire signature seemed to increase a bit in slant with age. The "i" can be dotted with a circle and in combination with the "c" can often resemble the letter "u". The "c" showed greater character definition in earlier examples. The ascender of the "k" was typically twice the height of the "d"'s ascender. The "k" in later examples can resemble and "h" and exhibits no flamboyant ending stroke.

Medwick was a very responsive signer and collectors should find the acquisition of his signature fairly easy.

Availability: Above average
Demand: Average

Cut signature	$18
Single-signature baseball	$330
3x5" index card	$25
Photograph/baseball card	$65
HOF plaque postcard	$85
Perez-Steele postcard	Impossible

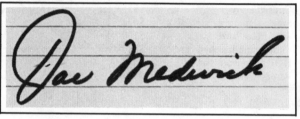

Johnny Mize

John Robert Mize
(Jan. 7, 1913-   )

The "Big Cat" was a power hitter who rapped 359 homers, 2,011 hits and drove in 1,337 runs during his career. A lifetime .312 hitter, Mize led or shared the National League home run title four times and in 1939 won the league's batting championship (.349).

Commonly signing "John Mize" or "Johnny Mize", his signature has varied primarily in capitalization. Consistent signature breaks fall between the "J" and the "o" in Johnny or John, also between the "M" and the "i" in Mize. The "J" is typically a single-stroke formation, although I have seen a two-stroke variation. The formation of the "J" commonly varies between a rounded stem character and a straight stemmed letter. The straight stemmed "J" may even have a loop in the ascender. The top of the "o" connects to the "h" to form the letter's ascender. The ascender of the "h" commonly varies in degree of right slant and can extend above the second "n" in Johnny. The descender of the "y" in Johnny typically forms a triangle at the bottom that can include two small loops. Earlier examples of Mize's signature will show a beginning looped construction to the "M" that resembles a "J", while later versions may or may not have this formation. the "M" can also vary in both size and slant. The "ize" in Mize has remained relatively consistent.

Mize has been very responsive to autograph requests and collectors should find the acquisition of his signature fairly easy.

Availability: Plentiful
Demand: Little

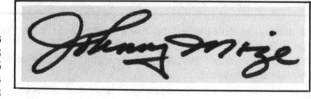

Cut signature	$3
Single-signature baseball	$18
3x5" index card	$6
Photograph/baseball card	$13
HOF plaque postcard	$8
Perez-Steele postcard	$25

Stan Musial

Stanley Frank Musial
(Nov. 21, 1920-   )

"Stan the Man" was a seven-time batting champion, who led the National League in RBIs twice, hits six times, runs five times, and slugging average six times. A three-time Most Valuable Player, he was named to 12 All-Star teams and ended his career with 3,630 lifetime hits at a batting average of .331.

Commonly signing "Stan Musial", his signature has varied primarily in character formation. Early examples (1940s) exhibit a signature break between the "M" and the "u" in Musial, while later examples only show consistent breaks in his first name between the "S" and the "t", and the "t" and the "a". The traditional capitalized "S" evolved into a stylized "S" that has remained relatively consistent for decades. The "t" became a separate two-stroke non-looped character, while the "an" remained fairly consistent. The "t" is typically crossed by a separate stroke that can begin from the middle of the letter "S", and extend to the "n" in Stan. The "n" typically resembles a "u" and can appear unrecognizable at times. the "M" evolved into the current letter formation, with earlier examples having an extended beginning stroke in the letter that slowly disappeared with age. The "M" also became less rounded in formation and generally smaller in size. The "usial" condensed a bit with age, with the "l" closing at the end, instead of forming an extended ending stroke. Each letter of the "usia" combination typically gets progressively smaller in character size. In later examples the ascender of the "l" in Musial may exceed the height of the "M". For some unknown reason, Musial also occasionally added one or two slashes at the end of his name.

Musial has been a very responsive and congenial signer. He commonly exerts extra effort to comply with fan requests and remains as popular today as he was during his playing days. Collectors should find the acquistion of his signature fairly easy.

Availability: Plentiful
Demand: Little

Cut signature	$4
Single-signature baseball	$24
3x5" index card	$7
Photograph/baseball card	$14
HOF plaque postcard	$12
Perez-Steele postcard	$60

Kid Nichols

Charles Augustus Nichols
(Sept. 14, 1869-April 11, 1953)

Nichols won 360 games, pitched 48 shutouts and posted a winning percentage of .639. He was a solid right-hander who won 30 or more games for seven consecutive seasons (1891-1897). Although he retired from the game in 1906, he was not inducted into the Cooperstown shrine until 1949.

Commonly signing "Charles A. Nichols" or "Charles Kid Nichols", his signature varied in character formation and slant. Consistent signature breaks fell between the "C" and the "h" in Charles, also between the "K" and the "i" in Kid. The "C" typically began with an upward extended stroke, from the signature's base line, which formed the first loop of the two-looped letter. The "h" could vary in ascender width and height. The "a" may or may not close on the top and the "r" could vary slightly in formation. The "l" in Charles exhibited inconsistencies in its slant and may resemble a "b" at times. The "s" was typically larger than the "e" and included a simple upward ending stroke. The "k" was a two-stroke character formation with the first stroke beginning from the base line and creating what resembled an upside down "V". The second stroke of the "K", which formed the arms of the letter, extended to the capitalization height and descended only to the signature's base line. The "id" could vary in size, with the "d" typically having a small hook at the end. A pair of quotation marks commonly surrounded his nickname. The capitalization in Nichols was a traditional formation and began from the top with a short hook formation. The "h", "l" and "s" in Nichols had the same characteristics as their predecessors in Charlie. The "o" may or may not close at the top of the letter.

Nichols signed meticulously and was responsive to autograph requests. His later signatures exhibited typical aging characteristics. After his retirement from the game he was active in many business partnerships including bowling alleys, motion pictures and real estate. Suprisingly, few samples of his signature surface in the autograph market.

Availability: Average
Demand: Above average

Cut signature	$120
Single-signature baseball	$2,700
3x5" index card	$180
Photograph/baseball card	$420
HOF plaque postcard	$325
Perez-Steele postcard	Impossible

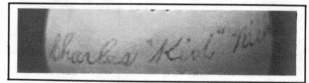

James O'Rourke

James Henry O'Rourke
(Aug. 24, 1852-Jan. 8, 1919)

"Orator Jim", a pioneer of the game, played for 19 years. He collected over 2,300 lifetime hits while compiling an average over .310. O'Rourke was well into his fifties before he decided to stop playing baseball in 1904.

Typically signing "Jas. H. O'Rourke" or "J.H. O'Rourke", his signature varied both in character formation and size during his lifetime. The only consistent signature break fell between the "R" and the "O" in O'Rourke. Occasional breaks occured between the "J" and the "a" in "Jas.", also between the "k" and the "e" (very rare) in O'Rourke. The "J" varied in size, but typically had a large descender. The "a" may or may not be closed at the top and the "s" was often left open a bit on the bottom. The "H" was a two-stroke formation, crossed in the center by the second stroke, which may or may not connect to the "O" in O'Rourke. The "O" varied in character formation and flamboyance, resembling a traditional capitalized "O" or an enlarged lower case version of the letter. The enlarged lower case formation of the "O" typically connected to the "R" in O'Rourke. The "R" in O'Rourke varied in flamboyance, but was fairly consistent in character formation. The ending stroke of the "R" typically extended below the signature's base line. The "our" varied in legibility, and like all O'Rourke lower case letters, was often four or five smaller than the capitalized characters. The "ke" could vary in slant and formation, but typically had no flamboyant ending stroke.

O'Rourke was a very intelligent man and a fairly prolific writer. As a practicing attorney in Bridgeport, Conn., he signed numerous correspondences. His handwriting is easily identified by his unique one- or two-stroke constructions of the letter "p", the extended crossing of his letter "t"s, and the unusually large and flamboyant descenders in his letters. Like all of baseball's pioneers his signature is highly sought after by collectors and may prove, despite his prolific writing habits, to be a challenging acquisition.

Availability: Scarce
Demand: Strong

Cut signature	$1,850
Single-signature baseball	$4,000
3x5" index card	$2,900
Photograph/baseball card	$3,775
HOF plaque postcard	Impossible
Perez-Steele postcard	Impossible

Mel Ott

Melvin Thomas Ott
(March 2, 1909-Nov. 21, 1958)

Ott led or shared the National League home run title six times while compiling a career total of 511. A lifetime .304 hitter, Ott smacked 2,876 hits over his 22 seasons with the New York Giants. His unique batting style of lifting his right foot became a personal trademark. Ott played in 11 All-Star games and three World Series contests.

Commonly signing "Mel Ott", his signature varied in character formation and size. There were no consistent signature breaks exhibited in his autograph. The "M" began from the top of the character, with a slight hook before the downward stroke which constructed the first loop of the letter. The first loop in the "M" was typically two or three times the width of the second loop in the first, and less rounded at the top of the loop. The "e" extended to the height of the second loop of the "M", while the "l" varied in both height and width. The beginning stroke of the "O" could originate from the inside or outside of the letter. The "O" could also vary in right slant. The "tt" formation varied in size and could be crossed by a separate stroke, or by an ending stroke which doubled back over the letter combination.

Ott was a responsive signer whose sudden death in an automobile accident at the age of 49 shocked the entire baseball world. Samples of his signature do periodically surface in the autograph market.

Availability: Average
Demand: Above average

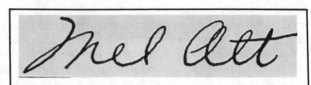

Cut signature	$100
Single-signature baseball	$625
3x5" index card	$140
Photograph/baseball card	$275
HOF plaque postcard	$375
Perez-Steele postcard	Impossible

Satchel Paige

Leroy Robert Paige
(July 7, 1906-June 8, 1982)

A popular figure, Paige was known most for his pinpoint accuracy and infinite base-ball wisdom. During his prime with the Pittsburgh Crawfords he won 31 games and lost four in 1933. The renowned barnstormer once struck out Rogers Hornsby five times during a single game. At the age of 42, he helped pitch the Cleveland Indians to the 1948 pennant.

Commonly signing "Satchel Paige", his signature varied in character formation, size and slant. Consistent signature breaks fall between the "S" and the "a" in Satchel, also between the "P" and the "a" in Paige. Occasional breaks also fall between the "t" and the "c" in Satchel, and the "i" and the "g" in Paige. The "S" could vary in size, although it was typi-cally the same height as the "t" or the "h" in Satchel. The top loop of the "S" may or may not be recognizable, depending on the character's width. The "a" may or may not close at the top and the "t" has an unusually large ascender which can exceed the height of the "l" in Satchel. The "t" is crossed by a separate stroke which may interesect the "h". The ascender of the "h" may vary in width and the "e" can vary in size. The slant of the "t", "h" and the "l" should all be similar. The "P" varied in character formation from a traditional styled capitalized "P", to an enlarged lower case "p". The traditional styled "P" was often 50% larger in size than the capitalized "S". The loop of the "P" may or may not be closed. The loop of the traditional styled capitalized "P" can extend above the "aig". The "g" often resembles the letter "y" and the "e" can vary in size. On occasion an extended upward ending stroke may follow the "i", when the letter breaks from te "g". Paige often added an underline to his signature.

The inconsistencies in Paige's signature can make authentication a challenge, however he was a very responsive signer and collectors should have little difficulty acquiring his autograph.

Availability: Above average
Demand: Above average

Cut signature	$25
Single-signature baseball	$275
3x5" index card	$40
Photograph/baseball card	$95
HOF plaque postcard	$75
Perez-Steele postcard	$1,650

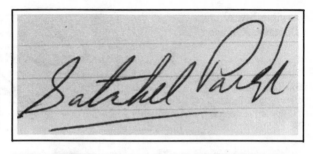

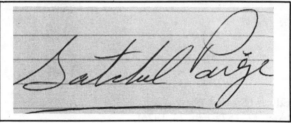

Herb Pennock

Herbert Jefferis Pennock
(Feb. 10, 1894-Jan. 30, 1948)

Pennock won 240 games and posted an ERA of 3.61 during his career. His post-season play was brilliant; he pitched 55⅓ innings at an ERA of 1.95 during five undefeated appearances.

Typically signing "Herb Pennock", his signature varied in character formation and size. Consistent signature breaks fell between the "H" and the "e" in Herb, also between the "P" and the "e" in Pennock. The "H" was a two-stroke formation that could vary in height, although the second stroke of the letter was always larger than the first. The "erb" condensed a bit with age, with the "er" often resembling a "u". The "b" varied in ascender width, but was similar in slant to the "H". The "P" was unique in its character formation, and could often vary radically in size. In earlier examples the descender of the "P" often extended well below the base line of his signature and formed a distinguishable loop. Later examples, however, show little distinction between the ascender loop and the much smaller descender loop. The "enn" combination often resembled a "nm" configuration and the "ock" varied in size, particularly the "c". The ascender of the "k" can vary in width, with the height of the character often falling just short of the capitalization. Both the "b" and the "k" will be fairly similar in slant.

Following his playing days he became vice-president and general manager of the Phillies
As a baseball executive he signed numerous documents, some of which occasionally sur
face in the autograph market.

Availability: Average
Demand: Average

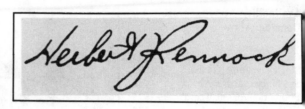

Cut signature	$95
Single-signature baseball	$1,075
3x5" index card	$160
Photograph/baseball card	$355
HOF plaque postcard	Impossible
Perez-Steele postcard	Impossible

Ed Plank

Edward Stewart Plank
(Aug. 31, 1875-Feb. 24, 1926)

Plank won over 300 games in his 17-year career at a winning percentage of .629. Plank
appeared in four World Series, pitching 54⅔ innings at an ERA of 1.30.

Commonly signing "Ed Plank" or "E.S. Plank", his signature varied in character formation and slant during his lifetime. A consistent signature break fell betwen the "l" and the
"a" in Plank. Occasionally a break also fell between the "P" and the "l" in Plank. The character formation of the "E" varied in both the beginning and ending stroke. The beginning
stroke of the "E" may have an extended line upward leading to the first loop, and the ending
stroke will vary both in flamboyance and size of the bottom loop. His middle initial of "S"
may or may not be closed on the bottom, and may have no distinguishable top loop to the
letter. The "P" originates from the top of the character as a downward stroke that doubles
back upward to form the variable sized loop to the letter. The "P" may or may not connect to
the "l". If the "P" does connect to the "l", the connection will intersect the stem in the
middle of the letter. The "l" commonly varies in size, but is consistent in slant. The "a" is
often left open and the "n" sometimes resembles a "v". The "k" was always a two-stroke
formation, with the second stroke varying in both size and the degree to which it intersects
the first stroke. It is not unusual for the "k" to show considerable flamboyance. The
upward stroke of the "P" and the stem of the "k" should be similar in slant.

The anomalies in Plank's signature can make it difficult to authenticate. He was an obliging signer but was never a prolific writer. Plank died at the young age of 50. Collectors should
find his signature a challenging acquisition.

Availability: Limited
Demand: Strong

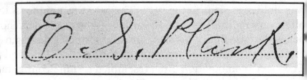

Cut signature	$1,925
Single-signature baseball	$4,000
3x5" index card	$3,250
Photograph/baseball card	$3,750
HOF plaque postcard	Impossible
Perez-Steele postcard	Impossible

Charles Radbourn

Charles Gardner Radbourn
(Dec. 11, 1854-Feb. 5, 1897)

"Old Hoss" pitched 308 winning games at a .617 percentage in just over a decade of seasons. In 1884, while playing in the National League at Providence, he won 60 games, eleven of which were shutouts. Equally impressive were his 441 strikeouts during that 1884 season.

Commonly signing "Chas. Radbourn", his signature varied in character formation and size. Consistent breaks fell between the "h" and the "a" in "Chas.", also between the "R" and the "a", and the "a" and the "d" in Radbourn. Radbourn's last name was mispelled for years, with an "e" added to the end. He also occasionally dropped the "o" in his last name, spelling it "Radburn". Uncertainty surrounds these spelling variations, adding unneeded complexity to an already difficult signature to authenticate. The "C" could vary in size and the formation of the beginning stroke of the letter. The beginning stroke of the "C" could be a small loop or a downward stroke. The ascender of the "h" varied in size, although it typically equalled or exceeded the height of the "C". The "a" on occasion could be open, however it was typically closed. The "R" was a stroke that doubled back to form the top loop. Worth noting in the lower case letter "a"s and the loop of the "d" was a sharpness on the bottom of the oval loop formation of the characters as they met the signature's base line. The ascender of the "d" was relatively short, due to the size of the character's loop. The "b" varied in ascender width, although its slant was similar to the "d". The "o" may be absent, with the "b" smoothly connecting to the "u". The "r" was an older style formation, similar to that used by Travis Jackson. The ending stroke, following the "n", was commonly a simple upward curl.

Following an illustrious career, he suffered a near fatal gun accident which disfigured his face. Suffering partial paralysis and the loss of one eye, along with the loss of his speech, Radbourn became a recluse and died at the age of 43. Mystery still surrounds many elements of Radbourn's life and collectors should find the acquisition of his signature one of the most difficult of all the inductees.

Availability: Scarce
Demand: Strong

Cut signature	$1,425
Single-signature baseball	$4,000
3x5" index card	$2,600
Photograph/baseball card	$3,750
HOF plaque postcard	Impossible
Perez-Steele postcard	Impossible

Pee Wee Reese

Harold Henry Reese
(July 23, 1918-   )

Reese played 16 seasons with the Dodgers recording over 2,100 hits at a batting average of .269. "The Little Colonel" led the Dodgers to seven pennants with his magnificent fielding and clutch hitting. Reese's finest season with the bat came in 1954 when he hit .309.

Commonly signing "Pee Wee Reese", his signature has varied in character formation, size and slant. Consistent signature breaks fall between the "P" and the "e", and the "W" and the "e" in "Pee Wee", also between the "R" and the "e" in Reese. During his playing years Reese's signature consisted of much larger capitalization (four to five times larger than his lower case letters), and less character slant. Over the years his capitalization has gradually reduced in size (two to three times larger than his lower case letters), while increasing the right slant of his signature. The end of the "e" in "Pee Wee" may connect to the "W", particularly in earlier examples. All the characters in his signature vary in size and the "s" in Reese is left open on the bottom of the letter. Generally speaking his signature has remained rather consistent.

Reese has been a responsive signer, however mail requests during recent years have had unpredictable results. Collectors should find his signature a fairly easy acquisition.

Availability: Plentiful
Demand: Little

Cut signature	$4
Single-signature baseball	$20
3x5" index card	$9
Photograph/baseball card	$14
HOF plaque postcard	$12
Perez-Steele postcard	$50

Sam Rice

Edgar Charles Rice
(Feb. 20, 1890-Oct. 13, 1974)

"Sam," a nickname bestowed by Clark Griffith, played for 20 seasons in the American League compiling a .322 batting average that included 2,987 hits. He helped guide the Washington Senators to three World Series contests, were he hit .302.

Commonly signing "Sam Rice", his signature varied primarily in character formation and size. Consistent signature breaks fell between the "S" and the "a" in Sam, also between the "i" and the "c" in Rice. The "S" can vary both in size and width of the looped character formation. The "a" may or may not be closed and can occasionally resemble a "u" in its formation. The "m" can vary in size, and quotation marks are commonly placed around his nickname. The beginning stroke of the "R" in Rice could vary both in size and flamboyance. The "i" could also vary in size and often resembles an "e". The "c" can appear in his signature as if it were a superscript, elevated slightly above the base line. The "e" commonly varied in size and may even dip slightly below the base line. The "R" is the highest point in his signature, and in combination with the "i", probably makes the best comparison point for authenticators.

Rice was a responsive signer and collectors should have little trouble acquiring his signature through autograph dealers or auction houses.

Availability: Above average
Demand: Average

Cut signature	$16
Single-signature baseball	$290
3x5" index card	$30
Photograph/baseball card	$70
HOF plaque postcard	$75
Perez-Steele postcard	Impossible

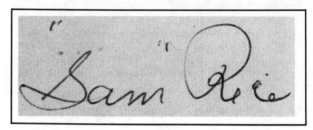

Branch Rickey

Wesley Branch Rickey
(Dec. 20, 1881-Dec. 9, 1965)

Rickey's career had a phenomenal impact upon the game of baseball. From breaking the color barrier to inventing the concept of a farm system, Rickey's overwhelming ambition was profound. A law graduate from the University of Michigan, he built both the St. Louis Cardinals and Brooklyn Dodgers into dynasties.

Commonly signing "Branch Rickey", his signature varied in character formation and size during his lifetime. Consistent signature breaks appeared between the "n" and the "c" in Branch, also between the "i" and the "c", and between both the strokes of the "k" in Rickey. The beginning stroke of the "B" began at the top of the letter, with a downward stroke that doubled back to form the rest of the character. The "B" commonly varied in size and can even be mistaken for an "E" at times. The "a" typically did not close at the top and the "n" often resembled a "u". The "ch" in Branch appeared like an "ile" combination, with a hooked ending stroke. The "R" could vary in size, but was relatively consistent in character formation. The "c" in Rickey seemed to have greater character definition when compared to the same letter in Branch. The "k" was a two-stroke formation, with the first stroke forming an unusually small ascender. The height of the "e" and the ascender of the "k" were often equal. The descender of the "y" was often a simple, slightly curved, downward stroke.

Rickey was an obliging signer and like most baseball executives his name adorned numerous pieces of documentation. Collectors should find his autograph a fairly easy acquisition.

Availability: Average
Demand: Average

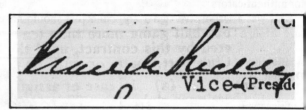

Cut signature	$75
Single-signature baseball	$550
3x5" index card	$140
Photograph/baseball card	$340
HOF plaque postcard	Impossible
Perez-Steele postcard	Impossible

Eppa Rixey

Eppa Rixey
(May 3, 1891-Feb. 28, 1963)

Rixey pitched in the National League from 1912 to 1933, winning 266 games at an ERA of 3.15. Not an overwhelming pitcher, despite his 6'5" size, he posted a career high 25 wins and 13 losses to lead the league in 1922.

Typically signing "Eppa Rixey" or "Eppa Rixey, Jr.", his signature varied in character formation and size. The only consistent signature break fell between the "R" and the "i" in Rixey. The "E" can vary in size, however was relatively consistent in character formation. The "pp" combination was the most notable element in his signature, with each letter having large extended ascenders. The ascenders of the "pp"s may exceed the height of the "E" in Eppa. The first "p" in Eppa may or may consist of a separate stroke for both the stem and the loop of the letter. The loop in the letter "p" does not typically close and the "a" in Eppa may vary in size. The "R" can vary in character formation, particularly in the beginning stroke of the letter. The "ixe" can vary in size and letter spacing. The descender of the "y" in Rixey can vary both in the formation and flamboyance of the ending stroke.

Rixey died at the age of 71 just one month after his election to the Baseball Hall of Fame. He was an obliging signer, however like most of the players who were not recognized by the Cooperstown shrine until late in their life, did not enjoy the long post-career fame which usually brings with it a flood of autograph requests. Collectors should find the acquisition of his signature a moderate challenge.

Availability: Average
Demand: Average

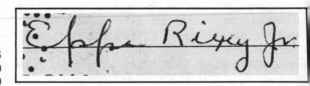

Cut signature	$55
Single-signature baseball	$360
3x5" index card	$90
Photograph/baseball card	$190
HOF plaque postcard	Impossible
Perez-Steele postcard	Impossible

Robin Roberts

Robin Evan Roberts
(Sept. 30, 1926-   )

Roberts posted 286 wins during his 19-year career, at an ERA of 3.41. He led or shared the National League title for pitching victories four consecutive years and led in innings pitched for five consecutive years.

Commonly signing "Robin Roberts", his signature has exhibited variation in both character formation and size. Early examples of his signature (1950s), show consistent breaks between the "R" and the "o" in Robin, also between the "R" and the "o" in Roberts. In later examples, following his retirement from baseball, he typically exhibited no signature breaks. The "R" in early autograph examples was more traditional in style, while later versions would show less width to the letter and a change to a two-stroke formation. The ending stroke of the "R" eventually evolved into a continuation of either his first or his last name by creating a looped character formation for the "o" The formation of the "b" was altered to accommodate the continuing stroke and often resembled an "h" in its appearance. The "in" has remained fairly consistent, except for a slight increase in its right slant. The "ts" combination was altered in order to cross the "t" with the ending stroke of the "s". Th ascender of the "t" varies in size, and on occasion can be crossed by a single separate stroke.

Roberts has been an obliging signer and like so many other inductees, has in recent years requested donations to scholarship funds or charities in exchange for his signature via an autograph request by mail. Collectors should find the acquisition of his signature fairly easy.

Availability: Plentiful
Demand: Little

Cut signature	$4
Single-signature baseball	$18
3x5" index card	$7
Photograph/baseball card	$12
HOF plaque postcard	$11
Perez-Steele postcard	$25

Brooks Robinson

Brooks Calbert Robinson
(May 18, 1937-   )

Robinson played his entire career with the Baltimore Orioles from 1955 to 1977, collecting 2,848 hits at a lifetime batting average of .267. "The Human Vacuum Cleaner", was one of the most graceful fielders to ever put on a glove. His defensive prowess at third base became legendary as he set numerous fielding records. Robinson was a clutch performer who batted .348 during his five World Series contests.

Typically signing "Brooks Robinson", his signature has varied in character formation and size. In earlier examples, those signed during his playing days, consistent signature breaks fell between the "B" and the "r" in Brooks, also between the "R" ad the "o" in Robinson. Later examples exhibit only one break, between the "R" and the "o" in Robinson. The "B" commonly varies in formation. Older examples will show the "B" originating from the top of the letter with a long downward stroke which doubles back to form the rest of the letter. Later examples typically find the "B" originating from below the signature's base line. The "roo" in Brooks has condensed a bit in character spacing and the "ks" combination resembles a "hi" formation. The top of the "o" may not totally close the letter. The "R" has remained fairly consistent, however I have occasionally witnessed a two-stroke variation. His entire last name has condensed a bit in size over the years. The "ob" can resemble an "eh" configuration and the "s" has decreased slightly in size from earlier examples. The most dramatic change in his signature to date has been in the "on" combination that ends his last name. The ending may appear like a superscript "m" or a capitalized "M", and can approach capitalization height. In earlier examples he may have dotted the "i" with a circle.

Brooks Robinson has always been an outstanding signer, even during his playing days he seldom turned away from an autograph request. He has been exemplary of every child's boyhood idol. Robinson's wonderful personality and congeniality make him one of the game's most popular players of all-time.

Availability: Plentiful
Demand: Little

Cut signature	$4
Single-signature baseball	$18
3x5" index card	$6
Photograph/baseball card	$12
HOF plaque postcard	$10
Perez-Steele postcard	$30

Frank Robinson

Frank Robinson
(Aug. 31, 1935-   )

This 1966 Triple Crown winner ended his career with 2,943 hits, 586 home runs, 1,812 RBIs and a career batting average of .294. Robinson is the only player to be presented the Most Valuable Player award in both leagues. Upon the conclusion of his playing career, he set his sights on managing and became the game's first black manager.

Commonly signing Frank Robinson, his signature has varied in character formation, slant and flamboyance. Consistent signature breaks fall between the "F" and the "r" an the "n" and the "a" in Frank. Also between the "R" and the "o" in Robinson. The "F" can vary in size and flamboyance, but has consistently been a two-stroke formaion. The "F" can occasionally resemble an enlarged "y" that has had a slash placed through its descender. The "r" has always been an individual letter and the "ank" has shown only slight variation in size. The "R" evolved from a single-stroke formation into a two-stroke construction. The somewhat unpredictable "R" can vary both in size and formation. The ascender of the "b" can vary in height, width and slant. The "inson" can be generally consistent, if it is legible, and the "s" can be dropped from his last name. The "s" is typically left open and the "i" may be dotted with a circle. The hallmark of his signature has been his unpredictable and flamboyant backward ending stroke, that can extend its loop beyond the "R" in Robinson.

Robinson has never been an easy autograph to acquire and collectors may find his occasional attendance at a baseball card shows the best forum to add his signature to a collection.

Availability: Plentiful
Demand: Little

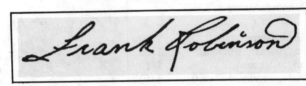

Cut signature	$4
Single-signature baseball	$20
3x5" index card	$7
Photograph/baseball card	$14
HOF plaque postcard	$14
Perez-Steele postcard	$40

Jackie Robinson

Jack Roosevelt Robinson
(Jan. 31, 1919-Oct. 24, 1972)

In a career that only lasted a decade with the Brooklyn Dodgers, Robinson stroked 1,518 hits and 137 home runs for an average of .311. This 1949 National League Most Valuable Player led Brooklyn to six World Series. Robinson terrorized pitchers on the base paths and will always be remembered for stealing home in the 1955 World Series.

Commonly signing "Jackie Robinson", his signature varied both in character formation and slant. Common signature breaks fell between the "J" and the "a" in Jackie, also between the "R" and the "o" in Robinson. The "J" may connect to the "a" in earlier examples, and the break between the "R" and the "o" is often inconsistent. Robinson's letter construction seemed to exhibit increased roundness with age, particularly evident in the "J". The ascender of the "J" is typically wider than the descender. The "a" can resemble an "o" at times and may or may not close at the top of the letter. The "c" can vary in its definition and can show little indication of a looped character. The ascender of the "k" can vary in width and typically equals or exceeds the height of the "J" in Jackie. The "R" can vary significantly in character formation, flamboyance and slant. The top loop of the "R" may or may not meet the stem of the letter and the beginning stroke of the letter may have a hook formation leading to a small loop before the first downward stroke is created. The top loop of the "R" shows increased slant in earlier examples and may extend almost to the "b" in Robinson. The "o" may or may not close at the top and the ascender of the "b" varied both in width and slant. The "ins" was relatively consistent in formation, but commonly varied in slant. The "o"could vary in character width and the "n"s can resemble a "v". The ending stroke of his signature was usually just a simple upward hook.

Robinson was a responsive signer and as his popularity grew, so did the demand for his signature. His autographs do periodically surface in the market and collectors should have little trouble acquiring a Robinson signature.

Availability: Above average
Demand: Above average

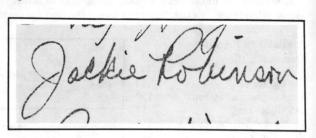

Cut signature	$100
Single-signature baseball	$800
3x5" index card	$150
Photograph/baseball card	$350
HOF plaque postcard	$360
Perez-Steele postcard	Impossible

Wilbert Robinson

Wilbert Robinson
(June 2, 1863-Aug. 8, 1934)

"Uncle Robbie," a star catcher for many years with the Baltimore Orioles (1890s), achieved greater fame as a manager and led the Brooklyn Dodgers from 1914 to 1931. He won 1,397 games and took his club twice to the World Series (1916 and 1920).

Commonly signing "Wilbert Robinson", his signature varied primarily in character formation. Robinson's unpredictable signature breaks were most consistent between the "W" and the "i" in Wilbert, also between the "R" and the "o" in Robinson. Occasional breaks also occur between the "n" and the "s", and the "s" and the "o" in Robinson. The capitalized rounded "W" formation remained fairly consistent, only occasionally adding or deleting a hooked formation at either end of the letter. The "l" could vary both in height and width, but was commonly smaller than the "b". The ascender of the "b" can be large, equalling or exceeding the height of the "W" in Wilbert. The crossing of the "t" was with a separate stroke which had a tendency to fall to the right-hand side of the letter. The "R" could vary in size and slightly in character formation. The "R" usually began near the top of the letter with a downward stroke which doubled back to form the top of the loop. The loop of the "R" may or may not intersect the stem of the letter. The right slant of the "R" allowed the character's loop to fall above the "o". The ascender of the "b" in Robinson was typically large, equalling or exceeding the height of the "R". The "b" in Robinson can often resemble a letter "h", and was typically larger than the "b" in Wilbert. The "ins" varied in character definition, with the "s" often left open on the bottom of the letter. The "on" often varied, resembling a "ue" combination in its appearance. The "o" may or may not close, and the ending stroke in Robinson was variable in length.

Robinson was an obliging signer, but not overly prolific. Collectors may find the acquisition of his signature a bit challenging, as relatively few samples surface in the autograph market.

Availability: Limited
Demand: Above average

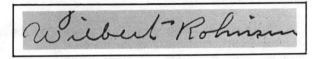

Cut signature	$775
Single-signature baseball	$2,425
3x5" index card	$1,075
Photograph/baseball card	$1,900
HOF plaque postcard	Impossible
Perez-Steele postcard	Impossible

Edd Roush

Edd J. Roush
(May 8, 1893-March 21, 1988)

Roush ended his career with a batting average over .320 which included over 2,100 hits, a considerable feat considering he used a 48-ounce bat. The winner of two batting championships (1917 and 1919), Roush hit over .300 for 11 consecutive seasons.

Typically signing "Edd J. Roush", his signature varied only slightly in character formation, size and slant. Consistent signature breaks fell between each letter in Edd, also between the "R" and the "o" in Roush. The "E" can vary in size, and begin from the signature's base line with a long upward stroke that formed the first loop of the letter. The character spacing between each letter in his first name can vary. The "d"s can vary in ascender width, and may or may not close where the loop meets the stem. Both the ascender and descender of the "J" could vary in size, but little in formation. The flamboyant two-stroke configuration of the "R" became the hallmark of his signature. Often beginning above the last "d" in Edd, the second flamboyant stroke of the "R" formed the loop and leg of the character. It is not uncommon for this long extended stroke of the "R" to intersect his middle initial. During the final years of his life, a three-stroke variation of the "R" occasionally surfaced in his signature. Earlier examples, those during his playing days, may show some flamboyance at the ending of the second stroke of the "R". The "o" began with a long upward extended stroke which originated from below the signature's base line, and may or may not intersect the second stroke of the "R". The typically small "o" and the "s" in Roush may or may not be closed. The letter spacing between the "s" and the "h" can vary, with the ascender of the "h" typically equalling or exceeding the height of the "R" in Roush.

Roush was a very responsive signer and a prolific writer. Collectors should have little trouble acquiring his signature through autograph dealers or auction houses.

Availability: Plentiful
Demand: Little

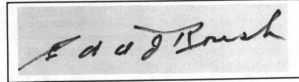

Cut signature	$9
Single-signature baseball	$65
3x5" index card	$11
Photograph/baseball card	$25
HOF plaque postcard	$20
Perez-Steele postcard	$160

Red Ruffing

Charles Herbert Ruffing
(May 3, 1904-Feb. 17, 1986)

Ruffing ended his career with 273 wins and 225 loses at an ERA of 3.80. He was selected to three All-Star teams playing for the New York Yankees. Following his career, which included seven World Series contests, he became a scout for Chicago and Cleveland, as well as a minor league manager.

Commonly signing "Red Ruffing", "Chas. Red Ruffing", or "Charlie Ruffing", his signature varied in character formation, size and slant. Consistent signature breaks fell between the "C" and the "h" in Charlie, the "R" and the "e" in Red, also between the "R" and the "u", and the "n" and the "g" in Ruffing. The "C" began with a stroke that originated from the signature's base line and extended to the top of the letter to form the character's loop. The ascender of the "h" and the "l" could vary in width, and the "a" was seldom identifiable as such, often resembling an "e". Earlier Ruffing examples, those signed during his playing days, exhibit capitalization five or six times the height of the lower case letters. With age these capitalized letters decreased in size to about three times the height of the lower case letters. The "R"s increased in slant with age, with the leg of the letter transforming from an outward stroke to an inward (concave) stroke. The "ed" varied slightly in size and the letters in the "ff" combination were typically not identical in size. The "g" decreased in size and flamboyance with age. Later "g" examples, those signed during the last ten years of his life, exhibit a small thin descender, in great contrast to his earlier version of the letter, which was very large with a flamboyant ending stroke. The "g" may or may not close at the top of the letter.

A stroke in 1973 confined him to a wheelchair, however he still corresponded with his fans. Mail requests during the last few years of his life were a bit unpredictable. Ruffing was an obliging signer, but not overly prolific. Collectors should find the acquisition of his signature fairly easy.

Availability: Plentiful
Demand: Little

Cut signature	$10
Single-signature baseball	$125
3x5" index card	$20
Photograph/baseball card	$45
HOF plaque postcard	$40
Perez-Steele postcard	$350

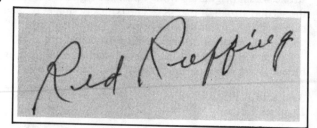

Amos Rusie

Amos Wilson Rusie
(May 30, 1871-Dec. 6, 1942)

Rusie played only 10 seasons in the National League, winning over 240 games at a percentage slightly above .600. He led or shared the National League title for shutouts four of his active 10 years, accumulating 30. Idolized during his playing days, Rusie's career was abruptly ended due to a mysterious arm problem. At the early age of 30 he retired from baseball and pursured a variety of occupations.

Commonly signing "Amos W. Rusie" or "Amos Rusie", his signature varied in character formation, size and slant. There were no consistent signature breaks exhibited in his autograph, however on rare occasions a break may fall between the "A" and the "m" in Amos. The "A" can vary in size, slant and character formation, however was typically two to three times larger than his lower case letters. Character variation in the "A" is common, particularly in the beginning stroke which originates from the bottom of the letter, but at a variety of lengths and angles. The "o" may or may not close at the top and the "s" creates a somewhat unique formation by being constructed from the tip of the "o". The "s" typically is left open, with only a small hook for an ending stroke. His middle initial of "W" can resemble a capitalized "U". The "R" in Rusie originates from the top, inside the character, with a downward stroke that loops over the beginning of the letter. The loop of the "R" may or may not touch its stem. The "usie" varied slightly in size, with little flamboyance in the ending stroke.

Injuries suffered in a 1934 automobile accident left him handicapped until his death. He was an obliging signer, however relatively few of his signatures surface in the autograph market. Collectors should find the acquisition of his signature a bit difficult.

Availability: Limited
Demand: Above average

Cut signature	$1,150
Single-signature baseball	$4,000
3x5" index card	$1,300
Photograph/baseball card	$2,165
HOF plaque postcard	Impossible
Perez-Steele postcard	Impossible

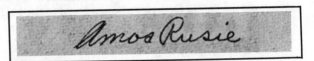

Babe Ruth

George Herman Ruth
(Feb. 6, 1895-Aug. 16, 1948)

Ruth led or shared the American League home run title 12 times, RBI title six times, and runs scored eight times. While recording an astounding career batting average of .342 that included 2,873 hits, he smashed a record 714 home runs. Ruth appeared in 10 World Series Contests, hitting 15 home runs and batting .326. He hit over 40 home runs 11 times during a career considered by most to be the greatest of all time.

Commonly signing "Babe Ruth" or "George H. Ruth", his signature varied in character formation, size, and slant, A consistent signature break can be found between the "B" and the "a" in Babe. There were no breaks exhibited in George, when he signed his first name. Like DiMaggio, Dickey and Mantle, the anomalies in his signature require a letter-by-letter analysis.

Letter	Variation
G	When he signed "George H. Ruth", the "G" was typically the highest point in his signature. The "G" resembles an enlarged "y" at times, with most of the samples I have measured right slanted between 55 and 65 degrees. The "G" began with a hook leading to the first loop in the character, followed by the second pinnacle which typically came to a point, rather than a loop. The second pinnacle in the letter was typically smaller than the first. The "G" was often left open on the bottom, and finished with a double backed stroke similar to the "B" in Babe. The beginning stroke of the letter will typically extend further left than the bottom double backed stroke. The "G" always rested on the signature's base line.
e	The "e" in George was a stylized reduced "E" similar to the "e" in Babe. The height of the "e" in George was often equal to the height of the lower case "g" in George. The bottom loop of the "e" may dip slightly below the signature's base line.
o	The "o" in George was small, typically half the height of the first "e". The "o" can be open or closed at the top of the letter.
r	The "r" typically began with a slight upward stroke that originated from the top of the "o". The top of the letter may have little character definition and could form only a point.
g	The top loop of the "g" was typically higher than the "or" and the last "e" in George. The letter's loop may or may not close and the descender can vary both in length and width. The slant of the descender and the slant of the "G" should be nearly identical. Any major variance in slant between these points should cause a collector to reconsider purchasing the signature.
e	The last "e" in George is usually traditional in style. The height of the "e" is usually equal to the height of the "r". The "e" can vary in width, with the finishing hooked stroke rising to the height of the letter.
H	His middle initial of "H" was a two-stroke construction, varying slightly in slant. The first stroke in the "H" typically began from the top with a loop, while the second stroke began as a simple downward line which doubled back to form the middle of the letter. The loop of the second stroke may not extend to the first stroke. The first stroke of the "H" may only extend as high as the "t" in Ruth, while the larger second stroke can reach the height of the "h" in Ruth.
B	The "B" in Babe is a difficult letter on which to base an authentication due to variations in slant and width. The hooked opening upward stroke began typically from the middle of the letter, then doubled back downward to the signature's base line, before turning upward at an unpredictable angle to form the top loop of the

letter. The middle loop of the "B" was often equal in height to the "a" in Babe. The top loop of the "B" typically extends beyond the bottom loop of the letter. The angle of the middle loop of the letter is unpredictable, either level to the signature's base line or slanted downward. The bottom loop of the "B" never closes the letter. The finishing stroke of the letter is typically a double backed curl that can resemble a "u". The double backed stroke of the curl may or may not be noticeable, depending upon how far apart the strokes lie from each other. Ghost-signed autographs commonly miss this typically pointed ending formation and will instead loop the stroke. Complicating matters even further is that Ruth himself occasionally looped the ending. Claire Ruth, Babe's wife, occasionally signed on the couple's behalf and she typically looped the bottom stroke of the letter. The "B" may or may not connect to the "a". The slant of the stem of the "B" should be very similar to the slant of the stem of the "R" (Within a few degrees).

a   The "a" in Babe may or may not close at the top of the letter. The "a" will rest on the signature's base line and extend in height to the middle formation of the "B". The width of the "a" equals or slightly exceeds the width of the "u" in Ruth.

b   The unusually large ascender of the "b" commonly exceeded the height of the "B" in Babe. The ascender of the "b" can vary in width, with the bottom loop typically stopping at equal height to the "a". The width of the bottom loop can vary and the height of the ascender of the "b" commonly exhibits less degree of right slant than the "t" or the "h" in Ruth.

e   The "e" in Babe was a stylized reduced "E" that resembled a "w" turned on it's side. The top loop of the "e" may begin slightly above the height of the "a". The slant and the formation of the bottom loop commonly vary. The finishing stroke of the "e" was typically a simple upward curl to the height of the first loop of the letter.

R   The "R", like the "B" in Babe, also varied in character formation and size. The letter typically began with a hooked stroke, similar to the "G" in George, which then turned downward to the signature's base line, then doubled back upward to form the character's extended top loop. The top loop of the "R" can extend as far as the "t" in Ruth. Once the top loop is formed, the stroke may or may not intersect its stem just above the letter's beginning hooked stroke. The gradual and slightly curled outward leg of the "R" can vary in length, however it is the only letter in his signature (Babe Ruth) that may dip slightly below the base line, with the occasional exception being the first stroke of the "B" or opening hooked stroke of the "u". The height of the "R" commonly varied. The spacing between the "R" and the "u" may also vary and occasionally the ending stroke of the "R" does intersect the beginning hooked stroke of the "u".

u   The "u" begins with a hooked stroke which occasionally can be wider than the letter. The bottom of the hooked beginning stroke of the letter may dip slightly below the signature's base line. The "u" is a two-looped construction with the second loop typically being slightly larger than the first. The slant of the "u" should be nearly identical to the slant of the "t", if it is not, the collector should reconsider purchasing the signature.

t   The "t" can vary in width, however it is typically about half to three quarters of the height of the "h". The ascender of the "t" commonly falls slightly below the opening hooked stroke of the "R". The "t" is typically crossed by a separate stroke which varies in length. The "t" may also be crossed by a flamboyant ending loop after the "h". Although crossing the "t" with the ending loop is not common, it can be noted in certain cases such as Ruth's autographed 60th home run ball (Sept. 30, 1927) on display in the Baseball Hall of Fame.

h   The "h" can vary in height, width and slant. The ascender of the "h" varies in height. On flat items it may exceed the top of the "R", while on baseballs it may only rise half the distance of the "R". The loop of the "h" typically lacks definition and may even resemble an undotted "i". The ending stroke of the "h" is typically a simple extended line, however as previously noted it can be flamboyant and double back to cross the "t". The height of the loop usually equals that of the first loop in the "u" in Ruth.

Ruth's handwriting is easily distinguished by his flamboyant two-stroke "T" and three-stroke "F" formations. Lower case letters such as "y" and "g" are often simple downward strokes which lack any loop formations. Much of his capitalization exhibits the familiar opening hooked stroke that is common in his signature's "B" and "R". Ruth commonly inserts a break between the capitalization in a word and the first lower case letters.

Complicating the task of authentication is the fact that Ruth employed the services of a ghost signer. Typically a ghost-signed autograph will be a bit larger with less attention paid to detail. The majority of Ruth's ghost-signed signatures appear on black and white photographs. Allegations of clubhouse personnel signing on behalf of "The Bambino" also haunt numerous pieces of autographed material, particularly team baseballs. Ruth's wife occasionally signed material on the couple's behalf, with her version of Babe's signature bearing incredible resemblance to an authentic sample. Add these three scenarios to the fact that his signature is often forged, and the collector is faced with and authentication nightmare. Purchasing a Ruth autograph is not recommended for the novice and collectors wishing to do so should approach such an acquisiton with prudence.

Fortunately for all collectors, Ruth was a willing and prolific signer. He would spend hours signing autographs, particularly for children. Although for many years he was often kidded by others that they never saw a baseball without his signature on it, today such an item is considered the supreme collectible. With Ruth autographed material constantly surfacing in the market, collectors should have little difficulty locating his signature.

Availability: Average
Demand: Strong

Cut signature	$425
Single-signature baseball	$2,000
3x5" index card	$525
Photograph/baseball card	$1,875
HOF plaque postcard	$3,350
Perez-Steele postcard	Impossible

Ray Schalk

Raymond William Schalk
(Aug. 12, 1892-May 19, 1970)

Schalk smacked 1,345 hits while compiling a lifetime average of .253. He spent 17 years with the Chicago White Sox as their premier catcher and exhibited outstanding defensive skills. Schalk played in both the 1917 and 1919 World Series where he hit a combined .286 that included 12 hits.

Typically signing "R. Schalk" or "Ray Schalk", his signature varied in character formation and size. A consistent signature break fell between the "R" and the "a" in Ray. The "R" typically varied in size, but was unique in formation. The "R" began with a long extended upward stroke that looped before moving downward to create the letter's stem, then circled backward and over or through the top loop of the stem to form the rest of the letter. The ending stroke of the "R" typically dipped below the signature's base line. The "a" can vary in size, but always began from the top of the letter. The "y" can vary significantly in length and descender flamboyance. The "S" could vary in size, but typically was equal to or smaller than the "R" in Ray. The "S" was usually left open on the bottom and included a characteristic ending loop that extended the stroke to connect to the "c" in Schalk. The "c" at times could resemble an "e". The ascender of the "h" was typically equal to or larger in height than the "S" in Schalk. The "a" resembled an "o" at times and was typically the smallest letter in Schalk. The "l" varied in width but was commonly smaller in height than both the "h" and the "k". The "k" could vary in both height and width with the ascender of the letter typically being equal to or larger in height than the "S" in Schalk. The loop of the "k" may or may not close and the ending stroke was usually a simple extended line from the "k".

Schalk was a very responsive signer and collectors should have little trouble acquiring his signature through autograph dealers or auction houses.

Availability: Above average
Demand: Average

Cut signature	$35
Single-signature baseball	$375
3x5" index card	$55
Photograph/baseball card	$115
HOF plaque postcard	$195
Perez-Steele postcard	Impossible

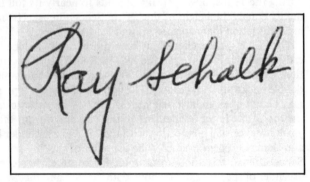

Red Schoendienst

Albert Fred Schoendienst
(Feb. 2, 1923-   )

Schoendienst compiled 2,449 hits for a career average of .289. He was an extra-base hitter, setting numerous records for doubles production including hitting eight in three consecutive games. He played 1,834 games at second base where he led or shared the National League fielding average title seven times, and assists three times. Schoendienst hit .342 with St. Louis in 1953 and led the league in hits in 1957 with 200.

Commonly signing "Albert Red Schoendienst", "Al Schoendienst", or "Red Schoendienst", his signature has varied in character formation, size and slant. A consistent signature break falls between the "S" and the "c" in Schoendienst. Occasional breaks also fall between the "A" and the "l" in Al, also between the "R" and the "e" in Red. The "A" in Albert or Al has varied in slant and may or may not be left open at the top of the letter. The "l" has varied in width and typically extends equal to or slightly below the height of the "A".

The "R" in Red has varied in character formation, slant and size. Older versions of his signature (circa 1950s), exhibit an "R" formation similar in style to that used by Babe Ruth, only with less right slant. The loop of the "R" in earlier versions may extend as far as the "d" in Red. Schoendienst's capitalization in earlier versions is commonly four to five times the height of his lower case letters. Later examples (circa 1980s), exhibit less right slant with capitalization that has been reduced in size to about two to three times the height of the lower case letters. The formation of the "R" in later versions shows the beginning stroke originating from inside the character and looping backward to form the major loop of the letter. Both the "e" and the "d" have varied in size, however the "e" typically equals the height of the "d"'s loop. The ascender of the "d", which reached half the height of the "R" during the 1950s, now typically ascends to nearly its full height. The "d" in Red now commonly equals the height of the "S" in Schoendienst. His nickname of Red may or may not have quotation marks placed around it.

The "S" in Schoendienst has been dramatically reduced in size with age and is now typically smaller in height than the "R" in Red. The "S" commonly varies in character formation, from a flamboyant loop (1950s), to a hooked backward line (1960s) and now to a slight double backward curl (1980s). The bottom of the "S" typically closes in earlier examples, but may be left open in later signatures. The "c" in earlier examples began with a small loop at the top of the letter (evident when the "S" broke from the "c"), but was dropped in recent years in favor of a connection with the "S". The ascender of the "h" has varied both in size and slant. In recent examples the ascender of the "h" has been equal in height to the "S" in Schoendienst. It is not uncommon for some earlier examples to have the right-slanted ascender of the "h" extend above both the "o" and the "e". The "oe" has varied primarily in size and both "n"'s in Schoendienst often resemble a letter "u" or "v". The ascender of the "d" has varied in size and the loop of the letter may or may not be closed. In recent examples the "d" has been equal in height to the "h" with a loop that has been increased in size (about 1½ times the size of the "o"). The "i" in often dotted above the "n" and the "s" may or may not be closed at the bottom. The "t" that was typically crossed with a separate stroke in earlier versions, is now crossed by an "L" shaped stroke that doubles back from the top of the letter. In earlier examples (1950s) the ascender of the "t" typically exceeded the height of the "h" or the "d". In recent examples the "t" has only extended to the top of the loop in the "d".

Schoendienst has been a responsive signer and collectors should have little trouble adding his signature to their collection.

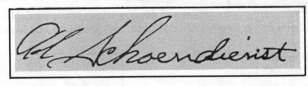

Joe Sewell

Joseph Wheeler Sewell
(Oct. 9, 1898-   )

Sewell joined the Indians in 1920, following the death of Ray Chapman who was hit by a pitched ball. In 1923 Sewell hit .353 with 195 hits. Sewell played in two World Series contests, in 1920 for the Indians and in 1932 for the New York Yankees. During the fall classic he compiled a batting average of .237 with nine hits.

Typically signing "Joe Sewell", his signature has varied in character formation and size. A break can fall between the "J" and the "o" in Joe. The "J" can vary in width, with both the beginning and ending strokes of the character typically intersecting the stem. The roundness of the loops of both the ascenders and the descenders of the "J" can vary. The ending stroke of the "J" typically intersects the "o". The "o" can occasionally be left open, however it is usually closed. The "e" is a noteworthy formation that can vary in size and often resemble a number "8" in its appearance. The bottom of the "S" is always left open and the often hooked opening stroke of the letter typically dips below the finishing loop of the character. The slant of the "S" can vary and the first "e" in Sewell is often larger than the "e" in Joe, but smaller than the last "e" in his name. The "w" can vary in size, but is typically equal in height to the first "e" in Sewell. The last "e" in Sewell is notably larger and commonly extends above the height of the "w". The "ll" formation commonly varies in width and may or may not exceed in height the "S" in Sewell. Joe's handwriting is easily distinguished by the unique formation of his capitalized "M", his extended ascenders in the letter "p", and his flamboyant capitalized "W".

At the age of 90 Joe attended the 1989 Induction Ceremonies in Cooperstown, where he wasted no time displaying why he is a favorite among collectors, by promptly attending every autograph session and congenially greeting each fan. He has always been a responsive signer and collectors should have little trouble adding his signature to their collection.

Availability: Plentiful
Demand: Little

Cut signature	$4
Single-signature baseball	$20
3x5" index card	$6
Photograph/baseball card	$13
HOF plaque postcard	$11
Perez-Steele postcard	$60

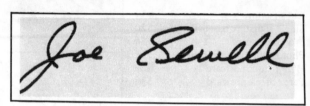

Al Simmons

Aloysius Harry Simmons
(Aloys Szymanski)
(May 22, 1902-May 26, 1956)

Simmons posted a lifetime .334 batting average that included 2,927 hits. He won consecutive American League batting titles 1930 and 1931. A three-time All-Star, Simmons guided his teams to four World Series contests, batting .329.

Commonly signing "Al Simmons", his signature varied in character formation, size and flamboyance during his lifetime. His signature breaks were inconsistent, with earlier versions exhibiting none, while later versions had occasional breaks between the "S" and the "i", between the "i" and the "m" also between the "m" and the "o" in Simmons. Earlier versions of his signature are easily recognized by the large flamboyant capitalization. The beginning stroke of the "A" began at capitalization height and at the end of Al. The flamboyant opening left stroke curved downward to form the loop and stem of the "A", followed by a nearly identical smaller loop for the "l". The formation of his first name was very similar in slant, with a dot commonly placed after the "l".

The often flamboyant "S" in Simmons varied in size and character formation. The beginning stroke of the "S" varied in size, and can originate over the second "m" in Simmons. The bottom loop of the "S" was often unpredictable in formation, with the top of the letter often being the highest point in his signature. The "S" may or may not connect to the "i" and the "i" can be dotted with a circle. The "mm" combination was unpredictable in formation and may resemble a "we" in its appearance. The "o" may or may not close and can break from the "m". The "n" can resemble a "v" at times and in combination with the "s" was always slightly above the base line, almost superscript height. The "s" may or may not close at the bottom of the letter, with the ending stroke usually a simple downward line. Later signature examples exhibited typical aging character formation from his earlier autographs. One of the only consistent elements of his signature has been the superscript appearance of the "ns" combination in Simmons.

Simmons was an obliging signer and although he died suddenly of a heart attack at age 54, samples of his signature do periodically surface in the autograph market.

Availability: Average
Demand: Average

Cut signature	$65
Single-signature baseball	$525
3x5" index card	$115
Photograph/baseball card	$225
HOF plaque postcard	$375
Perez-Steele postcard	Impossible

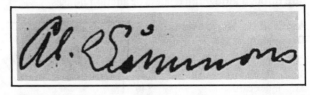

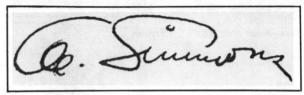

George Sisler

George Harold Sisler
(March 24, 1893-March 26, 1973)

Sisler posted a .340 lifetime batting average that included 2,812 hits. An outstanding batsman, Sisler topped the .400 mark twice in his career, first in 1920 and then again in 1922. In addition to his skills as a fielder or batter, Sisler also took a shot at pitching in 1915 and 1916, posting a record of 5-6 at an ERA of 2.13.

Commonly signing "George Sisler", his autograph varied in character formation, character spacing and size. Earlier signatures, during his playing days (circa 1920s), exhibited a consistent signature break between the "G" and the "e" in George. Later versions of his signature may or may not indicate this break, and will commonly add a break between the "S" and the "i" in Sisler. The "G" can vary in size, as well as the length of its beginning stroke which may originate from below the signature's base line. The opening stroke of the "e" can vary in length, and may also begin from the base line of his signature, but only when the character breaks from the "G". The "e" can vary in width and typically was a bit larger in height when compared to either the "o" or the "r". The "o" was often left open and the "r" can vary in its definition. The descender of the "g" was usually not looped, instead it was a simple double backed stroke which connected to the "e". The last "e" in George was always smaller than the first and gradually reduced in size with age.

The "S" may show a bit more flamboyance in earlier versions, however remained relatively consistent in character formation. The "i" in Sisler had the same characteristics as the "e" in George. The "s" in Sisler was typically left open on the bottom and the "e" could vary in size. The ending stroke in earlier versions of his signature commonly showed greater flamboyance. The character spacing in his signature seemed to increase with age. Sisler's handwriting is easily recognized by the long beginning strokes of the first lower case letters, which typically break from the capitalization in many words.

He was a very responsive signer and remained active in baseball as a scout for Brooklyn until a few years before his death. Collectors should have little trouble acquiring his signature through autograph dealers or auction houses.

Availability: Above average
Demand: Average

Cut signature	$20
Single-signature baseball	$185
3x5" index card	$40
Photograph/baseball card	$110
HOF plaque postcard	$95
Perez-Steele postcard	Impossible

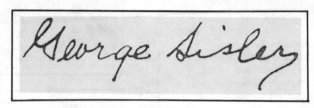

Enos Slaughter

Enos Bradsher Slaughter
(April 27, 1916-   )

"Country" played from 1938 to 1959 with four different teams and compiled 2,383 hits for a career batting average of .300. Known primarily for his hustling performance and solid fielding, Slaughter batted .291 in five World Series contests.

Typically signing "Enos Slaughter", his signature has exhibited only slight variation in character formation and size. The only consistent break in his signature falls between the "S" and the "l" in Slaughter. Capitalization that is six or seven times larger than his lower case letters is common in his signature, as are flamboyant strokes from his extended characters' ascenders and descenders. The top opening formation of the "E" resembles a "v" and often begins above the "o" or "s" in Enos, due to the very steep right slant of the capitalization. The middle loop of the "E" falls above the "n", with the bottom loop of the capitalized letter resting on the signature's base line. The "n" has varied little and is typically larger than the "o" or the "s" in Enos. The characteristically small "s" may be left open at the bottom.

The "S" originates from below the signature's base line to form both loops of the letter, which can vary in size. The "l" typically equals or exceeds the height of the "S" and the small "au" combination has remained relatively reduced in size with age. The "h" has remained fairly consistent, however the ascender of the "t" varies in height and may even be the highest point in his signature. The flamboyant ending stroke of the "r" doubles back to cross the "t". In earlier examples, the "t" may be crossed by a separate stroke.

Slaughter has been a very responsive signer. A regular attendee at baseball card shows, his wonderful personality and congenial response to his fans has made him a favorite among collectors.

Availability: Plentiful
Demand: Little

Cut signature	$3
Single-signature baseball	$20
3x5" index card	$7
Photograph/baseball card	$12
HOF plaque postcard	$10
Perez-Steele postcard	$25

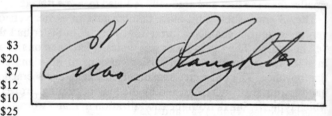

Duke Snider

Edwin Donald Snider
(Sept. 19, 1926-   )

Snider slugged 407 career home runs and led the National League in 1956 with 43. A lifetime .295 hitter he compiled 2,116 hits and helped lead the Dodgers to six World Series. During the 1952 fall classic Snider hit .345 with 10 hits, four of which were home runs.

Commonly signing "Edwin D. Snider" or "Duke Snider", his signature has varied in character formation and slant. There are no consistent signature breaks exhibited by his autograph. Earlier examples (circa 1950s) will show a break between the "E" and the "d" in Edwin, while later examples may show an occasional break betwen the "i" and the "d" in Snider. His entire signature has increased in left slant with age. The two-stroke "D" formation can vary in size and slightly in slant, but is typically left open at the bottom. The ascender of the "k" can vary in width and occasionally in slant. The height of the "k"'s ascender typically falls slightly below the "D" in Duke. The "e" in Duke may or may not connect to the "S" in Snider.

The "S" in Snider varies between two styles, a traditional capitalized "S" which is often connected to the "D" in Duke, or a stylized "S" that looks like the second stroke of the "D" in Duke with a hook added to the top of the letter. The "u" in Duke and "n" in Snider are usually identical in formation. The ascender of the "d" can vary in height, and the "er" combination also resembles the "u" in Duke. An excellent reference point for authenticators is to compare the left slant of the second stroke of the "D" in Duke, to the left slant in the formation of the stem and bottom loop of the "S" in Snider. They should be identical.

Snider has been an obliging signer and collectors should have little trouble adding his signature to their collection.

Availability: Plentiful
Demand: Little

Cut signature	$4
Single-signature baseball	$25
3x5" index card	$7
Photograph/baseball card	$14
HOF plaque postcard	$12
Perez-Steele postcard	$45

Warren Spahn

Warren Edward Spahn
(April 23, 1921-   )

Spahn won 363 games during his career at an ERA of 3.09. He led or shared the National League title in wins eight times and strikeouts four times. Spahn led his team to three World Series battles, 1948, 1957 and 1958.

Commonly signing "Warren Spahn", his signature has varied primarily in size and slant. A consistent signature break falls between the "W" and the "a" in Warren. In earlier examples, an occasional signature break fell between the "p" and the "a" in Spahn. The "W" has varied in slant, particularly in the beginning looped downward stroke which starts from the top of the letter. The "a" may or may not close at the top and the "rr" letter combination seemed to condense in character space with age. Other than decreasing in right slant over the years, the "en" has remained relatively consistent. Occasionally he connects the "n" in Warren to the "S" in Spahn.

The "S" has also decreased in right slant with age and may or may not close at the bottom of the letter. The "S" commonly varies in the size of both the top and bottom loop. The descender of the "p" has varied a bit with age, showing less right slant than earlier versions. The "p" may or may not be connected to the "a" in Spahn. The "a" in Spahn may or may not close at the top of the letter and is typically smaller than the "a" in Warren. The ascender of the "h" can vary in size and also will exhibit greater right slant in earlier examples. The "n" has remained fairly consistent with no flamboyance displayed in his ending stroke. In earlier examples, the "S" was typically the highest point in his signature, while later versions will vary the apex between the "S" and the "W".

Spahn has been a very responsive signer and collectors should have little trouble adding his signature to their collection.

Availability: Plentiful
Demand: Little

Cut signature	$3
Single-signature baseball	$18
3x5" index card	$6
Photograph/baseball card	$12
HOF plaque postcard	$10
Perez-Steele postcard	$30

Al Spalding

Albert Goodwill Spalding
(Sept. 2, 1850-Sept. 9, 1915)

Spalding did it all, from a noted pitcher, manager and club president, to founder of a worldwide sporting goods company. His leadership helped pace the Red Stockings to four National Association pennants. His business recognition brought him an appointment by President McKinley to a position as a United States Commissioner to the Olympic Games in 1900.

Commonly signing "Albert Spalding" or "A.G. Spalding", his signature varied in character formation, size and slant during his lifetime. His signature breaks were often inconsistent and later versions may exhibit none. An occasional break was found between the "S and the "p", and even between the "d" and the "i" in Spalding. The "A" had two styles, a traditional styled format or a stylized version that resembled a capitalized "S". Both "A"s could vary in right slant and size. The stylized version began with an extended upward stroke that originated from just below the signature's base line. The traditional styled "A" began from the top of the letter and may or may not be left open. The middle of the stylized "A" was a loop that was formed by the downward stroke of his signature. This loop may or may not intersect the first upward stroke of the letter. Spalding's stylized "A" extended upward to just below the height of the "S" in Spalding. The "l" could vary in both height and width, but was typically equal to or a bit smaller than the height of the "b" in Albert. The "b" could also vary in width and the "er" remained relatively consistent. The large ascender of the "t" could vary in width, but often exceeded the height of the "l" and the "b" in Albert. The "t" may or may not connect to the "S" in Spalding or to his middle initial. When he used abbreviations for his first two names, the traditional styled "A" connected to the "G" from the base line of his signature, while the stylized "A" was not connected and often had its middle loop formed by the separate beginning stroke of the "G" at lower case height. The ending stroke of the "G" may or may not dip slightly below the signature's base line.

The "S" was typically the highest point in his signature and typically had a much smaller top loop when compared to the letter's bottom loop formation. The "S" often varied in degree of right slant and may even extend as far as the "a" in Spalding. The "S" may or may not close at the bottom of the letter and can be connected to the "p". The "p" had an unusually large ascender that could often extend to the top of the bottom loop of the "S" in Spalding. The descender of the "p" often varied in its length and was typically a single-stroke format formed by a double backed line. The "a" may or may not close at the top and the "l" commonly varied in size. The ascender of the "d" could vary in height and character formation. Occasionally Spalding would curl the top of the "d"'s ascender backward over the top of the "l". If the "i" broke from the "d" then it may begin with a curled stroke which makes it appear like an "a". The "n" often resembled a "u" and the "g" often varied significantly in the flamboyance of its ending stroke. The descender of the "g" could resemble a backward "J" attached to the loop of the letter, or a simple downward line.

Spalding was a prolific writer and took delight in expressing his ideas with a pen and paper. His greatest literary contribution is no doubt *America's National Game*, a history of baseball that he authored based upon his numerous experiences during the game's infancy. His signature is highly sought after and suprisingly few samples have surfaced in the autograph market. Collectors may find his signature a challenging acquistion.

Availability: Limited
Demand: Strong

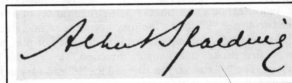

Cut signature	$1,400
Single-signature baseball	$4,000
3x5" index card	$2,000
Photograph/baseball card	$2,500
HOF plaque postcard	Impossible
Perez-Steele postcard	Impossible

Tris Speaker

Tristram E. Speaker
(April 4, 1888-Dec. 8, 1958)

Speaker stroked 3,515 hits for a lifetime batting average of .344. Speaker helped pace two clubs to the World Series, where he hit a career .306 in three appearances. Speaker hit over .350 nine times in his career, topping out at .389 in 1925.

Typically signing "Tris Speaker", his signature varied primarily in character formation and size during his lifetime. A consistent signature break fell between the "S" and the "p" in Speaker. Occasional breaks also fell between the "T" and the "r" in Tris, also between both strokes of the "k" in Speaker. A rare break also occurred between the "e" and the "a" in Speaker. The "T" is typically a two-stroke formation, however, I have seen a single-stroke variation. The "T" commonly varies in width and may or may not be connected to the "r". The "r" could vary significantly in size from a character equal in height to the "i", to a letter reaching the peak of the stem stroke of the "T" in Tris. The "is" could vary a bit in size, with the "i" typically dotted with a circle.

The "S" is the most inconsistent letter in his signature, varying radically in character formation and size. The "S" varied from a traditional styled letter to a stylized enlarged version. The traditional "S" had an elongated loop on the top of the letter, which could vary in size. The stroke of the traditional "S" intersected the stem in the middle of the character, then may intersect the stem with its bottom loop. The stylized "S" could intersect the stem twice before completing the first loop of the letter, then twice again with the creation of the flamboyant bottom loop. Speaker also utilized a variation of the stylized "S" which begins the top loop of the letter just above the "p" in Speaker. The "p" in Speaker is the hallmark of his signature and is easily recognized by its flamboyant looped descender which can extend as far left as the "i" in Tris. The ascender of the "p" is unusually large and often is equal to or slightly below capitalization height. The "p" begins with a loop that forms the ascender, then turns downward extending well below the base line, before forming the flamboyant descender that may intersect the "s" in Tris and usually the "S" in Speaker. The descender of the "p" can be two and a half times the size of the "S" in Speaker. The loop of the "p" is typically closed, with the "ea" occasionally varying in character formation. The "k" can either be a traditional single-stroke variety or a two-stroke flamboyant construction. The two-stroke "k" formation may begin the second stroke from above the "r" in Speaker, with an extended left downward line that may or may not loop before nearing the letter's simple first stroke, and changing direction. The traditional styled "k" may or may not close its loop. The "e" can vary in size and the "r" can vary in formation. Speaker typically added a period to the end of his name.

After completing his major league career he managed an International League team (Newark), bought a minor league team (Kansas City) and broadcast major league games (Chicago and Cleveland). He was a responsive signer and samples of his signature do periodically surface in the autograph market.

Availability: Average
Demand: Above average

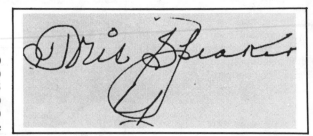

Cut signature	$120
Single-signature baseball	$1,150
3x5" index card	$185
Photograph/baseball card	$350
HOF plaque postcard	$550
Perez-Steele postcard	Impossible

Willie Stargell

Wilver Dornel Stargell
(March 6, 1941-   )

Stargell played for the Pittsburgh Pirates from 1962 to 1982. A charismatic leader who shared the National League's Most Valuable Player award in 1979, Stargell batted a lifetime .282. He smashed 475 home runs and 1,540 RBIs during a career that included two World Series appearances.

Commonly signing "Wilver Stargell" or "Willie Stargell", his signature has varied in character formation, size and slant. Earlier signature samples (circa 1960s) exhibit breaks between the "W" and the "i" in Wilver, also between the "S" and the "t", the "t" and the "a", the "g" and the "e", the "e" and the "l" and between both "l"'s in Stargell. Signatures samples from the 1970s commonly exhibit breaks between the "W" and the "i" in Willie, also between the "S" and the "t", the "r" and the "g", and the "g" and the "e" in Stargell. Recent autographs exhibit all the breaks shown by his signature in the 1970s with the only exception being a now continuous stroke between the "r" and the "g" in Stargell.

The "W" in Willie has varied considerably in character formation over the years, from a letter that now begins typically with a stroke at lower case height. The "W" has increased in width and left slant over the years. The ending stroke of the "W", which now is a steep left-slanted stroke that extends beyond the entire letter, was a simple slightly left slanted line that rose slightly above the "l" in Wilver. The "i" may or may not begin with a short upward curled stroke. The "l"'s in Willie have decreased in both size and slant. The stylized "e" in Willie has varied little and now is often equal in height to the "l"'s in Willie.

The formation of the stylized "S" was changed from a single-stroke simple formation (circa late 1960s, early 1970s), to a flamboyant two-stroke formation where the bottom of the letter is constructed with the beginning stroke of the "t". The ascender of the "S" is now the highest point in his signature and the descending stroke is the lowest. During the 1970s, the descender of the "g" was often the lowest point in his signature. The "S" can vary slightly in size and slant. The "t" can vary in width and is now commonly equal in height to the "a", in stark contrast to earlier examples where the ascender of the "t" usually reached capitalization height. The "t" is now haphazardly crossed by a separate stroke which may not even intersect the stem. Both the "a" and the "r" have varied little and typically are equal in height. The "g" has decreased in size, particularly in the descender and now exhibits little flamboyance. The descender of the "g" is now typically a simple downward stroke that dips slightly below the base line. The stylized "e" in earlier versions has been modified and now resembles a number "2" in its construction. Both the "l"'s have decreased in height and width.

Stargell has been an obliging signer and collectors should have little trouble acquiring his signature.

Availability: Plentiful
Demand: Little

Cut signature	$3
Single-signature baseball	$20
3x5" index card	$6
Photograph/baseball card	$15
HOF plaque postcard	$11
Perez-Steele postcard	$25

Casey Stengel

Charles Dillon Stengel
(July 30, 1889-Sept. 29, 1975)

As a player Stengel hit a lifetime .284 with 1,219 hits. He played in three World Series contests — 1916, 1922 and 1923 — hitting .393. Stengel's reputation, however was built as a manager. Casey won 1,926 games and took the New York Yankees to 10 World Series. His last management challenge came in 1962, at the age of 72, for the New York Mets.

Commonly signing "Casey Stengel", his signature varied in character formation and size during his lifetime. In earlier examples, those signed during his playing days, a consistent signature break fell between the "S" and the "t" in Stengel, while later versions typically exhibit none. The "C" varied both in size and character formation. In earlier examples the "C" began from below the signature's base line, with an extended stroke upward that formed an "s" shape, before looping at the top and beginning the major portion of the character's formation. This "C" formation may extend as far as the "e" in Casey. Later examples show less flamboyance in the "C" and a simplified version of the beginning stroke. Additionally, later versions show less definition, with the top loop varying in size. The "a" may or may not be closed and the "s" was typically left open at the bottom of the letter. The "e" could vary in size and the descender of the "y" was often unpredictable in length and formation. Early examples of Stengel's signature will show a well extended descender that flamboyantly loops to form a triangular formation, while later versions were in sharp contrast showing a very short descender that typically dropped only slightly below the base line.

The "S" varied in formation from a traditional capitalized form to a stylized version. When Stengel used the stylized version, as he did often during his playing days, there was typically a break with the "t". The "t" varied a bit in width, but typically had a long ascender that exceeded the height of the "S" in Stengel. The "t" was typically crossed near the top of the ascender with a fairly long separate stroke. Both "e"s in Stengel could vary in size and the "n" remained relatively consistent. The descender of the "g" could vary a bit in width, but was often conservative in its length by extending only a short distance beyond the base line. The loop of the "g" may or may not be left open. The "l" usually extended to the ascender height of the "t" and could vary in width. The ending stroke of his signature varied in flamboyance and he may place a dot or mark at the end of the "l".

Stengel was a very responsive signer and an extremely popular personality. Collectors should have little trouble acquiring his signature through autograph dealers or auction houses.

Availability: Average
Demand: Above average

Cut signature	$18
Single-signature baseball	$350
3x5" index card	$40
Photograph/baseball card	$110
HOF plaque postcard	$75
Perez-Steele postcard	Impossible

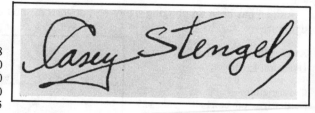

246

Bill Terry

William Harold Terry
(Oct. 30, 1896-Jan. 9, 1989)

In 14 seasons with the New York Giants, Terry cracked 2,193 hits while compiling a career average of .341. He batted over .300 for 11 seasons and became the last National Leaguer to bat over .400 in 1930. Terry paced the Giants to three World Series battles — 1924, 1933 and 1936.

Typically signing "Wm. H. (Bill) Terry", his signature varied only slightly in character formation during his lifetime. Consistent signature breaks fell between the "B" and the "i" in Bill, also between the "T" and the "e" in Terry. The "W" began from the bottom with an upward extended stroke, which doubled back to form the first loop of the letter. The "W" also varied in width, with both loops of the letter seldom being symmetrical. The superscript "m" varied in both size and flamboyance, but was always connected to the "W". Earlier examples of his signature will exhibit greater flamboyance in the "W" to "m" connection. The superscript "m" always has a short underline placed below it. The two-stroke "H" formation could vary slightly in size. The middle crossing of the letter "H" was a small loop made by the second stroke, which may or may not intersect the first stroke. The second stroke of the "H" commonly exceeded the height of the first stroke.

In his signature, "Bill" was surrounded by parentheses, the first of which was typically straighter and longer than the second. The second stroke of the "H" and the first parenthesis should be identical in slant. The "B" commonly varied in character formation, size and slant. The "ill" varied in height, width and slant of each letter. The last "l" typically equalled or exceeded the height of the first "l" in Bill.

The "T" commonly varied in size and was much larger in earlier examples. The "T" began from the top of the letter with a small loop, before creating the major formation of the character. The "T" could resemble a "2" in its formation and the ending stroke of the letter varied in flamboyance. The "T" in Terry was gradually reduced in size and flamboyance with age. Later versions of his signature commonly dropped the small loop on the top of the letter "T". The "err" varied in degree of right slant (decreasing with age), but changed little in character formation. The descender of the "y" in earlier versions was a longer single stroke that did not have a slash added. The slash that intersected the descender of the "y" was common in later versions of his autograph.

Terry was a very responsive signer and collectors should have little trouble acquiring his signature through autograph dealers or auction houses.

Availability: Plentiful
Demand: Little

Cut signature	$7
Single-signature baseball	$80
3x5" index card	$15
Photograph/baseball card	$30
HOF plaque postcard	$25
Perez-Steele postcard	$145

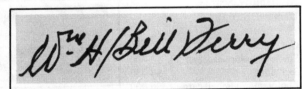

Sam Thompson

Samuel Luther Thompson
(March 5, 1860-Nov. 7, 1922)

"Big Sam" ended his career with nearly 2,000 hits and a batting average above .330. Thompson hit over .300 nine out of 15 seasons, and in 1894 compiled a career high .404. One of the game's earliest sluggers, Thompson also became recognized for his strong fielding, with cannon-like throws from the outfield.

Typically signing "Sam Thompson" or "Sam L. Thompson", his signature varied in character formation and size. The most consistent signature break fell between the "p" and "s" in Thompson. The right-slanted, traditionally styled "S" in Sam was often three to four times the height of the lower case letters and typically the highest point in his signature. A bottom looped formation to the "S" closed the letter and allowed his stroke to change direction and connect to the top of the "a" in Sam. The "a" often closed and the "m" could resemble a "uu" letter configuration. Thompson's capitalization typically began slightly below his signature's base line and should be similar in slant.

The "T" in Thompson was most often a two-stroke construction, with the base resembling an upside-down "V" and the crossing of the letter constructed by a looped stroke which connected to the ascender of the "h". The ascender of the "h" can vary in size and may or may not exceed the height of the "T" in Thompson. Characteristic of Thompson's handwriting is the lack of a rounded loop construction to his letters, particularly noticeable in the lower case characters of "h" and "m". The "o"s in Thompson may or may not close, and like his "m"s, the letter "n" often resembles a "u". In addition to being a unique breaking point, the "p" in Thompson possessed a large ascending stroke which reached nearly capitalization height. The width of the "p"s descender could vary, as could the length of the finishing stroke of the letter's loop. The "s" was a traditional style, similar to the "S" in Sam and often began with a stroke originating from slightly below the signature's base line. Comparing the slant of the letters "S", "T" and "p" can be particularly helpful to the authenticator; all should be very similar.

Thompson died suddenly from heart disease at the age of 62. His retirement job as a United States Marshal did require numerous signatures on legal documents, however few of these documents have surfaced in the autograph market. Like so many of the game's pioneers, his signature is highly sought by collectors who realize the difficulty in acquiring his autograph.

Availability: Scarce
Demand: Strong

Cut signature	$2,350
Single-signature baseball	$7,000
3x5" index card	$3,750
Photograph/baseball card	$6,000
HOF plaque postcard	Impossible
Perez-Steele postcard	Impossible

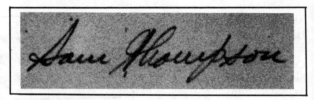

Joe Tinker

Joseph Bert Tinker
(July 27, 1880-July 27, 1948)

Alphabetically the last member of the famous double play combination "Tinker to Evers to Chance", he cracked nearly 1,700 hits while compiling a batting average above .260. He helped lead Chicago to four World Series contests and was known most for his clutch hitting and superb fielding.

Commonly signing "Joe B. Tinker" or "Joe Tinker", his signature varied in character formation, slant and size. Consistent signature breaks fell between the "J" and the "o" in Joe, also between the "T" and the "i" in Tinker. The "J" was typically a two-stroke formation, however he also used a single-stroke variation. The descender of the "J" typically exceeded the size of its ascender. The "o" can vary in width and the stylized "e" occasionally resembels a "u" because of its slant. His middle initial of "B" could vary in size and was typically left open at the bottom of the letter.

Tinker's large two-stroke "T" formation became the hallmark of his signature. The top stroke of the "T" could extend twice the height of the capitalization and as far as the "n" in Tinker, The "in" remained relatively consistent, with the "n" often resembling a letter "u". The unusually large looped "k" can resemble a capitalized "R" and was often two or three times larger than the surrounding lower case letters. The middle loop of the "k" may or may not intersect the stem. It is not unusual for the height of the loop in the "k" to equal that of its ascender. The "e" in Tinker was a traditional formation that remained relatively consistent, while the "r" may be unrecognizable as a letter.

Tinker was involved in a number of enterprises following his playing days, from extensive Florida land holdings to operating a billiard parlor in Orlando. He suffered for years with diabetes, which eventually led to the amputation of his left leg and death on his 68th birthday. He was an obliging signer, however mail requests could be a bit unpredictable at times, and collectors may find the acquisition of his signature somewhat challenging.

Availability: Average
Demand: Average

Cut signature	$275
Single-signature baseball	$2,500
3x5" index card	$325
Photograph/baseball card	$700
HOF plaque postcard	$1,075
Perez-Steele postcard	Impossible

Pie Traynor

Harold Joseph Traynor
(Nov. 11, 1899-March 16, 1972)

Traynor had 2,416 career hits for a lifetime batting average of .320. This exciting fielder was perhaps the finest third baseman of his day. Pie hit a career high 208 hits in 1923 and managed the Pittsburgh Pirates from 1934 to 1939.

Typically signing "Pie Traynor", his signature varied in character formation, size and slant during his lifetime. Consistent signature breaks can be found between the "P" and the "i" in Pie, also between the "T" and the "r" in Traynor. An occasional break may also fall between the "y" and the "n" in Traynor. The flamboyant "P" was often three to four times larger than the surrounding lower case letters. The right slant of the large loop of the "P" commonly extended beyond the "e" in Pie. The descender of the "P" typically dipped slightly below the signature base line, and the "ie" could vary a bit in slant and size.

The "T" was typically a single-stroke formation, although I have seen a two-stroke variation. The letter "T" typically begins from the top with a downward left stroke which looped then changed direction to form the top of the letter, before looping a final time to form the character's stem. The ending stroke of the "T" commonly varied in size and flamboyance. The right slant of the "T" allowed the top formation of the letter to extend above the "a" in Traynor. The "r" began with an extended line which originated from slightly below the signature's base line. The "a" may or may not close at the top of the letter. The descender of the "y" can vary in length and flamboyance, but its slant should be very similar to that of the "T" in Traynor. The "n" may resemble a "u" and the "o" may or may not be closed at the top of the letter. The "r" could vary in size and the ending stroke was typically a simple upward hook which also varied in measure. Traynor's handwriting is easily identified by flamboyant ending strokes of capitalization that extend well below the signature's base line, and the unique character formation of ending letters in words, such as the "t", which may resemble an "h" or "s" that has been crossed by a separate stroke.

Traynor was a responsive signer and an extremely popular figure in Pittsburgh. The acquisition of his signature, through autograph dealers or auction houses, should be fairly easy for collectors.

Availability: Above average
Demand: Average

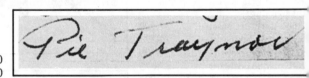

Cut signature	$40
Single-signature baseball	$500
3x5" index card	$70
Photograph/baseball card	$175
HOF plaque postcard	$325
Perez-Steele postcard	Impossible

Dazzy Vance

Clarence Arthur Vance
(March 4, 1891-Feb. 16, 1961)

Vance won 197 games at an ERA of 3.24. He led the National League twice in wins and three times in ERA. Vance spent 10 years in the minor leagues before being given a chance by Brooklyn to exhibit his incredible pitching speed. The National League Most Valuable Player in 1924, Vance led the league in strikeouts seven straight years from 1922 to 1928.

Usually signing "A.C. Dazzy Vance" or "Dazzy Vance", his autograph varied in character formation, slant and flamboyance. Consistent signature breaks fell between the "D" and the "a", between both "z"s, and the "z" and the "y" in Dazzy, also between the "V" and the "a", and the "n" and the "c" in Vance. The enlarged lower case "a" which formed his first initial, resembled Cap Anson's character formation and may or may not close at the top of the letter. The "C" was relatively consistent and when compared to the "A", often slightly larger in height.

The "D" could vary in the formation of the top and bottom loop of the letter, however was fairly consistent in slant. The "a" may or may not be closed at the top and the "z"s varied in the size and the formation of their descenders. The character formation of the "z" resembled a number "3", with both "z"s in Dazzy typically identical in slant. The "y" began with a short upward stroke from the base line that formed the top of the letter, and the character's descender typically equalled or exceeded the length of the "z"s' descenders. The descender of the "y" typically varied in the formation of its ending stroke and was typically different from that exhibited by either of the "z"s. The slant of the "y"'s descender should be similar to the slant exhibited by the "z"s in Dazzy.

The "V" varied primarily in the size and flamboyance of the beginning and ending stroke. The "V" was typically the highest point in his signature, with the ending stroke possibly extending as far as the "c" in Vance. The "a" may or may not close and the "n" often resembled a "u" in its formation. The "n" typically broke from the "c" and connected to the "e", however on rare occasions the "e" may be a separate letter. The "e" commonly varied in its character formation (stylized "e" or traditional) and ending stroke (simple curl or a hooked descender close).

Vance was an obliging signer and periodically samples of his signature do surface in the autograph market.

Availability: Average
Demand: Average

Cut signature	$70
Single-signature baseball	$950
3x5" index card	$130
Photograph/baseball card	$315
HOF plaque postcard	$465
Perez-Steele postcard	Impossible

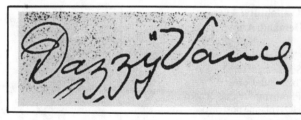

Arky Vaughan

Joseph Floyd Vaughan
(March 9, 1912-Aug. 30, 1952)

Vaughan spent 14 seasons in the National League, smacking 2,103 hits while batting .318. His best season came in 1935, when he hit .385 to win the National League batting title. A refined individual, this shortstop was seldom in the spotlight, letting his statistics speak for themselves. Arky drove in 90 runs four times and during his 10 years with the Pirates never batted below .300.

Commonly signing "Arky Vaughan" or "Floyd Vaughan", his signature varied in character formation, size and flamboyance. Consistent signature breaks fell between the "F" and the "l" in Floyd, also between the "V" and the "a" in Vaughan. The large "A", which was often four times the size of his lower case letters, began from the top of the letter at the signature's base line. The "A" was typically a thin formation that was left open at the top. The "r" varied a bit in size and was similar in style to the "r" formation used by Travis Jackson. The "k" originated from the top of the "r" and formed a long ascender that typically fell slightly below the height of the "A". It was not unusual for the "k" to extend above the "y" because of the degree of right slant. The loop of the "k" was generally small and may or may not intersect the letter's stem. The "y" had a well extended descender that varied in size, however was similar in slant to the stem of the "k".

The "V" in Vaughan varied in size and flamboyance, with the ending stroke of the letter possibly being twice the height of the character's first stroke. At times excessive flamboyance in the "V" made it appear similar to the letter "S". The two-looped "a" typically did not close at the top and the "u" could vary in size. The "g" may or may not close at the top and the letter's descender can vary in size. The "g" may or may not close at the top and the letter's descender can vary in both length and slant. The long ascender of the "h" can typically be the highest point in his signature and varies both in slant and width. The second "a" in Vaughan is often left open and is typically smaller than the first "a". The sharpness of the stroke of the "n" may appear like a "v" with a hooked ending stroke.

At the age of 40, Vaughan died tragically in a drowning accident. He was a responsive signer, however death at such an early age contributes significantly to the scarcity of his autographed material. Collectors should find the acquisition of his signature a bit challenging.

Availability: Average
Demand: Above average

Cut signature	$150
Single-signature baseball	$950
3x5" index card	$165
Photograph/baseball card	$375
HOF plaque postcard	Impossible
Perez-Steele postcard	Impossible

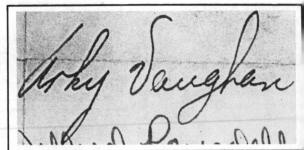

Rube Waddell

George Edward Waddell
(Oct. 13, 1876-April 1, 1914)

Waddell won 191 games in his career, 50 of which were shutouts. Known for his unusual behavior, Waddell was difficult for most managers to control. It took all Connie Mack's time and direction to guide Waddell to his landmark 1905 season of 26 wins, 11 loses and seven shutouts.

Typically signing "Rube Waddell" or "G. Waddell", his signature varied significantly in character formation, size and slant. Consistent signature breaks fell between the "R" and the "u" in Rube, also between the "W" and the "a", and between both "d"s in Waddell. The "R" could vary in both size and slant. The "R" often began from the top with a downward stroke that doubled back up at the signature's base line (at inconsistent angles) to create the character's loop. The loop of the "R" could vary in formation and may extend above the "u" in Rube, depending upon its variable slant. The "u" could vary in slant and size. The ascender of the "b" could vary in width and typically extended to capitalization height. The "e" could also vary in size and slant.

The capitalization of the "W" was unpredictable, exhibiting variation in character formation, slant and size. The "W" varied from a simplistic, almost printed, format, to a traditional style that could be twice his typical capitalization height and extremely flamboyant. The "a" may or may not close at the top of the letter and both the "d"s can vary in width, however are similar in slant. The ascenders of the "d"s can vary in height and the loops of the character may or may not close. The "l"s also commonly vary in both height and width.

Waddell's signature was very inconsistent and can be a real authentication challenge. From relatively few samples I have viewed, it is clear that his erratic behavior no doubt had an impact on his autographing habits. His death came at the early age of 37 from tuberculosis. Collectors should find the acquisition of his signature a bit difficult, however a limited number of examples have surfaced in the autograph market over the past few years.

Availability: Scarce
Demand: Strong

Cut signature	$1,750
Single-signature baseball	$6,000
3x5" index card	$1,950
Photograph/baseball card	$4,500
HOF plaque postcard	Impossible
Perez-Steele postcard	Impossible

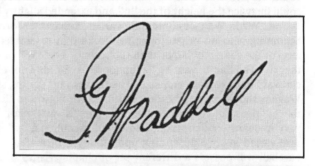

Honus Wagner

John Peter Wagner
(Feb. 24, 1874-Dec. 6, 1955)

Wagner hit 3,430 hits for a career average of .329. A brilliant hitter, Wagner was the National League's batting champion eight times. In his first year with the Pirates in 1900 he hit a career high .381 that included 201 hits. Considered by most to be the National League's greatest shortstop of all-time, Wagner had 17 straight seasons hitting above .300 "The Flying Dutchman" was an extremely popular figure whose face and name endorsed many a product.

Often signing either "John H. Wagner", "Hans Wagner", or "J. Honus Wagner", his signature varied in character formation, size, slant and flamboyance. Consistent signature breaks fell between the "J" and the "o" in John, also between the "H" and the "o" in Honus and occasionally between the "W" and the "a", and the "g" and the "n" in Wagner. His flamboyant quadruple-looped capitalized "J" varied in height, width and slant. The "J" typically begins at or near the top with a hook that may or may not loop before it moves upward to form the ascender of the character. The stem of the "J" varies in size and slant with the flamboyant ending stroke resembling a number "2" set on its side. The "o" varied in size and connects to the "h" via the top loop of the letter. The "h" can vary in size and its degree of right slant that allows the ascender to fall above the "n" in John. The "n" in John remained relatively consistent and possesed a simple upward curl for an ending stroke.

The three-stroke formation of the "H" could vary in size and slant, often resembling a "J" in its appearance. The second stroke of the "H" varied in size and flamboyance, and originated from capitalization height before descending well below the signature's base line. The second stroke of the "H" may or may not have a flamboyant looped formation added to it. The "H" was crossed by a simple stroke that may or may not intersect either of the other two strokes. The "o" begins with a small upward stroke extending from the base line, and may or may not be closed at the top of the letter. The "n" remained relatively consistent and the "u" could vary in size. The "s" also varied in size, particularly in earlier versions, where it could be twice the height of the "u" and extended slightly below the signature's base line.

The "W" in Wagner commonly varied in character formation and flamboyance. Typically beginning with an ornate opening stroke that resembled a "J", he often created the first loop of the character larger than the second. The "W" may or may not connect to the top of the "a". The flamboyant "g"'s top loop may or may not close and the descender of the letter can vary both in slant and size. The flamboyant ending stroke that was added to the "g" in Wagner should be nearly identical in its formation to that of the "J" in John, especially if the "g" does not connect to the "n". The "e" was relatively consistent, while the "r" could vary in character definition, and often resembled a "v". Like most players Wagner's signature varied in style depending upon the type of material he signed. A Wagner autographed baseball will possess a different set of characteristics when compared to his signature on a flat item.

Wagner served as a coach for the Pirates from 1933 to 1951 and took particular pride in reminiscing about his numerous achievements as a player. He was a responsive signer and collectors should be able to acquire his signature through autograph dealers and auction houses.

Availability: Average
Demand: Strong

Cut signature	$150
Single-signature baseball	$1,825
3x5" index card	$250
Photograph/baseball card	$550
HOF plaque postcard	$875
Perez-Steele postcard	Impossible

Bobby Wallace

Roderick John Wallace
(Nov. 4, 1873-Nov. 3, 1960)

Wallace played from 1894 to 1918, compiling over 2,300 hits at a batting average of .267. Playing with Cleveland in 1897 he hit .339 with 177 hits. He was the first American League shortstop elected to the Hall of Fame.

Commonly signing "Roderick J. Wallace", his signature varied in character formation, size and slant during his lifetime. Consistent signature breaks fell between the "R" and the "o" in Roderick and between the "W" and the "a" in Wallace. Occasional breaks also may occur between the "i" and the "c" in Roderick, also between the "l" and the "a" in Wallace. The unusually large "R", often five or six times the height of his lower case letters, originated from slightly beneath the signature's base line before extending upward to form the top loop of the character. The top loop of the "R", because of the degree of its right slant, could extend above the "o" and part of the "d" in Roderick. The finishing stroke of the "R" commonly extended well below the signature's base line. The "o" and the loop of the "d" may or may not be closed and the ascender of the "d" often equalled the height of where the loop meets the stem of the "R" in Roderick. The "eri" varied slightly in character formation and slant. The "k" could be either a single- or two-stroke construction, with its ascender often falling slightly lower than the height of the "d". The stem of the "d" and the stem of the "k" should be similar in slant.

His middle initial of "J" was a traditional formation that varied in size and slant, however the descender of the letter was typically larger than its ascender. The "W" could vary in its height and width. The "W" began from the top of the letter with a curled downward stroke that doubled back to about three-quarters of the height of the letter before forming the middle pinnacle, then turned downward to repeat the task. The ending stroke of the "W" usually showed little flamboyance. The height of the "W" typically exceeded the height of the "l"'s. The "a" could vary a bit in size and may or may not close at the top. Both "l"'s in Wallace could vary a bit in size, however were fairly consistent in slant. The first "a" in

Wallace was typically larger than the second. The "ce" could vary in size, with little flamboy ance shown at the end of his signature.

Thirty-five years after he stopped playing baseball, Wallace was elected to the Hall o Fame. Signatures generated later in his life (following his induction), show typical agin; characteristics. He was an obliging, but not prolific, signer. Collectors may find the acquisi tion of his signature a bit more challenging than might be expected from someone who diec during the 1960s.

Availability: Average
Demand: Average

Cut signature	$165
Single-signature baseball	$1,775
3x5" index card	$225
Photograph/baseball card	$500
HOF plaque postcard	$900
Perez-Steele postcard	Impossible

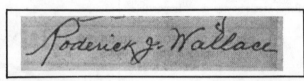

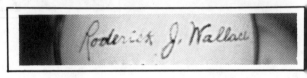

Ed Walsh

Edward Augustine Walsh
(May 14, 1881-May 26, 1959)

A notorious spitball pitcher, Walsh won 195 games during his career, 57 of them shut outs. His best season came in 1908 when he won a career high 40 games, 11 of them shutouts, while only losing 15. Walsh was an iron man on the mound, pitching 2,964 caree innings that finally ended with the Boston Braves in 1917. Walsh twice pitched and won twc games in one day.

Commonly signing "Ed. A. Walsh", his signature varied in character formation, size anc slant during his lifetime. Consistent signature breaks fell between the "E" and the "d" iz Ed, also between the "W" and the "a" in Walsh. The "E" began with a long stroke that ori ginated near the signature's base line and extended upward to form the first loop of the "E' in Ed. The top loop formation of the "E" typically was larger than the bottom formation although this may vary depending on the material being signed. The significant right slant o the letter often extended above the loop in the "d". The bottom loop formation of the "E' and the loop of the "d" are nearly identical in slant. This slant comparison is an excellen reference point for authenticators, especially for autographed flat items. The ascender of the "d" can vary both in height (typically equalled the height of the "E") and width, with the loop of the letter occasionally left open. His middle initial of "A" can vary in size and slant but was commonly left open at the top of the letter.

The "W" typically began with a flamboyant loop upward which originated from lower casa height near the middle of the letter, then turned downward to create the bottom loop of the letter. Occasionally the "W" resembled a "U" because of Walsh's tendency at times tc not complete the last loop of the letter. The "a" may or may not close at the top and the "l' commonly varied in size. The "s" may or may not close at the bottom of the letter and the "h" varied in both size and slant. The slant of the "l" and the "h" should be nearly identical, as should their height. The majority of Walsh's signatures have the ascenders of the "l" and the "h" extend to capitalization height. His later signature examples exhibit typical aging characteristics.

Walsh was very responsive to signature requests and signed material does periodically surface in the autograph market. Collectors should be able to acquire his signature through autograph dealers or auction houses.

Availability: Average
Demand: Average

Cut signature	$115
Single-signature baseball	$2,500
3x5" index card	$175
Photograph/baseball card	$325
HOF plaque postcard	$500
Perez-Steele postcard	Impossible

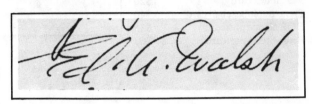

Lloyd Waner

Lloyd James Waner
(March 16, 1906-July 22, 1982)

"Little Poison" stroked 2,459 hits while batting a career .316 average. In 1927, his rookie season, Waner collected over 200 hits while batting .355. Lloyd was three years younger than his brother Paul, both of whom are appropriately enshrined at Cooperstown. They played together for 14 years in the Pittsburgh outfield.

Typically signing "Lloyd Waner", his signature varied in character formation, size and slant during his lifetime. A consistent signature break fell between the "L" and the "l" in Lloyd. The two-looped "L" formation varied in size, but was relatively consistent in character formation. The ending stroke of the "L" typically extended well below the signature's base line, often beyond the descender of the "y". The "l" typically originated from inside the hooked ending stroke of the capitalized "L" and commonly varied in height. The "o" could vary in character formation and may or may not be left open at the top of the letter. The descender of the "y" varied in both the length and the width, however its slant should be similar, if not identical, to the slant of the first stroke of the "W" in Waner. The ascender of the "d" varied in size and slightly in its character formation, but commonly added a flamboyant upward ending stroke to the letter.

The "W" began from the top and typically intersected the ending stroke of the "d". The "W" commonly varied in height and connected to the top loop of the "a", from the end of its last loop. The "a" was often left open and typically exceeded the height of the "n". The "e" could vary in size, while the "r" could vary in character formation. Waner typically added a flamboyant upward ending stroke that extended equal to or above the capitalization height.

Waner was a very responsive signer and collectors should have little trouble acquiring his signature through autograph dealers or auction houses.

Availability: Plentiful
Demand: Little

Cut signature	$12
Single-signature baseball	$150
3x5" index card	$20
Photograph/baseball card	$40
HOF plaque postcard	$35
Perez-Steele postcard	$1,700

Paul Waner

Paul Glee Waner
(April 16, 1903-Aug. 29, 1965)

"Big Poison" spent 20 years in the major leagues and collected 3,152 hits while batting .333. He won the National League batting title three times and hit over .300 for 14 seasons. Complementing his batting skills were speed on the base paths and a strong left arm in the outfield.

Commonly signing "Paul Waner", his signature varied primarily in character formation and size during his lifetime. A consistent signature break fell between the "P" and the "a" in Paul. Occasionally a break could also be found between the "W" and the "a" in Waner. His capitalization was often four to five times the size of his lower case letters. The "P" in Paul began from the top, inside the loop of the character. The loop varied in size and degree of right slant. It is not uncommon for the loop of the "P" to extend as far as the "l" in Paul. The ending stroke of the "P" commonly varied in its size and formation. The "a" typically began with a variable sized stroke that originated from below the signature's base line. The "a" is often left open at the top and the "u" can vary in size. The ascender of the "l" could often be mistaken for an "e", since it occasionally rose only to the height of the "a".

The flamboyant "W" formation began from near the top of the letter with a large oval shaped loop, then created a smaller second loop before intersecting the first or being completely inside of it. The opening loop gradually decreased in size with age and the ending stroke, which often connected to the top of the "a", grew in height, while typically finishing below the signature's base line in later versions. Particularly in early examples of his signature, the "W" could resemble a large "a" in its formation, with the ending stroke of the letter connecting to the "a" in Waner. The "a" may be left open at the top of the letter and the "e" could vary in size. The "r" varied in its character formation from a traditional style to one which resembled a letter "s". The ending stroke often varied in size, formation and direction.

Waner, who had a passion for late nights out, was an obliging but occasionally unpredictable signer. Samples of his signature periodically surface in the autograph market.

Availability: Average
Demand: Above average

Cut signature	$50
Single-signature baseball	$550
3x5" index card	$85
Photograph/baseball card	$225
HOF plaque postcard	$245
Perez-Steele postcard	Impossible

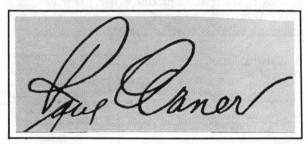

John Ward

John Montgomery Ward
(March 3, 1860-March 4, 1925)

A pioneer of the game, Ward was an accomplished pitcher, hitter, manager and owner. He won 158 games for Providence and New York and during a 17-year career compiled 2,123 hits while batting .278. His finest season came in 1890 when he led the Players League, a league that lasted for one season in competition against the National League, in hits while batting .369.

Typically signing "John M. Ward, his signature varied in character formation, size and slant. His signature exhibited no consistent signature breaks, however on occasion one could fall between the "W" and the "a" in Ward. The "J" in John varied significantly in character formation from a wide traditionally styled "J" that had flamboyant ascenders and descenders, to a very thin, straight-stemmed letter. When Ward used the wide traditionally styled "J" it often resembled an enlarged "d", due do its right slanted descender. The "o" was relatively consistent and connected to the ascender of the "h" from the top of the letter. The "h" varied slightly in character formation and was inconsistent in height. The "n" varied in character formation and at times appeared illegible. The "M" began from the top with a formation that could resemble a rounded number "7", before continuing to form the two pinnacles of the "M". The first pinnacle of the "M" commonly exceeded the height of the second.

The "W" often resembled a number "2" connected to a "V", because of the large middle loop of the letter. The opening formation of the "W" should be similar in slant to the beginning of the "M". The "W" and the "M" are typically the same height. The "W" may or may not connect to the "a", with the "a" often left open at the top of the letter. The "r" varied in size and the "d" varied in size, slant and formation. The loop of the "d" may or may not be left open and the ending stroke of Ward's signature varied in length, flamboyance, and origin.

Following his retirement from baseball at the age of 34, he became a seccessful attorney and in 1911, Ward became partner in ownership and president of the Boston Braves. He was an obliging signer and a prolific writer. (He published *Baseball, How to Become a Player* in 1888.) Although he authored numerous pieces of correspondence, few have surfaced in the autograph market. Collectors should find the acquistion of his signature a bit challenging.

Availability: Limited
Demand: Strong

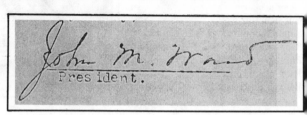

Cut signature	$1,550
Single-signature baseball	$6,500
3x5" index card	$1,825
Photograph/baseball card	$3,500
HOF plaque postcard	Impossible
Perez-Steele postcard	Impossible

George Weiss

George Martin Weiss
(June 23, 1895-Aug. 13, 1972)

Known most as an architect of championship teams, Weiss served as club executive in both the major and minor leagues from 1919 to 1966. As farm manager for the New York Yankees from 1932 to 1947, he is largely credited for the team's baseball dynasty. The Yankees won 10 pennants and seven World Series from 1947 to 1960 while Weiss served as the team's general manager. Weiss also served as president of the New York Mets from 1961 to 1966.

Commonly signing "George Weiss", his signature varied in character formation, size and slant. A fairly consistent signature break fell between the "W" and the "e" in Weiss, however early examples of his autograph commonly exhibit none. The flamboyant "G" in George became the hallmark of his signature. It was not uncommon for the "G" to be 10 to 12 times the size of his lower case letters. The "G" could either be a one- or two-stroke construction. If the "G" was a two-stroke version, the loop of the letter was an oval stroke, while the second stroke, which formed the stem and descender of the letter, resembled a "j". The "e" can vary in size and was often located close to the stem of the "G". The "o" may or may not close at the top or even at the side of the letter and the "r" varied a bit in size. The loop of the "g" in George may or may not close and in some instances may exhibit little definition. The descender of the "g" could vary in length, however should be nearly identical in slant to the "G". The "e" exhibited only slight variation in size.

The "W" in Weiss varied in character formation and size. The nearly nonexistent middle of the "W" gave the character an appearance like a "U". The "W" may connect to the letter "e", particularly in earlier examples. The "e" and the "i" may vary in both size and slant. The first "s" in Weiss typically showed less definition than the last. The first "s" in Weiss was often illegible. It was common for Weiss to add an underline beneath his signature.

As a baseball executive he signed a vast number of letters and contracts, some of which periodically surface in the autograph market. He was obliging to autograph requests and collectors should have little trouble acquiring his signature through autograph dealers or auction houses.

Availability: Above average
Demand: Average

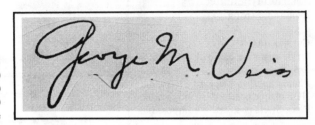

Cut signature	$45
Single-signature baseball	$550
3x5" index card	$50
Photograph/baseball card	$140
HOF plaque postcard	Impossible
Perez-Steele postcard	Impossible

Mickey Welch

Michael Francis Welch
(July 4, 1859-July 30, 1941)

"Smiling Mickey" ended his 13-year career with 311 wins at an ERA of 2.71. He accumulated 40 shutouts during his career, seven of which came during his remarkable 1885 season. During the 1885 season he posted 44 wins and 11 loses at an ERA of 1.66.

Typically signing "Mickey Welch", "M. Welch" or "Smiling Mickey Welch", his signature varied in character formation and size during his lifetime. Consistent signature breaks fell between the "M" and the "i" in Mickey, also between the "W" and the "e" in Welch. The flamboyant "M" in Mickey could vary both in size and slant, occasionally even resembling a letter "h" in its appearance. The first pinnacle of the "M" is typically larger than the second and due to the letter's degree of right slant, may even extend entirely above it. The ending stroke of the "M" may dip below the base line and the "ic" could vary in size. The ascender of the "k" could vary in size and due to its right slant may extend as far as the "y" in Mickey. The bottom loop of the "k" may be left open and the "y" can vary in definition and size.

The elaborate "W" in Welch at times resembles a "3V" character combination, with the middle of the letter commonly rising to capitalization height. Due to the degree of right slant exhibited by the "W", it was not uncommon for the ending stroke of the letter to extend above the entire "e". The "l" was very inconsistent in height, but should be similar in slant to the "h". The "h" was also erratic in both height and width, with the right-slanted ascender commonly rising above the simple ending stroke of the letter. His later signature samples exhibit typical aging characteristics.

Welch was a responsive signer and like so many of the pioneer of the game is a highly sought-after autograph, particularly because he reached the illustrious 300-win pitching plateau. Collectors should find the acquisition of his signature a bit challenging.

Availability: Limited
Demand: Strong

Cut signature	$2,175
Single-signature baseball	$5,000
3x5" index card	$3,250
Photograph/baseball card	$4,000
HOF plaque postcard	Impossible
Perez-Steele postcard	Impossible

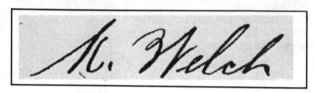

Zack Wheat

Zachariah Davis Wheat
(May 23, 1886-March 11, 1972)

Wheat finished his 19-year career with 2,884 hits at a batting average of .317. He batted over .300 for 14 seasons and won the National League batting title in 1918. He helped lead Brooklyn to two World Series contests, in 1916 and in 1929.

Commonly signing "Zach D. Wheat", his signature varied primarily in character formation and size during his lifetime. The only consistent signature break fell between the "W" and the "h" in Wheat and even between the "a" and the "c" in Zack. The "Z" often resembled a number "3" and had a flamboyant ending stroke attached to it which could extend as far as his middle initial. The "Z" could vary in size and slant particularly in the descender. The "a" may or may not be closed at the top and the "c" could vary in size. The "k" was unusually small, with an ascender that typically reached only to the height of the "c". Depending on the type of writing instrument used, the "k" may or may not be recognizable as a letter. The "a" in Zack commonly rested on or next to the flamboyant ending stroke of the "Z".

The "D" varied in size, particularly in the top loop formation of the letter, however the slant should be similar to the slant of the last upward stroke in the "W". The first stroke of the "W" was typically just a simple line that doubled back and showed little or no space between the first and middle stroke of the letter. The second loop of the "W" was recognizable and was always larger in size than the first. The "W" may connect to the "h" to form a large ascender that rose above his last name as far as the "t". The bottom loop formation of the "h", like the "e", typically varied in size, as did the "a". The "t" resembled a "v" and had little likeness to the intended letter. Wheat commonly placed two dots below his signature, one underneath the "DW" and one underneath the "t".

Wheat was a responsive signer and collectors should have little trouble acquiring his signature through autograph dealers and auction houses.

Availability: Above average
Demand: Average

Cut signature	$20
Single-signature baseball	$400
3x5" index card	$40
Photograph/baseball card	$120
HOF plaque postcard	$140
Perez-Steele postcard	Impossible

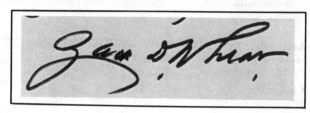

Hoyt Wilhelm

James Hoyt Wilhelm
(July 26, 1923-   )

Wilhelm appeared in over 1,000 games while compiling 143 wins, over 120 of which were won in relief. He spent 21 years in the major leagues with a variety of clubs and became baseball's premier relief pitcher. His elusive knuckleball became his hallmark and allowed him to amass 227 saves while posting a lifetime ERA of 2.52.

Typically signing "Hoyt Wilhelm", his signature has varied in character formation, slant and size. A consistent signature break falls between the "W" and the "i" in Wilhelm. The two- stroked "H" formation has varied primarily in character formation and flamboyance. In earlier versions of his signature, those signed during his playing days, it was not uncommon for the first curled stroke of the "H" to resemble a number "9". The second stroke of the "H" commonly exceeds the height of the first and often varies in its formation, particularly at the top of the letter, which may or may not open with a loop. The bottom of the second stroke of the "H" loops to form the middle of the letter, and may or may not intersect the first stroke. The top of the second stroke of the "H" is often the highest point in his signature. Both strokes of the "H" commonly dip sightly below the signature's base line. The "o" may or may not close at the top and the "y" has decreased in size with age. The descender of the "y", which was often the lowest point in his earlier signatures, now dips slightly below the base line and may not even reach the bottom of the "H" in "Hoyt". The slant of the descender of the "y" has decreased with age and the connection to the "t" in later versions has changed to a formation that often makes a sharp 90-degree angle before forming the letter's stem. The ascender of the "t" has always been large and in recent examples exceeds the height of the "W" in Wilhelm. The "t" is commonly crossed by a separate stroke.

The "W" in Wilhelm has decreased in size with age and in recent versions may only slightly exceed the height of the "i". Both the first "l" and the "h" commonly vary in width and slant. The "h" commonly exceeds the height of the first "l" and the "e" has increased in size with age. The last "l" in Wilhelm has decreased in size and slant, with recent examples having the letter equal in height to the first "l". In earlier examples of his signatures the second "l" in Wilhelm may occasionally be the highest point in his last name. The "m" in Wilhelm has varied considerably in character formation, with recent versions often resembling a letter "r". The ending stroke in Wilhelm is usually a fairly simple hooked stroke.

Wilhelm has been an obliging signer and collectors should find the acquisiton of his signature fairly easy.

Availability: Plentiful
Demand: Little

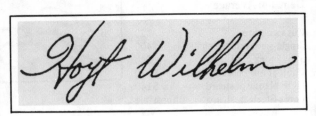

Cut signature	$3
Single-signature baseball	$20
3x5" index card	$5
Photograph/baseball card	$13
HOF plaque postcard	$10
Perez-Steele postcard	$25

Billy Williams

Billy Leo Williams
(June 15, 1938-   )

Williams smacked 2,711 hits, 426 of which were home runs, on his way to a career batting average of .290. Always a clutch performer, this 1961 National League Rookie of the Year hit over .300 five times and won the leagues's batting title in 1972.

Commonly signing "Billy Williams", his signature has varied in character formation, size and slant. Earlier examples, those signed during his playing days, exhibit consistent signature breaks between the "B" and the "i" in Billy, also between the "W" and the "i" in Williams. Recent examples of his signature typically exhibit no breaks. The "B" in earlier examples resembles a character formation used by Babe Ruth, with a similar hooked beginning stroke. The character can vary in size, often being left open at the bottom. In recent versions, the "B" resembles a capitalized formation used by Yogi Berra, and begins with a looped stroke which originates from inside the letter before forming the character. The "i" in recent examples varies in both height and width, but typically does not exceed the apex of the "B" in Billy. The "y" has gradually decreased in definition with age and now is often only a simple downward stroke that lacks upper character formation.

The "W" has also decreased in size with age and in recent examples is often smaller in height than both the "l"s in Billy. Both of the letter "i"s in Williams may or may not be recognizable in recent versions and are often left undotted. Both "l"s in Williams can vary in size, however are commonly similar in slant. The "iams" in recent examples shows little character definition and may resemble a "w" with a flamboyant ending stroke added. Earlier versions of his signature are far more legible.

Williams' recent signatures will no doubt eventually prove to be difficult to authenticate because of their variations. Fortunately he is a responsive signer and collectors should have little difficulty adding his autograph to their collections.

Availability: Plentiful
Demand: Little

Cut signature	$4
Single-signature baseball	$20
3x5" index card	$7
Photograph/baseball card	$15
HOF plaque postcard	$13
Perez-Steele postcard	$30

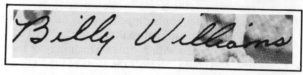

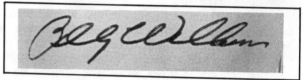

Ted Williams

Theodore Samuel Williams
(Aug. 30, 1918-   )

"The Splendid Splinter" spent his entire 18-year career with the Boston Red Sox where he compiled 2,654 hits, 525 home runs, and 1,839 RBIs at a batting average of .344. Williams hit over .300 every season of his career but one (1959). He won the American League batting title six times and was the last player in the major leagues to bat above .400 (1941 - .406). He played in 18 All-Star games and was named player of the decade 1951-1960.

Typically signing "Ted Williams", his signature has varied in character formation, size and right slant. Early examples of his signature (circa 1950s) typically exhibit consistent signature breaks between the "T" and the "e" in Ted, also between the "W" and the "i" in Williams. An occasional break between the "i" and the "a" in Williams is also worth noting. The anomalies in his signature necessitate a character-by-character analysis.

Letter	Variation
T	The "T" in Ted can be either a single- or two-stroke construction.
	Single-stroke version

The single stroke version of the "T" is common in his later signatures. The opening stroke of this version is often unpredictable, varying from a downward double backed stroke which begins at or near the top of the letter, to a simple single-stroke upward which may or may not loop at the top before changing directions. The height of either version may or may not exceed that of the "W". The stem structure of either version resembles a "J" in its appearance, with the bottom of the character varying in the degree of roundness. The finishing stroke can vary from an elongated loop that ends by intersecting the stem, to a simple backward stroke. Although any part of this character can vary in size, the slant of the "T" has been relatively consistent.

Two-stroke version

The two-stroke version is common in his earlier signatures (circa 1950s). The first stroke, or the top portion of the letter, began with an elongated loop, then extended upward at a variety of angles. The extension of the first stroke varied, but typically rose beyond the "e" in Ted. The stem of the two- stroke version had the same characteristics as the single-stroke variation.

The "T" commonly dipped slightly below the signature's base line. The slant of the "T" should be similar to that of the "d" in Ted.

e   The "e" began with a stroke which may or may not originate from below the base line, and could intersect the stem of the "T". The "e" is often equal in height to the loop of the "d".

d   The "d" can vary from a curved double backed line for the loop of the letter to an "e"-shaped loop that slants to form the bottom of the character. The ascender of the "d" varies in height and is often smaller than the "l"s in earlier versions, but may be equal in later examples. The ending stroke of the "d" in earlier versions was often a simple curled stroke, while later versions would extend the curl to capitalization height, form a loop to change direction, then create the "W". The size and flamboyance of the "d" to "W" connection has varied over the years. The looped connection can fall directly above the "d" or in between both characters slightly above the height of the letter's ("d") ascender. The height of the "d" and the size and position of the looped connection are often unpredictable and do not make good authentication reference points.

W   The "W" has changed from a separate stroked character which begins with a small loop at the capitalization height (earlier versions), to a letter that connects to the "d" via a flamboyant looped formation (later versions). The height of the middle stroke of the character commonly varies in size and may be looped or rounded at the top. The "W" varies in symmetry with little consistency in the width or slant of either side of the letter. The ending stroke of the letter varies in length and final direction. It is not unusual for the ending stroke of the "W" to exceed the height of the flamboyant looped connection. The beginning looped formation in earlier examples commonly varies in size and slant.

i   The "i" seems to have increased in size with age. Later versions are often undotted.

ll   In earlier versions, both "l"s will vary in height and width, but often reach the apex of the "W". In his later signatures the "l"s have been reduced in size and may be equal in height to the "i"s in Williams. Both "l"s should be consistent in slant.

a   The "a" is typically a two-looped formation that joins together at the top. Some earlier versions exhibit a break between the "i" and the "a", at which time the "a" then begins from the top of the letter with a simple stroke downward to form the character's loop.

m   The "m" varies in character formation and size. Often the letter is condensed and resembles a "uu" formation.

s   The "s" can also vary in character formation, size and slant. The "s" may or may not loop at the end, with the bottom letter resting at a variety of heights and angles. The height of the "s" in recent examples has exceeded that of any other lower case letter in Williams.

During the 1980s, Williams has gradually reduced the height of the lower case letters in his last name, and in recent signatures, they appear nearly equal. Perhaps the best methodology to authenticate his signature is via slant comparison, particularly that of the "T" and the "d" in Ted (should be similar), and the "illi" combination in Williams (should be similar). The numerous variations in his signature can add to the complexities of authentication. Fortunately for collectors, Williams has been a responsive signer and thus the acquisition of his signature should be fairly easy.

Availability: Plentiful
Demand: Average

Cut signature	$10
Single-signature baseball	$50
3x5" index card	$15
Photograph/baseball card	$30
HOF plaque postcard	$30
Perez-Steele postcard	$150

Hack Wilson

Robert Lewis Wilson
(April 26, 1900-Nov. 23, 1948)

During 12 seasons in the National League, "Hack" compiled 1,461 hits while batting .307. Wilson drove in 100 or more runs six times and smacked 244 lifetime home runs. He established a major league record in 1930 by driving in 190 runs.

Commonly signing "Lewis Hack Wilson" or "Hack Wilson", his signature varied in character formation, slant and size during his lifetime. Consistent signature breaks fell between the "L" and the "e" in Lewis, also between the "W" and the "i" in Wilson. The two-looped "L" in Lewis could vary in size and slant. The top loop of the "L" was typically larger than the bottom loop and was often the highest point in his signature. The steep right slant of the "L" allowed its top loop to extend above both the "e" and the "w" in Lewis. The "e" can vary in size and typically began with a line that originated from slightly below the signature's base line. The "w" can vary in width and the "i" originated from the top of the finishing stroke of the "W". The "s" can vary in size and is often smaller than any of the surrounding lower case letters.

The "H" in Hack was a two-stroke construction, with the first stroke often resembling a number "7" and the second a simple downward stroke that looped backwards at the bottom to form the middle of the letter. Both strokes of the "H" were typically the same height and nearly identical in slant. The "a" originated from the top of the character and the loop of the letter may or may not close. The "c" had little curvature to the loop and could resemble an "e" at times. The ascender of the "k" was very large and typically extended higher than the "H" in Hack. The slant of the "k" should be very smilar to that of the "H".

Each progressive pinnacle of the "W" commonly increased in size. The beginning stroke of the "W" resembled a number "7" and the bottom loops of the letter varied in degree of roundness. The finishing stroke of the "W" could vary in style and direction, however was typically the highest point in his last name. The "i" begins from the base line with a curved upward stroke and the "l" can vary in size. The slant of the "l" and the "k" should be very similar. The "o" may or may not close at the top and occasionally resembles a "u" in its formation. The ending stroke of his signature is typically a simple curl upward.

Following his retirement from baseball he held an assortment of jobs but was never able to regain financial stability and eventually died penniless in 1948. He was a popular player and an obliging signer. Collectors should find the acquisition of his signature a moderate challenge.

Availability: Limited
Demand: Above average

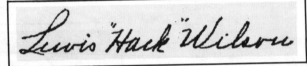

Cut signature	$240
Single-signature baseball	$1,550
3x5" index card	$300
Photograph/baseball card	$525
HOF plaque postcard	Impossible
Perez-Steele postcard	Impossible

George Wright

George Wright
(Jan. 28, 1847 — Aug. 21, 1937)

One of baseball's earliest stars, Wright was a member of the game's first professional team, the Cincinnati Red Stockings of 1869. He revolutionized the position of shortstop while playing on seven championship teams.

Typically signing "Geo. Wright" or "G. Wright", his signature varied in character formation, size and slant. A consistent signature break fell between the "W" and the "r" in Wright. The "G" began with a long upward stroke from the signature's base line, which formed the first pinnacle of the letter with a loop, then the second pointed pinnacle before moving downward. The finishing strokes of the "G" descended below the base line and may or may not create a looped formation before extending to the "e". The "eo" combination in George remained relatively consistent, however the "r" could vary slightly in slant and size. The "g" in George could have its descender vary in size and may or may not have its top loop closed.

The "W" often varied in its formation from a rounded loop style to a sharply pointed letter structure. The "W" can also vary in slant and the flamboyance of its ending stroke. It was common for the ending stroke to extend to the "g" in Wright. The "r" seemed to increase in size with age and may have its beginning stroke originate from slightly below his signature's base line. The "i" could vary in slant and the "g" in Wright, similar to the "g" in George, could vary in both length and width. The steep right slant of the "h" often allowed its descender to extend above the main formation of the "t", particularly in earlier examples. The unusually large "t" often exceeds the height of the capitalized "W" and may or may not be crossed by a double backed stroke that intersects the letter. The "t" can resemble a letter "s" when the ending stroke loops at the bottom of the letter, rather than intersecting the stem. Wright's later signatures exhibit typical aging characteristics and a lesser degree of right slant. It was not uncommon for him to add an underline to his signature.

Wright was an obliging signer and a frequent spectator at games in Boston. Like all of baseball's pioneers, his signature is highly sought by collectors who may find the acquisition of his autograph a challenge. Wright's signature does, however, surface occasionally in the autograph market and of all the pioneers, his is one of the most prevalent.

Availability: Limited
Demand: Strong

Cut signature	$900
Single-signature baseball	$3,000
3x5" index card	$1,700
Photograph/baseball card	$2,750
HOF plaque postcard	Impossible
Perez-Steele postcard	Impossible

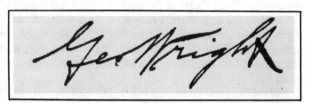

Harry Wright

William Henry Wright
(Jan. 10, 1835 — Oct. 3, 1895)

Harry Wright was a manager and center fielder for the famous Cincinnati Red Stockings. As manager with Boston of the National Association he won four straight pennants (1872-1875). Wright was an accomplished player, who along with his brother George, terrorized many teams with their aggressive play. His greatest feat as a player came in 1867 when he hit seven home runs in a game while playing against Newport, Kentucky.

Commonly signing "W. Harry Wright" or "Harry Wright", his signature varied in character formation, size and slant. Consistent signature breaks fell between the "H" and the "a" in Harry, also between the "W" and the "r", and the "i" an the "g" in Wright. The two-stroke "H" formation could vary in slant, with the second stroke commonly exceeding the height of the first. The middle of the "H", formed by the second stroke, may or may not intersect the first. Both strokes of the "H" commonly rest on the signature's base line. The "a" began from the top of the letter and may or may not be closed. The older styled "r"s could vary in size, with the second of the two letters often slightly smaller than the first. The descender of the "y" could also vary in width and was typically the lowest point in his signature.

The flamboyant "W" in Wright began with a hooked opening stroke that descended to the signature's base line, then turned upward extending beyond any other character in his name to form the letter's middle loop. The "W"'s stroke then descended from the middle loop downward to the base line forming a point before ascending to nearly the height of the hooked opening while curling outward. The "ri" in Wright often resembled a number "2", tilted on its bottom loop, with a "c" attached to the end. An occasional signature break may occur beween the "r" and the "i" in Wright. The "g" began from the top of the letter and may or may not have the loop closed. The descender of the "g" could vary in size as could the ascender of the "h". The "g" can vary in character formation and may resemble a capitalized "G" that rests on his signature's base line. The "t" was often similar in style to his brother George's letter formation, either doubling back to cross the "t" or adding a simple loop to the end. Wright may also use a single-stroke crossing for the letter "t". Wright's signature breaks are often unpredicatable and should not be used as a sole indicator of an authentic example. Wright handwriting is often recognizable by the small descenders of his characters (later examples), flamboyant capitalized letter "A"s, and his large middle-looped letter "W".

During the final years of his life, failing eyesight contributued to some interesting variations of his signature (primarily character spacing, formation, and signature breaks), making authentication of these later examples a bit difficult. Collectors should find his highly sought-after autograph a considerable challenge.

Availability: Scarce
Demand: Strong

Cut signature	$1,600
Single-signature baseball	$3,000
3x5" index card	$2,450
Photograph/baseball card	$3,500
HOF plaque postcard	Impossible
Perez-Steele postcard	Impossible

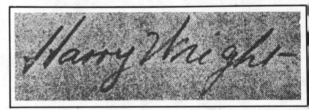

Early Wynn

Early Wynn
(Jan. 6, 1920-   )

Wynn spent 23 years in the American League compiling 2,334 strikeouts and 300 wins. He led the American League twice in wins, while recording 20 or more victories for five seasons. Wynn pitched 49 career shutouts and led the league twice in strikeouts.

Typically signing "Early Wynn", his signature has varied only slightly in size and flamboyance. A consistent signature break fell between the "W" and the "y" in Wynn. Occasionally a break also fell between the "E" and the "a" in Early, also between the "y" and the "n" in Wynn. The degree of right slant in his signature has allowed the "E" in Early to extend as far as the "r". The top loop formation of the "E" was typically smaller than the bottom loop and may or may not slip slightly below the signature's base line. The "E" seemed to increase in size with age and in later versions often exceeds the height of the "W" in Wynn. Earlier examples of his signature may have both the "E" and the "W" equal in height. The "arl" letter combination has remained relatively consistent, while the descender of the "y" has decreased in slant wih age and increased in the flamboyance of his ending stroke. In earlier versions of his signature, the long descender of the "y" may extend as far left as the "a" in Early, while later versions commonly travel only to the "r". The "y" in Early and the "y" in Wynn may show little similarity in slant, length or ending stroke formation. When he occasionally signed his nickname of "Gus", a break could be found between the "G" and the "u".

The "W" has varied only slightly in the formation of the bottom two loops in the letter. The ending stroke of the "W" often curled above the "y" in Wynn. The "y" often varied in slant and flamboyance, while typically being a bit shorter in its descender length when compared to the "y" in Early. The "nn" letter combination remained relatively consistent, with a simple extended ending stroke.

Wynn has been an obliging signer, however somewhat reluctant at times to sign various types of materials, such as cards. Collectors should have little difficulty adding his signature to their collections.

Availability: Plentiful
Demand: Little

Cut signature	$4
Single-signature baseball	$18
3x5" index card	$6
Photograph/baseball card	$15
HOF plaque postcard	$15
Perez-Steele postcard	$30

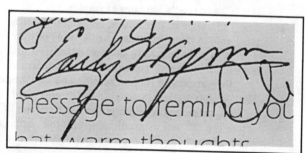

Carl Yastrzemski

Carl Michael Yastrzemski
(Aug. 22, 1939-   )

During 23 years with the Boston Red Sox, "Yaz" smacked 3,419 hits and 452 home runs. He won the Triple Crown and the Most Valuable Player award in 1967 while leading his team to the pennant. A winner of six Gold Gloves, Yaz displayed equally impressive fielding skills and was named to 18 All-Star teams.

Typically signing "Carl M. Yastrzemski" or "Carl Yastrzemski", his signature varied significantly in character formation, size, slant and flamboyance. Not until late in his career did his signature exhibit any breaks. Consistent signature breaks in samples signed during the 1980s fell between the "Y" and the "a" and the "z" and the "e" in Yastrzemski. His signature increased in right slant and flamboyance with age.

During the 1960s, Yaz's autograph, "Carl M. Yastrzemski", showed greater definition and less slant when compared to later versions. By the 1970s, he had dropped his middle initial of "M", decreased his signature slant to an almost vertical positioning, and began to show less definition in the individual characters in his last name, particularly in the letters "m", "s", "k" and "i". The 1980s have seen his signature increase in degree of right slant and flamboyance, particularly notable in his capitalized letter "Y".

The significant variation exhibited by his signature requires a character-by-character analysis.

Letter	Variation
C	Earlier versions (circa 1960s), typically had the "C" beginning at the top of the letter. By the late 1960s or early 1970s, the stroke shifted to originate from the base line. Autographs signed later in his career and following his retirement have the beginning stroke of the "C" originating from below the base line (with no curvature), then forming the small top loop (may or may not close), before beginning the large main formation of the "C" which intersects the beginning stroke. The right slant of the "C" radically varies from an average of about 55 degrees to 65 degrees, to as dramatic as 35 degrees. The "C" commonly varies in size, although it is typically six or seven times larger than his lower case "a". The "C" may extend above the "a" and the "r" in later examples.
a	The "a" varies in formation, being better defined in earlier examples and indistinguishable in later versions. The "a" may or may not close at the top.
r	The "r" has decreased in size and definition with age. If the "a" is distinguishable in his signature, it will typically be larger than the "r". Little attention is paid to the "ar" formation and it often resembles a "uu" letter combination.
l	The "l" has varied in height, width and slant. Earlier versions will have the "l" equal to or exceeding slightly the height of the "C". During the last few years of his career the "l" was unpredictable and may occasionally exceed both the height and width of the "C". His recent signatures have had the "l" extend only to the beginning of the first loop in the "C", with little width to the character. (Note: It is common for his first name to rise gradually above the signature's base line with each subsequent letter in Carl.)
Y	The "Y" has varied dramatically in character formation, size, slant and flamboyance. Earlier versions (circa 1960s and early 1970s) have a traditional styled formation with a descender that extends well below the base line before forming a simple loop upward to connect to the "a". The descender of the "Y" gradually increased in flamboyance and width until (circa late 1970s) it had formed a large loop that extended backwards beyond the beginning of his first name, and as high as the top loop of the "C" in Carl. The loop typically intersects the "C" and the "l" before finally extending through the stem of the "Y". The top formation of the letter has

gradually decreased in size and by the 1980s resembled a letter's serif rather than a character. The top formation of the "Y" commonly varies and can be a simple line or even a small loop. The height of the "Y" is also unpredictable and in recent examples has a tendency to equal that of the "C" in Carl. In recent examples, the slant of the "Y" often equals that of the "t". The "Y" is typically connected to the "a" in earlier examples.

a   The "a" has increased in size over the years and now typically exceeds the height of the "s". The slant of the "a" varies with the major slant of his signature.

s   The "s" has decreased in size and character definition over the years. In recent examples the "s" resembles an "r" and is often half the size of the "a".

t   The ascender of the "t" has always been unusally large and commonly exceeds the height of the "Y". The "t" can vary in width, with its slant often similar to that of the "k" or the "Y". The "t" is crossed by a separate stroke that varies in length and placement.

r   The "r" is distinguishable only in his earlier examples (circa 1960s). By the 1970s it resembled an undotted "i" or simply a bump upward in his stroke.

z   The "z" has always resembled a "y" and varies in slant and the formation of its descender. In recent examples the descender has been a simple line downward with no major loop construction. The looped descender is prevalent primarily in signatures where the "z" doesn't break with the "l". The length of the "z"'s descender is typically equal to that of the "Y".

e   The "e" has varied in size and slant. In earlier examples (circa 1960s and 1970s), the "e" may extend as high as half the length of the ascender of the "t". In recent examples the "e" has shown an increase in right slant and often equals the height of the "a".

m   The "m" has only displayed sharp character definition in 1960s' examples of his signature. Recent versions often resemble a letter "u".

s   Like the "m", the "s" has been recognizable most in his earlier signatures. By the 1970s, the "s" often was indistinguishable as a character.

k   The "k" often resembles a "b" or an "l", with the height of the ascender of the letter usually equal to that of the "t". The "k" also commonly varies in width. The slant of the "k" should be similar to that of the "t".

i   Since the mid 1970s, the "i" at the end of Yastrzemski's name has typically been non-existent. When the "i" is occasionally included it resembles an "r". The ending stroke in his name is typically an extended line that may be dotted at the end.

Yastrzemski has been a responsive signer and often appears on the baseball card show circuit. Collectors should have little trouble adding his signature to their collections.

Availability: Plentiful
Demand: Little

Cut signature	$4
Single-signature baseball	$20
3x5" index card	$7
Photograph/baseball card	$13
HOF plaque postcard	$13
Perez-Steele postcard	$75

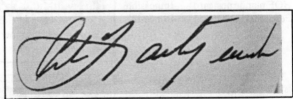

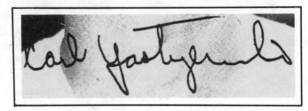

Tom Yawkey

Thomas Austin Yawkey
(Feb. 21, 1903-July 9, 1976)

Yawkey was owner and president of the Boston Red Sox from 1933 to 1976. His honesty, pride and perseverance were respected by all in baseball, but particularly by his players. His teams won pennants in 1946, 1967 and 1975, while narrowly missing during three other years (1948, 1949 and 1972). Yawkey also served as vice-president of the American League from 1956 to 1973.

Often signing "Thomas A. Yawkey" or "Tom Yawkey", his signature varied in character formation, size and slant during his lifetime. Consistent signature breaks fell between the "T" and "o" in Tom, also between the "Y" and the "a" in Yawkey. The large two-stroke "T" in Tom could vary in size and slant, particularly in the top stroke. The top stroke commonly exended well above his entire first name and could originate from lower case level, while finishing at the capitalization height of the "Y" in Yawkey. The "o" began from the top of the letter and may or may not be left open. The "m" varied little and was typically smaller in height than the "o".

The "Y", often four to five times larger than the height of his lower case letters, began from capitalization height with an opening curved stroke that formed the character's loop before extending well below the signature's base line to form the letter's descender. The "Y"'s descender was typically slashed with a separate stroke. The "a" could vary slightly in formation and may or may not be closed at the top of the letter. The "w" varied a bit in size, however was often smaller in height than the "a". The slant of the descender of the "y" and the ascender of the "k" should be similar. The "k" commonly varied in both height and width. The descender of the "y" in Yawkey fluctuated between two styles, a looped version or a simple downward stroke with a slash intersecting it. The slant of both the "Y" and the "y" in Yawkey should be similar.

Yawkey was a very popular figure in baseball and a responsive signer. Collectors should have little trouble acquiring his signature through autograph dealers and auction houses.

Availability: Average
Demand: Average

Cut signature	$70
Single-signature baseball	$650
3x5" index card	$115
Photograph/baseball card	$200
HOF plaque postcard	Impossible
Perez-Steele postcard	Impossible

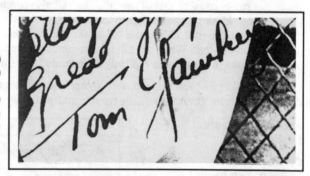

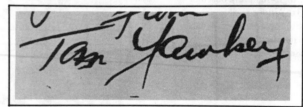

Cy Young

Denton True Young
(March 29, 1867-Nov. 4, 1955)

Considered by most to be the greatest pitcher of all-time, Young compiled a record 511 wins at an ERA of 2.63. He struck out 2,799 batters during his 22 years in the major leagues and pitched more innings than anyone to ever play the game. For 16 season he won over 20 games and led the league in victories four times.

Commonly signing "Cy Young", his signature varied in character formation, size and flamboyance during his lifetime. Consistent signature breaks fell between the "Y" and the "o", and the "n" and the "g" in Young. The "C" varied in size and may be equal to or slightly exceed the height of the "Y" in Young. The opening stroke of the "C" varies in formation from a small curl originating inside the letter to a looped formation beginning outside of the major construction of the character. The "C" connects to the first pinnacle of the "y", creates the character's loop and forms a point or loop at the second peak, before the stroke descends to form the pointed bottom loop of the letter. The descender of the "y" varies in length, formation and flamboyance. The "y"'s descender varies in formation from a simple downward stroke to a flamboyant loop at the bottom. The "y" is Cy can be similar to the "Y" in Young, particularly in slant.

Both the "y" and the "Y" can vary in size and character formation although the "Y" in Young is usually slightly larger. The "o" varies slightly in the size of the top loop of the letter and is typically closed. The "u" and the "n" vary in the degree of roundness in their formation and may be nearly identical in appearance. The "g" begins at the top of the letter and may or may not be closed. The descender of the "g" exhibits the same characteristics as the descender of the "y". The flamboyant ending strokes of the descenders, when used, varied in size and style. It is not uncommon for every letter in his signature to be nearly identical in height. Later versions of his signature exhibit typical aging characteristics.

Young's signature was not very graceful and later versions can be unpredictable in character formation, adding significant challenge to the authentication of his autograph. Fortunately Young was a responsive signer and his signatures do periodically surface in the autograph market.

Availability: Average
Demand: Strong

Cut signature	$165
Single-signature baseball	$1,900
3x5" index card	$225
Photograph/baseball card	$355
HOF plaque postcard	$875
Perez-Steele postcard	Impossible

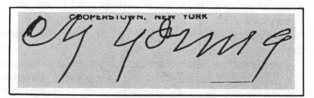

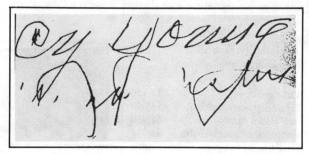

Ross Youngs

Royce Middlebrook Youngs
(April 10, 1897-Oct. 22, 1927)

"Pep" played 10 years in the major leagues and compiled 1,491 hits while batting a career .322. He batted over .300 every season he played but one (1925). He was the star right fielder of the champion New York Giants who reigned from 1921 to 1924. Youngs twice made over 200 hits in a season and led the league in doubles in 1919.

Typically signing "Ross Youngs", his signature varied in character formation, slant and size. A consistent signature break fell between the "n" and the "g" in Youngs. Additionally, an occasional break also fell between both "s"s in Ross. The "R" began with a small loop at the top of the letter, which then extended to the base line before doubling back at a variable angle to form the major loop of the letter. The "R" is somewhat reminiscent of the capitalization style of Babe Ruth, with the exception being Young's long ascender that typically extends to well above the height of the loop in the letter. The right slant of the "R" allowed its loop to extend above the "o" in Ross. The "o" varied a bit in size and the first "s" was typically left open at the bottom the letter. The second "s" typically closed and may at times resemble an "e". An occasional break can fall between each "s", and the bottoms of the two letters may not rest level with the signature's base line. The "oss" is typically the same height.

The flamboyant capitalized "Y" is often four to five times the size of his lower case letters. The "Y" begins from the top of the letter with a right slanted oval loop formation, before extending downward and forming a point near the base line. This stroke then continues upward to form the second pinnacle of the top formation. The well extended descender of the "Y" may vary in length and width, but should be very similar in slant to the stem of the "R" and the "g". The formation of the "o", which varies in size, may intersect the letter's stem. Both the "u" and the "n" can be nearly identical in formation, however vary in size. The "g" may be left open at the top of the loop and the descender of the letter can vary a bit in size. The "gs" formation in Youngs is similar in style to a Willie Mays closing configuration, with the "s" varying in size and finishing slightly above the base line, with a backward ending stroke. The ascender of the "R" is typically the highest point in his signature and the descender of the "Y" the lowest point. Young's handwriting is distinguishable by his long extended descenders in letters such as the "Y", elaborate opening character formations in letters such as the "k" or "R". The best reference point for authenticators is perhaps matching the slants in the letters "R", "Y" and "y" in his signature; they should be nearly identical.

Youngs suffered from a serious kidney ailment that eventually claimed his life in 1927 at the young age of 30. He was a responsive signer, however his sudden death at such an early age contributes significantly to the scarcity of his signature. Collectors should find the acquisition of his signature a challenge, however they do on rare occasions surface in the autograph market.

Availability: Scarce
Demand: Strong

Cut signature	$1,150
Single-signature baseball	$4,000
3x5" index card	$1,450
Photograph/baseball card	$1,675
HOF plaque postcard	Impossible
Perez-Steele postcard	Impossible

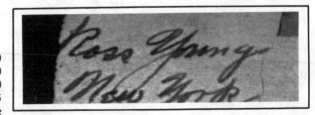

Frequently requested addresses

Adirondack/Rawlings
52 McKinley Avenue
Dolgeville, NY 13329

American Baseball Cap
310 Station Road
Media, PA 19063

Baseball Hall of Fame
P.O. Box 590
Cooperstown, NY 13326

Champion Products Inc.
P.O. Box 850
3141 Monroe Avenue
Rochester, NY 14603

Cooper Canada Ltd.
501 Alliance Avenue
Toronto, Ontario M6N 2J3

J. DeBeer & Sons, Inc.
5 Burdick Drive
P.O. Box 11570
Albany, NY 12211

W.A. Goodman
2419 E. 28th Street
Los Angeles, CA 90058

Hillerich & Bradsby Co.
P.O. Box 35700
Louisville, KY 40232

MacGregor Sand-Knit
330 Trowbridge Drive
Fond du Lac, WI 54935

Majestic Athletic Wear
636 Pen Argyl Street
Pen Argyl, PA 18072

New Era Cap
8061 Erie Road
Derby, NY 14047

Nike, Inc.
3900 S.W. Murray Blvd.
Beaverton, OR 97005

Perez-Steele Galleries
Box 1776
Ft. Washington, PA 19034

Rawlings Sporting Goods Co.
(Div. of Figgie Int. Inc.)
2300 Delmar Blvd.
St. Louis, MO 63166

Street & Smith's
304 East 45th Street
New York, NY 10017

Wilson Sporting Goods
2233 West Street
River Grove, IL 60171

Worth Inc.
P.O. Box 88104
Tullahoma, TN 37388

Major League Team Addresses

Baseball Commissioner's Office
350 Park Avenue
New York, NY 10022
(212) 371-2211

American League Office
350 Park Avenue
New York, NY 10022
(212) 371-7600

Baltimore Orioles
Memorial Stadium
Baltimore, MD 21218
(301) 243-9800

Boston Red Sox
Fenway Park
4 Yawkey Way
Boston, MA 02215
(617) 267-9440

California Angels
P.O. Box 2000
Anaheim, CA 92803
(714) 937-6700

Chicago White Sox
Comiskey Park
324 West 35th Street
Chicago, IL 60616
(312) 924-1000

Cleveland Indians
Cleveland Stadium
Cleveland, OH 44114
(216) 861-1200

Detroit Tigers
Tiger Stadium
2121 Trumbell Avenue
Detroit, MI 48216
(313) 962-4000

Kansas City Royals
P.O. Box 419969
Kansas City, MO 64141
(816) 921-2200

Milwaukee Brewers
Milwaukee County Stadium
201 South 46th Street
Milwaukee, WI 53214
(414) 933-7323

Minnesota Twins
Hubert H. Humphrey Metrodome
501 Chicago Avenue South
Minneapolis, MN 55415
(612) 375-1366

New York Yankees
Yankee Stadium
East 161st Street and River Avenue
Bronx, NY 10451
(212) 293-4300

Oakland A's
P.O. Box 2220
Oakland, CA 94621
(415) 638-4900

Seattle Mariners
P.O. Box 4100
Seattle, WA 98104
(206) 628-3555

Texas Rangers
P.O. Box 1111
Arlington, TX 76010
(817) 273-5222

Toronto Blue Jays
3000 Esplanade West, Suite 3200
Toronto, Ontario, Canada M5V 3B3
(416) 341-1000

National League Office
350 Park Ave.
New York, NY 10022
(212) 371-7300

Atlanta Braves
P.O. Box 4064
Atlanta, GA 30312
(404) 522-7630

Chicago Cubs
Wrigley Field
1060 West Addison Street
Chicago, IL 60613
(312) 281-5050

Cincinnati Reds
Riverfront Stadium
Cincinnati, OH 45202
(513) 421-4510

Houston Astros
P.O. Box 288
Houston, TX 77001
(713) 799-9500

Los Angeles Dodgers
Dodger Stadium
1000 Elysian Park Avenue
Los Angeles, CA 90012
(213) 224-1500

Montreal Expos
P.O. Box 500, Station 'M'
Montreal, Quebec, Canada H1V 3P2
(514) 253-3434

New York Mets
William A. Shea Stadium
126th Street & Roosevelt Avenue
Flushing, NY 11368
(212) 507-6387

Philadelphia Phillies
P.O. Box 7575
Philadelphia, PA 19101
(215) 463-6000

Pittsburgh Pirates
P.O. Box 7000
Pittsburgh, PA 15212
(412) 323-5000

Saint Louis Cardinals
P.O. Box 8787
250 Stadium Plaza
St. Louis, MO 63102
(314) 421-4040

San Diego Padres
P.O. Box 2000
San Diego, CA 92120
(619) 283-7294

San Francisco Giants
Candlestick Park
San Francisco, CA 94124
(415) 468-3700

Acknowledgements

First and foremost, I would like to thank everyone at Krause Publications, especially Pat Klug for her professionalism and confidence during this project. I also owe a great deal of gratitude to Bob Lemke, Steve Ellingboe and Tom Mortenson at Krause for their acceptance of so much of my work during the past three years.

A special thanks to Tom Heitz, librarian for the National Baseball Library and his entire staff, especially Pat Kelly and Bill Deane. Also a special thank you to Peter Clark, the Hall of Fame's registrar who allowed me access to many of the treasures not on display.

To Joe Sewell, Susan Sewell and the entire Sewell family, I am indeed so grateful for your acceptance and contribution to this project.

Additionally, I would like to thank Bill Williams at Hillerich & Bradsby; Mike York, Donna Baker, Michelle McCord at Worth Sports Company; Anna Graniero at Cooper; Scott Smith at Rawlings; James Muhlfelder at J. deBeer & Son, Inc.; Alan Schultz at Wilson; Peggy and Frank Steele at Perez-Steele Galleries.

To all my co-workers at the Genigraphics Corporation and Pansophic Corporation who were supportive and understanding during this project — thank you.

For the time and support from all my friends, especially those who I have met through this wonderful hobby, I am indeed grateful.

A special thank you to Thomas C. Gilhooly, a good friend and talented artist, who contributed art direction, graphic design and many hours of photography support.

A heartfelt thank you to my entire family who gave me the time and necessary support to complete this project. Finally, to my wonderful wife Christine Orioli Baker, who contributed hours of valuable editing, fine photography and much appreciated tolerance of a difficult project, I am proud to share this book with you. Thank you very much.

About the author

Mark Allen Baker holds a B.A. degree from the State University of New York. He has been published in various books and over 20 periodicals including: Computer Graphics World, Byte, Computer Pictures, CFO, Public Relations Journal, Computer Graphics Review, Personal Computing and Sports Collectors Digest. During his career Mr. Baker has worked in a variety of finance, marketing, sales and executive management positions for the General Electric Corporation, Genigraphics Corporation and Pansophic Systems, Incorporated.

Formal museum studies, including training in paper preservation and conservation, have proven particularly helpful during his 20 years of autograph collecting. Additionally, Mr. Baker has been involved in the design and manufacture of computer-based image processing systems that can be used for autograph authentication purposes.

Additional biographical data can be found in numerous professional directories including "Who's Who in the East."

Additional source material and notes

Foreward

Prepared exclusively for this book by Joseph W. Sewell, March 23, 1989.

Chapter 1

Material provided by the National Baseball Hall of Fame & Museum and the National Baseball Library. Rules for election to the Baseball Hall of Fame by both the Members of the Baseball Writers' Associaton of America and the Committee on Baseball Veterans reprinted by permission from the National Baseball Library. (See also Bibliography)

Chapter 2

(See Source Notes)

Chapter 3

(See Bibliography) Specific dates on the invention or development of certain writing materials may vary by source. Materials Analysis Charts provided by the author. "Sharpie" is a registered trademark product of the Sanford Corporation of Bellwood, Ill. Pen-touch is a product of the Sakura Color Products Corporation of Japan.

Sports Collectors Digest — "Authenticating Autographs" by Mark Allen Baker, June 19, 1987.

Chapter 4

(See Bibliography) Abbreviations may vary by periodical. Definitions may vary by source.

Chapter 5

(See Bibliography)

Chapter 6

(See Bibliography) Don Mattingly signature comparisons reference *Yankee Magazine* cover Nov. 3, 1983, and *Esquire* magazine's, "Man at His Best" promotional advertisements, 1987.

Sports Collectors Digest —"Learn What to look for when verifying signatures" by Mark Allen Baker, Nov. 6, 1987.

Chapter 7

(See Bibliography

Sports Collectors Digest — "Authenticating Autographs" by Mark Allen Baker and Scott Dockendorff, April 17, 1987.

Chapter 8

(See Bibliography) Information also provided by the National Baseball Hall of Fame and Museum.

Chapter 9

(See Bibliography) Information also provided by the National Baseball Hall of Fame and Museum.

Chapter 10

This chapter is a subjective commentary and reflects only the views of the author. Hobbyists are encouraged to establish their own collecting ethics.

Chapter 11

(See Bibliography)

Chapter 12

(See Bibliography) Information also provided by the National Baseball Hall of Fame and Museum.

Chapter 13

Information also provided by *Baseball Cards* magazine, by Krause Publications and Perez-Steele Galleries. Checklist information and photographs courtesy Perez-Steele Galleries. All postcard images copyright Perez-Steele Galleries.

Chapter 14

(See Bibliography)

Sports Collectors Digest — "Starting an Autographed Baseball Collection", by Mark Allen Baker, March 10, 1989.

The Sporting News — "Set The Standard", March 4, 1905.

The *New York Times* — "From Spalding to Reach to Aaron — There's Been Only One Baseball", by Reginald Stuart, April 8, 1974.

The *Daily Press* (Utica) — "The National Pastime Is a Losing Proposition for Baseball Maker", by Murray Olderman, March 30, 1972.

Springfield Republican — "Baseballs 'Farmed Out' to Haiti", March 18, 1973.

The Sporting News — "Official Baseball Rules", 1988 (Reference Only)

Chicago Tribune — "Manufacturing baseballs is no game to Rawlings officials", April 26, 1987.

"Sharpie" is a registered trademark product of the Sanford Corporation of Bellwood, Ill.

Advertisements are courtesy of the various manufacturers and reproduced for historical reference only.

Information also provided by the National Baseball Library.

Chapter 15

(See Bibliography)

Materials courtesy of Cooper Canada Limited: Executive Summary — Overview of Cooper Canada Limited; Material used for an article by the *Toronto Star* — "Cooper Canada Ltd. hopes for home run from the big leagues", by Adam Mayers, March 10, 1989; Spring/Summer 1989 Product Catalog.

American Legion Monthly — "It's in the Bat" by Rud Rennie, June, 1935.

The Sporting News — "Brett Retrieves 'That' Bat for Royals" by Mike Fish, Aug. 20, 1984.

Street & Smith's — "The 'Whip' Bat," 1960.

Material provided by Hillerich & Bradsby Company: Historical Dates in the History of Hillerich & Bradsby; Hillerich & Bradsby Company History; 1989 Sporting Goods Catalog; Reprint of an article from: The *Wall Street Journal* — "The Ball and Glove May Be Imported; The Bat is American," by John Heylyar, Oct. 9, 1984.

The Sporting News — "From Broken Bat in '84 to 4 Million a year" by Ralph Ray, Feb. 10, 1960.

Information also provided by the National Baseball Library: Correspondence from Jack McGrath — Hillerich & Bradsby, 1962; "Bat Timber for Louisville Sluggers".

Material provided by Worth Sports Company: 1988-1989 catalog; fact sheet; assorted brochures; press releases: NCAA Grants Final Approval to Worth Graphite Bat; Graphite Takes Crack at Solving Future Bat Shortage; Worth Graphite Bat: Chronological History of Development; The Pro Bat Story; Making the Big Leagues; Celebrating 75 Years Worth of Quality; Martha Cruce Makes the Major Leagues.

The Sporting News — "Official Baseball Rules", 1988 (Reference Only)

The following bats are registered trademark products of A.G. Spalding & Bros.: "Trade-Marked", "Wagon Tongue", "Axeltree", "Sacrifice", "Burnt Finish or Antique", "Black End Willow", and "Mushroom".

The following bats are registered trademark products of the A.J. Reach Co.: "Reach Burley", "Special Pro-Finish", and the "Frankie Frisch Model".

"Louisville Slugger" is a registered trademark product of Hillerich & Bradsby Company of Louisville, Ky.

"Sharpie" is a registered trademark product of the Sanford Corporation of Bellwood, Ill.

"Adirondack — Pro Ring" is a registered trademark product of the Rawlings Sportin Goods Company.

Advertisements are courtesy of the various manufacturers and reproduced for historica reference only.

Chapter 16

Samples courtesy of the National Baseball Library or assorted private collections.

Source Notes

( ) = Page

(9) "Patriotism and research . . . " Baseball Hall of Fame Fourty-Ninth Annual Pro gram, 1988 - "Doubleday's Legend: Did He or Didn't He? by Lowell Reidenbugh.

(9) "Baseball is of . . . ," "the first scheme . . . " Spalding's Official Baseball Guide 1908 from an article by James E. Sullivan.

(10) "I now declare . . . " transcript from Baseball Hall of Fame opening - 1939, the National Baseball Library.

(16-17) The inspiration for the poem on this page was in tribute to Ernie Harwell's - "The Game for All America."

(55) "I was served with a notice . . ." letter from Ban Johnson to August Hermann, July 1, 1921 (National Baseball Library)

(56) "That gambling thing comes to me . . ." letter from Kenesaw Landis to Connie Mack, June 19, 1939 (National Baseball Library).

Chapter 15

(59) "Hugh Duffy - Brilliant as a defensive . . . " from bronze plaque in the Gallery o the Baseball Hall of Fame.

Chapter 16

(66) "We are only trustees . . . ," "We have built up an . . . " from a conversation witl Frank Steele of Perez-Steele Galleries, May, 1989.

Section IV

( ) "You know that I always . . . " letter from Fred Clarke to Walter Littell, July 23 1947 (National Baseball Library).

Selected bibliography

Astor, Gerald and The National Baseball Hall of Fame and Museum, Inc., The National Baseball Library. The Baseball Hall of Fame 50th Anniversary Book. New York: Prentice Hall Press, 1988.

Beckett, James and Dennis W. Eckes. The Sports Americana Baseball Memorablia and Autograph Price Guide. Lakewood, Ohio: Edgewater Book Company, Inc., 1982.

Benjamin, Mary A. Autographs: A Key to Collecting. New York: R.R. Bowker, 1946; rev. ed., 1963.

Berkeley, Edmund, ed., Klingelhofer, Herbert, coed., Rendell, Kenneth coed., Autographs and Manuscripts: A Collector's Manual. New York: Charles Scribner's Sons., 1978.

Carter, Craig, ed. The Sporting News - The Complete Baseball Record Book. St. Louis: The Sporting New Publishing Company, 1988.

Carvalho, David N., Forty Centuries of Ink, or a Chronological Narrative Concerning Ink and Its Background. New York: Banks Law Publishing Co., 1904.

Clapp, Anne F. Curatorial Care of Works of Art on Paper. Oberlin: Intermuseum Conservation Association, 1973.

Doloff, Francis W., and Roy L. Perkinson. How to Care for Works of Art on Paper. Boston: Museum of Fine Arts, 1971.

Eckes, Dennis & R.J. Smalling. The Sport Americana Baseball Address List, No. 5. Cleveland: Edgewater Book Company, Inc.

Einstein, Charles, ed. The Fireside Book of Baseball. New York: Simon and Schuster, 1956.

Harrison, Wilson R. Suspect Documents: Their Scientific Examination. London: Sweet and Maxwell, 1958.

James, Bill. Historical Abstract of Baseball. New York: Villard Books, 1986.

Kathpalia, Yash Pal. Conservation and Restoration of Archive Materials. Paris: UNESCO, 1973.

Lanigan, Ernest, The Sporting News, Record Book for 1939. St. Louis: Charles C. Spink & Son, 1939.

Reach Official Baseball Guide(s), edited by Francis Richter. Philadelphia: A.J. Reach Sporting Goods Company.

Reichler, Joseph, ed., The Baseball Encyclopedia, 6th ed. New York: Macmillian Publishing Company., Inc., 1985.

Reidenbaugh, Lowell, Take Me Out To The Ball Park, St. Louis: The Sporting News Publishing Company, 1983.

Reidenbaugh, Lowell, Baseball's Hall of Fame, Cooperstown, Where Legends Live Forever, New York: Arlington House, Inc., 1986.

Rogosin, Donn. Invisible Men - Life in Baseball's Negro Leagues. New York: Antheneum, 1983.

Spalding Official Baseball Guide. New York: American Sports Publishing Company 1890 1941.

Webster's 9th New Collegiate Dictionary. Springfield: Miriam-Webster Inc., 1986.

Periodicals

Sports Collectors Digest. Iola: Krause Publications, Inc., 700 East State Street, Iola, WI 54990

Street & Smith's Baseball. New York: Conde Nast Publications Inc., Street & Smiths Sports Group, 304 East 45th St., New York, NY 10017.

The Autograph Collector's Magazine, P.O. Box 55328, Stockton, CA 95205.

The Autograph Review, 305 Carlton Road, Syracuse, NY 13207.

Index